AMERICA ON TRIAL

ROBERT R. REILLY

America on Trial

A Defense of the Founding

With a Foreword by
Larry P. Arnn

IGNATIUS PRESS   SAN FRANCISCO

Cover art
Signing the Declaration of Independence, July 4th, 1776
by John Trumbull (1756–1843)
Capitol Collection, Washington, D.C./Bridgeman Images

Cover design by John Herreid

© 2020 by Ignatius Press, San Francisco
All rights reserved
ISBN 978-1-58617-948-9 (HB)
ISBN 978-1-64229-114-8 (eBook)
Library of Congress Control Number 2019947393
Printed in the United States of America ∞

To the memory of my uncle Major Robert R. Egan,
U.S. Army Air Forces (d. 1943, Morocco),
whom I never had the privilege of meeting,
and with great love to
Michael, Catherine, Matthew, and Teresa,
who will carry on from here

May this notification, by some faithful record, be handed down to the yet unborn descendants of Americans, that nothing but the most fatal necessity could have wrested the present inestimable enjoyments from their ancestors. Let them universally inculcate upon their beloved offspring an investigation of those truths, respecting both civil and religious liberty, which have been so clearly and fully stated in this generation. May they be carefully taught in all their schools and may they never rest until, through a Divine blessing upon their efforts, true freedom and liberty shall reign triumphant.

—Recommendation of Townships of
Monmouth County, New Jersey, 1774

Cease to accept as a matter of course your blessings, your rare good fortune.

—General George C. Marshall, 1951

CONTENTS

FOREWORD

This book is about a "trial", the trial of America. A trial can mean any kind of ordeal, but the archetype is a defendant set in a dock before a judge, prosecuted for violating some standard of law or right or both. Robert Reilly, a friend of mine for decades, argues that America faces that kind of trial. He is not quite the prosecutor, for he would rather rescue than convict. The American people are in the dock, but also they are almost like the judge, for they must decide and thereby determine their own fate.

This book is part of a genre, one of the grandest in American political thought and history. This genre depicts America as an experiment or a quest, a journey to reach a goal that is perfect even if life on this earth cannot be. The first paragraph of *The Federalist* says that Americans are appointed "to decide the important question, whether societies of men are really capable or not of establishing good government from reflection and choice, or whether they are forever destined to depend for their political constitutions on accident and force". Lincoln said that the central principle of America is to be "constantly *approximated* and thereby constantly spreading and deepening its influence, and augmenting the happiness and value of life to all people of all colors everywhere". To approximate is not quite the same thing as to match or to attain.

This effort to approximate is the specific activity of America, the function that gives it life, the calling that gives it direction. Its justification under the "Laws of Nature and of Nature's God" makes the trial cosmic in scope. It is a drama across all time.

Representative of a genre, this book is still unique. It is not really about the trial itself, nor is it even a statement of the indictment. We can face the trial and answer the indictment only after we understand the law under which we are accused. The purpose of this book is to explain that law, show its preciousness, and begin to contrast it with our contemporary ways. It prepares us to formulate the case to save ourselves.

It will not be easy, because so much is lost. To recover what is lost, Reilly digs down very deep into the past, down before America, down before Christ, down before philosophy, down to the revelation of the Hebrew God. To understand the law that informs America yet transcends time, we must begin with that God. He is eternal. He is wholly good and therefore holy. He is Almighty, yet he created us free. He is the ultimate source of the transcendent law available to human reason, the "Laws of Nature and of Nature's God". Under these laws, America was formed. The charge being made against America, however, is the reverse—that she abandoned these laws.

The application of these laws to America cannot be understood, Reilly argues, without understanding Christ, who although one with God, amended the Hebrew understanding of God in two ways. First, he is fully and completely the God not only of the Jews but of everyone. Second, he does not give laws in the ordinary sense. He says: "My kingdom is not of this world." He does not form a polity, a political entity giving and enforcing laws. The regular laws must come from our instructed conscience and our judgment, if we can muster them.

Nonetheless the ordinary law will still control the monopoly on power that makes it law. The law will therefore be especially dangerous to this new kind of religion that crosses national boundaries and has no army of its own. All governments are jealous of competing authorities, and tyrants in particular hate anything that invites us to look over their heads. There is plenty of talk among American elites these days to the effect that the government is our church and our political leaders the priests. Against this the dispensation of Christ favors freedom, especially freedom of religion. The followers of Christ have a right to those beliefs. The business of government is to protect that right.

But can it any longer? Or rather, will it? Some argue that a terrible rupture took place between the political philosophy that arose from the triad of Jerusalem, Athens, and Rome and that of the Enlightenment. They say that America is hopelessly founded upon the latter and that her current existential crisis is the logical result of that flawed beginning. The story that Reilly tells, however, disrupts the neatness of many accounts of the history of political philosophy. In his view, the break is not simply between the ancients and the moderns: there are differences within antiquity and within modernity, and there are similarities that cross the boundary between them. It is not just an eternal quarrel between reason and revelation: the understanding of the relationship between them alters; sometimes it is sound and sometimes it goes astray.

One of the strengths of this book is its transhistorical or even cosmic outlook. For Reilly it is decisive that the classics, in giving a rational articulation of the whole, described a perfect being at the top or the center of it, necessary to its completion. The medieval Christian thinkers, a kind of classic group in their own right, included in their account of the God who revealed himself in Christ the many things that can be known about him by reason.

This means that philosophy rightly understood is teleological: it looks for the end; and theology rightly understood is rational first and faithful once the ground is laid for the ascent to the heights. When some Christians discarded philosophy, and with it the view that God was understandable through his creation as well as through his revelation, God became only a will. This Reilly calls "voluntarism", and in his account it lays the ground for the concentration on power alone that is the increasing drive of modern philosophy and politics. When philosophy ceases its interest in "imaginary republics", meaning the best life for human beings, it seeks not to know but to make, not to understand but to change. Nature, like chance, is now the subject of a campaign of conquest. This will lead to the disappearance of the human, the person who acts in nature in accord with its standards.

Reilly has been a Roman Catholic for as long as I have known him, and devoted—but not, thereby, an anti-Protestant. His criticisms of Luther will repel some of goodwill and conscience, but they need not. He quotes Luther saying that a thing is good if God says it is good and it ceases to be good if God says it is not; that we cannot by our own understanding see the way to our own salvation; that Aristotle and the classics in general are misleading or worse. In Reilly's reading, this grounds ultimate goodness not in the very nature of God, but rather in the will of God. If God were only a changeable will, then he would be hard for us either to understand or to obey. Reilly describes this God-as-will to be of a piece with the virulent modern philosophy of the will to power.

I say these opinions need not repel those who admire Luther. I am no Luther scholar myself, but I consulted some of my colleagues, both Catholic and Protestant, who study and talk about these things intensely. Some of them admire Luther deeply for precisely the reason that Bob admires Thomas Aquinas: that he explains both God and rightness in a way that supplies a ground both of belief and of action. They admit the truth of Reilly's quotes of Luther, and they present other quotes, also accurate, that cut in the opposite direction. This means that Reilly and my colleagues who admire Luther are actually after the same thing: a faith compatible with reason that can defend itself, morality, and freedom. Given the current crisis, this is not the time for them to quarrel. Reilly himself holds out the olive branch by exempting many of the closest students of Luther from his criticisms. He also offers another Protestant theologian, Anglican prelate Richard Hooker, as a remedy for what he sees lacking in Luther.

Reilly has learned all of this from a lifetime of thought that owes a debt to several teachers. There is Harry Jaffa, the political philosopher who taught his students Aristotle, Lincoln, and the Founding (to use the order in which Professor Jaffa discovered those things). There is the priest Fr. James Schall, S.J., lately passed, who explained the natural law in the Catholic context as well as anyone in modern times. There are several conservative thinkers especially Gerhart Niemeyer. They do not all agree with one another on all points, but Reilly finds an agreement among them to form his own understanding.

Not many people could cover the ground that Reilly has in this book. He is able because of the way he has lived his life. I met him in graduate school, decades ago. He struck me right away as a remarkably learned man for the station we both occupied. He had read many things about which I had only heard. He was, for example, already far along in understanding how reason and faith dance together to produce Western civilization.

To put that story together, one must be faithful, which Reilly is. One must be deeply read in the best philosophy, which he also is. And it seems to help if one is in fact a dancer, and he is the organizer of the Annual Evening of Viennese Waltzing in the nation's capital. I have seen him teach the waltz to stumbling young graduate students, not without the occasional smack with the baton.

Moreover Reilly is a cultured man. He is widely published in classical music periodicals. And to complete the picture, he has served his country as an officer in the First Squadron of the Eighteenth Armored Cavalry Regiment and has held high positions in several administrations in Washington.

Before we go to trial, we should study what Reilly has written. He has proved throughout his life that he will be standing there with us when sentence is passed, whatever it is.

Larry P. Arnn, Ph.D.
President of Hillsdale College
November 15, 2019

PREFACE

This is primarily a work of intellectual history, analysis, and synthesis. It covers a broad expanse, from the prephilosophical world to contemporary times. It is hardly comprehensive, however, nor is it meant to be. To keep things within the limited scope of a relatively short book, I have had to be highly selective in choosing representative thinkers. Some may object to the selection and be upset by what has been left out. Also, I have had to compress and simplify—some may say distort—complex ideas and events. I have done my best not to misrepresent them. My aim has been to present the essential character of things insofar as they relate to the overall topic of this book. My endeavor has been to trace some golden strains of thought as they threaded their way through history to the American Founding. I ask the reader's indulgence regarding the amount of repetition required to demonstrate that the *same* principles, however differently articulated, perdured and developed through centuries of turmoil to reach fruition in the American Founding. Considering the depth and the complexity of the issues involved, what is offered here might best be thought of as a sketch or a primer.

I make no claim to originality. I am both a recipient and a student of the heritage of which I write. I have undying gratitude to those who handed it on to me—such as Gerhart Niemeyer, Harry V. Jaffa, Fr. James V. Schall, and many others. Of course, there is no single authorship of this heritage. The goal is to make it one's own and, having done so, to pass it on. The only possibility of extending this legacy is to understand it from its roots. That is what I am trying to do here. I do not wish to embarrass all my teachers by naming them, but this work is more theirs than mine. I take full blame, however, for any errors contained herein.

I am especially beholden to my senior editor at Ignatius Press, Vivian Dudro, for insisting that I write this book (our third together), despite my objections to doing so, and to my publisher, Fr. Joseph Fessio, S.J., for his patience in waiting for me to get it done.

I especially wish to thank Angelo Codevilla, who has been a friend and guide for innumerable years, John Zmirak, William Layer, Dennis Teti, Richard Bastien, Tom Blau, Donald Devine, Katharine Gorka, Carson Daly, Benjamin Wiker, Msgr. Robert Sokolowski, and Carl Olson—all of whom read some draft chapters and provided invaluable counsel and encouragement. To James Gaston I owe a debt of gratitude for introducing me to the works of Joseph F. Costanzo, S.J., and to my wife, Blanca, for her heroic help with research. I also wish to acknowledge the *Claremont Review of Books* for permission to reprint portions of my 2017 article "For God and Country", found here revised and enlarged in chapters 1 and 11. Some of the latter portions of chapter 10 come in modified form from parts of my monograph *Ideas Matter: Restoring the Content of Public Diplomacy*. I am obliged to the Heritage Foundation for allowing their use.

I am also grateful for the grant from the late, greatly lamented Earhart Foundation for the writing of this book. I may not have finished it in time for Ingrid Gregg, Earhart president, and Montgomery Brown, director of program, to have seen it while still in office, but I hope they know how much I appreciated the generous help they gave.

INTRODUCTION

Do We Hold These Truths?

This book is about the lineage of the ideas that made the United States possible. It traces the origin of certain truths without which the American Founding would have been *inconceivable*. The story of the discovery of these truths—and the contemporaneous, sometimes violent opposition to them—over a span of several thousand years is at the heart of this endeavor. It is a long, sometimes difficult, but necessary journey if we are to see the significance of these discoveries, which now seem ordinary because we are habituated to them. But they were considered extraordinary by the world upon which they burst. By considering the character of the times in which they were introduced, we will try to recapture their newness and revolutionary qualities. For instance, monotheism shocked a world immersed in polytheism. Creation *ex nihilo* (out of nothing) shattered pantheism. The idea that existence is good violated Manichaean dualism. Philosophy's discovery that all things operate with a purpose confounded the randomness of things. Freedom challenged fatalism. The Greek idea of logos—a divine intelligence behind reality—was startling enough before the arrival of an incarnate Logos that scandalized the world. These things may seem a long way from the American Founding, but ultimately they are not. They are its bedrock.

Ideas, of course, are not the only influence on the development of events, but, as C. S. Lewis said, "Different beliefs about the universe lead to different behavior."[1] Ideas do have consequences, and it is on these that I primarily concentrate because it is only through ideas that one can come to understand the meaning of things. I hope that I capture some of the drama inherent in the intellectual battles with

---

[1] C. S. Lewis, *Mere Christianity* (New York: Macmillan, 1960), 58.

which this book deals. The stakes in them were, and continue to be, enormous. The tension between the primacy of reason, as it was theologically, philosophically, and politically elaborated, versus the primacy of will, as it was expressed in these same areas, is the driving engine of this book. The drama hinges on two opposing conceptions of reality: Is it constituted by reason or by will? The answer will determine, in turn, whether *law* is the product of reason or of will. The political ramifications of this are enormous. Primacy of reason means that *what is right* flows from objective sources in nature and the transcendent, from *what is*, as Plato proposed. Primacy of will, on the other hand, means that *what is right* flows from power, that will is a law unto itself. It is a conflict of *might makes right* versus *right makes might*. Knowledge of the sources of these contending schools of thought is necessary to gauge accurately their influence on the character of America's creation.

The reason for this undertaking is a controversy that goes to the heart of what the United States is—from where did it come, and what is its meaning? These may seem like questions from an elementary civics class, the answers to which were settled long ago. What was thought to have been settled, however, is now unsettled. The reason for this is the national convulsion resulting from America's current morally degraded condition—the effect of which is an identity crisis. "To be an American is not to be someone", wrote American historian Gordon S. Wood regarding the Founding generation, "but to believe in something."[2] What might that "something" *now* be?

Today, a number of thinkers dispute America's lineage and claim that the United States is a creature of the primacy of will, the very opposite of what it claimed itself to be. The quarrel can be posed by these questions: Was the American Founding rooted in the Judeo-Christian heritage and natural law, or was it infused with notions of the radical autonomy and the perfectibility of man and, therefore, inimical to the Christian and natural law conception of reality? Was the Founding America's Original Sin? Are present-day evils simply the logical outcome of this fatal flaw, or do current maladies result from a fundamentally sound principle gone awry for other reasons?

---

[2] Gordon S. Wood, *The Idea of America: Reflections on the Birth of the United States* (New York: Penguin Press, 2011), 322.

The responses to these questions are fraught with consequences. They will reveal whether America was founded on basic principles that are true and just—ones that we can unqualifiedly support—or whether the republic was based on ideas that are false and unavoidably lead to corporate and individual evil. If the United States is founded on high moral principles, then we owe her and those principles our grateful support and should fight to preserve and, if necessary, restore them. If, on the other hand, America is founded on principles that are malign, then anything we do to advance them makes us complicit with evil. In other words, can one concomitantly be a good person and a good American?

Whose Fault Is It?

This controversy is not new, although it has become more heated. More than two decades ago, I contributed to the volume *We Hold These Truths and More*, titled after Rev. John Courtney Murray's famous book, *We Hold These Truths*. Even at that time, strong currents in Christian thought condemned the American Founding for, as contributing author John A. Gueguen put it, "the philosophical errors that are embedded in the American civil religion". The task for Christians, he said, is to destroy the "erroneous philosophy of man and society which underlies the American Proposition and the currently reigning gnosis of pragmatism and positivism which grew out of that philosophy".[3] In other words, the American Founding was a poison pill with a time-release formula. We are its victims.

This view of a fatally flawed foundation has grown stronger because the decline in American public life and morals has dramatically accelerated, gaining it an attention it would otherwise not have had. Policies that many Christians and others of similar mind find repugnant and alien—in fact, hostile to their religion, such as abortion, pornography, and same-sex "marriage"—are publicly put forth as essential parts, even *requirements*, of the American principle

---

[3] Donald J. D'Elia and Stephen M. Krason, eds., *We Hold These Truths and More: Further Catholic Reflections on the American Proposition: The Thought of Fr. John Courtney Murray, S.J., and Its Relevance Today* (Steubenville, Ohio: Franciscan University Press, 1993), 41–42.

of equality. That those who advance these views have succeeded in the Supreme Court, which has ruled that these very things are essential to the Constitution, leads many Christians to suspect even more intensely that these faults are not deviations from the Founding principles, but the expression of a fundamentally corrupt regime performing its corrupt acts in perfect consistency with its malevolent principles. The more odious Christianity becomes to the dominant forces of American contemporary thought and jurisprudence—the more its beliefs are denounced as "hate crimes"—the greater the inclination of Christians and other religious people to find America odious in return.

Witness the *New York Times* bestseller *The Benedict Option: A Strategy for Christians in a Post-Christian Nation* by Rod Dreher, who is convinced by Notre Dame professor Patrick Deneen that the American "purpose of government is to liberate the autonomous individual".[4] What this means, as he states elsewhere, is that "the summum bonum of our American civil religion is maximizing the opportunities for individuals to express and satisfy their desires—a belief that orthodox Christianity by nature opposes."[5] A broad range of Christians endorsed *The Benedict Option*, from the Catholic archbishop of Philadelphia, Charles J. Chaput, to such notable figures in the Southern Baptist Convention as Russell Moore. There is, in other words, a growing faith-based critique of the republic's origins, constructed on premises accepted offhandedly by many of its followers, including Dreher. This is fraught with danger. If Christians come to believe that America is congenitally their enemy, they will cease to defend it and join in its destruction for their own reasons. This is true, as well, of many non-Christians who are equally appalled by this moral disarray.

This is why it is necessary to deal with this controversy anew, and why this book is subtitled as it is. It attempts to defend the Founding and show how deeply the American Proposition was rooted in the Judeo-Christian and natural law tradition. We will examine the premises of

---

[4] Rod Dreher, *The Benedict Option: A Strategy for Christians in a Post-Christian Nation* (New York: Sentinel, 2017), 90.

[5] Rod Dreher, "Christian and Countercultural", *First Things* (February 2015), https://www.firstthings.com/article/2015/02/christian-and-countercultural.

the critique of America by looking at some of its leading theoreticians. I have chosen two thinkers frequently referred to by Dreher: Patrick Deneen, associate professor of constitutional studies at Notre Dame University, and Michael Hanby, a scholar at the Vatican's Pontifical John Paul II Institute for Studies on Marriage and Family. Both are major contributors to *First Things* magazine and prominent members of the conservative Catholic cadre that holds to the poison-pill thesis. Deneen thinks that the Founding is based on a lie about humanity, a false anthropology. Hanby believes that it is based on an error about the nature of reality, a false metaphysics. Their arguments, considered together, provide the central elements of the poison-pill thesis, which is why writers such as Dreher invoke them sympathetically.

Their thesis would have shocked John Courtney Murray. In *We Hold These Truths*, he insisted that the men who forged the country "thought the life of man and society under government is founded on truths, on a certain body of objective truth, universal in its import, accessible to the reason of man, definable, defensible. If this assertion is denied, the American Proposition is, I think, eviscerated at one stroke."[6] Deneen and Hanby would not deny the necessity of objective truths as the basis for man's life under government. What they deny is that the American Proposition held such truths—thus, as Murray predicted, eviscerating it at one stroke. He would find this development ironic. Murray had expected that if the growing forces of voluntarism (meaning law as will rather than reason) further imperiled the Founding, "guardianship of the original American consensus, based on the Western heritage, would have passed to the Catholic community, within which the heritage was elaborated long before America was."[7] By this, he meant that the Catholic natural law tradition had formed the grounding for the American Proposition and was still strong enough to resist modern corrosives. If America lost her way, she could be recalled to her better self by Catholic intellectuals steeped in that tradition.

This is exactly what should have happened in light of what Murray called "the evident coincidence of the principles which inspired

---

[6]John Courtney Murray, S.J., *We Hold These Truths: Catholic Reflections on the American Proposition* (New York: Sheed and Ward, 1960), ix.

[7]Ibid., 43.

the American Republic with the principles that are structural to the Western Christian political tradition".[8] And it is what happened with thinkers such as George Weigel and the late Michael Novak, who did indeed follow the path of guardianship. It apparently did not occur to Murray, however, that some Catholic intellectuals would do the opposite—*refuse* the guardianship because they disavowed the paternity. Because they explicitly deny the coincidence of American principles with those of the Western Christian political tradition, they have abandoned the American Founding as an illegitimate child. As a result, the Founding has become a foundling. In 1960, Murray wrote that "there has never been a schism within the American Catholic community, as there was among French Catholics, over the right attitude to adopt toward the established polity."[9] Now there is.

Deneen and Hanby are rightly repulsed by the radical individual autonomy that has infected American life, exemplified in Justice Anthony Kennedy's notorious statement in *Planned Parenthood v. Casey* (1992) that "at the heart of liberty is the right to define one's own concept of existence, of meaning, of the universe, and of the mystery of human life."[10] This right, according to Kennedy, allows for abortion. In *Lawrence v. Texas* (2003), he wrote that "liberty presumes an autonomy of self that includes freedom of thought, belief, expression, and certain intimate conduct."[11] He used *this* freedom to advance sodomy as a constitutional right. Later, in the widely applauded *Windsor* case, he applied similar reasoning to assert the legitimacy of homosexual "marriage", as he did again in *Obergefell v. Hodges*. It appears that the job of government is to create a safe space in which our strongest passions are allowed to rule us. Almost anything can be justified with this "autonomy of self". In an article appropriately titled "Rights without Right", philosopher David Walsh points out that "the relentless extension of the liberal language of autonomy has removed a common moral framework from our society."[12]

---

[8] Ibid.

[9] Ibid.

[10] Planned Parenthood of Southeastern Pa. et al., v. Casey, Governor of Pennsylvania, et al., 505 U. S. 833, 851 (1992), https://www.law.cornell.edu/supct/html/91-744.ZS.html.

[11] John Geddes and Tyron Garner, Petioners v. Texas (02-102) 539 U.S. 558 (2003), https://www.law.cornell.edu/supct/html/02-102.ZO.html.

[12] David Walsh, "Rights without Right", *First Things* (November 1996), https://www.firstthings.com/article/1996/11/002-rights-without-right.

Ironically, Deneen and Hanby are in full agreement with Justice Kennedy as to what the Founding holds. Kennedy sees radical autonomy there, and so do they. The only difference is that they excoriate it, while Kennedy celebrates it. They all agree as to its substance and source. But Kennedy and his fellow justices *fabricated* an "autonomy of self" out of the Constitution's penumbras. Those who subscribe to Justice Kennedy's views have made themselves antithetical to the Founding, but others delude themselves by trying to make the Founding antithetical to itself. Where, for instance, do Deneen and Hanby locate the presence of this radical autonomy in America's origins? We will examine their answer to this question in chapter 11. Although I agree with their withering and eloquent appraisal of modernity, they are entirely mistaken in finding the Founding complicit in it. Their misdiagnosis diverts attention from the real causes of decline and therefore frustrates, in fact nearly eliminates, any hope of recovery.

If it is not the Founders' fault, whose is it? In the epilogue, I will suggest an answer to this question. For now, I will simply propose that the reason for our current decline is not that the nation's original principles have finally reached fruition, but that the Christian and natural law perspective that animated its Founders is being lost—for only by abandoning the general principles of Christianity and natural law can one imagine liberty as "autonomy of self". The men who set forth "a new nation" would have found completely objectionable Justice Kennedy's misunderstanding of freedom. The total dependence of liberty on virtue—both Aristotelian and Christian—was abundantly, unmistakably clear from their frequent writings, as we shall see in chapter 10. The idea of freedom as contentless choice was totally alien to them, as would be the idea that liberty is the right to define one's own meaning of the universe. For them, the meaning of the universe originates not in ourselves but in "the Laws of Nature and of Nature's God".

Sources of the Founding

To understand the Founding as those who built it did, we need to recover the context in which they thought. In several places in *We Hold These Truths*, Murray made allusions to deep Western traditions by referring to Thomas Aquinas and the great English jurists Henry of Bracton (ca. 1210–1268) and Sir John Fortescue (ca. 1385–ca. 1479), but he did so sparingly. It was not his purpose to explicate that heritage's legacy. A fuller development of these and other sources is required in order to rescue America from the controversies that are devouring it.

Too often, arguments about the Christian and natural law influences on the country's origins degenerate into itemizations of the specific religious beliefs or affiliations of each signer of the Declaration and the Constitution—as if such affiliations make or break the case.[13] Also, the historical perspective is pulled back only as far as the seventeenth century to examine the influence of John Locke. To understand the foundation, the perspective needs to be pulled back much further, as far as the first century A.D., if not even earlier—because that is where its roots are.

John Adams' remarks indicate this direction. In his June 28, 1813, letter to Thomas Jefferson about the basic concepts on which independence was achieved, Adams asked:

> And what were these principles? I answer, the general principles of Christianity in which all those sects were united and the general principles of English and American liberty in which all these young men united.... Now I will avow that I then believed and now believe that those general principles of Christianity are as eternal and immutable as the existence and attributes of God. And that those principles of liberty are as unalterable as human nature.... I could, therefore, safely say consistently with all my then and present information, that I believe they would never make discoveries in contradiction to these general principles.[14]

In this remarkable passage, Adams refers to no specific thinker; rather, he implicitly acknowledges certain presuppositions. These were the

---

[13] For the record, more than half, perhaps up to two-thirds, of the signers of the Declaration were Anglicans. See Rod Gragg, *By the Hand of Providence: How Faith Shaped the American Revolution* (New York: Simon and Schuster, 2011), 69; and Leonard P. Liggio, "Catholicism in the Era of American Independence", *Catholic Dossier* (1999): 14, https://leonardliggio.org/wp-content/uploads/downloads/2011/10/CATHOLICISM%20IN%20THE%20ERA%20OF%20AMERICAN%20INDEPENDENCE.pdf.

[14] John Adams to Thomas Jefferson, June 28, 1813, Founders Online, National Archives, https://founders.archives.gov/documents/Jefferson/03-06-02-0208.

commonsense beliefs of the people: the immutability of human nature; the constancy of the universe; the basic goodness of creation; the existence of a benevolent God; the indispensability of Christian morals and the eternal destiny of man in the transcendent, along with their implied limitations on the role of politics in man's life. By itself, of course, Christianity does not necessarily lead to the American Founding (or to any founding, because it is not a political doctrine), but it would not likely have happened without Christianity.

Athough Christians have sometimes been ambivalent, if not hostile, toward democratic constitutional order, we shall see that Christianity provided a bedrock of realist (Thomist) metaphysics and theological doctrine that allowed for its evolution and legitimacy. This entailed the natural integrity of the world, as asserted by Aquinas and others, and the partial autonomy of man within it, as allowed by Jewish and Christian revelation. The conception of natural law, essential for the development of constitutionalism, was assisted by the biblical doctrine of man made in the image of God. Absent this likeness, man had no grounds for the exercise of sovereignty. Also, Christianity itself supported and defended the secularization necessary for the development of constitutionalism. The distinction between God and Caesar, so essential to the separate sovereignties of church and state, has only one fount. As British scholar Larry Siedentop writes, "Secularism is Christianity's gift to the world."[15] The very idea of "secular" is Christian in origin. In short, constitutionalism is based on the constitution of man's nature, and it is the history of its apprehension, particularly in the baptized form of classical philosophy that appeared from Saint Augustine onward, that is critical to understanding the basis of the American nation.

These are among the ideas and principles that made the nation *conceivable*. We will trace the genealogy of these ideas, each of which was unique at the time of its introduction. To show just what are the principles of which Adams wrote, we will examine the thought of some of those who produced the definitive Christian and natural law ideas on man's relationship to a transcendent God, the limited power of the sovereign, the sovereignty of the people, the requirement of consent, representation, and the rule of law (all of which were in

---

[15] Larry Siedentop, *Inventing the Individual: The Origins of Western Liberalism* (Cambridge, Mass.: Harvard University Press, 2014), 360.

place well before the Enlightenment and therefore clearly not products of it).

This book, then, is not so much about the Founding itself as about the provenance of its ideas. Its purpose is to demonstrate that the ideas of democratic constitutional government have only one set of roots in human history. Christendom (strongly influenced by its antecedents in Jerusalem and in Athens), and only Christendom, has ever indigenously produced modern constitutional government.

Here is a summary of what we will present in greater detail—though in a necessarily limited way, as each topic by itself would require, and has produced, its own library. The aim is to provide the reader with glimpses into the essentials that derive respectively from Athens, Jerusalem, and Rome. From Athens: the existence of universal truth, a rational universe ordered by a divine intellect, the primacy of reason in man's moral life, the existence and immutability of human nature, and the existence and immortality of the human soul. From Jerusalem: monotheism, creation ex nihilo, the fundamental goodness and reliability of creation, man made in the *imago Dei* (image of God), and salvation history. Finally, from Rome (Christianity): the universalization of the truths of Judaism stated above, the Incarnation and the culmination of salvation history in Christ, the dedivinization of the world (the final end of pantheism), the separation of the sacred from the secular, and the recognition of the inviolability of the individual person.

After surveying the contributions of these three cities in chapter 1, we will see in chapter 2 how medieval thinkers, starting in the late eleventh century, began to advance the notions of popular sovereignty, representation, and the requirement of consent, first in canon, then in secular, law. These developments rested on the dual sovereignties of church and state—known as the "two swords" teaching. The defined limitations of each restrained power from being absolute in either. Representative bodies began to rule abbeys, religious orders, and church councils. Early parliaments were formed in their image, based on the idea that political sovereignty is derived from the people. The rule of law, jury trials, the protection of rights, and the moral obligation to oppose tyranny became hallmarks of the political and legal order of the Middle Ages. This was the common sense of Western civilization, at least at the level of principle, by the medieval period. Nor was there any shortage of such principles being put into practice during those centuries. After all, when Americans referred to ancient rights, they were referring to realities, not just theories. As political scientist Ellis Sandoz remarked, "The whole of medieval Christian constitutional and political theory ... lay squarely behind the American determination [to achieve independence]."[16] In any case, I will endeavor to show that the Lockean DNA theory of the Founding is radically reductionist. It would be more accurate to say, as did Murray, that the DNA of the American Founding is in Christian political theory going back to the eleventh century and, I would add, to Jewish revelation in Genesis and to ancient Greek philosophy from the sixth century B.C. onward.

In chapter 3, we will examine how the influence of William of Ockham and his fellow nominalists eroded much of the medieval achievement by diminishing the status of reason and, in fact, denying reason's ability to know the essences of things. In chapter 4, we will see how his disciple Luther applied these teachings to the bifurcation of faith and reason that ultimately led to the effective end of Christendom and, concomitantly, of the dual sovereignty of church and state, with its baneful political consequences. The "two swords" became one with the prince as the head of the church. The great medieval synthesis of faith and reason was torn asunder. Faith (fideism) now stood alone, but it was armed, and it was no longer necessarily reasonable. Certainty in faith and doubt in reason removed the means by which to reach understandings or agreements on the basis of what is reasonable, leaving force as the adjudicator. Since, according to fideism, there is no moral law inscribed in nature—or at least not one discernable by man's intellect—it was one understanding of divine revelation pitted against another. This was a recipe for the religious wars that ripped Europe asunder.

In England, however, due to the strength of its medieval legacy, a powerful intellectual defense of the integrity of reason and its relationship to faith was offered in the Anglican Church by its first theologian, Richard Hooker (1554–1600). In chapter 5, we will examine how he restored Aristotelian and Thomistic thought to Anglican Protestantism, defended medieval political principles, and preserved the heritage that made a return to constitutionalism possible.

---

[16] Ellis Sandoz, "Classical and Christian Dimensions of American Political Thought", *Modern Age* (Winter 1981): 17.

An intervening age of absolutism arose, however, based on the primacy of will—in God, on the one hand, and in the ruler, on the other. Secular absolutism came from Thomas Hobbes' degraded view of man in the state of nature in which there is a war of all against all—the solution to which was the power of the Leviathan, the omnipotent state (chapter 6). In the Divine Right of Kings version of absolutism, as articulated by James I and Sir Robert Filmer, the ruler received his sovereignty directly from God and was accountable to no one. With secular and spiritual power conjoined, Divine Right absolutism shattered constitutionalism, as we will see in chapter 7. The law of reason was replaced by the will of the ruler. In the latter part of chapter 7, we will see that the Divine Right notion did not go unchallenged. Robert Cardinal Bellarmine (1542–1621) and Spanish Jesuit Francisco Suárez (1548–1617) powerfully rebutted it through a rearticulation of the Christian natural law tradition and the medieval principles of constitutional government. In the English Protestant world, Algernon Sidney (1622–1683), did the same, drawing upon the works of Richard Hooker. All emphatically insisted that secular authority is received not directly from God but indirectly from the people in whom it is vested, as had been the medieval teaching. In chapter 8, we will examine how John Locke (1632–1704) obliterated the Divine Right argument, while offering novel foundations for republican government. In chapter 9, we shall see how all these influences were channeled into colonial America and the creation of the American republic.

Chapter 9 will examine how these influences grew to fruition in the words and deeds of the Founding Fathers. That absolutism had moved from the English monarchy to the English parliament by the late eighteenth century did not change its nature—it was still rule without the consent of the ruled and outside the bounds of natural law, as far as the American colonists were concerned. Therefore, they revolted. Murray claimed that the American Revolution "was less a revolution than a conservation".[17] But there would have been no conservation *unless* there had been a revolution. If Americans had surrendered to the absolutism that was being imposed on them, they would have had nothing left to conserve. Peter F. Drucker called

---

[17] Murray, *We Hold These Truths*, 31.

it "the Conservative Counter-Revolution of 1776".[18] Ellis Sandoz broadly views the Founding as "an anti-modernist rearticulation of Western civilization".[19]

It was all of these, because the truths set forth by the Founding Fathers were not new. As John Quincy Adams would later say, their "theory of government had been working itself into the mind of man for many ages".[20] But the Founding was also something new. What was revolutionary about it was that, for the first time in history, the effort was made to found a regime on these truths, for, as Adams remarked, they "had never before been adopted by a great nation in practice".[21]

Victory enabled the Founders, through "reflection and choice", as *Federalist* No. 1 states, to establish a constitutional republic that constrained governmental power by the consent of the governed.

What had been fought for was the primacy of reason, and what had been fought against was the primacy of will. Christian and natural law assumptions formed the basis of a revolution that was against not only George III and the absolutism of kings (or, in this case, of parliaments) but also the absolutism of Hobbes and Machiavelli, who undermined these truths.

In chapter 10, we will contrast the American Revolution with the French Revolution to illustrate the true character of each, as against those who conflate the two as essentially similar in ideological inspiration. In chapter 11, we will return to the Founders' critics to examine the soundness of their thesis in light the foregoing.

What was lost constitutionally by Divine Right and secular absolutisms after the collapse of Christendom was regained by the American Founding, which returned to Western civilization's deeper roots in Athens, Jerusalem, and Rome. To the unique contributions of these three cities we turn next, with a brief preamble to what the world was like before their existence.

---

[18] Peter F. Drucker, *The Future of Industrial Man* (New York: John Day, 1942), 156.

[19] Ellis Sandoz, *A Government of Laws: Political Theory, Religion, and the American Founding* (Columbia, Mo.: University of Missouri Press, 2001), 25.

[20] John Quincy Adams, "The Jubilee of the Constitution: A Discourse (1839)", Lonang Institute, https://lonang.com/library/reference/jqadams-jubilee-constitution-1839/.

[21] Ibid.

I

The Legacies of Athens, Jerusalem, and Rome

To appreciate the fundamental presuppositions of the American Founding, we must first see what the world was like *without* them—before philosophy discovered the order of nature and the role of reason, before the book of Genesis and monotheism, and before the Incarnation literally embodied the truths of Jewish revelation *and* Greek philosophy. At our distant remove, it is difficult for us to grasp how differently people understood the universe and themselves before these changes. But it is necessary for us to do so if we are to imagine what sort of world the collapse of American order—insofar as it remains the inheritor of these legacies—would impose on us.

We must look far backward in order to understand how unique is the way of life we enjoy and how precariously dependent it is on the fact that, when America's Founders revolted against the world's most powerful government, they really did so in accordance with "the Laws of Nature and of Nature's God", which they regarded as self-evidently true, *rooted in these legacies*. We will deal here with the revelations and discoveries that fundamentally transformed the West into the one and only place in which the establishment of the United States would become possible.

This journey into the past may at times take us down byways that seem to have no immediate relevance to our topic, but I hope to show that ultimately they do, because, as suggested earlier, only a certain anthropology, philosophy, and theology can support the kind of constitutional thinking that led to the American Founding. And regarding each of these areas, they were the *exceptions* to the rule of human thought and history. We will address how they developed in Athens, Jerusalem, and Rome (Christianity)—three cultures without which it might never have occurred to man that he ought to rule himself according to reason, rather than simply be subject to force and accident—as was the case throughout most of recorded history. This journey may also provide the deeper lesson that, when these presuppositions are removed, so too will be what they supported.

First, we will explore what the ancient prephilosophical world was like—a tribal, polytheistic realm of mythologies and superstitions. Second, we will look at the classical Greek world, as it emerged from under these tribal mythologies with the ascendancy of philosophical reasoning. Third, we will consider the unique contribution of monotheistic Judaism and its understanding of a transcendent God. And fourth, we will examine Christianity's claimed fulfillment of Jewish prophecy, its universalization of Judaic monotheism, and its eventual assimilation of the truths of Greek philosophy. Then we will be better able to appreciate how Greek philosophy, Jewish monotheism, and Christianity contributed indispensable notions to America's foundations.

The Prephilosophical World

We begin with what life was like without philosophy, monotheism, or Christ. In the prephilosophical world of city-states or cosmological empires, there was no demarcation between civic order and religious life. They were the same. There was no such thing as "secular" as distinct from "sacred". The city had a *religious* status. As Benedict XVI explained, ancient religion was "a rite and observance that ultimately guarantee[d] the identity of the state".[1] Participating in religious life was essentially a civic duty. Religion was a function and a requirement of the state and was subordinate to it. The ruler reigned because he originated in, or had a special relationship with, the gods. The local gods ruled the harvest and upheld the city. One participated in the divine scheme of things by fulfilling one's role in the city or the empire, centered on the person of the divine or semidivine ruler. A personal relationship with the gods was not possible for individuals. The city or empire was man's only access. In *The Ancient City*, Numa Denis Fustel de Coulanges explained,

[1] Benedict XVI, *Faith and Politics* (San Francisco: Ignatius Press, 2018), 16.

"Man felt himself at every moment dependent upon his gods, and consequently upon the priest king, who was placed between them and himself.... He it was who knew the formula and the prayers which the gods could not resist.... A king was a sacred being ... the man without whose aid no prayer was heard, no sacrifice accepted."[2] This was a period of history to which George Bernard Shaw's quip might appropriately apply: "The art of government is the organization of idolatry."[3]

In the cosmological empires of, for example, the pharaohs, the political order was supposedly an analogue of the divine order. This was replicated, point by point, by the divinity of the pharaoh, who issued out of the body of the sun god, and then, in rippling concentric circles, by the order of the court, society, and the political schema, which derived their importance from proximity to the divine pharaoh—an order duplicated even in the next world by the precise placement of the courtiers' tombs around the pharaoh's. The issue of physical proximity was taken so literally that Egyptian soldiers were existentially anxious about fighting outside Egypt, lest, if they be killed, their souls would be lost, unable to find their way back from a foreign land. Likewise, since the city or the empire was considered a mirror of the cosmos, any disturbance in the political order would produce profound existential disorientation, because it would be seen as a reflection of a disruption in the cosmic order that could threaten the structure of reality itself.

In the ancient world, men could not conceive of themselves *outside* this order. The fulfillment of man's destiny was possible only within the political order. This is why exile was the worst possible punishment. It was worse than death because it meant banishment from the only source of order and meaning. Cut off from the ruler and the order he had established, one was concomitantly cut off from the gods as well. Speaking of ancient man's attachment to the polis, Fustel de Coulanges said, "Let him leave its sacred walls, let him pass the sacred limits of its territory, and he no longer finds

---

[2] Numa Denis Fustel de Coulanges, *The Ancient City* (Kitchener, Ontario: Batoche Books, 2001), 149.

[3] George Bernard Shaw, *Man and Superman: A Comedy and a Philosophy* (London: Archibald Constable, 1903), 227.

for himself either a religion or a social tie of any kind. Everywhere else, except in his own country, he is outside the regular life and the law; everywhere else he is without a god, and shut out from all moral life."[4] By providing man with his only source of meaning, the ancient city or empire subsumed him entirely. Fustel de Coulanges remarked, "The ancients, therefore, knew neither liberty in private life, liberty in education, nor religious liberty."[5] The human person counted for very little.

Just as there was no distinction between the sacred and the secular, there was none between nature (*phusis*) and convention or custom (*nomos*). For instance, when the Egyptians buried their dead in brightly painted caskets, one said, "That is the way of the Egyptians." When a dog wagged its tail, one likewise said, "That is the way of a dog." The ancients did not, in fact could not, discriminate between what happens by nature and what happens by custom. Because they were prephilosophical, they did not have the conceptual means of understanding that what the dog does grows out of its nature as a dog, whereas the Egyptians bury their dead in painted boxes because that is simply a custom they made up.

In the prephilosophical world, the inability to distinguish the nature of things from man-made convention was at the basis of the tribal mentality. People deemed actions to be right or proper only to the extent that they conformed to the customary ways in which things had been done before; they deemed actions to be wrong to the extent that they differed. There was no standard other than "the ways of our fathers". One was only a tribal member, with duties to one's tribal gods and ancestors, and nothing beyond. Consequently, nothing could be right or wrong in and of itself. People who worshipped other gods and lived by different standards—members of other tribes or subjects of other empires—simply did not belong to one's "species", as it were. They had different "fathers" and different "ways". The poet Labid ibn Rabi'ah al-'Amiri, from pre-Islamic Arabia, put this perspective in verse: "We have leaders, noble and generous, men who come from a tribe that follows a sunnah, a way of life laid out for us by our fathers and their fathers before them. For every tribe,

---

[4] Fustel de Coulanges, *The Ancient City*, 166.
[5] Ibid., 187.

after all, has a sunnah and a model to follow."[6] The identification of the individual and the tribe was total.

To enslave or slaughter a member of another tribe fit perfectly within the order of the tribal view. For example, when the Egyptians successfully sallied forth to conquer another empire, they would also defeat the gods of that empire. The ancient understanding was that your city would do only as well as your gods were powerful. After all, what were the local gods for if not to protect their votaries? If a city lost a war, the ancients assumed that its gods had been defeated and subjugated by the greater powers of the victors' gods. When one people conquered another, the typical modus operandi was mass execution or enslavement. No one could imagine moral grounds on which to object to this. Significantly, there was often no word for "human being", no concept of personhood. An appeal to "mankind" would not have been intelligible to either the victors or the vanquished, because they both suffered from the incapacity to see another person as a human being.

From his observations of the American Indian tribes in 1793, Nathaniel Chipman touched upon some of the invariable characteristics of the tribal mentality:

> Among their different tribes, the injuries of an individual are resented as national. The possession of a hunting ground is, to them, the possession of an empire. These are sources of frequent wars, waged with the most savage ferocity. The butchering and scalping of old men, women, and children, the torturing and burning of prisoners, in cold blood, with the most shocking circumstances of cruelty, are among their pastimes. These are not secret acts of violence. They are by none considered as wrong. They are public transactions, performed, under what is, to them, the law of nations.[7]

Speaking of other kinds of tribes, including ancient ones, Chipman observed: "So universal is the state of war among such a people, that

---

[6] Cited in David Pinault, *The Crucifix on Mecca's Front Porch: A Christian's Companion for the Study of Islam* (San Francisco: Ignatius Press, 2018), 26.

[7] Nathaniel Chipman, *Sketches of the Principles of Government* (Rutland, Vt.: J. Lyon, 1793), 24, Evans Early American Imprint Collection, https://quod.lib.umich.edu/cgi/t/text/text-idx?cc=evans;c=evans;idno=N19425.0001.001;view=text;rgn=div1;node=N19425.0001.001%3A8.

in almost every language, the same word, originally, signified both foreigner and enemy."[8]

Those unfamiliar with the ancient lineage of tribal thinking often do not understand it when they encounter it today. Tribal thinking still exists in a few areas of the world, including some parts of Africa and remote regions in South America. Tribes there continue to define themselves in terms of their gods. These tribes name themselves, and other tribes, but they have no term for "human being" (the legacy of which allowed tribal Hutus to kill hundreds of thousands of tribal Tutsis in Rwanda in the space of several months in 1994). Consequently, they cannot recognize themselves or other people as human persons. Indeed, their own wives are often slaves.

A contemporary example of tribal mentality comes from Iraq's Al Anbar province. Speaking of what will be done to his tribal opponents, a leader said in late 2014, "This is a tribal issue for us right now. There's no way to let them live. I'm not going to leave any of them alive. It's them, their family members and all their property. We're going to destroy them all."[9] He might as well have been speaking in the prephilosophical world of ninth century B.C. Note that tribal vengeance can be taken on *any* member of an offending tribe—not necessarily upon the tribal members responsible for the grievance—because what really exists is the tribe, not the individuals who are part of it. Therefore, it is the tribe that must be punished, and any part of it will do for that purpose. This helps explain what otherwise would seem like random attacks upon the West by Islamist terrorists who are happy to kill *any* Westerner in retaliation for their perceived "humiliation". These terrorists, including those with graduate degrees, are mostly still living under the mores of prephilosophical Arab tribal culture, which justifies revenge against any member of the opposing tribe—meaning, in this case, the West or the "Romans", as they often call Westerners.

Wherever and so long as the tribal mentality prevails, constitutional order is difficult, if not impossible, to develop. Reflecting on the Aden British Protectorate in southern Yemen in the 1930s, colonial administrator Harold Ingrams reported, "Thus we had upwards of 1,400 separate tribal 'governments' in the two states. There were

---

[8] Ibid., 28.

[9] Matt Bradley, "War Carves Divisions among Iraq's Sunnis", *Wall Street Journal*, December 10, 2014, A10.

also several hundred autonomous towns of unarmed men.... Altogether I calculated there were about 2,000 separate 'governments' in the Hadhramaut."[10] Fighting is endemic to such situations. In Saudi Arabia, a country that formally abolished slavery only in 1962, King Salman explained why his country cannot consider democracy: "If Saudi Arabia adopts democracy, every tribe would be a party" and the country would be impossible to govern.[11] The tribal mentality is obviously inimical to the principle of equality, which is at the foundation of constitutional rule. One cannot say that "all men are created equal" until one knows what man is, which requires, as well, knowledge of the differences between nature and convention, the human and the nonhuman, and the human and the divine. These differentiations are essential to defining what *is* human.

Without an idea as to what exactly a human being is, tribal man was (and is) often unable to demarcate clearly between the human and the nonhuman—between man and animals or things—and between these things and the divine. They fluidly blended together along a continuum and were often thought to shift their shapes from one to another. (This was especially so in ancient Egypt. See Henri Frankfort's *Before Philosophy*.) Amid this confusion, it was not unusual for tribal man to take animals or things, such as trees and rocks, as idols and worship them. As Athenagoras of Athens noted, even as late as the second century A.D., "the Egyptians regard even cats, crocodiles, snakes, asps, and dogs as gods."[12] The sine qua non of democratic, constitutional order is the knowledge of *what* a human being is—as distinct from what an animal is, or what the gods are. The metaphysical mix-up of these things obviated any such possibility for tribal man.

Magic Time: The Problem with Pantheism

For the ancients, the divine order, far from transcending the world, was part of it. Without the transcendent, they considered the world as

---

[10] Cited in Tim Mackintosh-Smith, *Arabs* (New Haven, Conn.: Yale University Press, 2019), v.

[11] Karen Elliott House, "A Smooth Saudi Succession, but a Rough Road Ahead", *Wall Street Journal*, January 24–25, 2015, A13.

[12] Cited in Timothy Samuel Shah and Allen D. Hertzke, eds., *Christianity and Freedom*, vol. 1, *Historical Perspectives* (New York: Cambridge University Press, 2016), 48.

the whole of reality. There was nothing outside it. Even the gods were within it. In their view of the cosmos, the ultimate good or the final end resided in the empyrean, the uppermost regions within, not above, the cosmos. The suggestion that something existed prior to or outside, and therefore above, the cosmos would not have made any sense to an ancient because, for him, the cosmos was eternal. If matter is eternal, then the world exists necessarily. If the world exists necessarily, it must be divine. This is the premise on which ancient man populated the world with gods and spirits. To illustrate its literal geography, here is a typical description given by Ocellus of Lucania, a Pythagorean philosopher, in the fifth century B.C.: "The course of the moon is the isthmus (*isthmos*) of immortality and generation. All that is above it, and upon it, the race of the gods occupies, that which is below the moon [is occupied by the race] of discord (*neikos*) and nature."[13]

In the pantheism of the ancient world, everything was animated by its own spirit or god.

> The whole of nature teemed with beings whom we find it hard to name.... These nature spirits ... were far from being the only super-human beings that encompassed man.... The whole world believed in divination.... The flight of birds, the entrails of beasts, rain, thunder, lightning, everything was a means of divination.... That superstition so gross was accompanied by a paralyzing belief in magic, enchant-ment, miracle, astrology and witchcraft generally is not surprising.[14]

Ancient Babylonians specialized in hepatoscopy—sheep-liver divina-tion. Reading omens in that era led to such pronouncements as this: "If a white dog urinates on a man, hard times will seize that man. If the red dog urinates on a man, that man will have happiness."[15] Elab-orate rituals were devised to ward off evil: "You shall make a dog of clay. You shall put [a piece of] cedar wood on its neck. You shall pour oil on its head. You shall clothe it in a goatskin."[16] In Québec, French

---

[13] Cited in Rémi Brague, *Wisdom of the World: The Human Experience of the Universe in West-ern Thought*, trans. Teresa Lavender Fagan (Chicago: University of Chicago Press, 2003), 107.

[14] T.R. Glover, *The Conflict of Religions in the Early Roman Empire* (Boston: Beacon, 1960), 18.

[15] H.W.F. Saggs, *The Babylonians* (London: Macmillan, 1988), 252

[16] Ibid.

Jesuit Paul Le Jeune provided an example of the animistic mind-set from the prephilosophical North American Indians. In a report to his superiors in 1634, he wrote, "I ask them about thunder; and they said they did not know what animal it was; that it ate snakes, and sometimes trees; that the Hurons believed it to be a very large bird."[17]

Because we may find these examples amusing, it is hard for us to comprehend how thoroughly reality was understood in this animistic way and how seriously it was taken by the prephilosophical mind. But it is necessary to do so if we are to realize the revolutionary impact of the advent of philosophy, which upended this magical view of things through the introduction of cause and effect in the natural world, as we shall see next in the section on Athens. So long as the magical interpretation of reality prevailed, reason could not assume its central role in determining how man ought to live or rule himself. Such questions were decided by divination, not reason. A miraculous view of things makes the world incomprehensible precisely because it *is* miraculous—the result of mysterious forces for which one is unable to give a rational account.

Also, if everything is sacred, as it must be in pantheism, then nothing is secular; there is no room for the notion of a secular state. The secular *requires* the transcendent for the integrity of its own status. Only the transcendent can lift from the world the otherwise necessary notion of its own divinity and allow room for the profane. (The current loss of the transcendent in the West has led to the Mother Earth or Gaia type of environmental movement, which is basically a return to a form of ancient pantheism. Its adherents may be unaware that this will lead ineluctably to a redivinization of the state, to which they will be subject.)

Another problem with the eternal world was that it was in a state of constant flux—a condition, as we shall see, not favorable to a conception of constitutional order. Many of the ancients understood creation as the result of a battle between the gods. Creation was neither ex nihilo nor entirely good. In a primeval conflict, a god of light and a god of darkness struggled for supremacy. The violent struggle of these demiurges manifested itself in the turmoil erupting in life and

---

[17] Harry W. Kirwin, ed., *The Search for Democracy: A Documentary Record of the American Republic* (Garden City, N.Y.: Doubleday, 1959), 13.

nature. Consequently, instability constantly threatened to overwhelm the very tentative order of the world with the chaos out of which it originally arose. A deep suspicion that there is an underlying malignity to things animated this bifurcated view of reality. Its Gnostic version identified matter with evil itself in battle with the principle of light or goodness. To free man from evil meant to free him from matter, so that he could become pure light again.

Man's principal preoccupation was placating the demiurges to prevent the collapse of the world back into chaos. This often required blood sacrifices. As a result, the ancient world hemorrhaged in torrents of human and animal blood. The burnt child offerings to Baal immediately come to mind, as do the bloody exertions of the Aztecs (also a prephilosophical people), who believed that the sun would not rise without the sacrifice of a torn-out, still-beating human heart. High holy days required the sacrifice of thousands. Somewhat like the Manichaeans, the Aztecs believed that "divine sun fragments" were entrapped in the human body. Released, they would rejoin the sun. The inherent instability of a world in flux that is kept only somewhat steady by constant human sacrifice to propitiate the angry gods is not a realm conducive to constitutional rule, whose basis is a rational universe made by a rational Creator.

The Problem with an Eternal Universe

The eternity of the world also made what we think of as history incomprehensible to ancient man. For him, history was simply a giant turning wheel, the endless circular repetition of events. All empires were fated to end, but once all possibilities had been exhausted, they were destined to repeat themselves: interminable cycles of rising and falling. History was not intelligible as a progression—with beginning, middle, and end. There was no beginning and no end and, therefore, no middle. Certainly, ancient man attempted to record the deeds of great and noble men for posterity, but there was an acknowledged futility to this effort.

Everything was subject to fate, and fate was inscrutable. According to the famous verse from Cleanthes' "Hymn of Zeus", translated from Greek into Latin by Seneca the Younger: "The fates lead the willing and drag the unwilling" (ducunt volentem fata, nolentem trahunt). Fatalism does not serve well as a foundation for constitutional rule. It subverts free will and makes man the victim of forces outside his control, rather than the subject of his own purpose, over which he has some control. Man does not go about creating legislative institutions in which he will decide things when he believes things have already been decided for him. Therefore, the idea of constitutional rule would not be naturally intelligible to cultures in which fate plays the primary role in man's destiny.

In this and other ways, the doctrine of an eternal pantheistic world had profound consequences for the status of the human person. Entrapped within it, he was diminished by it. Romano Guardini wrote that ancient man "was neither able to view nor to shape his world from a vantage point which transcended it".[18] The eternal cosmos was indifferent to his fleeting existence. It rendered him insignificant. The eternity of the world was incompatible with the notion of a personal, providential God who values the individual person. Christianity's idea that every individual's soul is immortal and ordered to a transcendent end invests man with eternal worth and places limits upon political power exercised over him. In fact, without immortality, there really is no reason for such limits, as the state would naturally assume *itself* as the proper end of man. Only if man's end can be placed in the transcendent is there a compelling reason to keep the state in its proper place.

In summary, the prephilosophical ancient world of tribes and cosmological empires was unsuitable for the development of constitutional rule for the following reasons. If man lives in a world of which he can make no sense, an irrational, magical world, he can choose only to surrender to fate or to despair. Reason and freedom become irrelevant. If man is not a political creature endowed with reason in a world accessible to his mind, why attempt to order political life based on deliberation? In such circumstances, man will not go about writing constitutions, for constitutions by their very nature imply a belief in a stable external order (not a free-for-all between demiurges), in man's reasonability, and in his ability to formulate and establish a

---

[18] Romano Guardini, *The End of the Modern World* (Wilmington, Del.: Intercollegiate Studies Institute, 2001), 2–3.

rational mode of government, grounded in a rational creation (not in divination).

The Philosophical World: Athens

Before seeing how Jewish monotheism subverted pantheistic polytheism, we will examine how Greek philosophy transformed the prephilosophical mentality. Athens offered what Benedict XVI called "the gift of the Greeks": philosophy, which made possible the discovery of natural law. Greek philosophy overthrew the tribal view of man with the idea that the mind can know things, as distinct from merely having opinions about them, because reality exists objectively, independently of what anyone may think about it. It is accessible to the intellect and can therefore be truly *known* as it is. Through reason, man can ascertain the truth of things. Most importantly, there seems to be some rational purpose implied in the world's order, and this purpose has to do with what is called "the good", toward which man's soul is ultimately ordered. The source of this "good" exists outside and above the political order and is therefore not determined by it. Rational laws of nature allow men to distinguish between nature and convention—why a dog wags its tail, for instance, versus why Egyptians paint their funeral caskets in bright colors. For the first time (under Cleisthenes), citizenship became a matter of locality rather than membership in a tribe.

How could Greek philosophy claim the aptitude to know these things? From where came its confidence that reason is a better guide to reality than the divination of animal entrails by a high priest? The suggested answers to these profound questions came before Plato and Aristotle in the sixth and fifth centuries B.C. Some claim it was Heraclitus who first grasped that the universe is an intelligible whole and that therefore man is able to apprehend its order. (Others say it was Anaximander.) How can man do this, and in what terms can it be articulated? Heraclitus said that the universe is intelligible because it is ruled by and is the product of "thought", or wisdom. As far as we know, Heraclitus and Parmenides were the first to use the word *logos* to name this wisdom. *Logos* means "reason" or "word" in Greek. Heraclitus meant that all things are animated by a rational principle. He stated that "all things come to pass in accordance with this logos."

If this is true, then man's inquiry into the nature of reality becomes possible. The very idea of "nature" becomes possible. Heraclitus said, "It is the highest virtue and true wisdom in speaking and acting to obey nature that is the common logos. Therefore, all human laws are nourished by this original divine law."[19] It is logos that makes the world intelligible to the endeavor of philosophy, in other words, reason, and it is why laws, in turn, must be reasonable. As Socrates later said, "The world is the product of a Mind which sets everything in order and produces each individual thing in the way that is best for it."[20] We can have thoughts about things that are the product of thought. We can also have thoughts about the Thinker, leading Aristotle to describe God as "thought thinking itself". The Maker is reflected in the things he made, since they are not made accidentally but according to logos. Through reason, said Socrates, man can know "what is".

Natural Law: *What Is*

Aristotle said that "what is" operates according to the laws of nature. What are these laws? Since the subject of natural law is central to our topic, we will closely examine what is meant by it. Aristotle taught that the essence, or nature, of a thing is what makes it what it is, and why it is not, and cannot be, something else. (No more Egyptian shape-shifting of one thing into another.) In the *Politics*, he said that "the 'nature' of things consists in their end or consummation; for what each thing is when its growth is completed we call the nature of that thing, whether it be a man or a horse or a family."[21] For example, as an acorn develops into an oak tree, there is no point along its trajectory of growth when it will turn into something other than an oak. That is because it has the nature of an oak tree and not of anything else. It is inwardly directed to be an oak tree. Hence,

---

[19] Heinrich A. Rommen, *The State in Catholic Thought* (St. Louis: B. Herder, 1945), 156.
[20] Plato, *Phaedo* 99d.
[21] Aristotle, *Politics* 1, 2, 1252b.

by nature or natural law, Aristotle meant the principle of development that makes any living thing what it is and, given the proper
conditions, what it will become when it reaches its fulfillment.
For Aristotle, "nature ever seeks an end."[22] He declared, "Nature
does nothing without purpose or uselessly."[23] This end state is
a thing's *telos*, the reason for which it is. The telos of the acorn is a
fully mature oak tree. As Msgr. Robert Sokolowski, a philosopher
at Catholic University of America, said, "The end of a thing is its
perfection; the nature is what is perfected. The nature and end of
a thing are normative for that thing; the end, in particular, is how
the thing should be."[24] The natural law for each thing is what allows
us to speak of what it "ought" to be.

This means that what is "good" for a thing are those things or
actions that assist it in reaching its perfection. For example, the right
kind of soil and moisture are good for the acorn in reaching its perfection as an oak tree. Likewise, those things that inhibit or prevent
something from reaching its end are "bad" for it, as drought or poi-
soned soil would be bad for an acorn. In each case, Aristotle would
refer to the things that are good for the growth of the oak tree as
natural to it, and the things that are bad for its growth as *unnatural* to
it. What is good or natural for something is, therefore, *intrinsic* to that
thing, internal to and inseparable from it. It is not imposed from the
outside, and it cannot be altered.

In nonhuman creation, this design by nature is manifested through
either physical laws or instinct. In plants or animals, this involves no
self-conscious volition. In man, it does. Man is the only creature
that has conscious knowledge of the end for which he was made.
In classical Greek thought, a "freeman" is one who is moved to act
according to an understanding of the nature of things.[25] Only the
freeman truly knows what he is doing. Man alone has the ability to
choose between the acts or things that are conducive to his end and
those that are not. Animals, plants, and rocks cannot do this. Only
man can act in defiance of his nature, which is what defines "evil"

---

[22] Aristotle, *Generation of Animals* I, 715b15.

[23] Aristotle, *Politics* I, 1256b20–21.

[24] Personal correspondence with the author, 2018.

[25] Charles Nicholas Reiten McCoy, *On the Intelligibility of Political Philosophy: Essays of
Charles N. R. McCoy*, eds. James V. Schall and John J. Schrems (Washington, D.C.: Catholic
University of America Press, 1989), 151.

for him. Since man freely chooses his behavior, he is the only one for whom the natural law is *moral*. This is why Aristotle said, "The moral activities are human *par excellence*."[26] Therefore, references to natural law in regard to man mean not so much the physical laws or instinct to which he is subject like the lower orders of being, but the *moral* law, which applies exclusively to him. Aquinas would later expand on this meaning in his *Summa theologica*:

> All things partake somewhat of the eternal law, insofar as, namely, from its being imprinted on them, they derive their respective inclinations to their proper acts and ends. Now among all others, the rational creature is subject to Divine Providence in a more excellent way, insofar as it partakes of a share of Providence, by being provident for itself and for others. Wherefore it has a share of the eternal reason, whereby it has a natural inclination to its proper act and end, and this participation of the eternal law in the rational creature is called the *natural law*.[27]

It is especially important to emphasize that Aristotle said man does not make himself to be man: "Statesmanship does not create human beings but having received them from nature makes use of them."[28] He meant that man does not fabricate his end or telos. Human nature is a given. Its meaning is not located in man's will or desires, but in preexisting reality—in *what is*. Consequently, while man can know what is good or evil, he does not have the prerogative to *determine* what is good or evil. "Oughtness" is already in the given nature of things. Therefore, man is morally *obliged* to choose the good that will bring about what "ought" to be. Otherwise, he will become less than fully human and what he "ought" *not* to be—perhaps even something worse than a beast, as Aristotle warned.

The End of Man and Morality

If everything human must be measured against it, what *is* man's telos? Aristotle answered: "Happiness is the highest good, being a realization

---

[26] Aristotle, *Nicomachean Ethics* 10, 8.

[27] Thomas Aquinas, *Summa theologica* I-II, q. 91, a. 2 (my emphasis).

[28] Aristotle, *Politics* 1258a21–22.

and perfect practice of virtue."[29] Having established the primacy of reason as the highest human faculty, Aristotle asked in what way it served man's end. He answered that the highest exercise of man's reason is contemplation of the highest good, which is divine. Aristotle wrote, "Contemplation is ... the highest form of activity (since the intellect is the highest thing in us, and the objects it apprehends are the highest things that can be known)."[30] He said that "the activity of God, which surpasses all others in blessedness, must be contemplative; and of human activities, therefore, that which is most akin to this must be most of the nature of happiness." If man is by nature in relation to a divine good, it must mean that he has within himself some means of coming to know it. With his finite mind, man can somehow apprehend, at least in part, the infinite. Though he is not divine, man must strive to be godlike through the exercise of his reason. Aristotle counseled that "we must not follow those who advise us, being men, to think of human things, and, being mortal, of mortal things, but must, so far as we can, make ourselves immortal, and strain every nerve to live in accordance with the best thing in us; for even if it be small in bulk, much more does it in power and worth surpass everything."[31]

We see in Aristotle's account an adumbration of Aquinas' definition of final and perfect happiness as "nothing else than the vision of the Divine Essence".[32] As Josef Pieper explained, "The ultimate perfection attainable to us, in the minds of the philosophers of Greece, was this: that the order of the whole of existing things should be inscribed in our souls. And this conception was afterwards absorbed into the Christian tradition in the conception of the beatific vision: 'What do they not see, who see Him who sees all things?' "[33]

Thus it was, thanks to Greek philosophy, that reason became normative. For the first time, instead of dreams, the entrails of dismembered birds, or signs in the night sky, reason came to be the arbiter of right and wrong. It is through reason—not from the gods of the city, tribal mores, or the spirits of things—that man can discern what

[29] Aristotle, *Politics* 1328a.

[30] Aristotle, *Nicomachean Ethics* 10, 1177a20.

[31] Ibid., 1177b20.

[32] Thomas Aquinas, *Summa theologica* I-II, q. 1, a. 7.

[33] Josef Pieper, *Leisure: The Basis of Culture* (New York: Random House, 1963), 82.

is just from what is unjust, what is good from what is evil, what is myth from what is reality. He can discern natural causality and ascribe to things their true causes, rather than assigning magical properties to everything. Red-dog urine, contrary to Babylonian belief, is not actually a causal factor in producing happiness. Behaving reasonably or doing what accords with reason should be the standard of moral behavior and, therefore, the standard of law. To do what is unreasonable is wrong. As Aquinas, reflecting Aristotle, would later say, the essential character of sin or vice is its *irrationality*. The *Catechism of the Catholic Church* states that "sin is an offense against reason" (1849). The rule of reason is necessary for human beings on account of their rational nature. This view is the foundation for the primacy of reason over the primacy of force—an essential prerequisite for the development of constitutional order.

The idea that all men are constituted in the same essential way, their souls directed to the same good grounded in the order of the divine, is fraught with enormous political consequences. Aristotle wrote, "Universal law is the law of Nature. There really is, as everyone to some extent divines, a natural justice and injustice that is binding on all men, even on those who have no association or covenant with each other."[34] If men are ordered to the same good, regardless of where they live or who they are, then there must be a single standard of justice that transcends the political standards of any city. It must be the same at all times, everywhere, for everyone.

The Order of the City and the Order of the Soul

Before Aristotle, Socrates had taught this lesson in a somewhat different form. He said that the order of the city is the order of the soul writ large. Disorder in the soul leads to disorder in the city, and likewise, order in the soul leads to order the city. It is not the city, however, that can move the soul to its ultimate destination. The order of the soul and the order of the city (the political order) are not the same; the one, in fact, transcends the other; and man, therefore, owes his final allegiance to the higher order. Socrates taught this lesson in

[34] Aristotle, *Rhetoric* I, 1373b6–9.

the *Republic* by transposing the order of the soul into the order of the polis to show what the attempt to meet its demands through political means would look like. Such a polis would destroy the family, engage in eugenics, militarize its citizens, and eliminate privacy. Any attempt to fulfill the soul's ultimate desires through political means would transform the polis into a proto-totalitarian enterprise. As classicist Eva Brann remarks, "Thus the inside teaching is that extremism, the attempt to institute ideal justice on earth, will end in disastrous injustice, for this city is extremely coercive."[35] In other words, the soul may not be subsumed by political ends. It is inviolate and supersedes the order of the polis because politics is unable to achieve the highest human end.

In one of the most moving passages in political philosophy, Socrates said, "In heaven there is laid up a pattern of it [the ideal city], methinks, which he who desires may behold, and beholding may set his own house in order. But whether such a one exists, or ever will exist in fact, does not matter; for he will live after the manner of that city, having nothing to do with any other."[36] For Socrates, life should be a preparation for residence in this heavenly city. As Fr. James Schall wrote, "To put this city in speech in our souls is the essence of what it is to know."[37] In other words, the good and the wise will live according to a spiritual order that transcends the actual and particular order in which the individual lives. Socrates' city in speech beautifully adumbrates the New Testament's description of Abraham as "look[ing] forward to the city which has foundations, whose builder and maker is God" (Heb 11:10). Socrates foresaw the truth of Paul's statement: "Our commonwealth is in heaven" (Phil 3:20).

We are so familiar with this teaching and have for so long been its beneficiaries that it is almost impossible for us to appreciate how revolutionary it was when first set forth. Because philosophy directed them to an ideal city in speech that transcended Athens, Socrates was accused of alienating Athenian youth from their patrimony.

---

[35] Eva Brann, "Plato's 'Republic': Impossible Polity", *Imaginative Conservative*, July 23, 2018, http://www.theimaginativeconservative.org/2018/07/platos-republic-impossible-polity-eva -brann.html?mc_cid=d8a48ab415&mc_eid=89abaa241c.

[36] Plato, *Republic* 592b.

[37] James V. Schall, *The Life of the Mind: On the Joys and Travails of Thinking* (Wilmington, Del.: Intercollegiate Studies Institute, 2008), 169.

He taught them to order their souls according to the ideal city, and not only to the city of Athens. The Athenians considered this blasphemous. It was an affront to the gods upon whose favor the city depended and therefore a threat to the civic order. For the impiety of suggesting that there could be a standard of justice independent of and above the city's gods, Socrates was put on trial. In rebuttal to the charges against him, he said, "Men of Athens, I honor and love you; but I shall obey God rather than you, and while I have life and strength I shall never cease from the practice and teaching of philosophy."[38] Nothing could have illustrated more dramatically, or taught more powerfully, the ultimate incongruity of the spiritual and political orders than the death of Socrates.

Socrates' location of the ideal city in the spiritual realm prefigured the separation of the sacred and the secular that Christianity eventually brought about, without which the United States would have been inconceivable. The ultimate ordering of man's soul to the transcendent is the principal impetus for limiting politics. Thus Aristotle insisted that politics is not the highest thing: "It would be strange to think that the art of politics, or practical wisdom, is the best knowledge since man is not the highest being in the world."[39] If man were the highest being, politics would be the highest science, and there would be no limits to the political. Fr. Schall warned, "Once we think contrary to Aristotle, that man is the highest being, it follows that the state is the highest being, if it wants to be."[40] Aristotle also said that the best constitution is the one aimed at "the best life that is possible" but that the constitution cannot define "best life", because it is "the complete activity and employment of virtue, and not conditionally but *absolutely*".[41] In other words, philosophy is a constraint on politics, which is why politics sometimes tries to destroy it, as it destroyed Socrates. Philosophy limits the range of politics by pointing to a higher truth, which is not within the polis' power to determine or reach, but only to reflect in its own order if properly constituted.

These profound insights of Greek philosophy prepared the grounds for the consummate act of civilization—the recognition by man of his

[38] Plato, *Apology* 29d.
[39] Aristotle, *Nicomachean Ethics* 1141a20.
[40] Correspondence with the author.
[41] Aristotle, *Politics* 1328a and 1332a (emphasis added).

fellow men as members of the same species. This acknowledgment is at the basis of Western civilization, which has since called barbarian those who are incapable of it, such as the tribal members referred to earlier. With philosophy, men can discern the difference between custom, which can be changed because it is a human contrivance, and nature, which cannot be changed. When man understands this difference, he is no longer tribal man.

Aristotle's concept of natural law has major implications for man-made, or positive, law: it should not be based simply on the "will" of the ruler. In the most powerful Roman articulation of Aristotelian teaching, Cicero said:

> True law is reason, right and natural, commanding people to ful-fill their obligation and prohibiting and deterring them from doing wrong. Its validity is universal; it is immediate and eternal. Its commands and prohibitions apply effectively to good men, and those uninfluenced by them are bad. Any attempt to supersede this law, to repeal any part of it, is sinful; to cancel it entirely is impossible. Neither the Senate nor the Assembly can exempt us from its demands; we need no interpreter or expounder of it but ourselves. There will not be one law in Rome, one in Athens, or one now and one later, but all nations will be subject all the time to this one changeless and everlasting law: for God, who is its author and promulgator, is always the sole author and sovereign of mankind.[42]

Cicero, who was a major influence on eighteenth-century American political leaders, said that "wicked and unjust statutes" are not laws because "in the very definition of the term 'law' there inheres the idea and principle of choosing what is just and true."[43] In other words, positive law—law made by legislatures or rulers—is legitimate only to the extent to which it harmonizes with natural law, which is the objective source of the distinction between what is just and what is unjust. A positive law made contrary to natural law would be, by definition, unjust.

The Founders frequently referred to and quoted Cicero. When John Adams started a book study group, the first work they examined

---

[42] Cicero, *On the Commonwealth* 3, 33.
[43] Cicero, *De Legibus* 2, 11.

was Cicero's *Pro Milone*. Adams quoted Cicero in his *Defence of the Constitutions of the United States*: "Those laws, which are right reason, derived from the Divinity, commanding honesty, forbidding iniquity; which are silent magistrates, where the magistrates are only speaking laws; which as they are founded in eternal morals, are emanations of the Divine mind."[44] In his *Lectures on Law*, James Wilson also cited passages from *Pro Milone*.

The Problem of Happiness

Aristotle's definition of happiness set up a major dilemma of which we must be aware if we are to understand the significance of the contribution made by Christianity (addressed after the next section, on Jerusalem). Both Socrates and Aristotle admitted that the attainment of wisdom was so difficult that few, if any, could achieve it. Aristotle said that leisure is a necessary condition for the contemplation of the good. As only a few possess leisure, this presents a huge problem. What is more, even those with leisure face nearly insurmountable obstacles in obtaining wisdom because human nature "is in many ways in bondage", such that "the possession of [wisdom] might be justly regarded as beyond human power."[45] This statement seems to be in tension with Aristotle's teaching that "nature ever seeks an end" and that "always the tendency in each is towards the same end, if there is no impediment."[46] How is it, then, that, in all of nature, only man's end seems practically unreachable because of seemingly insurmountable "impediments"? If the possession of wisdom is the final perfection of man, how is it that even in the best regime, the many will never be wise? What about peasants, workers, and slaves who do not have the possibility of reaching the height of human attainment because they have no leisure to pursue wisdom? What is the purpose or end of their lives—only to support the leisure of those who do pursue it? Then most people are left out, doomed to frustration. As

---

[44] *The Works of John Adams: Second President of the United States*, 10 vols. (Boston: Charles C. Little and James Brown, 1850–1856), 6:56.

[45] Aristotle, *Metaphysics* 1, 982b28.

[46] Aristotle, *Generation of Animals* 1, 715b15; Aristotle, *Physics* 2, 8, 199b15–18.

twentieth-century political philosopher Leo Strauss observed, "If striving for knowledge of the eternal truth is the ultimate end of man,... the man who is merely just or moral without being a philosopher appears as a mutilated human being."[47]

As Aquinas would later say, "To strive for any end that cannot be secured is futile."[48] Therefore, the happiness to which all men are naturally ordered as their final perfection cannot consist in the happiness of only a few. That would indeed be futile. Thus, philosophy raised a question that it could not answer: How could man have a nature whose end is practically unobtainable? This question seemed in itself unreasonable on the very basis of the rational nature that the Greek philosophers had discovered through logos. It is the very keenness of this conundrum that made Christian revelation intelligible to the Hellenistic world that first received it, because it addressed the problem that man seemed to be made for something beyond his reach. Christianity would not have been as comprehensible without the philosophers' question preparing the way for it, as we shall see.

The immense importance of the Athenian legacy for eighteenth-century Americans was that the new nation would not have come into being without the understanding of nature as normative. It would be difficult to overstate the impact of the classical Greek thinkers (often conveyed through their Roman disciples) on the Founders, whose education was in large part informed by their works. Thomas Jefferson listed Aristotle, along with Cicero, as one of the classical sources that influenced the writing of the Declaration of Independence, which famously declares "the Laws of Nature and of Nature's God" as its authority. Also, Aristotle's concept of natural law was adopted and expanded upon by Aquinas, from whom Richard Hooker then received it. Hooker, in turn, was a major influence on Algernon Sidney, John Locke, and others directly associated with the intellectual lineage of the American Founding.

The higher standard that the Founders invoked against the depredations of the British Empire was what is right by nature. It is the objective standard to which they appealed against the arbitrary

---

[47] Leo Strauss, *Natural Right and History* (Chicago: University of Chicago Press, 1965), 151.
[48] Thomas Aquinas, *Summa contra gentiles* 3, 44.

exercise of British power. Aristotle's and Cicero's view of the relationship between natural and positive law motivated the American Founders in their revolution against Great Britain and was used to justify it. For them, there could not be one law in London for the British and another law in Philadelphia for them, but only one law based on the higher natural law, which they argued that the British had violated.

Jerusalem: Transcendent Monotheism

In the ancient Middle East, only one tribe, the Jews—regularly beaten by other tribes—formulated a far different cosmogony from the prevalent mythologies. Immersed in a sea of polytheism, Judaism was unique in its monotheism and ferocious in its condemnation of the surrounding idolatry: "Hear, O Israel: The LORD our God is one LORD" (Deut 6:4). The Wisdom of Solomon expressed Hebrew revulsion at idol worship, in which men

> bestowed on objects of stone or wood the name
>   that ought not to be shared.
> Afterward it was not enough for them to err
>   about the knowledge of God,
> but they live in great strife due to ignorance,
> and they call such great evils peace.
> For whether they kill children in their
>   initiations, or celebrate secret mysteries,
> or hold frenzied revels with strange customs,
> they no longer keep either their lives or their
>   marriages pure, . . .
> For the worship of idols not to be named
> is the beginning and cause and end of every evil.
>
> (14:21–24, 27)

Even when the Jews were defeated in battle or conquered by Assyrians, Babylonians, Persians, Greeks, and Romans, they quite extraordinarily did not consider their God defeated. There was no other god to defeat him. If the Hebrews were overcome by the Babylonians and taken as their captives, it was not because their

God had failed them, but because they had failed their God. Jewish Scripture reveals the Israelites' dawning consciousness that their God is not the god of their city or their tribe, but is the wholly transcendent, omniscient, omnipotent God. "He Who Is", Yahweh, is worshipped not only to bring victory in battle or abundance to the harvest, but because he is the God of all people and all things. Through the prophet Isaiah, God implored: "Turn to me and be saved, all the ends of the earth! For I am God, and there is no other" (Is 45:22).

What is more, Yahweh entered into a covenant with Abraham that was at other times renewed, as with Moses. The unprecedented aspect of the covenant is that it defined a *reciprocal* relationship. God was every bit as bound by it as was man: "You shall be my people, and I will be your God" (Ezek 36:28). The covenant contained an astonishing level of personal intimacy between Yahweh and man as between lover and beloved. Abraham questioned God over what he would be justified in doing to the cities of Sodom and Gomorrah. When Jacob wrestled with a divine presence, he held him fast and demanded, "I will not let you go, unless you bless me" (Gen 32:26). Then Jacob was told that his new name was Israel, meaning "he who struggles with God". When Job was afflicted with great suffering, he exclaimed, "But I would speak to the Almighty, and I desire to argue my case with God" (Job 13:3). Of all the figures in the Old Testament, Moses had the greatest intimacy with Yahweh. When God revealed himself in the burning bush, Moses asked him to tell him his name, and God replied: "I AM WHO I AM.... Say this to the sons of Israel, 'I AM has sent me to you'" (Ex 3:14). In the wilderness, Moses persuaded God to relent in his punishment of the Hebrews for their infidelity.

This covenantal relationship was unlike anything before it or around it in Mesopotamia or anywhere else in the ancient world. Hebrew revelation is charged with the extraordinary drama of the development of the relationship between Yahweh and his people, as they come to understand more fully who I AM *is*. The journey of the Jewish people drew its meaning from the covenant betweem them and God, which also had a profound influence upon the agreements men would establish among themselves as creatures made in God's image. (It certainly profoundly affected what the early Americans thought of themselves as doing, as it likewise affected the Founders, who envisaged themselves in an analogous covenant.)

The Goodness of Creation and the *Imago Dei*

Jewish revelation was also uniquely distinctive in that Yahweh exists not within the universe but outside it. He is transcendent. The world has not always existed; it is not eternal. Made out of nothing by Yahweh, it had a beginning and will have an end. This was the death knell of pantheism. (Christianity would later deliver the coup de grâce. Against the Roman pantheists, Saint Augustine said, "In the true theology, the earth is the work of God, not his mother."[49]) This emancipated man from the mythical. At the same time, Genesis makes clear that Yahweh did not create out of any necessity. He creates freely out of his goodness. "By the word of the LORD the heavens were made.... For he spoke, and it came to be; he commanded, and it stood forth" (Ps 33:6, 9). What is more, he made it well: nothing exists that he did not make, and *all* of it is good. As the six days of creation are recounted in Genesis, we hear the majestic refrain after each: "And God saw that it was good." And then finally, "God saw everything that he had made, and behold, it was very good" (1:31). One thing that is especially good is man, who we are told was created in the *imago Dei* (image of God). No one else had ever imagined man made in his Maker's image. In Genesis we immediately see the irreducibility of man to material causes or to this world alone. The Genesis revelation that "God created man in his own image, in the image of God he created him" (1:27) formed the basis of Western civilization. The book of Wisdom repeats this revelation: "For God created man for incorruption, and made him in the image of his own eternity" (2:23). This is the fount from which sprang the sanctity of the individual person as invested with the divine image in his reason, free will, and immortality.

There is no notion of genuine human rights that does not in some way hearken back to this revelation. Preceding any constitutional effort to protect the inviolability of the human person comes

---

[49] Augustine, *The City of God* 6, 8.

the grounds for that inviolability in the ineradicable imago Dei. The notion that government may not violate human persons rests soundly only on the recognition that each individual is in God's image. As David Goldman writes, "Life has a sanctity that no human agency has a right to impair."[50] It is wholly impossible to imagine the Western world without this foundation stone.

Our very familiarity with Old Testament texts has robbed us of the astonishing uniqueness of the biblical idea that creation is *good*. Since all that exists is good, matter is good. Because it was made by God, creation is stable and reliable: "All his works are trustworthy" (Ps 33:4, NABRE). Yahweh's creation is not threatened by some evil demiurge who is equal to him and with whom he is in constant struggle for supremacy. Monotheism provided an assurance against the Zoroastrian or Manichaean bifurcation of creation into coequal forces of good and evil. Man may build confidently upon creation. It provides the necessary requisite for man's enterprise and exploration. It is impossible to find a comparable vision of creation expressed in the creation myths of the Assyrians, the Babylonians, the Persians, or any other ancient people. Moreover, as mentioned, in many polytheistic creation myths, evil threatens to overwhelm the universe, which would then dissolve back into primeval chaos.

In Israel's revelation of creation, God's handiwork is so well made that man can come to know the Creator by studying his works. The book of Wisdom called "foolish by nature" those men who "were unable from the good things that are seen to know him who exists, nor did they recognize the craftsman while paying heed to his works" (13:1). This well-made creation offers an invitation to natural theology (an invitation later taken up by the Declaration of Independence). The book of Wisdom also makes it clear that the Creator who reveals himself in his works has called his creatures and works into being ex nihilo out of love. The Scripture says of God:

> You love all things that exist,
> and you loathe none of the things which you
>   have made,
> for you would not have made anything if you
>   had hated it.

[50] David P. Goldman, "A Leap of 'Faith'", *Tablet*, August 31, 2018, https://www.tablet mag.com/jewish-life-and-religion/269596/scott-shay-leap-of-faith.

> How would anything have endured if you had
>   not willed it?
> Or how would anything not called forth by you
>   have been preserved?
> You spare all things, for they are yours, O Lord
>   who love the living.
> For your immortal spirit is in all things.
> (Wis 11:24–12:1)

This God is not indifferent to the destinies of individuals. Yahweh is a personal God whose providence extends over each man—a notion inconceivable to the non-Hebrew ancient world. Though transcendent, he involves himself in his creation for its benefit. A benign God guides a benevolent creation within which man's reason and free will have ample scope to operate in fulfillment of the ultimate goal of communion with God himself. The fundamental optimism of this perspective stands in stark contrast to the fatalistic views of reality surrounding it in the ancient Middle East.

The Origin of Evil

Unlike the ancient cosmologies, Genesis makes it very clear that evil does not derive from God, from an evil demiurge, or from matter, but from man's free will. Echoing Genesis, the writer of the book of Sirach exhorts:

> Do not say, "Because of the Lord I left the right way";
>   for he will not do what he hates.
> Do not say, "It was he who led me astray";
>   for he has no need of a sinful man. . . .
> It was he who created man in the beginning,
>   and he left him in the power of his own inclination.
> (15:11–12, 14)

Therefore, according to the biblical vision, man is responsible for disorder in creation, which originally resulted when he first used the gift of his freedom to disobey God. Locating the source of evil in the world rather than in man's will was the foundation of various Gnostic enterprises, as philosopher Eric Voegelin so powerfully

pointed out. Locating evil in man's will, as Genesis did, undermined
the Gnostic schemes and the peculiar political apparatuses that were
erected to achieve them, all of which required total control in order
to transform being itself. The Jewish and then Christian teaching on
the origin of evil became the most powerful antidotes to fanatical
political projects aimed at the metaphysical renovation of reality. This
was as true in the ancient world as it turned out to be in the twentieth
century's struggles against the modern Gnosticisms of Nazism and
Communism.[51]

Though given its accurate origination, evil still presented an enormous problem. The creation account in Genesis is followed by the
Fall, what Christians call Original Sin, a cataclysmic dislocation in
the relationship between God and man. Death entered the world
through it, and as Saint Paul said, "the whole creation has been groan-
ing" as a consequence of this breach (Rom 8:22), which is not within
man's power to repair. What would this created, finite being have to
offer the infinite Being, whom he had offended? Man knows he is incapable of offering anything of sufficient worth in reparation. So, God
responds: I will send you a Messiah; I will send you a Savior who will
do this for you. In the Old Testament, the prophets foretell who this
person will be and what he will do. The Jewish people still await his
arrival to complete this mission. The promise of redemption sparked
salvation history, which is the foundation of all modern history. History begins with the Jews. As Franz Rosenzweig wrote, "Revelation is
the first thing to set its mark firmly into the middle of time; only after
Revelation do we have an immovable Before and Afterward."[52] For
the first time, history became linear instead of cyclical. It now moved
with purpose from the beginning toward a consummation. As Eric
Voegelin wrote, "Without Israel there would be no history, but only
the eternal recurrence of societies in cosmological form."[53]

---

[51] One need only recall Hitler's proclamation in *Mein Kampf* of "a declaration of war against
the order of things which exist, against the state of things which exist, in a word, against the
structure of the world which presently exists". Cited in Kyle-Anne Shiver, "Obama's Politics
of Collective Redemption", *American Thinker*, February 11, 2008, http://www.american
thinker.com/articles/2008/02/obamas_politics_of_collective.html#ixzz3TTu6srY4.

[52] Cited in David P. Goldman, "Love with No Future", *First Things*, January 2017, https://
www.firstthings.com/article/2017/01/love-with-no-future.

[53] Eric Voegelin, *Order and History*, vol. 1, *Israel and Revelation* (Baton Rouge: Louisiana
State University Press, 1956), 168.

God's transcendence also had a dramatic effect on the political character of man's rule, which could no longer properly be theocratic. As intimated earlier, it allowed for the emergence of the secular. Henri Frankfort wrote:

> The Hebrew king normally functioned in the profane sphere, not the sacred sphere. He was the arbiter in disputes and the leader in war. He was emphatically not the leader in the cult.... He did not interpret the divine will; that again was the task of the priests.... [Hebrew religion] bereft kingship of a function which is exercised all over the near East, where its principal task lay in the maintenance of harmony with the gods of nature.... The transcendentalism of Hebrew religion prevented kingship from assuming the profound significance which it possessed in Egypt and Mesopotamia.[54]

When King Saul overstepped these boundaries and presumed to perform the sacred rites, the prophet Samuel upbraided him: "You have not kept the commandment of the LORD your God" (1 Sam 13:13). Jan Assmann calls the new order created by the Mosaic Law "a revolt against the political system of ancient Near Eastern sacral kingship".[55] Alfred North Whitehead said the Jews were "the first example of [a people's] refusal to worship the State".[56] The Judaic desacralization of the ruler, in contradistinction to the character of political rule surrounding the Hebrews, was an essential step in establishing the integrity of the secular sphere and in introducing the distinction between the religious and the civic, without which constitutional rule could not eventually develop.

The impact of all of this on the foundations of Western civilization, including the American Founding, is immeasurable. Such was its significance that, in 1809, John Adams wrote:

> I will insist that the Hebrews have done more to civilize men than any other nation. If I were an atheist, and believed in blind eternal fate, I

---

[54] Henri Frankfort, *Kingship and the Gods* (Chicago: University of Chicago Press, 1978), 342–43.

[55] Cited in Benjamin Balint, "Out of Egypt", review of *The Invention of Religion: Faith and Covenant in the Book of Exodus*, by Jan Assmann, *Claremont Review of Books* (Summer 2018): 66.

[56] Alfred North Whitehead, *Science and Philosophy* (New York: Philosophical Library, 1948), 75.

should still believe that fate had ordained the Jews to be the most essential instrument for civilizing nations. If I were an atheist of the other sect, who believe, or pretend to believe, that all is ordered by chance, I should believe that chance had ordered the Jews to preserve and propagate to all mankind the doctrine of a supreme, intelligent, wise, almighty Sovereign of the universe, which I believe to be the great essential principle of all morality, and consequently of all civilization.[57]

Elsewhere, he proclaimed, "As much as I love, esteem, and admire the Greeks, I believe the Hebrews have done more to enlighten and civilize the world. Moses did more than all their legislators and philosophers."[58]

Rome: Christianity—The Nuptials of Jerusalem and Athens

With the one true God, Jerusalem freed man from polytheism; and with philosophy, Athens freed him from the grip of tribal mores and superstition. The Greeks with their reason and the Jews with their revelation, however, seemed to abide in wholly separate realms. "What has Athens to do with Jerusalem?" Tertullian famously asked. These separate realms were conjoined in the most astonishing way by Christianity, which Friedrich Nietzsche sneeringly referred to as "Plato for the masses". There was some truth in Nietzsche's remark. While Christianity universalized the transcendent monotheism of Judaism and extended salvation to all, it embraced and elevated the philosophical truths of Greek philosophy. In effect, Christianity achieved the marriage of Athens and Jerusalem. We shall now turn to how this happened and its enormous significance for our topic.

Logos Incarnate

Against the preceding Greek philosophical background, one can come closer to realizing the electrifying effect of the opening of the

[57]John Adams to F.A. Vanderkemp, February 16, 1809, Founders Online, National Archives, https://founders.archives.gov/documents/Adams/99-02-02-5302.

[58]Undated marginalia in Marie-Jean-Antoine-Nicolas Caritat, Marquis de Condorcet, *Outlines of an Historical View of the Progress of the Human Mind* (1795), cited in Jon Meacham, *American Gospel: God, the Founding Fathers, and the Making of a Nation* (New York: Random House, 2007), 40.

Gospel of John, which was written in Greek. The English translation uses "Word" for *Logos*, but it can be rendered just as well by "Reason". For our purposes here, let us leave the Greek word *Logos* in the quotation: "In the beginning was the Logos, and the Logos was with God, and the Logos was God. He was in the beginning with God; all things were made through him" (1:1–3). Revelation confirmed Heraclitus' intuition that logos makes the universe comprehensible because all things were made by and through Logos. Logos is not an *it*—an intelligible principle or a cosmic force—but a *who*. This is what John announces so majestically: the Word incarnate. The startling thing about Christianity is that Logos does not simply remain the Wisdom behind the world but enters into it: "Logos became flesh and dwelt among us" (1:14). What if Heraclitus, having speculated on logos, encountered Logos walking through the door? The face of Logos made visible is the transforming experience of a Hellenized Christianity or of a Christianized Hellenism. It moved the classical world from an impersonal logos to a personal Logos. Heinrich Rommen remarked: "The purely deistic *Nous* of Aristotle became the Creator-God who transcends the world, but who continually sustains it through His omnipotence, directs it through His providence, and governs it according to His eternal law."[59] As Benedict XVI wrote, "The encounter between the biblical message and Greek thought did not happen by chance."[60] So profound was its impact that the Incarnation became the foundation for a new civilization.

As mentioned earlier, the Judeo-Christian tradition shaped the West by assigning the source of evil to Original Sin—the cataclysmic dislocation in the relationship between God and man, which resulted in "fallen nature". The essence of that sin is a disorder within man, the preference of himself to God: pride. From the New Testament, of course, Christians believe that the Messiah came in the figure of Jesus Christ, the acceptable sacrifice, through whose offering this terrible breach with God was repaired. The unbearable burden of sin

---

[59] Heinrich A. Rommen, *The Natural Law: A Study in Legal and Social History and Philosophy* (Indianapolis: Liberty Fund, 1998), 33.

[60] Benedict XVI, lecture at a meeting with the representatives of science, Regensberg, Germany, September 12, 2006, Vatican website, http://w2.vatican.va/content/benedict-xvi/en /speeches/2006/september/documents/hf_ben-xvi_spe_20060912_university-regensburg.html.

is lifted because he "takes away the sin of the world" (Jn 1:29). The irredeemable becomes redeemable. God undertook to "re-create" man and to remedy his disordered will and restore creation in a new and everlasting covenant, which could be achieved only by the sacrifice of Christ, and then by man's renouncing evil with good works in cooperation with God's mercy and grace. So long as man does not rebel against, and attempt to displace, the imago Dei within himself, he will be united with God in the afterlife, in which he will find fulfillment even beyond the limits of his nature. God's having become man sanctifies human life in a new way. Even the offscouring of mankind becomes ineffably precious—each individual the object of infinite Love.

The Christian view was thus comprehensive: it explained man's origins in God's creation, the existence of evil from Original Sin, and the final triumph of salvation in Christ over evil and death. Life was understandable in these terms: it had a meaning and purpose with which man could transform his sufferings into something endurable and ultimately salvific. If man could not feel at home here, he had the reassurance that he was meant for elsewhere. "Thou hast made us for Thyself, O Lord, and our hearts are restless until they rest in Thee."[61] Man's end, then, was outside of history in personal union with a transcendent, loving God, something man could not dare to have hoped for, much less imagined, until God revealed himself in Christ as desiring nothing more than to share his inner life with his creatures, to impart to them his divinity.

We shall now see how and in what ways Christianity shaped this new civilization through the elevation of the status of reason, the dedivinization of the world, and the recognition of the inviolability of the human person and the freedom of the human will. Christianity opened the way for the eventual development of the notions of popular sovereignty and consent, which stem from the realization of the dignity of the individual person. As we shall see, it also provides indispensable support for man's equality—the moral principle underlying the rule of law and constitutional government.

The disclosure of Christ as Logos could not be a clearer message that revelation involves Reason. We also know that creation was

---

[61] Augustine, *Confessions* I, I.

made by way of his divine intellect. God willed creation into being, but it was, and is, according to his *Word*. At the level of revelation, we now know why the world is rational—because God *is* Reason. God speaks to man with equal force through his reason, as he does through divine revelation. Early Church Father Clement of Alexandria (ca. 150–ca. 215) insisted on the relevance of reason to faith: "Philosophy, therefore, was a preparation, paving the way for him who is perfected in Christ."[62] The mid-second-century *Second Epistle of Clement*, also known as *The Recognitions*, spelled out the necessity of reason to faith, which is worth hearing at length:

> Do not think that we say that these things are only to be received by faith, but also that they are to be asserted by reason. For indeed it is not safe to commit these things to bare faith without reason, since assuredly truth cannot be without reason. And therefore he who has received these things fortified by reason, can never lose them; whereas he who receives them without proofs, by an assent to a simple statement of them, can neither keep them safely, nor is certain if they are true; because he who easily believes, also easily yields. But he who has sought reason for those things which he has believed and received, as though bound by chains of reason itself, can never be torn away or separated from those things which he hath believed. And therefore, according as any one is more anxious in demanding a reason, by so much will he be the firmer in preserving his faith.[63]

Also in the second century, Justin Martyr wrote:

> The Logos is the preexistent, absolute, personal Reason and Christ is the embodiment of it, the Logos incarnate. Whatever is rational is Christian. And whatever is Christian is rational. The Logos endowed all men with reason and freedom, which are not lost by the fall.... Those who lived reasonably and virtuously in obedience to this preparatory light were Christians in fact, though not in name; while those who lived unreasonably were Christless and enemies of Christ.[64]

---

[62] *The Sacred Writings of Clement of Alexandria*, vol. 1, trans. Philip Schaff and William Wilson (Altenmünster, Germany: Jazzybee Verlag, 2017), 224.

[63] *The Epistles of Clement* (Woodstock, Ontario: Devoted Publishing, 2017), 136.

[64] Cited in Philip Schaff, *History of the Christian Church*, vol. 2 (Brandon, Fla.: Revelation Insight, 2011), 558.

Justin claimed, according to Henry Chadwick, that "the gospel and the best elements in Plato and the Stoics are almost identical ways of apprehending the same truth."[65] The congruence between the questions asked by Greek philosophy and the answers given by Christianity led Clement of Alexandria to say, "Both slave and free must equally philosophize, whether male or female in sex ... whether barbarian, Greek, slave, whether an old man, or a boy, or a woman.... And we must admit that the same nature exists in every race, and the same virtue."[66] "Heaven forbid", Saint Augustine would later exclaim, "that we should believe in such a way as not to accept or seek reasons, since we could not even believe if we did not possess rational souls."[67] Or as Etienne Gilson wrote, "Thomas Aquinas saw philosophy, in Eusebius of Cesarea's own words, as a kind of *praeparatio evangelica* by which divine providence prepared the mind of men to receive the truth of the Gospel."[68]

In summary, Christianity contains an invitation to reason because God's rationality guarantees reason's integrity. Msgr. Robert Sokolowski articulates the resulting complementary perspective on reality:

> We must maintain the natural intelligibility of the goods in question [in the natural order] and must bring out this intelligibility on its own terms, with its own moral syntax. The revelation and grace present in the Church may make us more sensitive to this intelligibility, but it must also be argued or disclosed through itself if we wish to make it clear to those who do not accept Christian revelation. Christian Revelation brings nature into a sharper light, but it does so at least in part on *nature's own evidence* and *on its own terms*. This is the interplay of faith and reason that is so characteristic of the best in Christian understanding.[69]

This is why Fr. James Schall wrote, "What is revealed does not demand the denial of intellect, but fosters it."[70]

---

[65] Cited in Rodney Stark, *How the West Won: The Neglected Story of the Triumph of Modernity* (Wilmington, Del.: ISI Books, 2014), 36.

[66] Clement of Alexandria, *The Stromata* 4.8, New Advent, http://www.newadvent.org /fathers/02104.htm.

[67] Stark, *How the West Won*, 39.

[68] Etienne Gilson, *The Spirit of Thomism* (New York: Harper and Row, 1966), 11.

[69] Holger Zaborowski, ed., *Natural Moral Law in Contemporary Society* (Washington, D.C.: Catholic University Press of America, 2010), 31 (emphasis added).

[70] James V. Schall, *Roman Catholic Political Philosophy* (Lanham, Md.: Lexington Books, 2004), 108.

If God is Logos, reason and revelation are not at an impasse. A division of labor defines them. The common objective is the search for and the apprehension of the highest things, and reason is given primacy in this search, including in its examination of the truths claimed by revelation. In Christianity, Fr. Schall said, "revelation itself has turned to philosophy precisely to explain more fully what is revealed." Christian revelation confirms reason in its authority. At the same time, revelation has a claim on reason. A philosophy that a priori excludes the possibility of revelation is a philosophy that is not true to itself. On its own terms, philosophy *must* remain open to revelation. Fr. Schall maintained that revelation, though it discloses truths beyond the ability of philosophy to arrive at unassisted, nonetheless "addresses itself to the same reason that philosophy considers".[71] They are complementary because the truth is harmonious. The *Catechism of the Catholic Church* recapitulates the relationship of reason to revelation: "Though faith is above reason, there can never be any real discrepancy between faith and reason. Since the same God who reveals mysteries and infuses faith has bestowed the light of reason on the human mind, God cannot deny himself, nor can truth ever contradict truth."[72]

Christianity also confirmed the great philosophical insight that what is reasonable constitutes what is morally good. Reason, therefore, is morally legitimate as a source of law, making all the more likely the future development of constitutionalism. But the Creator does more than reason could expect. He enters his creation to save it from the otherwise fatal harm that man has brought upon himself. Logos is also Agape, the overflowing, unconditional love of God for man. The gift of reason prepares for the more astonishing revelation of the Logos who loves each person intimately and individually. Though he had an inkling of it, Socrates did not know that there is a greater gift than philosophy. But without the philosophical endeavor, could man have come to understand the overwhelming significance of this greater gift? If the puzzle of man's purpose had not been posed by Aristotle, could man have adequately appreciated the solution to it?[73]

---

[71] Ibid., 154.
[72] *CCC* 159, quoting *Dei Filius* 4:DS 3017.
[73] I am indebted to Fr. James Schall for this thought.

The Solution to Happiness

As mentioned earlier, Aristotle saw the need to, in "so far as we can, make ourselves immortal, and strain every nerve to live in accordance with the best thing in us".[74] Yet he clearly perceived that only the few with leisure could even attempt to reach so far. What of the vast majority of mankind, who are incapable of the philosophical life? Christianity solved the terrible dilemma posed by Aristotle by offering, as Fr. Schall noted, "to encompass a destiny that might include all men, even the non-philosophers.... This conclusion meant that the highest things were intended for more than just the philosophers."[75] Indeed, "resurrection accomplishes that final personal happiness which political theory initially proposes for man" but for which it had no answer.[76]

What Aristotle could only vaguely intimate regarding man's striving to imitate the divine comes to startling fruition in Christ's offer to share his divine life with each person. Individual man moves from paltry insignificance to inestimable worth. In the eyes of the world, man is seen as next to nothing in the brief span of his life. Christianity reveals otherwise. For the first time, the hidden identity of man is disclosed. His natural end is superseded by a supernatural one in which he partakes of divine life. John made the extraordinary statement: "We are God's children" (1 Jn 3:2). Now there is a familial relation between every person and God: he is our Father; we are his children. In the same verse, John also said, "It does not yet appear what we shall be, but we know that when he appears we shall be like him, for we shall see him as he is." The implication is very clear that man's destiny is to share in God's divine life. Hence, Paul proclaimed, "We are children of God, and if children, then heirs, heirs of God and fellow heirs with Christ" (Rom 8:16–17). It is hard to imagine a more shattering announcement to the pagan Roman world. Thus, the great Christian contribution to the question of man's nature and his ultimate end is the revelation that man's soul is drawn not only

---

[74] Aristotle, *Nicomachean Ethics* 10, 1177b27–1178a.

[75] James V. Schall, *At the Limits of Political Philosophy* (Washington D.C.: Catholic University of America Press, 1996), 137.

[76] James V. Schall, *The Politics of Heaven and Hell* (Lanham, Md.: University Press of America, 1987), 28.

to the good but to goodness itself, which is God. His true home is not the polis, but the City of God, in which he will truly become Godlike. Socrates' "city in speech" finds its true location and reality in Augustine's *City of God*.

This validation and elevation of the profoundest insights of Greek philosophy also confirmed the limits of the political, at which Socrates and Aristotle had hinted. Since Christ is a personal Savior, interested in each individual soul, in love with each person, each person could participate in the divine order of salvation *as* an individual, not through his participation as a citizen of his state or the mediation of a semidivine ruler, but through union with Christ. As the Romans implicitly recognized when they executed Christians who refused to sacrifice to the emperor as a god, Christ's identity as a personal Savior was totally incompatible with the ancient cosmological view of the universe and the political legitimacy it bestowed on the ancient city or empire. Just as Socrates was killed for his insistence on his citizenship in the city in speech, so too were the early Christians martyred for insisting on the primacy of their citizenship in the heavenly city. In a powerful echo of Socrates' statement that he would obey God rather than the men of Athens, Peter and the other apostles answered the Sanhedrin's attempt to silence them: "We must obey God rather than men" (Acts 5:29).

The Primacy of the Person

As Fustel de Coulanges remarked, this is why Christianity spelled the end of ancient society: "Man felt that he had other obligations besides that of living and dying for the city. Christianity distinguished the private from the public virtues. By giving less honor to the latter, it elevated the former; it placed God, the family, the human individual above country, the neighbor above the city."[77] Indeed, Heinrich Rommen wrote: "From now on the idea of man no longer finds its absolute fulfillment in the citizen. Man's end transcends the state."[78]

---

[77] Fustel de Coulanges, *The Ancient City* (Baltimore: Johns Hopkins University Press, 1991), 387.

[78] Cited in James V. Schall, *Christianity and Politics* (Boston: St. Paul Editions, 1981), 263.

The primacy of the political was over. The most important aspect of man's life, his salvation, was marked off from the state and was not to be reached through its agency. Because of this, the claims of the polis were permanently diminished, its jurisdiction forever narrowed. As historian Edward Gibbon noted disapprovingly, "Every Christian rejected with contempt the superstitions of his family, his city, and his province."[79] Man is no longer subsumed by the polis; rather the polis exists to serve man. The terrestrial good of man does not become irrelevant, but it is subordinated to the goal of his eternal happiness, which is beyond any temporal good in the prerogative of the state. Here was a powerful new concept for limiting government and taming it constitutionally.

The foundation of this distinction was Christ's introduction of the novel notion of the duality of the civic and spiritual realms. The Pharisees and Herodians attempted to trick Christ by asking whether it was lawful to pay the census tax to Caesar. After examining a denarius, Christ questioned them in turn: Whose image was on it? Caesar's, they said. He then responded, "Render to Caesar the things that are Caesar's, and to God the things that are God's" (Mk 12:17). Matthew's Gospel records that "when they heard it, they marveled" (22:22). Indeed, anyone in the ancient world would have been amazed, since such a statement had never been made. Why was not everything Caesar's? Because, unlike the coin given to Christ, Caesar's image was not stamped on man; God's was. From this crucial difference sprang the distinction between the sacred and the secular. The secular is not antithetical to Christianity; it is a *product* of it. Christianity created the secular. It insists on it.

This was the ultimate basis for the constitutional principle of separation of ecclesiastical and secular authority. By a long road, it eventually led to religious freedom—something that would have been inconceivable unless the political order had been secularized. (Ultimately, it was the basis for the First Amendment.) The fact that some things are God's limits the reach of political authority. Jesus' words, Lord Acton said, gave to the civil power "bounds it had never acknowledged; and they were the repudiation of absolutism and the

[79] Edward Gibbon, *The History of the Decline and Fall of the Roman Empire*, vol. 1 (Cincinnati: J. A. and U. P. James, 1851), 183.

inauguration of Freedom.... The new law, the new spirit, the new authority, gave to liberty a meaning and a value it had not possessed in the philosophy or in the constitution of Greece or Rome before the knowledge of the truth that makes us free."[80]

Jesus' statement, however, has a dual edge. Recognizing that some things are God's, it otherwise grants legitimacy to political authority as some things properly are Caesar's. Fr. Schall observed, "Granting to Caesar genuine authority ... may well have been Jesus's most revolutionary political contribution."[81] In other words, Christ himself acknowledged a realm within which man is rightly semiautonomous and legitimately sovereign aside from, but not opposed to, divine revelation and God's sovereignty. In the affairs of the world, man is expected to use his reason to figure out how to rule it and himself. Religion may not use man's transcendent end as an excuse to trespass upon legitimate temporal authority. To the disappointment of many, Jesus said, "My kingship is not of this world" (Jn 18:36). He did not come as a political liberator. Thus, he had no pretension to exercise political power. Christ no more expected man to install his Kingdom on earth than Socrates expected the Athenians to instantiate his "city in speech" on the Greek peninsula.

Limiting the Political to Be Itself

Yet Christianity made the prospect of constitutional order all the more probable *because* it removed from the political order any pretension to fulfill man's highest end through its own means. Augustine was quite clear on the subject: "What we seek is not here" since "salvation, such as it shall be in the world to come, shall itself be our final happiness."[82] Ironically, by offering a vision that transcends politics, Christianity saved politics from itself, or rather from trying to be something other than itself, by enabling it to focus on its proper realm—how best to govern man in the temporal world by arranging

---

[80] John Emerich Edward Dalberg Acton, *The History of Freedom and Other Essays* (London: Macmillan, 1907), 29.

[81] Schall, *Politics of Heaven and Hell*, 23.

[82] Augustine, *The City of God* 19, 4.

the things of this life so that man could pursue his transcendent end. "Christianity", stated Fr. Schall, "was able to give a reason why politics ... did not have to be concerned with man's highest destiny or virtue. Resurrection and the Kingdom of God suggested both that man's deepest desires would be fulfilled—the sting of death was not absolutely defeating—and that politics could, consequently, pursue a temporal good in a human, finite fashion."[83] Since man's ultimate human happiness lies in God, and a transcendent God is, by definition, outside of history, man cannot make his home in this world. Thus, politics is not the salvific engine for the transformation of mankind and the elimination of evil. Christ is. This is what ultimately limits (and therefore makes possible) politics.

Without this limiting view of politics, constitutional thinking would not be possible. Only such a vision gives impetus to the effort to restrain political power, and it profoundly affected the Founders' desire to do so. It is also the staunchest guardian against the ever present temptation for politics to displace the spiritual order and take upon itself man's salvation. Benedict XVI warned, "Wherever politics tries to be redemptive, it is promising too much. Where it wishes to do the work of God, it becomes not divine, but demonic."[84] The truth of his statement was amply illustrated by the horrors of Nazi Germany, the Soviet Union, and Communist China, regimes that attempted to eliminate Christianity to clear the way for their own efforts at man's self-deification.

Dedivinization of the World

Christianity included the Genesis teaching of creation ex nihilo, but the Incarnation dramatically reemphasized that the world is contingent and not eternal. Saint John revealed Christ as the "only-begotten" (*unigenitum*) of the Father. John's wording, explained theologian and physicist Fr. Stanley Jaki, made the exclusivity of Christ's generation by God clear in terms that the ancient world could not fail to

---

[83] Schall, *Politics of Heaven and Hell*, 287.

[84] Joseph Cardinal Ratzinger, *Truth and Tolerance: Christian Belief and World Religions* (San Francisco: Ignatius Press, 2004), 116.

understand. It meant that the world was *not* "begotten" by him. God did not beget anything but Christ. The world is not made up of God. It is not an emanation of his being, as the pagan classical world believed, but is made by him and is separate from him. The cosmos does not exist necessarily. Thus, the Incarnation delivered the coup de grâce to the ancient world; it made pantheism impossible. Pan was dead, and the spirits inhabiting trees, groves, and grottos fled forever. Since Christ is the "Only Begotten Son of God", the ruler, whether pharaoh or king, was not, and could not be, divine. Only Christ is. Dedivinizing the world dedivinized its rulers and punctured their theocratic pretensions to rule as gods.

The doctrine of creation ex nihilo, coupled with the Incarnation, also removed the futility inherent in the view of an eternally cyclical universe, the ever-turning wheel, and the constant flux with no beginning or end. The human aspiration for eternity could not be met within a pantheistic world of endless recurrence, but only outside of it. In the ancient world, as we have seen, there was no *eschaton*—no final summing up of things toward which everything was moving. The universe was endlessly looped in on itself. The ancients, remarked Eva Brann, "never, never, thought of history as having an intelligible purposeful movement; they never thought that time contained moments of revelation, or bore a spirit, or had in it a beginning and an inevitable end."[85] The Incarnation split fatalism asunder. In its stead came freedom, release from the loop. "The stars, in their unalterable courses", said Henri de Lubac, "did not, after all, implacably control our destinies.... No more circle! No more blind destiny!"[86] In the "Addition" to his translation of Boethius, King Alfred of England wrote: "I say, as do all Christian men, that it is a divine purpose that rules, and not fate."[87] In fact, history did not so much begin anew with the birth of Christ, as truly begin for *everyone*. Christ is the Lord of history, and its unfolding leads to its end in

---

[85] Eva Brann, "The Roots of Modernity in Perversions of Christianity", *Imaginative Conservative*, September 17, 2018, http://www.theimaginativeconservative.org/2018/09/the-roots-of-modernity-in-perversions-christianity-eva-brann.html?mc_cid=1c76c2c21d&mc_eid=89abaa241c.

[86] Henri de Lubac, *The Drama of Atheist Humanism* (San Francisco: Ignatius Press, 1995), 23.

[87] Cited in Harold J. Berman, *Law and Revolution: The Formation of the Western Legal Tradition* (Cambridge, Mass.: Harvard University Press, 1983), 63.

him—the Parousia and the establishment of his Kingdom, the eternal City of God. The inscrutability of fate disappeared like a shadow in the light.

Man's Freedom

Within this view of salvation history, man's freedom took upon itself greater meaning than it had ever had. Irenaeus called Christ's apostles "the apostles of freedom". The Incarnation invested man's actions with extraordinary significance and moral dignity. "The old servitude had passed and the day of free will had dawned", wrote Augustine, "and man was fitly and helpfully taught how he had been created with free will."[88] In an early intimation of freedom of religion, Augustine wrote: "No one is ... to be compelled to embrace the faith against his will."[89]

Man's self-rule now becomes conceivable, inimitably tied to his ability to discern a rational moral order in creation. Fr. Jaki concluded:

> Finally, man figured in the Christian dogma of creation as a being specially created in the image of God. This image consisted both in man's rationality as somehow sharing in God's own rationality and in man's condition as an ethical being with eternal responsibility for his actions. Man's reflection on his own rationality had therefore to give him confidence that his created mind could fathom the rationality of the created realm.[90]

The personal responsibility of each individual soul before God necessarily involved a broad sphere of freedom in the acts for which the person is to be held accountable. Christianity presumed freedom in this sense:

> Created of God as a distinct individuality ... man is henceforth the protagonist of a drama, which is none other than that of his own

---

[88] Augustine, *Earlier Writings* (Louisville, Ky.: Westminster John Knox Press, 2006), 239.

[89] Augustine, *Against the Book of Petilian the Donatist* 2, 84, cited in Greg Forster, *Starting with Locke* (New York: Continuum International, 2011), 137.

[90] Stanley Jaki, *Christ and Science* (New Hope, Ky.: Real View Books, 2000), 23.

destiny.... From the opening of the Christian era it is no more of man that we speak but of the human person.[91]

The Christian primacy of the person stands out in this spiritual drama in a way beyond the imagination of the ancients. It represented a total transformation in attitude toward the value of others, making the misuse of any person all the more grievous an offense. This changed the relationship among men as the basis of community was radically altered. It was no longer necessarily a matter of where one was born or to whom. As Eric Voegelin said:

> The Christian idea of mankind is the idea of a community whose substance consists of the Spirit in which the members participate.... Only because the Spirit is transcendentally out of time can it be universally present in time, living in each man equally, irrespective of the age, or place in which man lives. Only because the source of the community is out of time is mankind a universal community within time.[92]

This gave a new understanding to the common good asserted by Aristotle and, therefore, to any commonwealth based on it.

The New Spiritual Genealogy: Equality

Christ made this new relationship understood in the famous parable of the Good Samaritan, in which he disclosed who one's neighbor is (Lk 10:29–37). The true neighbor turns out to be not a fellow Jew but a much despised Samaritan. The lesson could not be clearer. Tribal relations and sectarian differences no longer define human relations. To the people gathered in the home of Cornelius, a Roman centurion, Peter said, "You yourselves know how unlawful it is for a Jew to associate with or to visit any one of another nation; but God has shown me that I should not call any man common or unclean." He then declared, "Truly I perceive that God shows no partiality, but in

---

[91] Etienne Gilson, *The Spirit of Medieval Philosophy* (New York: Charles Scribner's Sons, 1940), 193, 206.

[92] *The Collected Works of Eric Voegelin*, vol. 26, *History of Political Ideas*, ed. David Walsh (Columbia: University of Missouri Press, 1999), 114–15.

every nation any one who fears him and does what is right is accept-able to him" (Acts 10:34–35). A tribal religion with a universal truth, Judaism now becomes transformed in Jesus to a universal religion without tribes. Saint John declared there is a new fraternity of people "who were born, not of blood nor of the will of the flesh nor of the will of man, but of God" (Jn 1:13).

Jesus also made clear that the genealogy that counts is no longer biological, but spiritual. "Who is my mother, and who are my breth-ern?" he asked. In answer to his own question, he said, "Whoever does the will of my Father in heaven is my brother, and sister, and mother" (Mt 12:48, 50). Paul also spoke of the new familial relation-ship with God: "And because you are sons, God has sent the Spirit of his Son into our hearts, crying, 'Abba, Father!' So through God you are no longer a slave but a son, and if a son then an heir" (Gal 4:6–7). The Our Father was a revolutionary prayer when Christ said it, and it remains so today. This was the new salvific framework within which men were to regard each other. The image of God in man was now specified as the image of Christ. It becomes even more personal than the intimate relationship between Yahweh and the Jewish people. The Christian exhortation was to serve Christ in *all* others. Emperor Julian the Apostate would complain to his pagan high priest Arsacius, "Why do we not observe that it is their [Christian] benevolence to strang-ers, their care for the graves of the dead and the pretended holiness of their lives that have done most to increase atheism [abandonment of the Roman pagan religion]? ... For it is disgraceful [that] when ... the impious Galilaeans support not only their own poor but ours as well, all men see that our people lack aid from us."[93]

This teaching, the most profound assertion of human equality ever offered, transformed everything, including the distinction between freeman and slave: "For by one Spirit we were all baptized into one body—Jews or Greeks, slaves or free—and all were made to drink of one Spirit" (1 Cor 12:13). Paul wrote to Philemon on how he ought to treat his runaway slave, whom Paul was sending back to his master: "I appeal to you for my child, Onesimus, whose father I

---

[93] Julian the Apostate, "To the High-Priest Theodorus", in *The Works of Emperor Julian*, vol. 3, trans. W. C. Wright (New York: G. P. Putnam's Sons, 1923), 20, The Tertullian Proj-ect, http://www.tertullian.org/fathers/julian_apostate_letters_1_trans.htm.

have become in my imprisonment.... I am sending him back to you, sending my very heart.... Perhaps this is why he was parted from you for a while, that you might have him back for ever, no longer as a slave but more than a slave, as a beloved brother ... both in the flesh and in the Lord" (Philem 10–16). Paul elaborated on the new spiritual brotherhood: "So then you are no longer strangers and sojourners, but you are fellow citizens with the saints and members of the household of God" (Eph 2:19). There are, of course, many other such passages. This central teaching was frequently repeated: "There is neither Jew nor Greek, there is neither slave nor free, there is neither male nor female; for you are all one in Christ Jesus" (Gal 3:28); "Here there cannot be Greek and Jew, circumcised and uncircumcised, barbarian, Scythian, slave, free man, but Christ is all, and in all" (Col 3:11). Though the gospel does not condemn slavery per se, it is clearly repugnant to its spirit. And this is what slowly transformed the attitude toward it.

The new basis for community is man's equality in the eyes of God as the bedrock for what later became the Declaration's proclamation that "all men are created equal." Translated politically, it made possible constitutional government, which is organized around the inestimable worth of the individual person. The understanding of equality came very slowly, as it was against the grain of centuries. But in the words of Benedict XVI, "Even if external structures remained unaltered, this changed society from within."[94] In the fourth century, not long after the Edict of Milan legalized Christianity in the Roman Empire, Gregory of Nyssa demonstrated this transformative power in his sermons against slavery. In a homily on Ecclesiastes, he reflected in inimitably Christian terms on the buying and selling of slaves. It is worth quoting at length for its extraordinary rhetoric and, of course, for its substance:

For what price, tell me? What did you find in existence worth as much as this human nature? What price did you put on rationality?... God said let us make man in our image, after our likeness. If he is in the likeness of God, and ... has been granted authority over everything on earth from God, who is his buyer, tell me? Who is his

---

[94] Benedict XVI, Encyclical Letter on Christian Hope *Spe Salvi* (November 30, 2007), no. 4.

seller? To God alone belongs this power; or rather, not even to God himself. For his gracious gifts ... are irrevocable. God himself would not reduce the human race to slavery, since he himself, when we had been enslaved to sin, recalled us to freedom.... Your origin is from the same ancestors, your life is of the same kind, sufferings of soul and body prevail alike over you who own him and over the one who is subject to your ownership—pains and pleasures, merriment and distress, sorrows and delights, rages and terrors, sickness and death. Is there any difference in these things between the slave and his owner? Do they not draw in the same air as they breathe? Do they not see the sun in the same way?... If you are equal in all these ways, therefore, in what respect, have you something extra, tell me, that you who are human think yourself the master of a human being and say, 'I bought male and female slaves,' like herds of goats or pigs.[95]

At our distance from it, it is hard for us to appreciate how singular this sermon was. Outside Christianity, no such statement against slavery had ever been made. From time immemorial, slavery had been the rule rather than the exception. No matter how long the process took, without Christianity, slavery most likely would have remained the norm of mankind.

Equally singular and without historical precedent before Christianity were the teachings about the poor. In the fourth century, Gregory of Nazianzus (ca. 329–390), archbishop of Constantinople, instructed his flock to regard the poor as "our brothers in God, whether you like it or not; whose share in nature is the same as ours; who are formed of the same clay from the time of our first creation ... more importantly, who have the same portion of the image of God just as we do and who keep it perhaps better, wasted though their bodies may be". Men were created "free and with free will", Gregory said, and Christians should therefore behave according to "the original equality of rights, not the subsequent inequities". [96]

If not always observed in practice, the teaching of human equality was consistent in the Church's history. Here are a few notable examples widely spaced over the centuries to illustrate this fact.

---

[95] Cited in Larry Siedentop, *Inventing the Individual: The Origins of Western Liberalism* (Cambridge, Mass.: Harvard University Press, 2014), 119.

[96] Cited in Shah and Hertzke, *Christianity and Freedom*, 141.

In the early fifth century, Saint Augustine taught that "this relationship is prescribed by the order of nature, and it is in this situation that God created man.... He did not wish the rational being, made in his own image, to have dominion over any but irrational creatures, not man over man, but man over the beasts.... And yet, by nature, in the condition in which God created man, no man is the slave either of man or of sin."[97] To Augustine, it is a "sinful soul that aspires to lord it even over those who are by nature its equal, that is, its fellow man. This is a reach of arrogance utterly intolerable."[98] In *The City of God* he wrote, "It is thus that pride in its perversity apes God. It abhors equality with other men under Him; but, instead of His rule, it seeks to impose a rule of its own upon its equals."[99] Augustine made it clear that these injunctions embrace all of mankind: "*What you do not wish to have done to yourself, do not do to another* cannot be varied on account of any diversity of peoples.... Since no one wishes to be harmed by another, he should not harm others."[100] He acknowledged man's equality as the foundation for the requirement for his consent in how he is governed. Consent, however, must operate within what the dictates of the natural law prescribe.

Likewise, Bishop Theodulf of Orléans (ca. 750–821) reprimanded the court of Charlemagne for its violations of equality: "Their sweat and their toil make you rich. The rich get their riches because of the poor. But nature submits you to the same laws. In birth and death you are alike. The same holy water blesses you; you are anointed with the same oils; the flesh and blood of the lamb (the Christ) nourishes you all together."[101] At the turn of the thirteenth century, Innocent III proclaimed that "it may be said that kings are to be treated differently from others. We, however, know that it is written in the divine law, 'You shall judge the great as well as the little and there shall be no difference of persons.'"[102] The political repercussions of

[97] Augustine, *The City of God* 19, 15.

[98] Augustine, *De doctrina Christiana* 1, 23, cited in Joseph F. Costanzo, S.J., "Catholic Politeia I", *Fordham Law Review* 21, no. 2 (June 1952): 109n43.

[99] Augustine, *The City of God* 19, 12.

[100] Augustine, *De doctrina* 3, 14, cited in Shah and Hertzke, *Christianity and Freedom*, 204.

[101] Cited in Siedentop, *Inventing the Individual*, 172.

[102] Decretal *Novit* (1204), cited in ibid., 218.

these teachings were manifested in provisions from the Law of the
Visigoths, promulgated in 653:

> The royal power, like the whole of the people is bound to respect the
> laws.... We decree that no king shall by any means, extort, or cause
> to be extorted, any documents whatever in acknowledgment of any
> debt, whereby any person can unjustly and without his consent, be
> deprived of his property.... No one has a right to hear a cause which
> is not authorized by the laws.... The judge, when inquired of by a
> Party, should be able to give a reason for his decision.[103]

In an extraordinary encyclical from 1537, Pope Paul III called
demonic those who denied the full humanity of the Indians. Though
it was observed largely in the breach, the encyclical is worth quoting
at length for its teaching:

> The enemy of the human race ... inspired his satellites who, to please
> him, have not hesitated to publish abroad that the Indians of the West
> and the South, and other people of whom We have recent knowledge
> should be treated as dumb brutes created for our service, pretending
> that they are incapable of receiving the Catholic Faith. We, who,
> though unworthy, exercise on earth the power of our Lord and seek
> with all our might to bring those sheep of His flock who are outside
> into the fold committed to our charge, consider, however, that the
> Indians are truly men and that they are not only capable of under-
> standing the Catholic Faith but, according to our information, they
> desire exceedingly to receive it. Desiring to provide ample remedy for
> these evils, We define and declare by these our letters ... that, not-
> withstanding whatever may have been or may be said to the contrary,
> the said Indians and all other people who may later be discovered
> by Christians, are by no means to be deprived of their liberty or the
> possession of their property, even though they be outside the faith of
> Jesus Christ; and that they may and should, freely and legitimately,
> enjoy their liberty and the possession of their property; nor should
> they be in any way enslaved; should the contrary happen, it shall be
> null and have no effect.[104]

---

[103] The Visigothic Code, bk. 5, cited in Joseph F. Costanzo, S.J., *Political and Legal Studies*
(West Hanover, Mass.: Christopher Publishing House, 1982), 77.

[104] Paul III, Encyclical on the Enslavement and Education of Indians *Sublimus Dei* (May 29,
1537), Papal Encyclicals Online, http://www.papalencyclicals.net/paulo3/p3subli.htm.

In 1839 Pope Gregory XVI reiterated his predecessors' teachings against slavery:

> We have judged that it belonged to Our pastoral solicitude to exert Ourselves to turn away the Faithful from the inhuman slave trade in Negroes and all other men.... Desiring to remove such a shame from all the Christian nations ... and walking in the footsteps of Our Predecessors, We warn and adjure earnestly in the Lord faithful Christians of every condition that no one in the future dare to vex anyone, despoil him of his possessions, reduce to servitude, or lend aid and favour to those who give themselves up to these practices, or exercise that inhuman traffic by which the Blacks, as if they were not men but rather animals, having been brought into servitude, in no matter what way, are, without any distinction, in contempt of the rights of justice and humanity, bought, sold, and devoted sometimes to the hardest labour. Further, in the hope of gain, propositions of purchase being made to the first owners of the Blacks, dissensions and almost perpetual conflicts are aroused in these regions. We reprove, then, by virtue of Our Apostolic Authority, all the practices abovementioned as absolutely unworthy of the Christian name. By the same Authority We prohibit and strictly forbid any Ecclesiastic or lay person from presuming to defend as permissible this traffic in Blacks under no matter what pretext or excuse, or from publishing or teaching in any manner whatsoever, in public or privately, opinions contrary to what We have set forth in this Apostolic Letter.[105]

Thus it was, because of changes "from within", that slavery, an institution that had existed for millennia, was first eliminated by Great Britain and eventually in America. The Declaration of Independence provided the moral principle of human equality for the ultimate extirpation of slavery in the United States. Without the revelation that man is made in the image of God and the concomitant teaching of spiritual brotherhood as revealed in Christ, it is doubtful that either of these things would have happened. It is one thing to proclaim that all men are endowed by their Creator with "certain unalienable rights", but those rights can be exercised only where they are recognized. The roots of that recognition came principally from the

---

[105] Gregory XVI, Apostolic Letter *In supremo apostolates* (December 1, 1839), EWTN, http://www.ewtn.com/catholicism/library/condemning-slave-trade-7859.

Christian religion. As Alexis de Tocqueville observed, "It was necessary that Jesus Christ come to earth to make it understood that all members of the human species are naturally alike and equal."[106] He also wrote, "Christianity, which has rendered all men equal before God, will not be loath to see all citizens equal before the law."[107] In this sense, Jacques Maritain was correct in saying that equality

> should be called Christian equality, not only because it issues from the Judeo-Christian tradition and conforms with the Christian conception of life, but also because, if it were not for the influence of the Christian leaven injected into secular history, and if it were not for the added stimulus, which in its own sphere temporal civilization receives from Christian energies, this equality could not succeed in coming to pass. As there is a flowering of the natural law, which can be attained only with the help of the virtues of the New Law, there is also a human flowering, a real humanism of civil life, which can be attained only with the help of these virtues.[108]

In a 1981 address to Catholic members of the German Bundestag, Joseph Cardinal Ratzinger summed up the invaluable lessons from Jerusalem, Athens, and Rome that we have sketched out here:

> The state is not the whole of human existence and does not embrace the whole of human hope. Men and women and their hopes extend beyond the thing that is the state and beyond the sphere of political activity.... This kind of politics that declares the kingdom of God to be the result of politics and distorts faith into universal primacy of the political is by its nature the politics of enslavement; it is mythological politics. To this, faith opposes the standard of Christian reason, which recognizes what man is really capable of creating as the order of freedom and can be content with this because it knows that man's greater expectation lies hidden in God's hands. Rejecting the hope of faith is at the same time rejecting the standard of political reason. To

---

[106] Alexis de Tocqueville, *Democracy in America*, ed. J.P. Meyer (Garden City, N.Y.: Anchor Books, 1969), 413.

[107] Alexis de Tocqueville, *Democracy in America*, trans. Harvey C. Mansfield and Delba Winthrop (Chicago: University of Chicago Press, 2002), 11.

[108] Donald Gallagher and Idella Gallagher, eds., *A Maritain Reader* (Garden City, N.Y.: Doubleday, 1966), 280.

renounce the mythical hopes of a society free of domination is not resignation but honesty that maintains men and women in hope. The mythical hope of a do-it-yourself paradise can only drive people into fear from which there is no escape; fear of the collapse of their promises and of the greater void lurks behind it; fear of their own power and its cruelty.[109]

Although this is a contemporary expression of what the structure of political life should be like in light of the triple Western legacies, it applies as well to the minds of the American Founders, who so carefully fashioned a limited government in light of these truths. In chapter 9, we shall hear them speak directly of these things. Now we turn to how these truths were incorporated and conveyed in the Middle Ages.

[109] Joseph Ratzinger, *Church, Ecumenism and Politics* (New York: Crossroad, 1988), 148–49.

2

The Medieval Roots of Constitutionalism

This chapter will show how and why representative, constitutional government grew out of the experience and thought of the Middle Ages. By its end, I hope it will have shown on what basis Ellis Sandoz could claim that "the whole of medieval Christian constitutional and political theory ... lay squarely behind the American determination [to achieve independence]."[1] This thesis rubs rawly against the grain of the popular imagination, which holds that Christendom was the source of absolutism, rather than its opponent. It also disturbs the widely held picture of the medieval period as part of the "Dark Ages". Therefore, we will go into some detail showing otherwise.

It cannot be emphasized enough that the doctrine and teaching of the intrinsic and inviolable worth of each person, propagated by Christianity, was the motive force in this development. Medieval man thought through the full implications of the imago Dei in terms of how he ought to live and how his society should be organized. At the center of this effort was his lived Christian faith, reconciled with reason in the extraordinary achievements of the Scholastics, especially Aquinas. The reconciliation of reason and faith, of natural law and Christianity, created the seedbed of constitutionalism. According to historians R. W. and A. J. Carlyle, the representative system was created by medieval civilization at its highest point and was "the natural and logical outcome of its political conditions and ideas".[2]

---

[1] Ellis Sandoz, "Classical and Christian Dimensions of American Political Thought", *Modern Age* (Winter 1981): 17.

[2] R. W. Carlyle and A. J. Carlyle, *A History of Medieval Political Theory in the West* (London: William Blackwood and Sons, 1950), 129.

No one has better captured the inner dynamics of this transformation than the nineteenth-century French historian Benjamin Guérard, who said:

> Christianity was the greatest benefactor of the Middle Ages.... The dogma of a common origin and destiny for all men alike was an unceasing argument for the emancipation of the people; it brought together men of all stations, and opened the way for modern civilisation. Men, though they did not cease to oppress one another, began to recognise the fact that they were all members of the same family, and were led, through religious equality, up to civil and political equality; being brothers in the sight of God, they became equal before the law, the Christian became the citizen. This transformation took place gradually and slowly, as being necessary and inevitable, by the continued and simultaneous enfranchisement of men and of land. The slave whom paganism, as it disappeared, handed over to the Christian religion, passed first from a state of servitude to a state of bondage, from bondage he rose to mortmain, and from mortmain to liberty.[3]

Indeed, the result was that in the Middle Ages, wrote nineteenth-century French writer Charles Forbes René de Montalembert, "the world was bristling with liberty."[4]

Dual Sovereignties

The vehicle for this transformation was the juridical development of the dual sovereignties of the spiritual and secular realms beginning in the late eleventh century. Almost the entire Middle Ages was a working out of what these dual sovereignties meant and of how to structure society in accordance with them. The "two swords" or "two powers" teaching meant separate sovereignties exercised over the *same* people. Though this was bound to create friction, it

---

[3] Cited in Paul Lacroix, *Military and Religious Life in the Middle Ages and at the Period of the Renaissance* (London: Bickers and Son, 1874), vi–vii, http://www.archive.org/stream/military religiouoojacouoft/militaryreligiouoojacouoft_djvu.txt.

[4] The Count de Montalembert, *The Monks of the West* (Boston: Patrick Donahoe, 1872), 126.

produced not only heat, but light. The struggle over the boundaries between ecclesiastical and secular authorities led to the articulation and enforcement of the all-important limits of the sovereignty of each. Legal scholar Harold Berman wrote, "If the church was to have inviolable legal rights, the state had to accept those rights as a lawful limitation upon its own supremacy. Similarly, the rights of the state constituted a lawful limitation upon the supremacy of the church. The two powers could only coexist peacefully through shared recognition of the rule of law, its supremacy over each."[5] This recognition developed slowly, painfully, and not always peacefully over the course of many years. At least in theory, if not always in practice, both sides agreed to the intrinsic autonomy of the other. This, in turn, created the conditions for the development of the principles of equality, the rule of law, popular sovereignty, the requirement for consent, the right to resist tyranny, and the grounds for representation in ecclesiastical and then secular government.

We first need to review the development of the two-swords teaching. As we saw in the last chapter, it was revolutionary to claim that Caesar's power was not absolute but was confined to certain temporal aspects of his subjects' lives. For several centuries, Caesar fought against the bifurcation of his power by persecuting Christians. After Emperor Constantine, public acknowledgment of the spiritual sword gradually grew in theory, if not in practice. In the mid-fifth century, Pope Leo I, according to Robert Cardinal Bellarmine, stated in a letter to Emperors Theodosius and Martin that "the emperor is elected and that his authority is from God, not from the Pope."[6] At the end of the fifth century, Pope Gelasius explicitly stated that man has dual citizenship under both sovereigns. The secular sword also has a divine source, but it is distinguished by its limited competence to things temporal. In 496, in a text widely used in the Middle Ages regarding the Church-state controversy, Gelasius wrote:

> For Christ ... distinguished between the offices of both powers [i.e., the Church and the state] according to their own proper activities and

---

[5] Harold Berman, *Law and Revolution: The Formation of the Western Legal Tradition* (Cambridge, Mass.: Harvard University Press, 1983), 29.

[6] *De Romano Pontifice* 5, 1, 2, 3, cited in Rev. John Clement Rager, *The Political Philosophy of St. Robert Bellarmine* (Spokane, Wash.: Apostolate of Our Lady of Siluva, 1995), 43.

separate dignities ... so that Christian emperors would need priests for attaining eternal life and priests would avail themselves of imperial regulations in the conduct of temporal affairs. In this fashion, spiritual activity would be set apart from worldly encroachments, and the "soldier of God" (2 Timothy 2:4) would not be involved in secular affairs; while on the other hand he who was involved in secular affairs would not seem to preside over Divine matters.[7]

If man's destiny is outside of time, then a timeless entity should oversee it: the Church. While man is living within time, however, there must also be a secular agency to oversee matters concerning his temporal needs: the state. Politics should focus on the goods proper to it: the earthly peace that both Augustine and Aquinas called "the tranquility of order". The fundamentals essential to constitutional order grew out of this dual perspective. Without it, limited government would have been unlikely. Christendom made it likely by allowing men to live simultaneously at two semiautonomous levels.

Rendering unto Caesar the things that are Caesar's and unto God the things that are God's was not an easy admonition to incorporate into medieval society because, as we have seen, it was a separation that had never been attempted. It was one thing to articulate it; it was quite another to institute it. There were many conflicting interests and ambitions involved on both sides of the new divide. It should be noted that some members of the two respective sides— ecclesiastical and royal—did not consistently support their respective sovereigns. This was a matter in constant flux. None too eager to see stronger papal control over their dioceses, some bishops occasionally supported the secular ruler against the pope. And sometimes princes and dukes would find it convenient to support the pope against the overweening ambition of their emperor. Since the two sovereignties oversaw the same congregants, occasional conflict and confusion were unavoidable. Also, since the divide between the two powers was permeable, they were bound to act upon and influence each other in profound ways.

---

[7] Gelasius, *On the Bond of Anathema* (496), cited in Benjamin Wiker, "Catholicism in the American Founding", *National Catholic Register*, July 3, 2013, http://www.ncregister.com /daily-news/catholicism-and-the-american-founding/#ixzz2Y688eLyM.

Wielding the Two Swords

When the Church was largely under imperial control, there were frequent, if ineffective, appeals to Gelasius' teaching. It is worth citing a couple of examples to see how they were phrased. Hincmar (806–882), archbishop of Reims, upbraided the Carolingian court:

> Some so-called wise men say that the prince, being king, is not subject to the laws or judgment of anyone, if not that of God alone ... and that in the same way he must not, whatever he has done, be excommunicated by his bishops; for God alone has the right to judge him.... Such language is not that of a Catholic Christian; it is full of blasphemy in the spirit of demons.... The blessed Pope Gelasius wrote to the Emperor Anastasius: "there are two principal powers by which the world is governed: pontifical authority and royal dignity; and the authority of the pontiffs is all the greater because they have to render accounts to the Lord for the souls of kings."[8]

Around the same time, Abbot Wala of Corbie, a cousin of Charlemagne, spoke of the parallel sovereignty of the Church, which should have "church properties, almost like a second public domain".[9] In a startling premonition of later political theory, Alcuin of York, perhaps the most prominent thinker and teacher in Charlemagne's court, spoke of the limitations of the state: "Since all men are by nature free, it follows that every government, whether it rests its authority on written law or on the living voice of the prince—derives solely from the common agreement and consent of the subjects."[10]

Between the collapse of the Roman Empire and the early Middle Ages, these appeals went largely unheeded. In the fractured state of Europe during those centuries, the secular sword dominated the spiritual. The Church became very much a local affair. Local lords and princes appointed bishops and abbots, gave the gift of Church

---

[8] Cited in Larry Siedentop, *Inventing the Individual: The Origins of Western Liberalism* (Cambridge, Mass.: Harvard University Press, 2014), 174.

[9] Cited in Robert Louis Wilken, *Christianity Face to Face with Islam* (New York: First Things Reprint Series, 2010), 32.

[10] John B. Morrall, *Political Thought in Medieval Times* (New York: Harper and Row, 1958), 129.

property to their followers, and sold ecclesiastical offices outright. For this reason, this era is sometimes termed the "feudalization" of the Church. In a decree of 1067, William the Conqueror even asserted royal power over the making of canon law and any ecclesiastical disciplinary actions concerning his barons and officials. Kings considered spiritual offices as fiefs held from them. Therefore, it was the king who invested the bishops. They would present the bishop with a crosier and a ring, saying: "Receive the Church [*Accipe Ecclesiam*]." The integrity and even the universality of the Church were seriously compromised. Who was the real Vicar of Christ—the king (*rex et sacerdos*) or the pope? Would temporal princes control the Church, or, as Gelasius had insisted, would the Church be supreme in her own realm?

The Investiture Conflict

When the cry arose for freedom for the Church, it meant release from secular control and the degraded condition into which the Church had fallen. In the late eleventh century, Pope Gregory VII began what has been called "the papal revolution". Its importance cannot be underestimated, noted Harold Berman:

> The first of the great revolutions of Western history was the revolution against domination of the clergy by emperors, kings, and lords and for the establishment of the Church of Rome as an independent, corporate, political, and legal entity, under the papacy.... This was, however, only one side of the Papal Revolution. Another side of it was the enactment of the secular political and legal authority of emperors, kings and lords as well as the creation of thousands of autonomous, self-governing cities.[11]

In a major reform effort, Gregory started to claw back the Church's authority. He forcefully rearticulated the two-swords teaching in both word and deed.

Until he regained control over it, Gregory could not reform the Church. To reassert spiritual authority, he created a universally

[11] Berman, *Law and Revolution*, 520.

applicable code of canon law. In his *Dictatus papae* of 1075, he declared that it was the pope—not secular princes—who decided whether any actions were canonical, and it was he who would select bishops. At the Lenten (Roman) Synod of 1075, he withdrew "from the king the right of disposing of bishoprics in future, and relieved all lay persons of the investiture of churches".[12] In 1078 he decreed: "No one of the clergy shall receive the investiture with a bishopric or abbey or church from the hand of an emperor or king or of any lay person, male or female [under threat of excommunication]."[13] The lines of battle were drawn.

To resacralize the Church, Gregory had to desacralize the princes and divest them of ecclesiastical function, authority, and power. This upset customary arrangements of the prior several centuries. Echoing Tertullian in the early third century, however, Gregory insisted: "Christ did not say, 'I am custom', but 'I am truth.' "[14] The claims of the papacy, indeed of Christianity, made a state *without* ecclesiastical functions necessary for its own authority. Ironically, the state became an unintended beneficiary of this effort, as, until this time, there had not been a clear conception of what a state is. In historian Joseph Strayer's words, "The Gregorian concept of the Church almost demanded the invention of the concept of the State."[15] The investiture controversy that led to the legal definition of the powers of the two swords took place over the course of more than a century in both England and the Holy Roman Empire.

The Struggle in England

In England, the problem developed in the following curious way. William II (1087–1100) had left the office of the archbishop of

---

[12] *Catholic Encyclopedia* (New York: Robert Appleton, 1910), s.v. "Conflict of Investitures", New Advent, http://www.newadvent.org/cathen/08084c.htm.

[13] Gregory VII, Decree of November 19, 1078, forbidding lay investiture, in Ernest F. Henderson, ed., *Select Historical Documents of the Middle Ages* (London: George Bell and Sons, 1910), 365–366, *Internet Medieval Sourcebook*, ed. Paul Halsall, Fordham University, https://sourcebooks.fordham.edu/source/g7-invest1.asp.

[14] Berman, *Law and Revolution*, 112.

[15] Ibid., 404.

Canterbury vacant when its occupant died in 1089, apparently so he could help himself to its revenues. When William thought he was dying in 1093, however, he recanted and chose Anselm as the successor. When Pope Urban II confirmed the appointment, a now recovered William denied Anselm's request to go to Rome to receive the pallium from the pope. William insisted that Anselm first recognize the authority of the king's grand council to decide which pope should be recognized, Urban II or the antipope Clement. Anselm replied, "In the things that are God's I will tender obedience to the Vicar of St. Peter; in things touching the earthly dignity of my lord the King I will to the best of my ability give him faithful counsel and help."[16] When the pallium was delivered to England by a papal legate, William insisted that he would be the one to give it to Anselm, but Anselm refused to accept it from him. In reaction, William vituperated, "Yesterday I hated him with great hatred, today I hate him with yet greater hatred and he can be certain that tomorrow and thereafter I shall hate him continually with ever fiercer and more bitter hatred."[17] Nevertheless, Anselm received his pallium from the altar of the cathedral.

Tensions continued under William's successor, Henry I (1100–1135). With an audacious claim to spiritual power, Henry's advocate asserted that "the anointing of a king at his coronation transforms the individual into another man", as described in the Bible (1 Sam 10:1–3, 6). The king becomes "the LORD's anointed" (christus Domini; 1 Sam 24:6), "another Christ, and, through grace, takes on the character of Christ himself".[18] In other words, the king was the real Vicar of Christ as he represented Christ's divine nature as ruler of the universe; therefore, it was he who would invest the bishops. At the instructions of Pope Urban II, Anselm denied King Henry's request for the royal investiture of bishops. In 1107, they finally compromised with the Concordat of London. Henry forswore the right

---

[16] Catholic Encyclopedia (New York: Robert Appleton, 1909), s.v. "England (Before the Reformation)", New Advent, http://www.newadvent.org/cathen/05431b.htm.

[17] Eadmer's History of Recent Events in England, trans. Geoffrey Bosanquet (London: Cresset Press, 1964), 53.

[18] "The Norman Anonymous Tract on Christian Kingship", Consitutions of Clarendon (blog), October 7, 2013, http://conclarendon.blogspot.com/2013/10/the-norman-anonymous-tract -on-christian.html.

of investiture of bishops and abbots, but he reserved the custom of having them present themselves to him beforehand in order to give homage in their temporal roles regarding their feudal properties and powers. In this ceremony, the king made the bishop a baron, with all the attendant duties to the king. The consecration as bishop by the Church followed.

With his Constitutions of Clarendon, Henry II (1154–1189) tried to restore royal supremacy over the Church. Thomas à Becket, his former chancellor who had become the archbishop of Canterbury, opposed him. In a letter (1166), Thomas instructed Henry that "you have not the power to give rules to bishops, nor to absolve or excommunicate anyone, to draw clerks before secular tribunals, to judge concerning churches and tithes, to forbid bishops to adjudge causes concerning breach of faith or oath, and many other things of this sort."[19] In reaction, Henry supposedly exclaimed, "Will no one rid me of this turbulent priest?" After Becket's subsequent murder, Henry recanted and renounced the offensive parts of his Constitutions that had made the king the supreme arbiter of canon law in England.[20]

An incident in 1185 is particularly instructive regarding the constitutional status that the two-swords controversy was taking on. When the abbot of Abington Abbey died, Henry II turned the abbey over to Thomas of Esseburn, who, in turn, conveniently proposed giving it and all its possessions to the king. The prior and the religious brothers of the abbey appealed to Ranulf de Glanvill, the chief justiciar, a position roughly equivalent to the king's chancellor. According to a contemporaneous account by the abbey's chronicler, "The grace of God finally prevailed to this extent, that Rannulphus de Glanvilla, the chief of the justices, turning to the other justices, said that our customary rights have been established reasonably and wisely, that

[19] James Bruce Ross and Mary Martin McLaughlin, eds., *The Portable Medieval Reader* (New York: Viking Press, 1949), 249–50.

[20] In November 1538, Henry VIII issued a proclamation whose final clause ordered that Becket's images, including his shrine at Canterbury, the pilgrimage site made famous by Chaucer's *Canterbury Tales*, be destroyed and his name erased from the Church's service books. His Office, Mass, and Collect were no longer to be said, and his feast days not to be kept. See "Henry VIII's Proclamation, 1538: The Unsainting of Thomas Becket", *Consitutions of Clarendon* (blog), October 4, 2013, http://conclarendon.blogspot.com/2013/10/henry-viiis-proclamation-1538.html.

nothing excessive could be found in them, and *that the lord king, neither wishes* NOR DARES to go against customs in some measure, so
ancient, and so just as to change anything respecting them."[21] Note
that by this time customs were considered an expression of natural
law in that they had "been established reasonably".

In 1205 King John revived the investiture dispute by attempting
to install his own candidate as the archbishop of Canterbury. Pope
Innocent III defied him by consecrating Stephen Langton as the new
archbishop instead. When John refused to accept Langton, Innocent
III excommunicated him and placed his kingdom under an interdict.
Further, Innocent threatened to depose him. At the pope's behest,
Philip II of France began preparing to do so through an invasion.
King John finally capitulated, surrendering England to the pope
by becoming his vassal. In 1213, Langton, called by British scholar
Ernest Barker the "father of English liberty", finally assumed his seat
at Canterbury.

Magna Carta

Nevertheless, the dispute continued with Langton's call for a renewal
of the Coronation Charter granted by Henry I in 1100. The charter
acknowledged the liberty of the Church but also recognized specific
liberties of the barons. At Saint Paul's on August 25, 1213, Langton
apparently read the charter to a gathering of barons. According to
English historian John Lingard, "Langton called the barons aside,
read to them the charter of Henry, and commented on its provisions. They answered by loud acclamations, and the archbishop,
taking advantage of their enthusiasm, administered to them an oath
by which they bound themselves to each other to conquer or die
in the defense of their liberties."[22] At the same time, Langton urged
the barons to make their demands reasonable and, if possible, to
eschew violence in pursuing them. This was the impetus that led
to the *Magna Carta Libertatum* (the Great Charter of Liberties) in 1215.

---

[21] Charles Howard McIlwain, *Constitutionalism: Ancient and Modern* (Ithaca, N.Y.: Cornell
University Press, 1947), 65 (emphasis in the original).

[22] John Lingard, *The History of England*, vol. 2 (London: J. C. Nimmo and Bain, 1883), 337.

Having set the barons in motion, Langton became the intermediary between them and the king, whom he served as a commissioner at Runnymede.

Langton helped draft Magna Carta and was the first witness to sign it. Its first provision stated:

> We have in the first place granted to God and by this our present charter have confirmed, for us and our heirs forever, that the English Church shall be free and shall have its rights entire and its liberties inviolate. And how we wish [that freedom] to be observed appears from this, that of our own pure and free will, before the conflict that arose between us and our barons, we granted and by our charter confirmed the liberty of election that is considered of prime importance and necessity for the English Church, and we obtained confirmation of it from the lord pope Innocent III—which [charter] we will observe ourself and we wish to be observed in good faith by our heirs forever.[23]

The freedom of the Church spoken of here meant, of course, freedom from royal control and freedom to govern herself, most especially through episcopal and monastic elections, rather than by royal appointment.

Magna Carta is also famous for laying the basis of due process, trial by jury, and the requirement that "scutage or aid shall be levied in our kingdom only by the common counsel of our kingdom" (article 12). The latter, as we shall see, is an expression of the *Quod omnes tangit ab omnibus tractari et approbari debet* principle in canon law, which developed into the requirment that taxes must receive the consent of those being taxed. The kernel of due process is in article 39: "No freeman shall be captured or imprisoned or disseised or outlawed or exiled or in any way destroyed, nor will we go against him or send against him, except by the lawful judgment of his peers or by the law of the land."[24]

Langton was most likely responsible for the preservation of what was then known as the Articles of the Barons, because he apparently

---

[23] Magna Carta (1215), Constitution Society, https://www.constitution.org/sech/sech_044.htm.
[24] Ibid.

took it with him from Runnymede for safekeeping.[25] Two months later, Pope Innocent III annulled the charter because John was "forced to accept" it. Revised versions of Magna Carta, however, were issued in 1216 and 1217 during the minority of King Henry III, who was a ward of the pope. The papal legate set his seal on these versions, indicating they had finally obtained papal approval. In 1225, Magna Carta received its definitive form, and Langton pronounced that violators of the charter of any rank would automatically be excommunicated.[26] In 1297, King Edward I confirmed Magna Carta as part of English statute law. By the early seventeenth century, it had been confirmed by English monarchs some thirty-two times.[27]

Because of its significance for later developments, one must interject here some reflections on the importance of the charter. Victorian historian William Stubbs claimed that "the whole constitutional history of England is little more than a commentary on Magna Carta."[28] Winston Churchill noted that Magna Carta was "entirely lacking in any spacious statement of the principles of democratic government or the rights of man", but that "throughout the document, it is implied that here is a law which is above the King and which even he must not break. This reaffirmation of a supreme law and its expression in a general charter is the great work of Magna Carta; and this alone justifies the respect in which men have held it."[29]

The influence of Magna Carta on the American colonies was pervasive, due to the efforts of Sir Edward Coke, who, in 1606, was tasked with drafting the First Charter of Virginia. "The Charter makes reference to 'Liberties, Franchises, and immunities' and was largely inspired by Magna Carta. The same language was used in the foundational charters of the colonies of Massachusetts, Maryland,

[25] "Archbishop Stephen Langton", British Library, http://www.bl.uk/people/archbishop-stephen-langton#.

[26] Dr. Sophie Ambler, "Stephen Langton", Magna Carta Trust, https://magnacarta800th.com/schools/biographies/magna-carta-bishops/stephen-langton/.

[27] Ellis Sandoz, *Republicanism, Religion, and the Soul of America* (Columbia: University of Missouri Press, 2006), 61.

[28] Cited in Daniel Hannan, "Eight Centuries of Liberty", *Wall Street Journal*, May 30, 2015, C1.

[29] Winston S. Churchill, *A History of the English-Speaking Peoples*, vol. 1 (New York: Dodd, Mead, 1956), 256.

Maine, Connecticut, Carolina, and Rhode Island."[30] British historian
Daniel Hannan points out that in 1638, "Maryland sought permission
to recognize Magna Carta as part of the law of the province."[31]

Magna Carta was repeatedly referenced during the American
movement for independence. Elisha Williams, writing in 1744 under
the pseudonym Philalethes, used it to insist on the primacy of natural law: "The rights of Magna Charta depend not on the will of the
prince, or the will of the legislature; but they are the inherent natural
rights of Englishmen: secured and confirmed they may be by the
legislature, but not derived from nor dependent on their will."[32] In
1766, a Son of Liberty in Bristol County, Massachusetts, toasted liberty by saying, "Our Toast in general is,—Magna Charta."[33] Samuel
Adams appealed to Magna Carta in "The Rights of the Colonists:
The Report of the Committee of Correspondence to the Boston
Town Meeting, November 20, 1772". Just as the barons had been
justified in raising their swords against the usurpations of the king, so
too might be the colonists, said Adams:

> Magna Charta itself is in substance but a constrained Declaration,
> or proclamation, and promulgation in the name of King, Lord, and
> Commons of the sense the latter had of their original inherent, inde-
> feasible natural Rights, as also those of free Citizens equally perdura-
> ble with the other. That great author, that great jurist, and even that
> Court writer Mr. Justice Blackstone holds that this recognition was
> justly obtained of King John sword in hand: and peradventure it must
> be one day sword in hand again rescued and preserved from total
> destruction and oblivion.[34]

In 1775, Massachusetts chose a depiction of a patriot carrying Magna
Carta in one hand and a sword in the other for its seal.[35]

---

[30] André P. DeBattista, "Magna Carta, Liberty, and the Medieval Mind", *European Conservative* 12 (Summer/Fall 2015): 15.

[31] Daniel Hannan, *Inventing Freedom, How the English-Speaking Peoples Made the Modern
World* (New York: HarperCollins, 2013), 114.

[32] Elisha Williams, *The Essential Rights and Liberties of Protestants* (March 30, 1744), Con
Source, http://consource.org/document/the-essential-rights-and-liberties-of-protestants-by
-elisha-williams-1744-3-30/.

[33] Clinton Rossiter, *Seedtime of the Republic: The Origin of the American Tradition of Political
Liberty* (New York: Harcourt, Brace, 1953), 360.

[34] *The Writings of Samuel Adams: 1770–1773* (New York: G.P. Putnam's Sons, 1906), 356–57.

[35] Hannan, *Inventing Freedom*, 116.

The constitutions of a number of states—Maryland, North Carolina, South Carolina, Massachusetts, and New Hampshire—contain paraphrases of Magna Carta's article 39, which also influenced the Fifth Amendment to the Constitution. In 1937 Hatton Sumners, a Texas congressman who served as the chairman of the House Judiciary Committee, said, "There is a straight road which runs from Runnymede to Philadelphia."[36] As well known as the influence of Magna Carta on the United States may be, few are probably aware of the role of a Catholic cardinal in instigating and drafting it. The straight road runs from *Rome* to Runnymede to Philadelphia.

The Struggle in the Holy Roman Empire

On the Continent, the investiture struggle was fought with particular vigor between Gregory VII and Emperor Henry IV, who refused to accede to the pope's commands on investiture—as a result of which the two tried to depose each other. Gregory instructed Henry that the pope's decree was to be received "as a necessary truth and light for regaining salvation ... [and] should be devoutly received and observed not only by thee and by those of thy kingdom, but by all the princes and peoples of the world who confess and cherish Christ."[37] Gregory proclaimed, "Let him [Henry] no longer imagine that Holy Church is his subject or his handmaid but rather let him recognize her as his superior and his mistress."[38] Henry fired back, "In virtue of my office as *Patricius Romanus* given to me by God and the Roman people, I revoke from thee all papal authority."[39] At the same time, however, it is illustrative of the strength of the two-swords teaching that Henry appealed to it for his authority. He accused Gregory of, "without God's knowledge", usurping "for himself the kingship and the priesthood. In this deed he held in contempt the pious ordinance

[36] Ibid.

[37] Gregory VII to Henry IV, December 1075, in Ernest F. Henderson, ed., *Select Historical Documents of the Middle Ages* (London: George Bell and Sons, 1896), The Avalon Project of the Yale Law School, http://avalon.law.yale.edu/medieval/inv01.asp.

[38] Richard John Neuhaus, ed., *The Second One Thousand Years* (Grand Rapids: William B. Eerdmans, 2001), 11.

[39] Cited in Heinrich A. Rommen, *The State in Catholic Thought* (St. Louis: B. Herder, 1945), 531.

of God, which especially commanded that these two—namely, the kingship and the priesthood—should remain, not as one entity, but as two."[40] At least implicitly, Henry acknowledged the integrity of the pope's sphere of authority. The argument was never over whether there ought to be two spheres, but over where the borders were located. Gregory responded by excommunicating Henry, who, with twenty-six of his bishops, tried to depose the pope, saying, "I, Henry, king by the grace of God, with all my bishops say to thee: 'Descend! Descend, thou ever accursed.' "[41] Gregory's excommunication, however, prevailed. In 1077, Henry, dressed as a penitent, knelt in the snow outside the Castle of Canossa, imploring the pope's pardon.

During this dispute, Manegold of Lautenbach, a Saxon monk who later became bishop of Chartres, delivered a forceful defense of Gregory VII's position. His letter is worth quoting at length because it shows how, early in the Middle Ages, ideas essential to the American Founding were rooted. It contains an early statement of social contract theory, asserting that the prince derives his power from a pact with the people and can be deposed if he violates it.

> King is not a name of nature but a title of office: nor does the people exalt him so high above it in order to give him the free power of playing the tyrant in its midst, but to defend him from tyranny. So soon as he begins to act the tyrant, is it not plain that he falls from the dignity granted to him? Since it is evident that he has first broken that contract by virtue of which he was appointed. If one should engage a man for a fair wage to tend swine, and he find means not to tend but to steal them, would one not remove him from his charge? . . . Since no one can create himself emperor or king, the people elevates a certain one person over itself to this end, that he govern and rule it according to the principle of righteous government; but if in any wise he transgress the contract by virtue of which he is chosen, he absolves the people from the obligation of submission, because he has first broken faith with it.[42]

[40] Cited in Siedentop, *Inventing the Individual*, 204.

[41] Ted Byfield and Paul Stanway, eds., *The Christians: Their First Two Thousand Years* (Edmonton: Christian History Project, 2004), 85.

[42] R. L. Poole, *Illustrations of Medieval Thought and Learning* (New York: Macmillan, 1920), 232.

The distance between this statement and John Adams' reference to the Declaration of Independence as the "moral thunderbolt, which melted the chains of allegiance that bound the colonists to his sovereign" is not so great.

Manegold was not the only twelfth-century thinker to circumscribe royal power. John of Salisbury (ca. 1115–1178) produced one of the most influential works of political thought in the early Middle Ages. In *Policraticus* (1159), he wrote that God's law is equity, which "is a certain fitness of things, which compares all things rationally, and seeks to apply like rules of right and wrong to like cases, being impartially disposed toward all persons, and allotting to each that which belongs to him. Of this equity, the interpreter is the law, to which the will and intention of equity and justice are known." Therefore, John concluded that the law is both "a discovery, and a gift from God".[43] He defended tyrannicide against any prince who usurps the law. John, who served as secretary to Thomas à Becket, stated:

> Jurists declare that "the prince's pleasure hath the force of law" [a famous Roman legal maxim]; but this maxim is false.... His power comes of God, and is still God's although it is exercised by a deputy. Thus we have the dependence of the royal power on the Divine law clearly enunciated; and as the interpreter of that law we have the Church.... The prince will always prefer the advantage of others to his private will, and will not seek his own good but that of others. It is in this that the difference between the prince and the tyrant partly consists, and so whilst the prince is to be honoured and revered, it is lawful to deceive and honourable to kill a tyrant, if he cannot be otherwise restrained.

John called a tyrant an "image of depravity ... [who] spring[s] from evil and should be cut down with the axe wherever he grows". He added, "If [the prince] is resistant and opposes the divine commandments, and wishes to make me share in his war against God, then, with unrestrained voice I must answer back that God must be preferred before any man on earth."[44] In chapter 19, he used ancient

---

[43] Ross and McLaughlin, *The Portable Medieval Reader*, 253.
[44] Cited in Berman, *Law and Revolution*, 281.

Rome to make his point again: "As for Comodus, he incommoded every one, and was finally murdered in the House of the Vestals, having already during his life-time been adjudged an enemy of the human race. And this is perhaps the best and fittest description of a tyrant and the one which explains the real significance of the name. Therefore, as it is lawful to kill a condemned enemy, so it is to kill a tyrant." Thus,

> to kill a tyrant, is not merely lawful, but right and just.... Therefore the law rightly takes arms against him who disarms the laws, and the public power rages in fury against him who strives to bring to naught the public force. And while there are many acts which amount to lèse-majesté, none is a graver crime than that which is against the body of Justice herself. Tyranny therefore is not merely a public crime, but, if there could be such a thing, a crime more than public. And if in the crime of lèse-majesté all men are admitted to be prosecutors, how much more should this be true in the case of the crime of subverting the laws which should rule even over emperors? Truly no one will avenge a public enemy, but rather whoever does not seek to bring him to punishment commits an offense against himself and the whole body of the earthly commonwealth.[45]

Here we find a twelfth-century premonition of Thomas Jefferson's famous motto: "Rebellion to tyrants is obedience to God." In the early thirteenth century, *The Mirror of Saxon Law* echoed these views. It stated that "God is himself law; therefore law is dear to him" and that, therefore, a person has a right "to resist a lawless decision of his king and of his judge, and also to help another to do so if he is his relative or his lord".[46]

By the reign of Innocent III (1198–1216), the papacy had more or less prevailed in the investiture controversy in Germany. In 1122, the Concordat of Worms ended lay investiture. At the same time, Innocent III recognized the limitations of his sovereignty: "Why should we wish to usurp foreign power when we are not sufficient to exercise our own jurisdiction? We do not intend to judge concerning a fief, but concerning sin, which undoubtedly pertains to us. The Pope

---

[45] Ibid., 282.
[46] Ibid., 504.

has full direct temporal power only in the patrimony of St. Peter, but not in other regions."[47] In adjudicating disputes, Innocent also showed how difficult it was to keep the lines of jurisdiction clear. In addressing a conflict between the kings of France and England, he declared:

> Therefore let no one think that we intend to infringe upon or diminish the jurisdiction and authority of the illustrious King of France, since he neither would nor should infringe upon our own jurisdiction ... but ... since the King of England, as he asserts, is sufficiently prepared to show that the King of France sinned against him ... how can we, who have been called by a supernatural disposition to the government of the Universal Church, fail to heed the divine mandate? ... For we do not intend to judge concerning the fief which lies in his jurisdiction ... but to judge concerning the sin, for this, without doubt we have judgment which we can and ought to exercise on anyone whomever.[48]

As mentioned earlier, there was bound to be tension between the dual jurisdictions, since they were exercised over the same persons. But it was a creative tension—the resolution of which defined and maintained the integrity of each to a workable degree. This was inspired by an overarching vision of temporal and spiritual powers operating together in a harmonious whole. In *Summa Decreti* (1159), Stephen of Tournai described it clearly:

> In the same city, under the same king, there are two peoples, and for the two peoples there are two ways of life, and for the two ways of life there are two governments, and in accordance with these two governments there is a twofold order of jurisdiction. The City is the Church; the King of the City is Christ; the two peoples are the two orders in the Church, clerics and layman; the two lines are the spiritual and the carnal; the two governments, the priestly and the regal; the twofold jurisdiction, divine and human law. Render to each its due, and all will be well.[49]

---

[47] Cited in Rager, *Philosophy of St. Robert Bellarmine*, 43.

[48] Jerome G. Kerwin, *Catholic Viewpoint on Church and State* (Garden City, N.Y.: Hanover House, 1960), 34–35.

[49] Ibid., 30.

About a century later, Thomas Aquinas elaborated on the distinction between the two powers, making clear why government may
not arrogate to itself control of the spiritual and religious:

> Furthermore, if [the state] could attain this [final] end by the power of
> human nature, then the duty of the king would have to include the
> direction of men to this end.... But because a man does not attain his
> end, which is the possession of God, by human power, but by divine
> power ... therefore the task of leading [men] to that end does not per-
> tain to human government, but to divine. Consequently, government
> of this kind pertains to that king who is not only a man, but also God,
> namely, to our Lord Jesus Christ.... Consequently, in order that spir-
> itual things might be distinguished from earthly things, the ministry of
> this kingdom has been entrusted not to earthly kings, but to priests,
> and in the highest degree to the chief priest, the successor of St. Peter,
> the Vicar of Christ, the Roman Pontiff.[50]

So long as this teaching obtained, no one could rightly combine
spiritual and temporal powers into one—the single most important
separation of powers that has ever existed. As a result, the one jurisdiction limited the other, with the consequence of greater freedom
for individuals, who could, on occasion, play the one off the other.
Indeed, in certain instances, ecclesiastical courts developed as an
alternative to civic or public courts.[51] Plural jurisdictions meant that
neither encompassed the totality of things regarding anyone. Limited authority meant limited obedience. As historian and medievalist
Brian Tierney explained:

> There was never just one structure of government, presided over by
> an unchallenged theocratic head, but always two structures, eccle-
> siastical and secular, always jealous of each other's authority, always
> preventing medieval society from congealing into a single, monolithic
> theocracy. Ecclesiastical criticism diminished the aura of divine right
> surrounding kinship; royal power opposed the temporal claims of the
> papacy. Each hierarchy limited the authority of the other. It is not
> difficult to see that such a situation could be conducive to a growth of

---

[50] Thomas Aquinas, *De regimen principium* (*On the Governance of Rulers*) 1, 14.
[51] Timothy Samuel Shah and Allen D. Hertzke, eds., *Christianity and Freedom*, vol. 1, *His-torical Perspectives* (New York: Cambridge University Press, 2016), 182.

human freedom, and the fact has often been pointed out. Lord Acton long ago wrote, "To that conflict of four hundred years we owe the rise of civil liberty."[52]

The legal definition of the limits of each sovereignty served to curb the arbitrary exercise of power. Legal scholar Harold Berman called it "a constitutional principle of the first magnitude".[53]

Another constitutional principle that we shall see developed in the Middle Ages was enunciated in the early eleventh century by Peter Damian, bishop of Gubbio, later declared a Doctor of the Church, who stated, "All political authority derives from God, but resides essentially in the people." (Potestas est in Populo / A Summo data Domino.)[54] This teaching was the foundation of popular sovereignty. As a complementary aside, one should also note that Jewish communities held to similar democratic principles, though they developed them somewhat differently. In the European ghettos of the Middle Ages,

> government was generally democratic. Although Jewish communities had all sorts of constitutions, there was never any approach to monarchy.... The sovereignty of the people ... was never contested; its only alternative was the sovereignty of God, whose power, however, was exercised through the people. The rabbi was subject to the general laws, as much as any layman. His rights and duties were those of every Jew. What superiority of position he might gain, was due to his personal eminence and the voluntary submission of others to his judgment.[55]

The Contribution of Canon Law to Constitutional Thinking

As the idea and development of dual sovereignty was a unique product of Christianity, it should be no surprise that other rudiments of

---

[52] Brian Tierney, *Religion, Law, and the Growth of Constitutional Thought 1150–1650* (New York: Cambridge University Press, 1982), 10.

[53] Berman, *Law and Revolution*, 213–14.

[54] Cited in R. L. Bruckberger, *Image of America*, trans. C. G. Paulding and Virgilia Peterson (New York: Viking Press, 1959), 97.

[55] Salo W. Baron, *A Social and Religious History of the Jews*, 3 vols. (New York: Columbia University Press, 1937), 2:103–4.

constitutional thinking first arose within the Church's conception of her own law. Canon law, the positive law of the Catholic Church, was the first systematic attempt at an ecclesiastical legal order based on Christian presuppositions of both natural and divine law. Canon lawyers thought through the legal implications of man's being made in the imago Dei—particularly in respect to equality, reason, and free will—which they gradually translated into the rule of law, popular sovereignty, representation, and the requirement for consent. Canon laws were not theoretical speculations as such. They were responses to real-life problems. They were as much a reflection of life in the Middle Ages as a formulation of it. But they implicitly contained theories that guided their development.

The eleventh-century rediscovery of the sixth-century Justinian Code, or *Corpus juris civilis*, around 1080, animated the development of canon law. The code contained ordinances and decisions of Roman emperors made before Justinian, Justinian's own laws, and a large collection of extracts from the opinions of Roman jurists in actual cases concerning a wide variety of legal propositions and issues. In the prologue, Justinian said:

> We have found the entire arrangement of the law which has come down to us from the foundation of the City of Rome and the times of Romulus, to be so confused that it is extended to an infinite length and is not within the grasp of human capacity; and hence We were first induced to begin by examining what had been enacted by former most venerated princes, to correct their constitutions, and make them more easily understood; to the end that being included in a single Code, and having had removed all that is superfluous in resemblance and all iniquitous discord, they may afford to all men the ready assistance of true meaning.[56]

This early effort at legal synthesis and comprehensibility inspired medieval canonists to attempt something similar in respect to Church law, which, until that time, was a mishmash of collections of rules of conduct taken from the Bible, the first-century *Didache*, the third-century *Teachings of the Apostles*, the fourth-century *Enactment of the*

---

[56] "Medieval Sourcebook: Corpus Iuris Civilis, 6th Century", Fordham University, https://sourcebooks.fordham.edu/source/corpus1.asp.

Apostles, and papal decretals (letters of the popes setting ecclesiastical law), as well as laws from many synods, ecumenical councils, and individual bishops.[57] Partial collections of these canons were occasionally published, with the canons usually arranged in chronological order, though not necessarily with any logical sequence or development. As Harold Berman pointed out, there was "a legal *order* within the church, but no *system* of ecclesiastical law, that is, no independent, integrated, developing body of the ecclesiastical legal principles and procedures, clearly differentiated from liturgy and theology".[58] Around 1140, this changed with the publication of Gratian's *A Concordance of Discordant Canons*, otherwise known as *Decretum*, which Berman called "the first comprehensive and systematic legal treatise in the history of the West, and perhaps in the history of mankind—if by 'comprehensive' is meant the attempt to embrace virtually the entire law of a given polity, and if by 'systematic' is meant the express effort to present that law as a single body, in which all the parts are viewed as interacting to form a whole."[59]

Gratian drew, first of all, upon the Golden Rule—"Do unto others as you would have them do unto you"—and the sources mentioned above, particularly prior canonical collections. As his title indicates, the objective was to reconcile conflicting canons and eliminate inconsistencies. His method was Scholastic dialectical analysis. It was based on the *disputatio*—the main pedagogical method used in medieval universities. It worked in a way familiar to anyone who has read Aquinas. The procedure was to pose a question (*quaestio*) or a dispute involving contradictory texts related to a certain issue. The question was followed by a *propositio*, giving the authority and the reasons for one side of the dispute. Then the *oppositio* would appear, giving the authorities and reasons for the opposing view. Finally, the *solutio* would discern whether one side or the other gave reasons that were not true or that needed to be adjusted or abandoned in light of the better reasons of the other.[60] The dialectical style operated like an intellectual court procedure aimed at discerning the truth. The

---

[57] Berman, *Law and Revolution*, 199.
[58] Ibid., 202 (emphasis in the original).
[59] Ibid., 143.
[60] Ibid., 148.

validity of this way of proceeding rested on the assumption, going back to Heraclitus, that reason is the basis of law. Since God is Reason (Logos), man ought to have reasons for his laws. What's more, Berman has written, "underlying the canon law as a whole was the belief in a God of justice who operates a lawful universe, punishing and rewarding according to principles of proportion, mercifully mitigated in exceptional cases."[61]

Gratian distinguished three main types of law and placed them in hierarchical order: divine law, natural law, and then human law. Divine law was from Scriptures, and natural law came from reason and was embedded in conscience. Of course, there could be no conflict between them as they ultimately came from the same source. At the beginning of the *Decretum*, he stated, "Natural law (*ius*) is what is contained in the law and the Gospel by which each is commanded to do to another what he wants done to himself and forbidden to do to another what he does not want unto himself."[62] Around 1160, the decretist Rufinus defined *jus naturale* as "a certain force instilled in every human creature by nature to do good and avoid the opposite".[63] Revelation, it was thought, even refers to natural law. Jeremiah states, "I will put my law within them, and write it upon their hearts" (31:33). And in the Letter to the Romans, Saint Paul wrote, "When Gentiles who have not the law do by nature what the law requires, they are a law to themselves, even though they do not have the law. They show that what the law requires is written on their hearts, while their conscience also bears witness and their conflicting thoughts accuse or perhaps excuse them" (2:14–15).

Human law, made by man, must be infused with both divine and natural law and be in accord with reason. Most importantly, Gratian wrote that "the law of princes ought not to prevail over natural law [*jus naturale*]." Neither, he said, should ecclesiastical laws. "Enactments, whether ecclesiastical or secular, if they are proved to be contrary to natural law, must be totally excluded."[64] Gratian also declared

---

[61] Ibid., 529–30. It should be noted that the Scholastic *disputatio* format persisted in the education provided by the colonial colleges and seminaries attended by the Founding generation.

[62] Cited in Charles J. Reid Jr., "The Medieval Origins of the Western Natural Rights Tradition: The Achievement of Brian Tierney", *Cornwall Law Review* 83, no. 2 (January 1998): 443, https://pdfs.semanticscholar.org/5602/bf20298571a0020f9e36820c975a65956819.pdf.

[63] Ibid., 444.

[64] Cited in Berman, *Law and Revolution*, 147.

that natural law required that "princes are bound by and shall live according to their laws."[65] This was a medieval innovation. Classical Roman law stated that "what has pleased the prince has the force of law" and "the prince is absolved from the laws."[66]

Gratian also made custom subject to natural law. Custom was to have no standing if it did not conform to reason and conscience. In canon 1, Gratian wrote, "The natural law prevails over custom and legislation in dignity. Anything that is accepted by custom or included in legislation which is against natural law is to be considered null and void. Therefore, Augustine says: No one may do anything against natural law."[67] One can easily see the huge significance of these teachings for the formation of constitutional thought and the rule of law. What is striking is the place Gratian gives to the primacy of reason and natural law in the political order—a teaching of great significance to the American Founding, even if the Founders might not have traced it specifically to Gratian. They said many things that sound like paraphrases of Gratian's statements.

These canons were not some airy speculations; they had practical applications in medieval jurisprudence. Natural and divine law, pointed out Paul Sigmund, "were cited in church courts in medieval Europe to annul arbitrary customs and local laws. With the existence of the ecclesiastical courts to give it application, the conception of natural law as a higher set of norms invalidating irrational legislation began for the first time to have an operative significance."[68] Gratian's work became the standard text for the study of canon law and constituted the most voluminous part of the *Corpus iuris canonici*, in use in Catholic ecclesiastical courts until 1917. It also inspired law professors, who came to be known as decretists, to pursue the dialectical approach further in search of even greater harmonization of the law. Their commentaries were known as glosses, collections of which came to be published with the *Decretum*.

As mentioned earlier, the canonists were not applying an abstract theory of constitutionalism to medieval society but were working out

---

[65] Ibid., 145.

[66] Ibid., 585.

[67] Cited in Paul E. Sigmund, *Natural Law in Political Thought* (Cambridge, Mass.: Winthrop Publishers, 1971), 50.

[68] Ibid., 38.

the practical problems of the day as they developed from how life was lived in the medieval polity. The principles sprang from the actions as much as the actions from the principles. The genius of medieval canonists was in taking elements of Roman law, which largely eschewed generalities and principles, and drawing out of them a general legal theory as needed. They did this in a way that transformed the original meaning of certain Roman legal terms that had applied only to private law in very specific ways. They patiently renovated them into moral and political principles that then shaped the form and practice of public life. From this effort evolved the laws of corporations and the requirements of representation and consent—especially, in another prefigurement of modern constitutionalism, in matters of taxation. What began in the Church eventually influenced practices in civil life and the early formation of parliaments. The impact of canon law on secular law was naturally facilitated by the fact that those engaged in civil administration (clerks) were at least in minor orders (and therefore clerics). They worked in both the ecclesiastical bureaucracy and the royal chanceries. Brian Tierney noted that "the juridical culture of the 12th century—the works of the Roman canon lawyers, especially those of the canonists where religious and secular ideas most obviously intersected—formed a kind of seedbed from which grew the whole tangled forest of early modern constitutional thought."[69]

Medieval canonists appropriated Roman corporate law to define the Church and apply her jurisdiction.[70] Unlike Roman corporate law, however, canon law did not require imperial recognition for the establishment of a corporation. Church associations were constituted by the *voluntary consent* of their members. What is more, it was not now only a *public* authority that "could have legislative and judicial jurisdiction over its members", but these new corporations could as well.[71] Berman claimed that "the church in the eleventh century was the first collective to call itself a corporation (*universitas*)."[72] Also, smaller groups within the Church, such as abbeys, cathedral chapters,

[69] Tierney, *Religion, Law*, 1.
[70] Berman, *Law and Revolution*, 150.
[71] Siedentop, *Inventing the Individual*, 234.
[72] Berman, *Law and Revolution*, 150.

and monasteries, were constituted as semi-independent corporations. Medieval society became honeycombed with many such voluntary, self-governing associations. This was a unique development.

The law of corporations, and its application to ecclesiastical polities, served as a proto-constitutional law. It gave the Church a legal identity independent from emperors, kings, and feudal lords.[73] Under corporation law, bishops and priests received their authority not solely from ordination, but from the jurisdiction given by the Church as a corporation.[74] Ordination conferred priestly powers on the individual; jurisdiction conferred legislative, administrative, and judicial authority to the bishop within his diocese or to the abbot in his abbey.[75] Jurisdiction pertained to the position, not to the person. This was also true of the pope, who held supreme legislative, administrative, and judicial authority over the Church as a whole. This supreme authority, however, was to be exercised only within the law that established it—including divine and natural law.

What Touches All Must Be Approved by All

The ingenuity of the canonists was most particularly displayed in their transformative usage of the Roman maxim *Quod omnes tangit ab omnibus approbari*—What touches all must be approved by all. Taken from the Code of Justinian (5, 59, 5, 2–3), this maxim was to become one of the most influential in the Middle Ages. In Roman law, it applied only to private law cases in which there were several legal guardians of the same ward or property, or in cases in which there were multiple persons who shared a common source of water. It stipulated that no single one of them could determine the emancipation of the ward or the disposition of the property under the joint guardianship without the consent of all the guardians. It otherwise had no political, civic, or constitutional significance. The canonists vastly expanded and applied this rule to ecclesiastical corporations in order to underpin the practice of self-government within

[73] Ibid., 218.
[74] Ibid., 150.
[75] Ibid., 207.

religious orders, dioceses, abbeys, and the entire Church, especially as it applied to taxation and legislation. According to Kenneth Pennington, a scholar of ecclesiastical and legal history, "The canonists first used this principle to define the legal relationship between a bishop and his chapter of canons. Later, they introduced the maxim into ecclesiastical government where it supported the rights of the lesser members of the ecclesiastical hierarchy to have a hand in the governing of the church."[76] Thus, the person affected should have some say in the matters affecting him. In his reign (1159–1181), Pope Alexander III emphasized that the "advice" or "consent" of the members of the chapter, meaning the clergy, was *required* in various kinds of proprietary cases.[77] *Quod omnes tangit* was gradually elevated to the status of a constitutional principle. (In *The Letters of a Pennsylvania Farmer* written on the eve of the American Revolution, author John Dickinson would explicitly refer to it.)

If consent is required, how is it to be exercised and by whom? Consent was expressed in the electoral principle and the operation of the *jus eligendi*, the right to vote. It was manifested in the selection of the pope by the cardinals, which, as defined by the Third Lateran Council in 1179, required a two-thirds majority vote. Bishops, in turn, were elected by their cathedral chapters—the canons and other clergy in the capital of the diocese—and abbots were elected by the monks of their monasteries. Canons also chose a provost or dean to preside over the assemblies of the clergy of the cathedral. Chapter officers were elected. The decretalists made clear that any coercion used to influence the decisions of the electors would invalidate the election. To ensure the integrity of free consent, voting took place in secret. In the cases of the bishops and the heads of religious orders and monasteries directly under the pope's authority, these elections were subject to papal approval.

Paul Sigmund explained:

In the mid-thirteenth century, Pope Gregory X decided that a vote in which the prevailing side was twice as large as those opposed—a

---

[76] Kenneth Pennington, "Bartolomé de Las Casas and the Tradition of Medieval Law", *Church History* 39 (1970): 157, https://scholarship.law.edu/scholar/653/.

[77] Berman, *Law and Revolution*, 220–21.

two-thirds majority—could be assumed to fulfill both the requirements of numbers and merit. This decision was incorporated in the *Liber sextus* (C. 9, I, 6) in 1298 and extended to episcopal elections a requirement that had already been applied to the election of the pope in the twelfth century (1179). Subsequently, the two-thirds requirement found its way into the proceedings of many deliberative bodies, but its origin seems to be the canonistic requirement of approval by the *maior et sanior pars*.[78]

Medieval family law also developed to reflect the requirement of consent, especially in its emphasis on the mutual consent of both spouses for the validity of a marriage.[79] The choice had to be a free one, without the forceful interference of the respective families, which, until that time, typically had had marriages arranged principally for the benefit of the family, irrespective of the interests or affections of the prospective spouses. Coercion now became grounds for annulment. Speaking of medieval marriage, Harold Berman said, "Before God the two parties to marriage were equal and this doctrine of equality was first taught by Christianity. In practice it meant, above all, that the obligations, especially that of fidelity, were mutual."[80] As we have seen elsewhere, the principle of equality ineluctably led to the requirement of consent.[81] As an illustration of Christendom's gradual movement of men from slavery to serfdom, and then to freedom, it is also significant that a serf was allowed to marry without his lord's permission. Pope Hadrian IV declared that such marriages were likewise valid and indissoluble.[82]

When joined with the notion of representation, the *quod omnes tangit* maxim developed into one of the foundations of constitutional government. To achieve that combination, canon law made a major change in the Roman concept of representation by proctor—in which one person could represent only one other person as an agent.

[78] *International Encyclopedia of the Social Sciences*, s.v. "Canon Law", by Paul E. Sigmund, Encyclopedia.com, accessed June 24, 2019, https://www.encyclopedia.com/social-sciences/applied-and-social-sciences-magazines/canon-law.

[79] Berman, *Law and Revolution*, 168.

[80] Ibid., 229.

[81] The great third-century Roman jurist Ulpian, whose writings constituted one-third of Justinian's Code, wrote, "As far as the law of nature is concerned, all men are equal."

[82] Berman, *Law and Revolution*, 322.

Hans von Rautenfeld points out that "political representation only arose after 1150 c.e. when the concept of the proctor was conjoined to the concept of a corporation, a fictive person comprised of a group of individuals with similar interests which was itself considered the seat of rights and interests."[83] A grant of *potestas* (power) or *plena potestas* (full power) allowed a proctor to represent and act on behalf of someone else. In Roman law, these Latin terms were usually applied to court proceedings. In the twelfth century, however, they were used exclusively in ecclesiastical affairs and law.[84] The elected representatives in Church bodies were fully empowered to represent their body of constituents and were, in turn, accountable to them. Again, the initial impetus for this was to ensure that there was no taxation without representation. This begins to look very much like representation in its modern constitutional meaning.

In 1216, a case arose that illustrates how the principles of representation and consent worked their way through the structures of the Church. An archbishop had forbidden representatives of certain cathedral chapters to participate in a provincial synod. The chapters appealed to Pope Honorius III. In his decretal deciding the case, *Etsi membra*, Pope Honorius found fault with the archbishop because he had denied the cathedral chapters representation at councils where matters touching their interests would be determined, a clear violation of the principle of *quod omnes tangit*.[85] He said, "We and our brothers the cardinals were in complete agreement that those chapters ought to be invited to such councils and their nuncios (*nuntii*) ought to be admitted to the business of the council, especially those about matters that are known to concern the chapters."[86]

Speaking of law, Aquinas captured the general sense of the maxim when he said, "The directing of anything to the end concerns him to whom the end belongs."[87] Honorius instructed the archbishop

---

[83] *New Dictionary of the History of Ideas*, s.v. "Political Representation", by Hans von Rautenfeld, Encyclopedia.com, accessed June 24, 2019, http://www.encyclopedia.com/doc /1G2-3424300690.html.

[84] John B. Morrall, *Political Thought in Medieval Times* (Cincinnati, Ohio: Benziger Brothers, 1928), 63.

[85] Kenneth Pennington, "Representation in Medieval Canon Law", *Jurist* 64 (2004): 370.

[86] *Etsi membra* X, 3, 10, 10, posted at Ken Pennington, http://legalhistorysources.com /LisbonRights/EtsiMembra2.html.

[87] Thomas Aquinas, *Summa theologica* II, q. 90, a. 3.

that "when the head gives the members their due the body shall not experience the ravages of schism but will remain whole in the unity of love."[88]

Etsi membra was absorbed into canon law in 1225. Shortly afterward, canonist Jacobus de Albenga remarked that Honorius' decision was clearly based on the principle that "what touches them ought to be decided by them."[89] Medieval historian Richard Kay describes Honorius' decretal as "a landmark in the development of representative government".[90] The reason is explained by Kenneth Pennington:

> The canonists immediately expanded the right to attend provincial councils by representatives of cathedral chapters into a more general right of persons whose interests were affected by the business of the council. During the thirteenth century provincial synods included representatives of cathedral chapters as a matter of course. *Etsi membra* became a key legal justification that persons and ecclesiastical institutions had the right to send representatives to assemblies that dealt with issues pertaining to their interests and that they, through their representatives, had the right to consent to new legislation.[91]

Next, said Joseph Costanzo,

> Innocent III set an extraordinary authoritative precedent when he joined together the principle of consent and the principle of representation in a limited matter of proprietary interests and, by the sixth and twelfth canons of the Fourth Lateran Council, enjoined the universal practice of representative assemblies amongst the metropolitans and the religious orders. The influence of papal pressure on the institutional evolution of the representative idea was exerted at the two oecumenical Councils of Lyons (1245 and 1274), the ligatine Council at Bourges of 1225, and in direct imitation of the latter, the English provincial Synod convened by Archbishop Langton in 1226.[92]

---

[88] Pennington, "Representation in Medieval Canon Law", 370.

[89] Ibid., 371.

[90] Ibid.

[91] Ibid.

[92] Joseph F. Costanzo, S.J., "Juridic Origins of Representation II", *Fordham Law Review* 23, no. 3 (1954): 296–97.

The net result of this was that these bodies exercised substantial self-government.[93] One ought to add that, in a case involving the Church in Troyes, Innocent III found that the majority in a corporate community could not deprive the minority members of their rights through majority vote.[94] Brian Tierney points out that "in spite of the persistent tendency towards papal centralization, the whole Church, no less than the secular states, remained in a sense a federation of semi-autonomous units, the union of innumerable greater or lesser corporate bodies."[95]

In addition, to assist with lawmaking, popes would occasionally convene councils, which Berman claimed "were Europe's first legislatures".[96] For the Fourth Lateran Council in 1215, Innocent III summoned not only archbishops and bishops, abbots, priors, and monarchs, but for the first time the chapters of the churches were asked to send a provost or dean to act on their behalf.[97] The reason for this novelty was that the business of the council—which, in this case, included financial taxes to support parochial teachers—would affect them. Therefore, the *quod omnes tangit* dictum—what touches all must be approved by all—applied. There was a gradual expansion of those included in such synods and councils that finally reached down to the parish level (at least in England)—the expanding enfranchisement always justified by the same principle.

The Development of Consent

Religious orders served as models of representative government at this time. The Dominican Order offered a particularly concrete example. In 1220, Saint Dominic summoned representatives from the dozen priories that he had founded to meet in Bologna at Pentecost. According to Marie-Humbert Vicaire O.P., "He expressly

---

[93] Berman, *Law and Revolution*, 215.

[94] Brian Tierney, *The Idea of Natural Rights* (Grand Rapids: William B. Eedermans, 1997), 184.

[95] Brian Tierney, *Foundations of the Conciliar Theory* (London: Cambridge University Press, 1968), 97.

[96] Berman, *Law and Revolution*, 208.

[97] Joseph F. Costanzo, S.J., "Catholic Politeia II", *Fordham Law Review* 21, no. 3 (1952): 264.

stated that in this major Chapter was vested the legislative authority of the Order, and that while in session it would have supreme powers of control and government, even over his own person.... It was he who decided to convoke the Chapter, and he made it abundantly clear that he regarded its authority as sovereign."[98] This elective system became the Dominican rule. Local communities elected their representatives, who would determine together the conduct of the affairs of the order. In 1228, the second master general of the Dominicans, Jordan of Saxony, summoned the provincial priors with two deputies each for a chapter meeting in Paris, stating that "every brother should without exception give their assent to them and grant plenary power to them [because] whatever they decided either by creating or by renouncing, or by changing—either by adding or subtracting—will remain permanent and stable."[99] The Dominican system soon spread to other religious orders.

After the arrival of the Dominican friars in England in 1221, there was a gradual growth of representation in the convocations from bishops and representatives of cathedral chapters to representatives from monasteries and other collegiate houses and, finally, proctors of diocesan clergy.[100] This, no doubt, was partly driven by the increasing frequency of royal appeals for financial grants from the Church and the reluctance of the bishops to allow them without the consent of those affected. This led Archbishop Langton, as early as 1225, to summon proctors of cathedral, collegiate, and conventual churches to attend his provincial synod. It was the first time representation from monasteries and other religious houses had been added. By 1283, in what has been called the Model Convention of the Province of Canterbury, Archbishop of Canterbury John Peckham took the final step by including diocesan clergy as well. Joseph Costanzo pointed out that

> bishops, abbots, priors and other heads of religious houses, deans of cathedral and collegiate churches, and archdeacons were summoned to appear in person or by proctors; and, the significant innovation,

---

[98] Marie-Humbert Vicaire, O.P., *The Genius of St. Dominic* (Nagpur, India: Dominican Publications, 1987), 42.

[99] Pennington, "Representation in Medieval Canon Law", 380.

[100] Costanzo, "Juridic Origins", 146.

bishops are enjoined to assemble and instruct the diocesan clergy to
the intent that they elect two proctors from each diocese, and the
cathedral and collegiate churches designate one proctor with plenary
powers and instructions of "treating and consenting" in the name of
their constituents.[101]

From all of these developments, Costanzo concluded that "the originality of representative governance is Catholic, papal in promotion,
religious in precedent and experience, [and] ecclesiastical in the syn-
odal convocations. Its growth in ecclesiastical and civil circles was
mutually compenetrant."[102] Indeed, something like the principle
of osmosis seemed to function between the ecclesiastical and civil
realms, as the principles of consent and representation began to pen-
etrate the conduct of government from that of the Church.

As Brian Tierney reported, "Given the whole background of
medieval thought and practice, it is not surprising that every major
work on law and political theory written around 1300 contains at
least some passing reference to consent."[103] As adumbrated in the
earlier remarks of Alcuin and Manegold, the issue of consent became
essential to the legitimacy of rule. This was laid out in the work of
Henry of Bracton, priest and jurist. In *On the Laws and Customs
of England*, written around 1259, he stated that "the king must not
be under man but under God and under the law, because the law
makes the king ... for there is no rex where will rules rather than
lex."[104] But what produces the laws? Bracton answered, "These laws,
since they have been approved by the consent of those using them
and confirmed by the oath of kings, can neither be changed nor
destroyed without the common consent of all those with whose
counsel and consent they have been promulgated."[105] Along with
the emphasis on consent in this text is the priceless notion of the king

[101] Ibid., 301.

[102] Joseph F. Costanzo, S.J., *Political and Legal Studies* (West Hanover, Mass.: Christopher
Publishing House, 1982), 202.

[103] Tierney, *Religion, Law*, 42.

[104] Henry de Bracton, *On the Laws and Customs of England* (ca. 1250), vol. 2, trans. Samuel
Thorne (Cambridge, Mass.: Belknap Press, 1968), 33, Harvard Law School Library, bracton
.law.harvard.edu/Unframed/English/v2/33.htm.

[105] McIlwain, *Constitutionalism*, 70.

as subject to the law. There is a direct line from Bracton and his pre-decessors to the American Founding, in which George III is accused of violating the laws to which he himself should have been subject.

The matter of consent was clearly expressed in medieval Scot-land, as well. The Scottish Parliament, in the struggle between the House of Bruce and the House of Plantagenet, informed the pope: "The due consent and assent of us all have made our Prince and King [Bruce].... Yet if he should give up what he has begun, and agree to make us or our kingdom subject to the King of England or the English, we should exert ourselves at once to drive him out as our enemy and a subverter of his own rights and ours, and make [elect] some other man who was well able to defend us our King."[106] The Declaration of Arbroath (1320) was sent to the pope, requesting that he recognize Scotland's independence and Robert the Bruce as the country's lawful king and explaining that he should do so because, among other reasons, "the due consent and assent of us all have made [him] our prince and king."[107]

The English Parliament spoke similarly on the matter of consent in 1322: "All those matters which were to be established for the king-dom and the people were to be treated, agreed upon, and determined in Parliament by the king, with the assent of the Prelates, Counts, Barons and the whole Commonalty of the kingdom."[108]

Though a proponent of monarchy, Aquinas said that, concerning the right ordering of rule in a state or nation, "all should take some share in the government: for this form of constitution ensures peace among the people, commends itself to all, and is most enduring, as stated in [Aristotle's] Polit. ii. 6."[109] Accordingly,

> the best form of government is in a state or kingdom, where one is given the power to preside over all; while under him are others having

---

[106] Declaration of Arbroath (April 6, 1320), National Records of Scotland, SP13/7, https://www.nrscotland.gov.uk/files//research/declaration-of-arbroath/declaration-of-arbroath-transcription-and-translation.pdf; also cited in John Emerich Edward Dalberg Acton, *The History of Freedom and Other Essays* (London: Macmillan, 1907), 36.

[107] Ibid.

[108] Cited in A.J. Carlyle, *Political Liberty: A History of the Conception in the Middle Ages and Modern Times* (London: Oxford University Press, 1941), 20.

[109] Thomas Aquinas, *Summa theologica* I-II, q. 105, a. 1.

governing powers: and yet a government of this kind is shared by all, both because all are eligible to govern, and because the rules are chosen by all. For this is the best form of polity, being partly kingdom, since there is one at the head of all; partly aristocracy, in so far as a number of persons are set in authority; partly democracy, i.e. government by the people, in so far as the rulers can be chosen from the people, and the people have the right to choose their rulers.[110]

Aquinas taught that if a people originally incompetent, by reason either of corruption or immaturity, come to "have a sense of moderation and responsibility and are most careful guardians of the common welfare, it is right to enact a law allowing such people to choose their own magistrates for the government of the commonweal."[111] Concomitantly, he who gains power by means other than consent rules illegitimately: "Whoever seizes power by violence does not become a true ruler." A ruler acquires legitimacy only by "the consent of his subjects" or by being appointed by a superior who has gained such consent; thus, a tyrant may be overthrown if he "has violently seized power against the will of his subjects, or has forced them to consent".[112] What is more, he may be removed on account of his malfeasance:

> If to provide itself with a king belong to the right of any multitude, it is not unjust that the king set up by that multitude be destroyed or his power restricted, if he tyrannically abuse the royal power. It must not be thought that such a multitude is acting unfaithfully in deposing the tyrant; ... because he himself has deserved that the covenant with his subjects should not be kept, since, in ruling the multitude, he did not act faithfully as the office of a king demands.[113]

By the thirteenth century, all of the key canonical terms regarding representation and consent were employed in political ways in the

---

[110] Ibid.

[111] Thomas Aquinas, *Summa theologica* I-II, q. 97, a. 2. The obverse of this is that if a people fall into incompetence due to a condition of corruption, then the allowance for them to choose their own magistrates is withdrawn: "The right of appointing their public officials is rightly forfeit to such a people." I-II, q. 97, a. 1.

[112] Thomas Aquinas, *Commentary on the Sentences of Peter Lombard* 2, 44, 2.

[113] Thomas Aquinas, *On Kingship: To the King of Cyprus*, trans. Gerald B. Phelan (New York: Sheed and Ward, 1938), 58–59.

civic arena. As mentioned, it is difficult not to discern the influence of the example of the Dominicans and the Church at large on the secular realm and its parliamentary development. "The first explicit recognition of political representation", said Hans von Rautenfeld, "is found on the occasion of the English Parliament of 1254, when knights of the shires were elected in county courts and empowered to speak for and bind the whole county."[114] Likewise, in the brief interregnum when Simon de Montfort was ruling England, he convened Parliament in 1265 to approve a new constitution. Uniquely, he insisted that representatives be elected, not appointed, and that they include two citizens from each city and two burgesses from each borough. Properly speaking, this was the first English Parliament.

De Montfort was overthrown shortly thereafter, and it was not until the Model Parliament of 1295 under Edward I that representatives from towns were regularly included in Parliament. When Edward summoned the Model Parliament, he ordered the representatives of the towns and boroughs to bring with them "full and sufficient power (*plenam et sufficientem potestatem*) from their communities", so that "the business in hand may not be held up in any way through lack of such power."[115] The king wished to ensure that the decisions reached by Parliament were binding on the constituents who sent the representatives.

The authority of such representation was repeatedly expressed. In 1365, the chief justice of England proclaimed, "Parliament represents the body of all the realm."[116] As Kenneth Pennington said, "By the beginning of the fourteenth century, kings all over Europe were summoning representative assemblies of their noblemen, clergy, and townsmen. When they did, the reason that they often gave for calling such assemblies was, 'what touches all must be approved by all.' Thus Quod omnes tangit became part of the theoretical basis for parliament."[117] Parliaments met in England, France, and the kingdoms of Spain—first in the kingdom of Leon in 1188. The nobles of Aragon were said to have selected their king with the following formula:

---

[114] von Rautenfeld, "Political Representation".
[115] Morrall, *Political Thought in Medieval Times*, 63.
[116] von Rautenfeld, "Political Representation".
[117] Pennington, "Bartolomé de Las Casas".

"We who are as good as you choose you for our king and lord, provided that you observe our laws and privileges; and if not, not."[118]
Hans von Rautenfeld stated:

> By the fourteenth century ... members of Parliament were expected
> to convey the grievances of their constituencies to the king and his
> counselors, giving rise to the formula "Redress of grievances before
> supply." Thus the function of the representative was to serve as a two-
> way channel of communication, expressing grievances and popular
> opinion, while garnering popular support for the policies of rulers.
> This in turn gave rise to the affirmation that rulers, in so far as they
> are representative, must act in the interests of those they represent.[119]

Aside from these considerable achievements, the Middle Ages also
introduced ideas often thought to be the exclusive property of the
Enlightenment. Four centuries before it, for instance, Pope Innocent
IV asserted, around 1250, that "by nature all men are free." He then
speculated, in light of this, as to how political rule had been instituted: "But how this jurisdiction first began I do not know unless
perhaps God assigned some person to do justice ... or unless in the
beginning the father of the family had complete jurisdiction over his
family by the law of nature though now he has it only in a few minor
matters.... Or again, a people could have princes by election as they
had Saul and many others." In any case, he concluded that, since "all
men are free", infidels may not be deprived of what is justly theirs
because they are no less men than any others: "I maintain, therefore,
that lordship, possession and jurisdiction can belong to the infidels
licitly ... for these things were made not only for the faithful but
every rational creature.... Accordingly, we say that it is not licit for
the pope or the faithful to take away from infidels their belongings
or their ... jurisdictions."[120] In the late fourteenth century, Jean Gerson, chancellor of the University of Paris, would reaffirm the case
that infidels enjoyed certain rights by natural law.[121] Likewise, it is

---

[118] Cited in Henry Hallam, *The View of the State of Europe during the Middle Ages*, vol. 2
(London: John Murray, 1878), 43.

[119] von Rautenfeld, "Political Representation".

[120] Cited in Siedentop, *Inventing the Individual*, 63.

[121] Reid, "Medieval Origins", 457.

curious to note that the idea of a "state of nature" was in currency at an early date. John XXII used it in the late 1320s to rebut the Franciscan position on the nature of private property. He said, "What God established at the very beginning of things in an ideal state of nature is not common possession but individual property."[122]

Here are some other examples of how constitutional principles permeated medieval societies. The right to overthrow tyranny not only existed as an abstract principle, as mentioned by Aquinas, but was occasionally codified. The Hungarian Golden Bull of 1222 ends with King Andrew II stating, "We also ordain that if We or any of Our Successors shall at any time contravene the terms of this statute, the bishops and the higher and lower nobles of Our realm, one and all, both present and future, shall by virtue thereof have the uncontrolled right in perpetuity of resistance, both by word and deed, without thereby incurring any charge of treason."[123]

Nothing could provide a better illustration of how deeply the idea of constitutional rule was rooted in the imago Dei than the language used by Philip the Fair for the enfranchisement of the bondmen in his Valois domain in 1311. No doubt Philip was motivated in part by the fees he would receive, as serfs had to purchase their manumission. Nevertheless, his words are revealing: "As a human creature who is formed according to the image of Our Lord must, in general, be free according to natural law, and in no country should this natural liberty be so effaced and obscured by the very hateful yoke of servitude, ... it moves us to pity, for the remedy and [for the] salvation of our soul and out of consideration for humanity and the common good."[124]

In 1315, Philip's son, King Louis X (1289–1316), drew similar conclusions from the law of nature regarding servitude within his territories of France and Navarre. He declared:

---

[122] Cited in Siedentop, *Inventing the Individual*, 291.

[123] Berman, *Law and Revolution*, 294.

[124] "Comme creature humaine qui est formee a l'image Nostre Seigneur doie generalement estre franche par droit naturel et en aucuns pays de cette naturelle liberte ou franchise par le jou de servitute qui tant est haineuse soit si effaciee et obscurcie ... nous meus de pitie pour le remede et salut de nostre ame et pour consideration de humanite et de commun profit." Cited in Frederick Pollock, "The History of the Law of Nature: A Preliminary Study", *Columbia Law Review* 1, no. 1 (January 1901): 22–23.

As according to the law of nature each must be born free, and that by
some usages and customs, which of great antiquity have been introduced and hitherto preserved in our kingdom ... many of our common people have fallen into servitude and diverse conditions which
very much displease us; we, considering that our kingdom is called
... the kingdom of the Franks [free men], and wishing that the fact
should be truly accordant with the name ... upon deliberation of
our great council, have ordered and order that generally through our
kingdom ... such servitudes be brought back to freedom and that to
all those who served from origin or recently from marriage, or from
residence in places of servile condition are fallen ... into bonds of
servitude, freedom be given.[125]

In declaring that "France signifies freedom", Louis proclaimed that
any slave setting foot on French territory should be freed. This was
not quite as attractive as it may sound, since the serfs, as mentioned
above, were required to pay for their release. Nonetheless, it is startling to hear the "born free" formulation at so early a date—and from
a king, no less.

After the death of Louis XI in 1423, Philippe Pot, the seneschal of
Burgundy, stated at a meeting of the French Estates-General that, in
the case of an incapacitated king, the right to rule lay in the people:

It is certain that the royal power is a dignity and not the property
(haereditas) of the prince. History relates that at the first the sovereign people created kings by its vote. It is in its own interest that
each nation gave itself a master. The whole world repeats that the
state is the creation of the people. If it is so, how could the people
abandon its charge? How can flatterers attribute supreme power to
the prince who exists only in virtue of the people? That being so,
what is the power in France which has the right of governing when
the king is incapable of doing so? Clearly this task reverts neither to
a sole prince, nor a handful of men, but to all, that is the people,
the giver of power. This task it must take up as it were its own,
all the more so because it is always the victim, the sole victim of a
bad government.[126]

---

[125] Cited in Siedentop, *Inventing the Individual*, 312.

[126] Cited in E. F. Jacob, "Political Thought", in C. G. Crump and E. F. Jacob, *The Legacy of the Middle Ages* (Oxford: Clarendon, 1926), 531.

Fifteenth-century Nicholas of Cusa, a cardinal, claimed, "All legitimate authority arises from elective concordance and free submission. There is in the people a divine seed by virtue of their common birth and the equal natural right of all men so that all authority—which comes from God as does man himself—is recognized as divine when it arises from the common consent of the subjects."[127] He also wrote, "Since all men are by nature free, it follows that every government, whether it rests its authority on written law or on the living voice of the prince—derives solely from the common agreement and consent of the subjects."[128] Lord Acton summed up the end result of all of this:

> Looking back over the space of 1,000 years, which we call the Middle Ages, to get an estimate of the work they had done, if not towards perfection in their institutions, at least towards attaining the knowledge of political truth, this is what we find:—Representative government, which was unknown to the ancients, was almost universal. The methods of election were crude; but the principle that no tax was lawful that was not granted by the class that paid it; that is, that taxation was inseparable from representation, was recognized, not as the privilege of certain countries, but as the right of all. Not a prince in the world, said Philip de Commines, can levy a penny without the consent of the people. Slavery was almost everywhere extinct; and absolute power was deemed more intolerable and more criminal than slavery. The right of insurrection was not only admitted but defined, as a duty sanctified by religion. Even the principles of the Habeas Corpus Act, and the method of the Income Tax, were already known. The issue of ancient politics was an absolute state planted on slavery. The political produce of the Middle Ages was a system of states in which authority was restricted by the representation of powerful classes, by privileged associations, and by the acknowledgment of duties superior to those which are imposed by man. As regards the realization in practice of what was seen to be good, there was almost everything to do. But the great problems of principle had been solved.[129]

---

[127] Nicholas of Cusa, *The Catholic Concordance* (Cambridge: Cambridge University Press, 1991), 230.

[128] Cited in Morrall, *Political Thought in Medieval Times*, 129.

[129] Lord Acton, "The History of Freedom in Christianity" (address delivered to the members of the Bridgnorth Institute, May 28, 1877), Acton Institute, https://acton.org/research/history-freedom-christianity.

In other words, there was a well-ensconced medieval aversion to the use of arbitrary power and an adherence to the framework of law, within which alone force could be legitimately exercised.

As was suggested at the beginning of this chapter, the fact that representative government became typical of the Middle Ages was due to the idea of the integrity of the human person and his transcendent destiny—which is the source of the "duties superior to those which are imposed by man". This is why German scholar Otto Gierke was able to say of the medieval period, "An ancient and generally entertained opinion regarded the Will of the People as the Source of Temporal Power. . . . Indeed that the legal title to all Rulership lies in the voluntary and contractual submission of the Ruled could therefore be propounded as a philosophic axiom."[130] He added, "Medieval theory therefore was unanimous that the power of the State stood below the rules of Natural and above the rules of Positive Law."[131] He also stated that

> during the Middle Age we can hardly detect even the beginnings of that opinion which would free the Sovereign (whenever he is acting in the interest of the public weal) from the bonds of the Moral Law in general, and therefore from the bonds of the Law of Nature. Therefore when Machiavelli based his lesson for the Princes[132] upon this freedom from restraint, this seemed to men of his time an unheard of innovation and also a monstrous crime.[133]

So closely associated with medieval Christendom were the fundamental doctrines of liberty that, in his attack upon them, Sir Robert Filmer, the foremost exponent of the Divine Right of Kings in the seventeenth century, explicitly assigned them to the Middle Ages:

> Since the time that school divinity [i.e., Catholic universities] began to flourish, there hath been a common opinion maintained as well by the divines as by the divers of learned men which affirms: "Mankind is naturally endowed and born with freedom from all subjection, and

---

[130] Otto Gierke, *Political Theories of the Middle Ages* (Cambridge: Cambridge University Press, 1900), 38–40.
[131] Ibid., 78.
[132] Machiavelli, *The Prince* (1532).
[133] Gierke, *Political Theories*, 86.

at liberty to choose what form of government it please, and that the power which any one man hath over others was at the first by human right bestowed according to the discretion of the multitude." This tenet was first hatched in the schools [medieval universities], and hath been fostered by all succeeding papists for good divinity.[134]

At the end of his paean to the Middle Ages, Lord Acton asked: "We come to the question: How did the sixteenth century husband the treasure which the Middle Ages had stored up?"[135] Why was there not a straight trajectory from medieval constitutional principles to the American Founding, which embraced the same principles? As we shall see, the close of the Middle Ages brought detectable movement in the direction of releasing the sovereign from the bonds of the "Moral Law and the Law of Nature". First, the bonds were loosened and then eventually broken, with disastrous consequences for constitutional rule. This is what made the American Revolution necessary as a *reestablishment* of those principles and practices.

In the way of a brief preview of the next chapter, we offer Alexis de Tocqueville's observation as to what replaced the limited notion of kingship in the Middle Ages:

> Royalty had nothing in common with medieval royalty; its prerogatives were different, its rank had changed, its spirit was new, the homage it received was unusual. The central power encroached on every side upon decaying local franchises.... All these new powers employed methods and took for their guide principles which the Middle Ages either never knew or rejected, and which, indeed, were only suitable for a state of society they never conceived.[136]

We shall now turn to these new principles and spirit, seeking an answer as to how political absolutism arose—not because of the Middle Ages, but in spite of them. Who conceived of this new state of society and government, and why?

---

[134] Sir Robert Filmer, *Patriarcha, or the Natural Power of Kings* (London: Richard Chiswell, 1680) I, I, Online Library of Liberty, https://oll.libertyfund.org/titles/filmer-patriarcha-or-the-natural-power-of-kings.

[135] Acton, "History of Freedom".

[136] Alexis de Tocqueville, *The Old Regime and the Revolution* (Mineola, N.Y.: Dover Publications, 2010), 33.

3

The Loss of Reason and Nature

Before we can come to a proper understanding of how political absolutism arose, we need to examine how reason was undermined after its medieval apogee. One could not have happened without the other. The loss of constitutionalism was a result of the loss of reason's standing. This chapter, concentrating on William of Ockham, and the next one, on Martin Luther, offer two illustrative thinkers (out of many) whose ideas undercut the powers of reason while enhancing the status of will.

In the fourteenth century, a school of thought called nominalism, after the Latin *nomen* or "name", arose. Its corrosive effects fatally fractured medieval Christendom, though the formal break within the Church did not come until Luther in the sixteenth century. Nominalism holds that natures or essences do not exist in reality but are only "names" or contrivances inhabiting the mind, with no correlation to what exists outside of it. Since naming is the principal means of knowing, the severance of the substantive connection between names and reality proved a devastating loss. Though this dispute may seem esoteric, it shook the foundations of Western theology and philosophy and, consequently, the political order. Nominalism undermined the metaphysical and epistemological foundations of medieval constitutionalism and the very concept of law as based on natural law and reason and replaced it with will (*voluntas*). Sundering words from reality also broke the connection between faith and reason and eventually led to the development of political absolutism, which, as we have seen, was entirely foreign to the Middle Ages. Absolutism provided the grounds for the despotism against which colonial America would revolt. To understand the American Founding, we need to recognize the sources of absolutism that it opposed—even as they first arose some four hundred years earlier. This can also aid in a correct appraisal of the resurgence of absolutism today, albeit in a democratic guise.[1]

To grasp the profundity of the change at hand, we will first sketch out the view of reality at the heart of the Middle Ages, known as the *via antiqua*, and then address the ways in which nominalism, called the *via moderna*, subverted it. In the *via antiqua*, Aquinas offered a synthesis of faith and reason. The rational order of creation, anchored in a rational God, pointed man to his end of happiness. Scripture revealed this end to be an actual sharing in divine life through the redemptive grace of Christ. Though marred by Original Sin, creation retained enough traces of its original harmony for man to read the score. As we saw in chapter 1, the ancient Greek philosophers, particularly Plato and Aristotle, noted this harmony in their apprehension of logos. Using Old Testament imagery from the psalms, Clement of Alexandria declared that Christ, Logos himself, is the "New Song". The logos of the ancient philosophers was a dim preview, even a preparation for, the revealed Logos. For Saint Thomas, there could be no real conflict between the philosophical logos and the theological Logos of revelation. The one completes the other. Reason and revelation rightly reinforce each other. Therefore, "believing is an act of the *intellect* assenting to the divine truth by command of the will moved by God through grace."[2] Grace perfects nature; it does not displace it. Grace needs nature, just as nature needs grace. As we shall see, they stand or fall together.

The Realist Metaphysics of Reality

The Thomist view of the relationship between creation and its Creator, between reason and revelation, required a realist metaphysics to anchor it. Commenting on Aristotle's *Metaphysics*, Aquinas remarked, "The little that is won here [in metaphysics] weighs more than all that is won in all the other sciences."[3] Like Aristotle, Aquinas said

---

[1] We will see that the resurgence has nothing to do with the American Founding (contra Deneen and Hanby) and everything to do with what it opposed.

[2] Thomas Aquinas, *Summa theologica* II-II, q. 2, a. 9 (emphasis added).

[3] Thomas Aquinas, *Commentary on the Metaphysics* 1, 3, cited in Josef Pieper, *Leisure: The Basis of Culture* (New York: Random House, 1963), 111.

that reality exists in individual things, but those individual things are defined by their natures or essences. Man's nature, in other words, does not exist outside its manifestation in individual men—it is not a Platonic ideal or universal existent independent of individual men—but it is what makes each man *what* he is. It makes him knowable *as* man. Of course, reason abstracts the idea of human nature from existing human persons, but human nature is *actually*—in the exact metaphysical sense—present in individual men. Knowledge of this is expressed in words, such as "man", that have a real intrinsic connection with what they represent. It is the *essence* of man to which the name is applied. Words signify forms or essences, which answer the question as to *what* things are.

How is it that our idea of, or our word for, something such as "man" can tally with what a man is? For this to be so, external reality must exist objectively, and it must contain within itself a rational principle that makes it intelligible. As we saw in chapter 1, it was Heraclitus or perhaps Anaximander who first grasped that the universe is intelligible and that, therefore, man is able to comprehend its order. The world is comprehensible precisely and only because it operates on a rational basis. As I have written elsewhere,

> It is by their *natures* that we are able to know what things are. Otherwise, we would know only specificities and be unable to recognize things in their genus and species. In other words, we would experience this piece of wood (a tree) only as opposed to that piece of wood (another tree), but we would not know the word *tree* or even the word *wood*, because we would not know the essence of either. In fact, although we might experience many things, we would know nothing.[4]

Like the ancient Greek philosophers, Aquinas said that we can know reality, or *what is*, because it was made by Logos and is a product of the divine intellect. Since it was through Logos that all things were made, creation carries the imprint of its Creator *as* reason. (In fact, this is why man, made in the image of God, is morally obliged to rule himself by reason, and not by his passions or will. To do what is unreasonable, as Aristotle and Aquinas said, is wrong.) Nature

---

[4] Robert R. Reilly, *Making Gay Okay: How Rationalizing Homosexual Behavior is Changing Everything* (San Francisco: Ignatius Press, 2014), 18.

bespeaks an intelligibility that derives from a transcendent, intelligible source. Benedict XVI referred to the "world as a product of creative reason", just as had Seneca in the first century A.D.[5] If creation is the product of intellect, then it can be apprehended by reason. This is the discernible connection between the Creator and creation, and why the Creator can be known through his creation.

Within this realist view, *naming* is essential to knowing. Echoing Aquinas, Josef Pieper said, "God's knowledge creates being."[6] Man gains access to the knowledge by which God created things by naming them. Etienne Gilson wrote:

> Man alone has been created with a knowing mind and a loving heart, in order that, by knowing and loving all things in God, he might refer them to their origin, which is at the same time their end.... His essential function is to lend his voice to an otherwise speechless creation, to help each thing in publicly confessing its deepest and most secret meaning, or rather its essence, for each of them *is* a word, while man alone can *say* it.[7]

This beautiful reflection means that each existing thing is the result of Logos, the Word of God. God said, "Let there be light, and there was light", and so forth. But light cannot speak. Only man can speak the names of things that *are* as God's Word constituted them. This is part of his being made in the image and likeness of God. He is the only creature in the universe that can speak the word that each thing *is* according to its end or telos. This is the powerful significance of man's naming the animals in Genesis. Saint Thomas wrote, "Man named the animals. But names should be adapted to the nature of things. Therefore, Adam knew the animals' natures."[8] The connection between words and things is real, metaphysical. Pieper put it this way: "Words convey reality. We speak in order to name and identify something that is real."[9] When God said "light", it came into being. When man says "light", he grasps, albeit dimly, the divine knowledge by which

[5] Seneca, *Epistles* 65, 2.

[6] Josef Pieper, *Happiness and Contemplation* (South Bend, Ind.: St. Augustine's Press, 1998), 37.

[7] Etienne Gilson, *The Unity of Philosophical Experience* (New York: Charles Scribner's Sons, 1965), 49–50 (emphasis in the original).

[8] Thomas Aquinas, *Summa theologica* I, q. 94, a. 3.

[9] Josef Pieper, *Abuse of Language, Abuse of Power* (San Francisco: Ignatius Press, 1988), 15.

light was made. When he names, he *knows*. What we understand when we know something is its essence.

Nominalism and the End of Essences

Nominalism, the *via moderna*, denied these things. William of Ockham (1280–1349) sundered the Thomist synthesis of faith and reason.[10] There are no complementary points of correspondence between them. Nor is there an intrinsic connection between words and reality. For Ockham, man does not share in God's creative knowledge through his power of naming. Contrary to Genesis, man has no such power. Although Ockham agreed with Aquinas that only individual things are real, unlike him he denied the existence of essences. Heraclitus had said that man gained knowledge through contemplation by "listening to the essence of things".[11] Now there was nothing to listen to. If there are no essences, names have nothing to apply themselves to in reality; they become unhinged. There are no forms for words to signify. Only singular dogs exist. The word "dog" and the concept of a dog's nature are only in man's mind and nowhere else. There are no species by nature. As Ockham put it, "No universal belongs to the essence or quiddity of any substance whatever."[12] What man observes in things are simply similarities—one dog looks like another—but there is no underlying metaphysical reason, such as dog's nature, for these similarities to exist. They exist only because God wills them to exist. The creation of each dog is accordingly an *individual* act of God's will unrelated to any other act of his will. Contrary to what Aquinas taught about the divine ideas, God does not harbor a divine idea of what a dog is and then make dogs from it. General ideas or universals do not correspond to anything in reality.

[10] There exists a lively dispute as to whether Ockham was a conceptualist or a nominalist. He may have been the former, but this is a distinction that need not detain us here. Ockham's most radical statements speak for themselves and will be seen to be compatible with the thinking of the clearly nominalist thinkers roughly contemporary with him, whom we will quote after dealing with Ockham.

[11] Pieper, *Leisure*, 26.

[12] Cited in Frederick Copleston, S.J., *A History of Philosophy*, vol. 3, *Late Mediaeval and Renaissance Philosophy*, pt. 1, *Ockham to the Speculative Mystics* (Garden City, N.Y.: Image, 1963), 69.

Nothing in reality seems intelligible in itself; it is *given* its intelligibility by man's mind.[13]

Voluntarism and the Primacy of Will

This view carries huge consequences. If things have no natures making and keeping them what they are, it must be God who directly does so without any intermediary causes. Nominalism ineluctably leads to voluntarism, the view that God's will is the first and only cause of things. What is more, his will is unbound by anything, including reason. To put it in another way, if God does everything directly, then things could have no natures. Natures become superfluous. As Fr. James Schall put it, a voluntarist believes that "what is behind all reality is a will that can always be otherwise. It is not bound to any one truth."[14] Of course, it would be just as accurate to say that voluntarism leads to nominalism. They go hand in hand, as they did in Ockham. It is God who directly constitutes things as they exist in and at any given moment—not their natures. If, for instance, a dog does not possess the nature of a dog, it might turn into something else—such as a fig tree or a cat. What prevents it from doing so? Only God's continuous and direct action keeps it as a dog for as long as it remains one, until it pleases him to make it something else. As only particular dogs exist, one can have certain knowledge of them only in their particularity. Since there is no such thing as "dogness", we are unable to relate one dog to another, or to anything else, really. We cannot even account for how one thing comes from another.

The larger consequence is that we cannot argue about nature as a cause of anything, much less base something upon "the Laws of Nature". The demonstration of truths through causes or principles is no longer possible. If there are no formal and final causes we can know, we have only probabilities. Philosophy is the study of *what is*, not only of how things are, but *why* they are—understanding them in terms of their causes. If God is the only cause of things and his will

---

[13] Gilson, *Unity of Philosophical Experience*, 67.
[14] James V. Schall, *On Islam: A Chronological Record* (San Francisco: Ignatius Press, 2018), 7.

is inscrutable, then there can be no philosophy. A voluntarist God removes the subject matter of philosophy from consideration. We are left with empiricism to probe for probabilities.

What was the attraction of this kind of thinking? Behind nominalism is Ockham's exaggerated concern for God's omnipotence and absolute freedom of will, and his detestation of what he thought was the contamination of Christianity by pagan (Aristotelian) metaphysics. He thought that God's freedom was compromised by the teaching that God's will proceeds from his divine intellect and not the other way around. This is the core issue. Aquinas argued that, since God is Logos or Reason itself, his "will follows upon intellect."[15] Reason rules; will follows. The Word precedes action. This was not a new teaching in Christianity. Going back to the third century, Hippolytus said of God: "He thought of it (the cosmos), willed it, spoke the word and so made it. It came into being instantaneously, exactly as He had willed it."[16] Even though for God all things are simultaneous and instantaneous, Hippolytus placed God's thought *before* his will, which then carried out God's thoughts. The primacy of intellect is clear.

Nominalism flips the relationship between intellect and will. God's will becomes primary, and his intellect subordinate to it as a mere instrument. It is no longer his knowledge that constitutes being; it is his will that does so. In fact, God knows *because* he wills; will *precedes* knowledge. It is the *act* that produces knowledge, not knowledge that produces the act. As Goethe's Faust says in his parody of the opening of the Gospel of John, "In the beginning was the deed," not the Word. Will becomes *the* ontological principle. This was a revolutionary change with seismic consequences. Unless the divine intellect is precedent to the divine will, logos cannot be imprinted in creation as its essential aspect. Spanish scholar J. A. Fernández-Santamaría said, "Occam has done away with the *Logos* ... and all that is left in God is will, a will that cannot be bound or limited by the reason-inspired actions or assumptions of man."[17]

---

[15] Thomas Aquinas, *Summa theologica* I, q. 19, a. 1.

[16] Cited in James V. Schall, S.J., "At a Moment of His Own Choosing", *Catholic Thing*, December 23, 2014, http://thecatholicthing.org/2014/12/23/moment-choosing.

[17] J. A. Fernández-Santamaría, *Natural Law, Constitutionalism, Reason of State, and War: Counter-Reformation Spanish Political Thought*, vol. 1 (New York: Peter Lang, 2005), 105.

The early sixth-century Christian philosopher Boethius wrote that "the human soul, in essence, enjoys its highest freedom when it remains in the contemplation of God's mind."[18] Ockham foreclosed this possibility. This highest freedom would no longer be possible, as access to God's mind is blocked. We can know only his will. Thomas Aquinas said that "the first cause of the universe is mind, and that the last end of the universe must be the good of the mind, that is truth, and that in the contemplation of truth man finds the principal object of wisdom."[19] For the nominalists, the first cause of the universe is will, not mind. Therefore, the last end of the universe cannot be the good of the mind. The overthrow of the Thomistic synthesis is complete. Man's final end is no longer rational. This has a direct bearing on the rise of absolutism (which is not to say Ockham was a political absolutist; he was not) and the concomitant loss of constitutionalism.

Parallels with Islamic Voluntarism

Ockham's rejection of Thomistic metaphysical realism parallels, and might well have been influenced by, a similar but earlier rejection of Aristotelian realism in Sunni Islam by Mohammed al-Ghazali (1058–1111). The striking similarities are worth exploring because they clearly demonstrate that, even across highly dissimilar cultures, the logic of voluntarism inexorably reaches the same conclusions with the same devastating results. Al-Ghazali's ideas help to account for the fact that constitutionalism never arose indigenously in the Muslim world; Ockham's ideas account for the decline of constitutionalism in the Christian world. Of course, one might argue that there is a difference between voluntarist man under Christianity and voluntarist man under Islam because of the substantially different character of their respective revelations. And this may be true so long as the tenets of faith hold and guide the ruler. A truly Christian king would behave differently from a genuinely Muslim sultan. But once the constraint of Christian faith is removed, it would be

---

[18] Pieper, *Abuse of Language*, 54.
[19] Thomas Aquinas, *Summa contra gentiles* 1, 1.

hard to distinguish between the two because of the shared primacy of the will.

Loss of Cause and Effect

Both Ockham's and al-Ghazali's efforts were purportedly undertaken for the same purpose: to protect a radical notion of the omnipotence and absolute freedom of God. For al-Ghazali, wrote Duncan Black MacDonald, "the fundamental thing in the world and the starting-point of all speculation is will."[20] Likewise for Ockham. One must reject the natural law order of the universe to protect God's power. God is not to be limited by any laws of nature. He can do anything other than violate the principle of noncontradiction. Essences are an affront to his freedom.

In *The Incoherence of the Philosophers*, al-Ghazali insisted that God is not bound by any order and that, therefore, there is no "natural" sequence of cause and effect, as in fire burning cotton. Fire does not burn cotton; God does. Similarly, Ockham wrote, "it follows from this that it cannot be demonstrated that any effect is produced by a secondary cause. For even though when fire is close to combustible material, combustion always follows, this fact is, nevertheless, consistent with fire's not being the cause of it. For God could have ordained that whenever fire is present to a close-by patient, the sun would cause combustion [in the patient]."[21]

The nominalist subversion of cause and effect in the natural world went directly against the teachings of Saint Thomas, who wrote that "whoever answers the question, why wood got hot, because God has willed it so, answers appropriately if he intends to carry back the question to the prime cause; but inappropriately, if he intends to exclude all other causes." Aquinas said that the latter position "is the mistake of those who believe that all things follow, without any rational plan, from God's pure will. This is the error of the exponents of the Law of the Moors, as Rabbi Moses [Maimonides] says;

---

[20] Duncan Black MacDonald, *Development of Muslim Theology, Jurisprudence, and Constitutional Theory* (New York: Charles Scribner's Sons, 1903), 231.

[21] Cited in Edward Feser, *Razor Boy*, March 8, 2011, http://edwardfeser.blogspot.com /2011/03/razor-boy.html.

according to them, it makes no difference whether fire heats or cools, unless God [directly] wills it so."[22] The example of fire was popular with nominalists. Robert Holcot, a doctor of theology at Oxford in 1332, also stated that one cannot prove that fire causes combustibles to burn. Indeed, like Ockham, he said that it cannot be proven with certainty that one thing is the efficient cause of another.[23]

Another nominalist, Nicholas of Autrecourt (1300–1350), seems to have been directly affected by al-Ghazali's thinking. In his introduction to his translation of Averroes' *The Incoherence of the Incoherence*, which is a refutation of al-Ghazali, Simon Van Den Bergh writes:

> It seems to me probable that Nicholas of Autrecourt, "the medieval Hume", was influenced by Ghazali's Ash'arite theories. He denies in the same way as Ghazali the logical connexion between cause and effect: "ex eo quod aliqua res est cognita esse, non potest evidenter evidentia reducta in primum principium vel in certitudinem primi principii inferri, quod alia res sit" [from the known existence of one thing it cannot be inferred, with evidence reducible to the certitude of the first principle, that another thing exists]; he gives the same example of *ignis* [fire] and *stupa* [coarse flax], he seems to hold also the Ash'arite thesis of God as the sole cause of all action, and he quotes in one place Ghazali's *Metaphysics*.[24]

From his voluntarist and nominalist premises stated above, Nicholas went so far as to say that the principle of causality is worthless and that the existence of the external world is indemonstrable. The problem with the nominalist view is that, if we cannot have knowledge of the causes of things, it is equally uncertain as to whether we can really know anything.

Indeed, Ockham said that we cannot even be sure who is human and who is not: "Thus, there is no effect through which it can be proved that anyone is a human being—especially through no effect that is clear to us. For an angel can produce in a body everything that we see in a human being—e.g. eating, drinking, and the like.... Therefore,

---

[22] Thomas Aquinas, *Summa contra gentiles* 3, 97, 15.
[23] Leonard A. Kennedy, C.S.B., "Philosophical Scepticism in England in the Fourteenth Century", *Vivarium* 21, no. 1 (1983), https://www.jstor.org/stable/42569749?seq =1#page_scan_tab_contents.
[24] Averroes, *Tahafut al-Tahafut (The Incoherence of the Incoherence)*, trans. Simon Van Den Bergh (Cambridge: Gibb Memorial Trust, 2008), xxx–xxxi.

it is not surprising if it is impossible to demonstrate that anything is a cause."[25] Likewise, radical nominalist Nicholas Aston (ca. 1317–ca. 1367), a doctor of theology at Oxford and its chancellor from 1359 to 1361, told his students that they "probably were not certain that Nicholas was really a human being".[26] The thing that distinguishes man most from the animal—naming and, therefore, knowing—has now been lost. Aston's position illustrates Swiss thinker Max Picard's dictum that "where the word comes to an end, man himself ends."[27]

If one cannot even tell what a human being is, or whether someone is human, what happens to the imago Dei and the political order based on it? They are obviously imperiled by this kind of radical skepticism, as is the whole notion of reality by Aston's further assertion that one could not be certain whether one is dreaming or awake.[28] At this, reality lapses into incoherence—which becomes especially evident in Aston's teaching that God can even change the past such that it never existed. He did this by arguing that contingent things are never necessary and that the past was once contingent; therefore, it is still contingent, not necessary, and can be changed. The logic of his premise led him to assert that God can simultaneously will two opposites—that "this does not exist" (*hoc non est*) and that "this will always be" (*hoc semper erit*).[29] Of course, this defies Aristotle's statement, repeated by Aquinas: "This alone is denied even to God: to make what has been not to have been." As Aristotle said, "It is impossible for the same thing to be and not to be at the same time."[30] With the denial of the principle of noncontradiction, the world becomes completely unintelligible, and nothing that makes sense can be said.

The nominalist view also logically spelled the end of ethics or moral philosophy. Ockham canceled the classical prescription that man is to live in accordance with nature because nature is rational and therefore normative. To live rightly insofar as one can through the guidance of nature becomes a metaphysical and epistemological

---

[25] Cited in Feser, "Razor Boy",
[26] Kennedy, "Philosophical Scepticism", 53.
[27] Max Picard, *Hitler in Ourselves* (Chicago: Henry Regnery, 1947), 99.
[28] Kennedy, "Philosophical Scepticism", 53.
[29] Ibid., 51.
[30] Aristotle, *Metaphysics* 1006a.

impossibility. Man must be able to perceive the good before willing it. If man cannot know the good, he cannot will it.[31] Man, Josef Pieper explained, "looks first at reality; and by virtue of and on the basis of his knowledge of reality he decides what is to be done and what not, and how it is to be done and how not." In other words, "realization of the good presupposes knowledge of reality [for] one who does not know how things really are cannot do good; for the good accords with reality."[32]

Without an inherent human end by which to judge the goodness or evil of his actions as taking him toward or away from the fulfillment of his nature, man is adrift. He has no natural good to guide him in reality. In fact, according to Ockham's metaphysics, reason cannot tell good from bad because all actions are morally indifferent or neutral. Intrinsically, acts are neither good nor bad, except insofar as God makes them so. God does not command certain behavior because it is good; it is good because he commands it. Likewise, he does not forbid murder because it is bad; it is bad because he forbids it. The goodness or badness of anything does not reside in God's intellect but in his will, which he can change. There is not anything objective in the character of acts themselves. Evil is only a rule, or rather, it is not obeying the rule. Things are morally obligatory or forbidden simply by God's decree through revelation. Ockham said, "Evil is nothing else than to do something when one is under an obligation to do the opposite. Obligation does not fall on God, since He is not under any obligation to do anything."[33] This statement could be a paraphrase of al-Ghazali's position on the same matter.

According to Ockham, God's choice of moral law is arbitrary because he could well have willed an entirely different moral order from the present one. Ockham argued that, however unlikely it may be, God could require one to do the very opposite of what he had previously commanded, such as to commit adultery:

Hatred, theft, adultery, and the like may involve evil according to the common law, in so far as they are done by someone who is

---

[31] See Michael Allen Gillespie, *The Theological Origins of Modernity* (Chicago: University of Chicago Press, 2008), 155.

[32] Josef Pieper, *The Christian Idea of Man* (South Bend, Ind.: St. Augustine's Press, 2011), 14.

[33] Copleston, *A History of Philosophy*, 3:115.

obligated by a divine command to perform the opposite act. As far as everything absolute in these actions is concerned, however, God can perform them without involving any evil. And they can even be performed meritoriously by someone on earth if they should fall under a divine command, just as now the opposite of these, in fact, fall under a divine command.[34]

What's more, wrote Ockham, "'Mortal sin' does not have a real essence. For there is no one real thing, whether positive or negative, that it signifies." God could require us to hate him and we would be obliged to comply, as all vices could be transformed into virtues "if they were to agree with the divine precept just as now, *de facto*, their opposites agree with the divine precept."[35] Thus, Ockham asserted that, while everything God commands is just, he can command something unjust. This assertion contravened the preceding medieval metaphysical view that God could do no such thing as it would violate his own nature or essence to order men to hate him or to act unjustly.

The nominalist view of morally indifferent acts was pregnant with two developments that occurred shortly afterward, within a few years of each other. The first was from Niccolò Machiavelli, who understood that, if nature no longer defines what is good for man (and there is no certain God to define it either), then man can. Man's will fills the vacuum left by nature; he can define his own end. Nominalism's moral indifference also provided a preview of Martin Luther's belief that man's actions are irrelevant to his salvation because there is no necessary connection between moral goodness and redemption. Ockham showed, said J. A. Fernández-Santamaría, that "God finds nothing in man's intrinsic actions deserving of reward and punishment, nothing that compels him to save the innocent or damn the guilty."[36] If this is so, what could man possibly do to assist in his salvation? Luther would soon answer: nothing.

In any case, the purpose of Ockham's epistemology was to demonstrate that man knows far less than he thinks he does. Ockham and the nominalists relegated anything that could not be philosophically proven to the realm of faith. This included natural theology, or what

---

[34] William of Ockham, *Commentary on the Sentences of Peter Lombard* 2, 15.

[35] Ibid.

[36] Fernández-Santamaría, *Natural Law*, 105.

Thomas Aquinas called the "preambles of faith", the rational proofs for God's existence, and, as we have seen, ethics. "Having expelled from the mind of God the intelligible world of Plato," Etienne Gilson said, "Occam was satisfied that no intelligibility could be found in any of God's works. How could there be order in nature, when there is no nature?"[37] The more inscrutable the divine will, the more opaque reality becomes as its product. This obstructs access to God through his creation. The end result, as summarized by Scott Hahn and Benjamin Wiker, is that

> since ultimately nothing can be read from nature (which was merely a particular expression of God's power) about His actual, inscrutable nature defined by His absolute power, then there could be no philosophical climbing from the contingent creation to an understanding of any necessary metaphysical principles or to God Himself. The only real connection that can be made is from the side of God, through revelation, and even here God's power is absolute and His ways ultimately inscrutable.[38]

Man still had revelation, the only source left for the moral order. As we have seen, the good is obedience to divine rules, whatever they may be. Divine law, however, is extrinsic to man. It is not located within—written in his heart, as it were—as something he could perceive even dimly without faith. Nature provides no guide. "Only faith gives us access to theological truths", said Ockham. "The ways of God are not open to reason, for God has freely chosen to create a world and establish a way of salvation within it apart from any necessary laws that human logic or rationality can uncover."[39]

Nominalism's moral agnosticism also seems to have provided the foundation for David Hume's famous is-ought distinction, made in the eighteenth century, or what later came to be called the fact-value distinction. These assert that there can be no moral guidance from what exists or what "is", to what "ought" to be. One cannot derive an "ought" from an "is". This is another consequence of claiming

---

[37] Gilson, *Unity of Philosophical Experience*, 85.

[38] Scott W. Hahn and Benjamin Wiker, *Politicizing the Bible* (New York: Crossroad, 2013), 51.

[39] Dale T. Irvin and Scott W. Sunquist, *History of World Christian Movement*, vol. 1, *Earliest Christianity to 1453* (Maryknoll, N.Y.: Orbis Books, 2001), 434.

that nature cannot be normative because there are no ends in it—no telos to guide things to become what they should be in their fullest, according to their essences. In short, there is no foundation in reality for what "ought" to be. Once one is rid of essences, there is not an "ought" in sight. We are simply left with what "is". (Machiavelli would take great advantage of this.) As a consequence, one gets to make up one's own "values". Moral truth is relocated to the will. This becomes a very dangerous teaching when it is politicized. If law is no longer reason, what is it? Man's law becomes its own standard, based only on the *will* of the ruler (whether one or many), predisposed to nothing but itself.

A voluntarist God ineluctably leads to voluntarist man. It is not so great a leap from the voluntarist exaltation of the will of God to the voluntarist exaltation of the will of man. If God is a voluntarist, we become voluntarists. After all, if God's intellect is subordinate to his will, why should man be any different in subordinating his reason to his will? As Bertrand de Jouvenel said, "The man who finds in God before all else will and power, will be disposed to the same view of human government."[40] As appalled as he probably would have been with the results, one wonders why Ockham did not see this coming from his premises.

Consequences for Law

We can now clearly see the consequences of these different ideas of God and reality for the conception of law itself. The reality of nature or essence was the basis of the medieval vision of the concept of law. As characterized by the eighteenth-century Scotsman Andrew Ramsay, it saw that "the law in general is nothing else than the Rule which each Being ought to follow, in order to act according to his Nature."[41] A thing's perfection is defined as the fulfillment of its nature.

---

[40] Bertrand de Jouvenal, *Sovereignty: An Inquiry into the Political Good* (Chicago: University of Chicago Press, 1957), 237.

[41] Cited in Rémi Brague, interview by Christophe Cervellon and Kristell Trego, in Rémi Brague, *The Legend of the Middle Ages: Philosophical Explorations of Medieval Christianity, Judaism, and Islam* (Chicago: University of Chicago Press, 2009), 12, University of Chicago Press, https://www.press.uchicago.edu/Misc/Chicago/070803.html.

Heinrich Rommen differentiated between the *lex ratio* and the *lex voluntas*, the first being law as reason, and the second, law as will. The first corresponds to the Thomist idea of God's primacy of intellect over will. The second corresponds to the Ockhamist notion of the primacy of will over intellect. In respect to *lex ratio*, Rommen points out, according to Russell Hittinger, that "the intellect's grasp of what ought to be done comes first; the force executing that judgment comes second, after the directive of reason."[42] In other words, man's law imitates the primacy of intellect in God. The intellect directs the will; the will then acts in accord with reason. Rational laws are first conceived and then enforced.

On the other hand, the *lex voluntas* idea of law "holds that law binds human liberty because of the superior power or will of the legal authority.... Thus, the *lex-voluntas* tradition insists that the will comes first, and reason, which guides the application of the command, comes second."[43] In imitation of a voluntarist God, man's reason is the servant of the will, rather than its director. The will asserts itself, and reason accommodates and supplies the will by finding the best way to accomplish what has been willed. (Building upon this notion, David Hume would later take it a step further, saying, "Reason is, and ought only to be, the slave of the passions and may never pretend to any office other than to serve and obey them.")[44] If there is no nature, there is no natural law. If there is no natural law, there is no rational means by which to judge positive law's adherence to a moral standard outside itself. Reason loses its job of distinguishing right from wrong when it is incapable of doing so. Reason is no longer a legislator. Law becomes law not because it is a work of reason but because it is the will of the stronger. Force is the adjudicator. It is easy to see which of these two views undergirds constitutionalism and which supports political absolutism.

Once one abandons essences, as Ockham did, one is left with only probabilities. We are simply reduced to applying "methods". In this way, empiricism is the necessary result of nominalism, which subjects everything that remains of reality to empirical treatment as the only

---

[42] Heinrich A. Rommen, *The Natural Law: A Study in Legal and Social History and Philosophy* (Indianapolis: Liberty Fund, 1998), xxvi.

[43] Ibid., xxvii.

[44] David Hume, *A Treatise of Human Nature* (1740) 2, 3, 3.

way of apprehending it. Apparently, Ockham did not have much interest in empiricism, but it did not take long for those who followed his thinking to catch on. It soon became apparent to Renaissance man that perhaps he could impose his purposes on things through the methods of empiricism and become, in a way, their cause. German philosopher Hans Blumenberg remarked, "When God becomes Nominalism's *Deus absconditus* [hidden God], the world loses its rational base and man is left to find whatever meaning and purpose he can through his own efforts [and] that leads to the modern project of self-affirmation and self-assertion."[45] Man's purpose is no longer to understand nature but, as Francis Bacon said, "to conquer nature". By substituting efficient for final causality, man becomes free from the metaphysical restrictions of essences and can make of things what he wills or has the power to do. In other words, the modern project of making man autonomous, or even or remaking him, by gaining power over the world begins here. In the *Oration on the Dignity of Man*, Giovanni Pico della Mirandola (1463–1494) sang the hymn to the new Renaissance man through the voice of God: "Thou, constrained by no limits, in accordance with thine own free will, shall ordain for thyself the limits of thy nature.... With freedom of choice and with honor, as though the maker and molder of thyself, thou mayest fashion thyself in whatever shape though shalt prefer."[46] One sees in this paean the terrible temptation of the perfectibility of man by his own powers. Empirical science is his instrument for this anthropocentric project. Man will now be "molder" of his own image, whatever that may be.

Moving so much of man's available knowledge from the realm of reason—in order to sanitize it from pagan philosophy—to the realm of faith did not disturb the nominalists (some of whom, like Ockham, were priests), since their faith was still secure and served as a guarantor of faith-based knowledge. As Frederick Copleston said, however, "The nominalists left faith hanging in the air, without (so

---

[45] Hans Blumenberg, *The Legitimacy of the Modern Age* (Cambridge, Mass.: MIT Press, 1983), 2–3.

[46] Giovanni Pico della Mirandalo, *Oration on the Dignity of Man*, in Ernst Cassirer, Paul Oskar Kristeller, and John H. Randall, eds., *The Renaissance Philosophy of Man* (Chicago: University of Chicago Press, 1948), The History Guide, http://www.historyguide.org/intellect/pico.html.

far as philosophy is concerned) any rational basis."[47] They did not suspect what would be loosed upon the world when faith faltered, and only the radical skepticism of their nominalist views remained. After denuding the landscape of the certainty of reason's truths, what is left when faith itself weakens or evaporates? The problem is that the retreat into fideism leaves faith open to charges of irrationality. When faith itself is doubted, there is nothing left underneath it, and a great danger looms. Fr. James Schall said:

> The evaporation of content from the natural order was the result of trusting nothing but God. This position, within a voluntarist and nominalist background, tended ... to leave the world itself open to a kind of atheism, since it became in this context a world with no authentic "signs", no "vestigia" of God within its internal structure. If then there is no link between God and the world, except through the internalization of scriptural faith, any philosophical or political denial of God as a proper object of intellect in some fashion would leave the world an open field for man's practical intellect to refashion as it chose. Such refashioning is then dependent on no prior objective norms of man or cosmos.[48]

Indeed, nominalism empowers man's mind to make of nature what he will. Names do not so much reflect reality as create it. Naming becomes an exercise of the will. It is the human mind that projects onto the world whatever order there is thought to be there. His choice is based only on his will and his passions. In other words, outside of revelation, it leaves everything relative, since man has nothing in natural law on which to base norms for his behavior. This means that, with the loss of his natural end, man loses the limits that that end would otherwise impose on the exercise of his will. One might wish to say that man is rescued from this moral relativity by the law of God, but that too turns out to be relative because God can change his mind at any moment.

To say that the "evaporation of content from the natural order" delivers a devastating blow to the underpinnings of constitutionalism

---

[47] Copleston, *A History of Philosophy*, 3:21.

[48] James V. Schall, "Luther and Political Philosophy", *Faith and Reason* 8, no. 2 (Summer 1982): 20–21.

is an understatement, since it leaves the arena open to the primacy of will and closed to the primacy of reason—the latter being the sine qua non of constitutional rule. If "ultimately nothing can be read from nature", then there can be no "Laws of Nature and of Nature's God"—as in the Declaration of Independence—on which to base a constitution. Indeed, the very grounds for opposing political absolutism disappear. As we will see, the American Revolution was based on a reestablishment of those rational grounds and could not have taken place without them.

Ockham's thinking spread to universities in Paris, Oxford, Heidelberg, Prague, and Cracow.[49] The *via moderna* was ascendant. Its logic would soon work its way through philosophy and politics with devastating consequences for Christendom and its nascent constitutional order.

---

[49] Larry Siedentop, *Inventing the Individual: The Origins of Western Liberalism* (Cambridge, Mass.: Harvard University Press, 2014), 342.

4

Enter: Martin Luther—Exit: Christendom

As we saw in chapter 2, in the Middle Ages the swords of church and state served one truth, producing Christendom. Dual sovereignty had meant *restricted* sovereignty, as neither church nor state could claim the whole man. The end of the Middle Ages brought about *two* truths—faith alone, or fideism, on the one hand; reason alone, on the other—with only *one* sword. This change considerably enhanced the burgeoning power of national states, since the remaining sword was theirs. Between them, Ockham and Luther (with the help of others) brought about the end of Christendom and laid the basis for *unrestricted* state sovereignty, which would soon claim the whole man for its own. As A.J. Carlyle observed, in this new era "there grew up a conception of political authority which was fundamentally different from that of the Middle Ages, for absolute monarchy was a new thing, an innovation which had no real relation to the past. It was indeed a revolutionary innovation."[1] We need to examine how and why this "new thing" happened. Political absolutism, divine or secular, did not arise out of thin air. It arose in rebellion against medieval teachings and was based on certain theological and philosophical doctrines diametrically opposed to them.

Of course, ideas are not the sole driving force of human affairs. Historical circumstances help create the environment within which certain ideas flourish as opposed to others. The strengthening of national states and the weakening of the Church through multiple scandals at the close of the Middle Ages (the Babylonian Captivity of the papacy in Avignon, the schism of the antipopes, etc.) were among those circumstances. Protestantism was partially the product of something that

[1] A.J. Carlyle, *Political Liberty: A History of the Conception in the Middle Ages and Modern Times* (London: Oxford University Press, 1941), 26.

went wrong in the Church. The ecclesiastical hypocrisy and corruption in the late medieval and Renaissance times left little doubt of the need for reform, but not necessarily for Reformation. Pope Adrian VI confessed as much in a message to a Diet at Nuremberg (1522):

> We know well that for many years things deserving of abhorrence have gathered around the Holy See. Sacred things have been misused, ordinances transgressed, so that in everything there has been a change for the worse.... We all, prelates and clergy, have gone astray from the right way, and for long there is no one that has done good, no, not one.... Therefore ... we shall use all diligence to reform.... The whole world is longing for such reform.[2]

Luther's ideas did not spread solely because of their intellectual allure but were somehow attuned to their times in a way even the pope recognized.

The purpose of this chapter is to consider these new ideas, particularly as they took shape in Martin Luther's theology. Lutheranism is relevant to our topic only insofar as certain of its teachings helped pave the way for political absolutism, although Luther never envisioned that concept. Ideas have consequences in ways unintended by their progenitors. The purpose of examining Luther at length is to reveal the philosophical and theological underpinnings of the ideas that brought down the medieval edifice, and to see the foundation on which the new one was constructed. The emphasis will not be so much on Luther the man (nor is this intended to be a comprehensive treatment of his thought) as on the ideas themselves—no matter their source. Thus, the intent is not to criticize Martin Luther or Lutheranism per se but to examine the consequences of the notions he embraced, principally from Ockham.

The problem with Luther is not that he was a Protestant (after all, nearly all the American Founders were Protestants), but that he was a nominalist and a voluntarist—the very opposite of Protestant theologian Richard Hooker, as will be seen in the next chapter. That is what is at issue here, not his beautiful prayers, hymns, and meditations on Christ's mercy. In his turn, however, Luther caused

---

[2] Cited in Will Durant, *The Reformation* (New York: Simon and Schuster, 1957), 381.

problems that had effects—including for constitutionalism—some of which, no doubt, went beyond the intentions of their author. Luther was a theologian, not a political philosopher—though he claimed his political thought was a product of his theology. (We shall see later how this makes perfect sense.) Luther redefined the nature of man and his relationship to God. In so doing, he ineluctably changed the way in which man thought of political order. Spiritual upheaval led to political upheaval.

Our general thesis is that Luther took the *via moderna* to its logical conclusion in religious terms. If Luther had not taken things as far as he did in his breach with the Church, someone else likely would have because of the prevalence of Ockham's thought at the time. Luther was simply working out Ockham's radical epistemology. Others then took these ideas to their political conclusion, which they were able to do effectively thanks to the Reformation's separation of religious from public life.

This fundamental change is important for our long-term theme because removing reason from faith (*sola fide*) opened the unforeseen possibility of reducing, if not eliminating, the pertinence of faith to political and civic life—a possibility exploited by Machiavelli and then by Hobbes in ways that would no doubt have shocked both Ockham and Luther. The principal beneficiary of nominalism's metaphysical demolition of reason and natural law as moral guides to ultimate ends was the primacy of the will—first God's, then man's. Luther scholar Thomas D. Pearson pithily observed that "in the end, nominalism's rendition of natural law replaces reason with will, nature with commands, teleology with obedience."[3] As we shall see, these are the grounds on which absolute rule has been argued.

In addition to the influence of the nominalist school on Luther, we will examine the diminishment of the imago Dei through his radical exaggeration of the effects of Original Sin, and how it logically led to the denigration of reason and the denial of free will. These, in turn, reinforced secular authority, which no longer had to contend with notions of popular sovereignty, the requirement of consent, or the right to revolution, all of which Luther denied.

[3] Thomas D. Pearson, "Luther on Natural Law", *Journal of Lutheran Ethics* 7, no. 12 (December 2007), https://www.elca.org/JLE/Articles/472.

Before looking at these consequences, however, we will examine the ideas behind them as they developed in Luther, partially through Ockham's influence, and partially as a consequence, it seems, of Luther's extreme scrupulosity, to which he sought a solution in salvation by faith alone.

As we saw in the last chapter, Ockham opened a fissure between nature and grace, between reason and revelation. They were now separate and disparate in an immiscible way. There is no longer an interpenetration of faith and reason to form a whole. Faith did not speak to reason, or reason to faith. The two truths were without any apparent relationship to each other. Thus ended the tremendously rich cross-fertilization of theology and philosophy so evident in Aquinas' thought. The new theology was without philosophy, and philosophy without theology.[4] Under Ockham's influence, Martin Luther embraced this disparity and reformulated Christianity based on it. Reformed Christianity was to be grounded on faith alone (*sola fide*), in Scripture alone (*sola scriptura*), by grace alone (*sola gratia*). Grace does not perfect nature, as Aquinas claimed; it simply covers it (*natura deleta*). Corrupted nature was on its own, irremediable.

Luther and Nominalism

The story begins in Erfurt. "By the time of Martin Luther," wrote Michael Gillespie, "there was only one university in Germany that was not dominated by the nominalists."[5] It was decidedly not the University of Erfurt, where Luther matriculated. Erfurt was a center of Ockhamist influence, which, Luther said, "I have absorbed completely."[6] Helping him in this direction was Luther's teacher, Gabriel Biel (d. 1495), a nominalist heavily indebted to Ockham. In *Table Talk*, Luther expressed his admiration for Ockham, whom he called

[4] James V. Schall, *The Mind That Is Catholic: Philosophical and Political Essays* (Washington, D.C.: Catholic University of America Press, 2008), 175.

[5] Michael Allen Gillespie, *The Theological Origins of Modernity* (Chicago: University of Chicago Press, 2008), 27.

[6] Cited in Scott W. Hahn and Benjamin Wiker, *Politicizing the Bible* (New York: Crossroad, 2013), 148.

[7] Cited in Philip Schaff, *The Protestant Reformation* (Grand Rapids: Wm. B. Eerdmans, 1963), 193.

"without doubt the leader and most ingenious of the Schoolmen".[7] He demonstrated his own understanding of the central issue between the *via antiqua* and the *via moderna*:

> The Terminists [another name for nominalists], among whom I was, is the name of a school in the universities. They oppose Thomists, Scotists, and Albertinists, and are called Occamists, from Occam their founder. They are the very latest sect and the most powerful in Paris, too. The dispute was over whether "humanitas" and words like it meant a common humanity, which was in all human beings, as Thomas and others believe. Well, say Occamists or terminists, there is no such thing as a common humanity, there is only the term "homo" or humanity meaning all human beings individually.... Occam is a wise and sensible man, who endeavored earnestly to amplify and explain the subject.[8]

Although he was later to reject parts of Ockham's theology, Luther spoke of "my master Occham" and kept a collection of Ockham's writings on his bookshelf. In his *Life of Luther*, Philip Melanchthon, Luther's disciple, stated that Luther "read Occam much and long and preferred his acumen to that of Thomas and Scotus".[9] In fact, said Luther, "Thomas Aquinas was only a talker and a brawler"— a conclusion he may have reached without reading Aquinas firsthand. Dr. Colin Brown suggested that "Luther read Thomas through the eyes of others, especially those of Gabriel Biel. Moreover, late medieval knowledge of Aquinas seems to have been based more on his commentaries than on the *Summa*."[10] Whatever the case may have been, Luther felt qualified to say that "Thomas wrote a great deal of heresy, and is responsible for the reign of Aristotle, the destroyer of godly doctrine."[11]

---

[8] Cited in T. Bruce Birch, ed., *The De Sacramento Altaris of William of Ockham* (Burlington, Iowa: Lutheran Literary Board, 1930), xxiii.

[9] Cited in James G. Kiecker: "The Influence of William of Ockham on Luther's Eucharistic Theology", Wisconsin Lutheran Seminary Digital Library, http://www.wlsessays.net /handle/123456789/2494.

[10] Colin Brown, *Christianity and Western Thought: A History of Philosophers, Ideas and Movements*, vol. 1, *From the Ancient World to the Age of Enlightenment* (Downers Grove, Ill.: Inter-Varsity Press, 1990), 150.

[11] *Luther's Works* (hereafter *LW*), trans. Jaroslav Pelikan (St. Louis: Concordia Publishing House, 1955–1986), 32:258.

The continuity of Luther's thinking with the preceding nominalism is apparent in his rejection of natural law as a moral guide and in
his voluntarist idea of divine will as the only source of moral law. "I
can find nowhere in Luther's writings", stated Pearson, "an endorse-
ment of the traditional notion that the value of natural law lies in
the prospect that individual members of the human species can use
reason to order their lives in accordance with the moral precepts of
the natural law."[12] For sure, Luther spoke of natural law but mostly as
an instinct of conscience, a matter of what God placed in the human
heart as an inclination. It was not something arrived at through reason. In his thinking, there was no ontological basis for natural law as
it was classically understood, in other words, as providing a rationally
apprehensible, teleological order of moral good. This was consistent
with his view of the divine. Luther wrote:

> God is He for Whose will no cause or ground may be laid down as its
> rule and standard; for nothing is on a level with it or above it, but it is
> itself the rule for all things. If any rule or standard, or cause or ground,
> existed for it, it could no longer be the will of God. What God wills is
> not right because He ought, or was bound, so to will; on the contrary,
> what takes place must be right, because He so wills it. Causes and
> grounds are laid down for the will of the creature, but not for the will
> of the Creator—unless you set another Creator over him![13]

Like al-Ghazali's Allah, Luther's God acts for no reasons. He is not
Logos in his essence. Therefore, *whatever* happens "must be right".
God must be right because right is the rule of the strongest. This is
pure voluntarism straight out of Ockham.

The Hidden God—*Deus Absconditas*

Like Ockham, Luther held the nominalist position on God's necessary inscrutability. In *The Bondage of the Human Will*, Luther wrote
that "God is absolutely incomprehensible in omnipotence and righteousness." This is as it should be, said Luther, "as He is the one

---

[12] Pearson, "Luther on Natural Law".
[13] Martin Luther, *The Bondage of the Will* (Grand Rapids: Revell, 1992), 209.

and true God, and moreover incomprehensible and inaccessible by human reason, it is right, nay, it is necessary, that His righteousness should be incomprehensible."[14] In his *Foundations of Modern Political Thought*, Quentin Skinner wrote that Luther "is forced to acknowledge that since we cannot hope to fathom the nature and will of God, His commands are bound to appear entirely inscrutable. It is at this point that he most clearly reveals his debt to the Ockhamists: he insists that the commands of God must be obeyed not because they seem to us just but simply because they are God's commands."[15] If God acts for no reasons, how could he possibly be understood? "For as in His own nature God is immense, incomprehensible, and infinite," wrote Luther, "so to man's nature He is intolerable."[16] He is the *Deus absconditas*, the hidden, unfathomable God (who so terrified Luther). Luther wrote, "God hidden in his Majesty neither deplores nor takes away death, but works life, death, and all in all. For there he has not bound himself by his word, but has kept himself free over all things."[17] God is unaccountable; he can do anything. Man cannot pretend to understand God or his commands; he can only submit to them.

This definition of an incomprehensible God *necessarily* involves the diminishment of man's reason, as it is no longer anchored in Logos. God is known only insofar as he is revealed and by no other means (shades of al-Ghazali). Like Ockham, Luther held that the truth of faith is not accessible to reason. In *Lectures on Galatians*, Luther stated: "Reason cannot think correctly about God; only faith can do so."[18] How could it? In the *Commentary on Romans*, Luther proclaimed: "The gospel is a teaching having no connection whatever with reason.... Reason cannot grasp an extraneous righteousness." In 1536, he wrote to Melanchthon: "In the things of God we must not hearken to reason." In fact, he held that "reason is contrary to faith."

[14] Martin Luther, *The Bondage of the Will* (Belfast, Northern Ireland: Ambassador Publications, 2007), 165.

[15] Quentin Skinner, *The Foundations of Modern Political Thought*, vol. 2, *The Age of Reformation* (Cambridge: Cambridge University Press, 1978), 5.

[16] Martin Luther, *Lectures on Galatians, 1535*, in *LW*, 26:29.

[17] Luther, *Bondage of the Will*, *LW*, 33:140.

[18] *LW*, 26:238, cited in Bryce P. Wandrey, "A Brief Introduction to Reason", *Lutheran Theology* (February 22, 2010), https://lutherantheology.wordpress.com/2010/02/22/a-brief-introduction-to-reason.

And then, even more forcefully he exclaimed, "Reason is directly opposed to faith, and one ought to let it be; in believers it should be killed and buried."[19] Some truths that God has revealed cannot be discovered through reason and must be accepted on faith, but Luther went beyond that when he denied that revelation is also *addressed* to man's reason. Luther's approach undermined the relationship between man's reason and the mind of the Creator. He was driven by his view of divine voluntarism to snap the connection.

Complete Corruption of Original Sin

To Ockham's metaphysical explanation for why reason is not connected to faith, Luther added that reason had been blinded through the corruption of nature and as a result is unable to understand "what belongs to the Spirit of God". Key to understanding Luther is the radical extent of that corruption. It is worth hearing from him at length on this central teaching:

> Conceived in sorrow and corruption, the child sins in his mother's womb. As he grows older, the innate element of corruption develops. Man has said to sin: "Thou art my father"—and every act he performs is an offense against God; and to the worms: "You are my brothers"— and he crawls like them in mire and corruption. He is a bad tree and cannot produce good fruit; a dunghill, and can only exhale foul odors. He is so thoroughly corrupted that it is absolutely impossible for him to produce good actions. Sin is his nature; he cannot help committing it. Man may do his best to be good, still his every action is unavoidably bad; he commits a sin as often as he draws his breath.[20]

What's more, Luther wrote, "I say that whether it be in man or devil, the spiritual powers have been not only corrupted by sin, but absolutely destroyed; so that there is now nothing in them but a depraved reason and a will that is the enemy and opponent of God, whose only

---

[19] *LW* (Erlangen edition), 44:158, cited in Jacques Maritain, *Three Reformers* (New Delhi, India: Isha Books, 2013), 34.

[20] *LW* (Wittenberg edition), 3:518, cited in John Hardon, S.J., "St. Peter Canisius on Christmas Joy", *Homiletic and Pastoral Review* 48, no. 3 (December 1947), Real Presence Association, http://www.therealpresence.org/archives/Saints/Saints_030.htm.

[21] Cited in Maritain, *Three Reformers*, 18.

thought is war against God."[21] Not surprisingly in this unrelievedly bleak landscape, Luther thought that "the natural condition of the world is chaos and upheaval."[22] Hobbes' degraded view of man and of the constant strife of the natural state in which he lives is not very far away. Indeed, like Hobbes after him, Luther thought that, absent strong government, "men would devour one another, seeing that the whole world is evil and that amongst thousands there is scarcely a single Christian.... The world would be reduced to chaos."[23]

With the imago Dei so obscured, if not obliterated, it should come as no surprise that its two principal manifestations, reason and free will, fade almost beyond recognition in Luther's thinking. He wrote, "Original sin really means that human nature has completely fallen; that the intellect has become darkened, so that we no longer know God and His will and no longer perceive the works of God."[24] As we have seen, nature is so deeply compromised by the Fall that it cannot be relied upon for any moral guidance. "No act is done according to nature that is not an act of concupiscence against God."[25] Man is so corrupted that his reason cannot discern right from wrong. To the limited extent that Luther thought there is such a thing as natural law, it was nonetheless morally irrelevant: "Evil lust and sinful love obscure the light of natural law, and blind man, until he fails to perceive the guide-book in his heart and to follow the clear command of reason."[26] What is reasonable no longer serves as normative. Heinrich Rommen wrote:

> Luther taught that original sin had so utterly destroyed the goodness of human nature that even grace did not reform its inner-most malignity, but simply covered it. He denied that reason is able to recognize natural law and that will can strive for it. The universe is broken up: the realm of nature is evil, separated from the realm of supernature. There is no bridge between religion as grace in the world and the field of reason and natural ethics.[27]

[22] Cited in Gillespie, *The Theological Origins of Modernity*, 122.

[23] Ibid.

[24] *LW*, 1:114.

[25] Martin Luther, *Disputation against Scholastic Theology*, no. 21, trans. H.J. Grimm, Check Luther.com, https://www.checkluther.com/wp-content/uploads/1517-Disputation-against-Scholastic-Theology.pdf.

[26] *Luther's Epistle Sermons* (Minneapolis: Luther Press, 1909), 73.

[27] Heinrich A. Rommen, *The State in Catholic Thought* (St. Louis: B. Herder, 1945), 63.

Reason is no longer in service to God. It is on its own, cut off from its source or, more accurately, with no source at all. Gone is the understanding contained in Justin Martyr's statement in the second century that "the Logos endowed all men with reason and freedom, *which are not lost by the fall.*"[28] Since reason has no role outside of its pragmatic or instrumental uses in the affairs of earthly life (of which Luther approved), man must turn to faith alone.

Faith Alone

Luther's extraordinary polemics against reason must be understood in light of his intention to discredit it so thoroughly that no alternative but faith remained. Luther did not abandon the use of practical reason in the secular sphere but left secular reason out of the sacred sphere. Such is the antipathy of reason to faith, he said, that "all the articles of our Christian faith, which God has revealed to us in His Word, are in the presence of reason sheerly impossible, absurd, and false."[29] Luther, averred Jacques Maritain, wanted "to *exterminate reason* in order to save faith".[30] The question as to whether Maritain's statement is an exaggeration should be considered in light of the ample quotations from Luther that follow.[31] Thus, Luther famously declared that "reason is the greatest enemy that faith has ... the whore of the devil. It can only blaspheme and dishonor everything God has said or done." "Does reason shed light?" he asked rhetorically and then answered, "Yes, like that which filth would shed if it were set in a lantern."[32] Therefore, "You must abandon your reason, know nothing of it, annihilate it completely or you will never enter heaven."[33] In his last sermon preached at Wittenberg, Luther even more energetically proclaimed: "Reason is the Devil's greatest whore; she is a prostitute, the Devil's appointed

---

[28] Philip Schaff, *History of the Christian Church*, vol. 2 (Brandon, Fla.: Revelation Insight, 2011), 558 (emphasis added).

[29] Cited in Durant, *The Reformation*, 370.

[30] Maritain, *Three Reformers*, 143 (emphasis in original).

[31] Their number disallows the likelihood that they are cherry-picked to make a point. Although Luther said many different, and sometimes conflicting, things in his voluminous writings, this many cherries indicate that there is a cherry tree.

[32] Cited in Maritain, *Three Reformers*, 32.

[33] Ibid., 34.

whore; whore eaten by scab and leprosy who ought to be trodden underfoot and destroyed, she and her wisdom.... Throw dung in her face to make her ugly. She is, and she ought to be, drowned in baptism; she would deserve, the wretch, to be banished to the filthiest place in the house, to the closets."[34] His regret was that "alas, in this life reason is never completely destroyed."[35] However, Luther did admit a role for "regenerate reason" when it is "serving humbly in the household of faith" in understanding Scripture.[36]

As stated at the beginning of this chapter, the end of the Middle Ages brought forth two truths instead of one. This is amply evident in Luther's splenetic attack against the Sorbonne, in which he expressed his opposition to the Thomist synthesis of faith and reason. In 1539, he declared, "That mother of all errors has defined, as badly as could be, that if a thing is true, it is true for philosophy and theology; it is godless in it to have condemned those who hold the contrary."[37] This was particularly offensive because, for Luther, "it is impossible to harmonize faith and reason."[38] Therefore, he proclaimed: "In short, it is impossible to reform the Church if Scholastic theology and philosophy are not torn out by the roots with Canon Law."[39]

Contra Aristotle and Philosophy

Philosophy, of course, is a work of reason, and Luther turned as vehemently against it as he did against reason itself: "I indeed believe that I owe to the Lord this service of barking against philosophy and urging to the study of Sacred Scripture.... One should learn philosophy only as one learns witchcraft, that is to destroy it; as one finds out about errors, in order to refute them."[40] (This was also al-Ghazali's strategy: to master philosophy in order to destroy it.)

[34] *LW* (Erlangen ed.), 16:142–48.

[35] Cited in Maritain, *Three Reformers*, 34.

[36] James V. Schall, "Luther and Political Philosophy", *Faith and Reason* 8, no. 2 (Summer 1982): 18.

[37] Cited in Maritain, *Three Reformers*, 31.

[38] Ibid., 34.

[39] Ibid., 31.

[40] Ibid.

Luther contemptuously inveighed against Aristotle, as he had against Aquinas, who, he said, "never understood a chapter of the Gospel or Aristotle".

Rejecting the medieval view that one could not be a theologian without the aid of Aristotle, Luther declared, "No one can become a theologian unless he becomes one without Aristotle."[41] In the same document he wrote, "In vain does one fashion a logic of faith."[42] Therefore, Luther concluded, "Aristotle is to theology as darkness to light."[43] In 1517, he wrote, "Should Aristotle not have been a man of flesh and blood, I would not hesitate to assert that he was the Devil himself."[44] In 1520, Luther again denounced Aristotle, saying,

> I venture to say that any potter has more knowledge of nature than is written in these books [of Aristotle]. It grieves me to the heart that this damned, conceited, rascally heathen has with his false words deluded and made fools of so many of the best Christians.... This dead heathen has conquered and obstructed and almost suppressed the books of the living God, so that when I think of this miserable business I can believe nothing else than that the evil spirit has introduced the study of Aristotle.... His book on Ethics is the worst of all books. It flatly opposes divine grace and all Christian virtues.[45]

Luther declared that "virtually the entire Ethics of Aristotle is the worst enemy of grace."[46]

Luther's vitriol against Aristotle was based on Luther's emphatic denial that virtue is attainable through the practice of good works. For him, Aristotelian virtue had to be impossible; otherwise, his teaching of salvation by faith alone would be imperiled. Peter Redpath explains that Luther

---

[41] Luther, *Disputation*, no. 44.

[42] Ibid., no. 46.

[43] Ibid., no. 50.

[44] Cited in Hahn and Wiker, *Politicizing the Bible*, 149.

[45] Martin Luther, *An Open Letter to the Christian Nobility* 3, 25, trans. C.M. Jacobs (Philadelphia: A.J. Holman, 1915), Project Wittenberg, https://christian.net/pub/resources/text/wittenberg/luther/web/nblty-07.html.

[46] Luther, *Disputation*, no. 41.

could not tolerate naturally-acquired virtues of the soul that were generated, maintained, and lost over time through habitual practice.... Because Aristotle was the chief source of the philosophical teaching about natural virtues and habits, Aristotle haunted Luther like the ghost of Banquo haunted Macbeth. These natural habits, virtues, simply had to go. While Luther could not drive Aristotle out of Athens, he did the next best thing. He tried to drive his ghost out of Western culture.[47]

Luther no doubt was worried about Pelagianism, the heretical teaching that man could effect his own salvation, but he took this concern to the extreme of denying that man's actions have *any* effect, either good or bad, on his salvation. Good works are not efficacious. Luther declared: "He that says the Gospel requires works for salvation, I say flat and plain he is a liar."[48]

It appears that Luther's extreme scrupulosity, which imbued him with such panic at the prospect of God's judgment, drove him to figure out some way to disassociate his acts from any moral significance. This seems likely to have inspired the solution that he could be saved by faith *alone*. Philosopher Edward Feser states: "The prospect of judgment by the terrifying God of nominalism and voluntarism—an omnipotent and capricious will, ungoverned by any rational principle—was cause for despair. Since reason is incapable of fathoming this God and good works incapable of appeasing Him, faith alone could be Luther's refuge."[49] Although this new doctrine no doubt provided him with enormous relief, the price was high: human actions become morally irrelevant. Exaggerating for effect, Luther urged:

Be a sinner and sin on bravely, but have stronger faith and rejoice in Christ, who is the victor of sin, death, and the world. Do not for a moment imagine that this life is the abiding place of justice: sin must be committed. To you it ought to be sufficient that you acknowledge

---

[47] Peter A. Redpath, *A Not-So-Elementary Christian Metaphysics* (Manitou Springs, Col.: Socratic Press, 2012), 233.

[48] Cited in Durant, *The Reformation*, 371.

[49] Edward Feser, "Razor Boy", *Edward Feser* (blog), March 8, 2011, http://edwardfeser .blogspot.com/2011/03/razor-boy.html.

the Lamb that takes away the sins of the world, the sin cannot tear you away from him, even though you commit adultery a hundred times a day and commit as many murders.[50]

It is worth reflecting for a moment on what a momentous change Luther represents from the Aristotelian-Thomist understanding of human nature at the heart of Western civilization heretofore. That understanding held that the natural end of the intellect is truth. In turn, the natural end of the will is the choice of those actions that bring one into conformity with the truth. The highest end of intellect is knowledge of God. Therefore, the highest end of free will is the choice of those means that make possible the attainment of knowledge of God. With Luther, all of this becomes anathema. In 1517, he wrote: "It is false to state that the will can by nature conform to correct precept.... One must concede that the will is not free to strive towards whatever is declared good."[51] This is because, as he said elsewhere, "men are flesh and have a taste for nothing but the flesh, it follows that free choice avails for nothing but sinning."[52]

Freedom from Free Will

Because salvation is by faith alone, Luther eliminated anything that smacks of good works, such as pilgrimages, penance, religious orders, monasticism, clerical celibacy, and fasting, or any other form of asceticism, all of which presume a relationship between acts and spiritual merit. The monasteries and convents were forcibly disbanded. Gone, too, were most of the sacraments, jettisoned for the same reason that they fraudulently offered a role in sinners' salvation. From the Old Testament, Luther expunged sections that violated this tenet, such as 2 Maccabees 12:45, because of its approval of prayers for the dead. All intercessory prayer was eliminated, including the last half of the Hail Mary. Luther also discreetly added to Scripture in his German rendition of the Bible. He translated Romans 3:28 to read

[50] Martin Luther to Melanchthon, Letter no. 99, August 1, 1521, *LW*, 48:281–82.
[51] Luther, *Disputation*, nos. 6 and 10.
[52] Skinner, *Foundations*, 6.

that "man becomes justified by faith alone." The word "alone" does
not appear in the original Greek. Certainly, said Luther, good works
were expected of those who had been "saved", but those works were
no more than the effect of being saved and absolutely were not
related to salvation as a contributory cause. Luther "freed" Christian
man from such a relationship. No longer could human suffering, if
intentionally joined to the sufferings of Christ, be in any way salvific. Luther scholar W. D. J. Cargill Thompson noted: "An inevitable
consequence of Luther's rejection of good works as a necessary factor
to salvation was that he no longer saw this world as being prepa-
ratory to the next, in the sense that what one does in this world con-
tributes directly to one's fate in the next."[53]

Although man was freed from the wages of sin by faith alone and
relieved of the need to do good works for his salvation, he was, in
fact, not free at all in terms of his will. As with Ockham, the nominalist notion of God's omnipotence led Luther to profound problems
with the existence of free will. He could not reconcile the two. Man
could not, for instance, *choose* to believe. Faith does not involve a free
act of the will. No one can choose God; therefore, God must predes-
tine whom he wills. This new doctrine was in contravention of the
long-standing Church teaching that the reception of the gift of faith
was indeed an intrinsically free and rational act of the will in cooperation with grace. Grace makes it possible, but there is an element of
human volition in *accepting* grace. Grace can be refused. Luther could
not abide this doctrine. For Luther, the receipt of faith and grace has
nothing at all to do with the recipient's actions, favorable or otherwise. Man's behavior cannot affect his fate.

In his dispute with Luther over free will, Erasmus wrote that if
Luther's teaching of God's sovereignty is taught, "Who will try
to reform his life?" Luther answered, "I reply, Nobody! Nobody
can! God has no time for your practitioners of self-reformation,
for they are hypocrites. The elect, who fear God, will be reformed
by the Holy Spirit; the rest will perish unreformed." Erasmus tried
again: "Who will believe that God loves him?" Luther insisted: "I
reply, Nobody! Nobody can! But the elect shall believe it; and the
rest shall perish without believing it, raging and blaspheming, as

---

[53] Cited in Hahn and Wiker, *Politicizing the Bible*, 124.

you describe them."[54] What is more, declared Luther, "God ... does all things by his immutable, eternal, and infallible will. Here is a thunderbolt by which free choice is completely prostrated and shattered, so that those who want free choice asserted must either deny or explain away this thunderbolt, or get rid of it by some other means."[55]

Luther did not flinch from the consequences of this view: "From this it follows irrefutably that everything we do, everything that happens, even if it seems to us to happen mutably and contingently, happens in fact nonetheless necessarily and immutably, if you have regard to the will of God."[56] Luther also enthusiastically endorsed Melanchthon's *Notes of the Lectures on Romans and 1 Corinthians*, which pithily reflected Luther's views: "Everything in every creature occurs of necessity.... It must be firmly held that everything, both good and bad, is done by God." Also, wrote Melanchthon, "God does not merely allow His creatures to act, but it is He Himself Who acts." As he does what is good, so also what is evil, "such as David's adultery and Manlius's execution of his son".[57] Ten years later, having reconsidered his views, Melanchthon repudiated his book and, in fact, endeavored to create a kind of Protestant scholasticism to fill in the gaps that Luther had left. Frederick Copleston remarked that "Martin Luther was very strongly anti-Aristotelian and anti-Scholastic; but Melanchthon, his most eminent disciple and associate, was a humanist who introduced into Lutheran Protestantism a humanistic Aristotelianism set to the service of religion."[58]

In further response to Erasmus, Luther dramatized the total subjection of man's will in this way: "Thus the human will is placed between the two like a beast of burden. If God rides it, it wills and goes where God wills.... If Satan rides it, it wills and goes where Satan wills; nor can it choose to run to either of the two riders or to seek him out,

---

[54] Cited in Brian G. Mattson, "Double or Nothing: Martin Luther's Doctrine of Predestination", The Highway, https://www.the-highway.com/Luther-on-predestination_Mattson.html.

[55] Luther, *Bondage of the Will*, *LW*, 33:37.

[56] Ibid., 33:37–38.

[57] Cited in Hartmann Grisar, S.J., *Luther*, vol. 4, trans. E. M. Lamond, ed. Luigi Cappadelta (London: Kegan Paul, Trench, Trubner, 1915), 435–36.

[58] Frederick Copleston, S.J., *A History of Philosophy*, vol. 3, *Late Mediaeval and Renaissance Philosophy*, pt. 1, *Ockham to the Speculative Mystics* (Garden City, N.Y.: Image, 1963), 32.

but the riders themselves contend for the possession and control of it."[59] Furthermore, Luther stated, God "loves and hates according to his eternal and immutable nature.... And it is this very thing which compels freewill to be a mere nothing—namely, that the love of God towards men is eternal and immutable, and his hatred towards them eternal.... And everything is wrought in us necessarily, according to his having either loved us or not loved us, from eternity."[60] Luther therefore concluded that "we do all things by necessity, and nothing by Freewill, so long as the power of the free will is nothing, and neither does nor can do good, in the absence of grace.... It follows from what has been said, that Freewill is a title which altogether belongs to God, and cannot join with any other being, save the Divine Majesty."[61] Man, he said, is as "unfree as a block of wood, a rock, a lump of clay, or a pillar of salt".[62] Here we see the total overthrow of Aquinas' position that since man is rational, "it is necessary that he should have free choice."[63] Luther's freedom through the justification and righteousness of God turns out to be freedom *from* freedom.

Far from being distressed by the deprivation of free will, Luther celebrated it: "I frankly confess that, for myself, even if I could be, I should not want 'free will' to be given me, not anything to be left in my own hands to enable me to endeavor after salvation."[64] Luther's determinism, however, creates problems with theodicy: If God is good, how is it that everything, both good and bad, is done by him? How could one justify the ways of God to man if God condemns persons who had no choice other than to do evil? In *The Bondage of the Will*, Luther asks, "Why does [God] not at the same time change the evil wills that he moves?" He answers, "This belongs to the secrets of his Majesty where his judgments are incomprehensible (Rom. 11:33). It is not our business to ask this question, but to adore these mysteries. And if flesh and blood is offended here and murmurs, by all means let

[59] Luther, *Bondage of the Will*, LW, 33:65.

[60] Martin Luther, *The Bondage of the Will*, sect. 27, trans. Edward Thomas Vaughan (London: T. Hamilton, Paternoster-Row and T. Combe, 1823). http://www.monergism.com/thethreshold/sdg/luther/Bondage%20of%20the%20Will%20-%20Martin%20Luther.pdf.

[61] Ibid., sect. 25.

[62] Cited in Durant, *The Reformation*, 375.

[63] Thomas Aquinas, *Summa theologica* Ia, q. 83, a. 1.

[64] Luther, *Bondage of the Will*, 33:288–89.

it murmur (cf. John 6:61); but it will achieve nothing; God will not change on that account."[65]

Luther solved this dilemma, as had al-Ghazali, through the nominalist disconnection between God's will, which defines justice as *anything* God does, and man's unrelated concept of what is right, which, by definition, is irrelevant to God's will. Luther said:

> Now, if you are disturbed by the thought that it is difficult to defend the mercy and justice of God when he damns the undeserving, that is to say, ungodly men who are what they are because they were born in ungodliness and can in no way help being and remaining ungodly and damnable, but are compelled by a necessity of nature to sin and to perish ... rather must God be honored and revered as supremely merciful toward those whom he justifies and saves, supremely unworthy as they are, and there must be at least some acknowledgement of his divine wisdom so that he may be believed to be righteous where he seems to us to be unjust. For if his righteousness were such that it could be judged to be righteous by human standards, it would clearly not be divine and would in no way differ from human righteousness. But since he is the one true God, and is wholly incomprehensible and inaccessible to human reason, it is proper and indeed necessary that his righteousness also should be incomprehensible.[66]

As we have seen, whatever God wills is righteous by definition, because will, not reason, is the source of right.

The Political Consequences

What were the consequences of Luther's views for constitutionalism? Needless to say, the loss of free will and the integrity of reason had a negative impact on constitutional principles. If man has no free will, why have free institutions? If even the prince behaves in a foreordained way, how could he be held accountable for his acts? As we shall see later, according to Luther, he could not be. But the most immediate consequence of Luther's thought in Protestant

---

[65] Ibid., 33:180.
[66] Ibid., 33:289.

lands was the destruction of the organizational structure of the Church. The logic of its elimination came from Luther's voluntarist theology. Why would God need a church or priests to effect his will? No intermediary between God and man is necessary or allowed. Every man becomes his own priest. Since the Church is no longer a mediator, she could not possibly have the authority of one. Without this authority, she could not possibly contest or hold accountable secular authority, even when it transgressed the Church's spiritual realm. The Church no longer had a realm in any terrestrial way.

This spelled the end of Christendom, which fell apart from the centrifugal forces Lutheranism unleashed. With Luther's elimination of the Church as intermediary between God and man, there was no real constraint left on what each individual might interpret from Scripture or on what he might decide constitutes Scripture. This was not Luther's intention, but it seems to have been an unavoidable consequence of his ideas. One of Luther's erstwhile supporters and later bitter enemies, Andreas Bodenstein von Karlstadt, pointedly warned Luther in 1520 about his denigration of the Letter of James in terms that forecast why Protestantism would suffer multiple fractures: "If it is permissible to make something great or little as one pleases, it will happen at last that the dignity and authority of [biblical] books depends on our power. And then, by whatever right any Christian is allowed to reject my ideas, I have the same right ... to esteem my own highly and trample down those of others."[67] In the priesthood of all believers, everyone shares religious authority equally. Everything is left to conscience and private judgment. This is obviously a recipe for division, which is what it produced. As Benjamin Wiker and Scott Hahn point out, Luther's *sola scriptura* "provided the catalyst for the splintering of Christendom, which would invariably preclude theological resolutions and thus provided the occasion for political ones".[68]

By 1525, Luther recognized the fissiparous forces he had let loose, supposedly admitting that "there are almost as many sects and beliefs

---

[67] Ronald J. Sider, *Andreas Bodenstein Von Karlstadt* (Leiden, Netherlands: E.J. Brill, 1974), 97.
[68] Hahn and Wiker, *Politicizing the Bible*, 13.

as there are heads."[69] Ironically, Luther lambasted Karlstadt as one who "seeks to destroy it [the gospel] with cunning interpretation of Scripture".[70] Karlstadt reciprocated by calling Luther the "malicious assassin of the Scripture".[71] He sarcastically referred to Luther as "the new Wittenberg pope".[72]

The End of Dual Sovereignty

On December 10, 1520, Luther burned the corpus of medieval canon law, the *Corpus juris canonici*, in front of the church at Wittenberg, disparaging it as "heretical, anti-Christian, and unnatural".[73] He urged German nobles to "tear down to the ground the whole of Canon law."[74] Up in flames went the ecclesiastical corporations that had hemmed in secular authority. With the elimination of canon law, the Church as a corporation disappeared. The destruction of the institutional Church had great consequences for the political order in both theory and practice. Brad S. Gregory notes, "A corollary to justification by faith alone was power exercised by secular rulers alone."[75] John Neville Figgis ironically observed that when Luther burned the *Corpus juris canonici*, "he destroyed, in fact, the metaphor of the two swords; henceforth there should be but one, wielded by a rightly advised and godly prince. It is a curious fact that Luther, whose fundamental motive was a love of liberty and care for the rights of one's neighbors, should have been so powerful a supporter of absolutism."[76] In fact, averred Figgis, "Luther denied any limitation of

---

[69] Cited in Dave Armstong, "Luther's Disgust over Protestant Sectarianism and Radical Heresies", *National Catholic Register*, September 8, 2017, http://www.ncregister.com/blog /darmstrong/luthers-disgust-over-protestant-sectarianism-and-radical-heresies.

[70] Cited in Benjamin Wiker, *The Reformation 500 Years Later: Twelve Things You Need to Know* (Washington, D.C.: Regnery, 2017), 120.

[71] Cited in ibid., 133.

[72] Cited in Durant, *The Reformation*, 267.

[73] Cited in *International Encyclopedia of the Social Sciences*, s.v. "Canon Law", by Paul E. Sigmund, Encyclopedia.com, accessed June 24, 2019, https://www.encyclopedia.com /social-sciences/applied-and-social-sciences-magazines/canon-law.

[74] Cited in Brad S. Gregory, *The Unintended Reformation: How a Religious Revolution Secularized Society* (Cambridge, Mass.: Belknap Press, 2012), 146.

[75] Ibid., 148.

[76] John Neville Figgis, *Political Thought from Gerson to Grotius: 1414–1625* (New York: Harper and Brothers, 1960), 73–74.

political power either by Pope or people; nor can it be said that he showed any sympathy for representative institutions; he upheld the inalienable and divine authority of kings in order to hew down the Upas tree of Rome."[77]

It was the institutional structures of the Church that had given teeth to its spiritual oversight of temporal power. The demolition of these structures left it toothless. A single sovereignty could now monopolize man. There was no second ecclesial sovereignty to which he could retreat or through which he could seek recourse. The only remaining courts were civil. Lutheran churches became state churches. In Protestant lands, all power transferred to the prince who appointed church personnel, and it was to him, not to any clerics, that Luther looked for church reforms.[78] Melanchthon wrote that "the prince is God's chief bishop (*summus episcopus*) in the church."[79] Legal scholar Harold Berman pointed out that "sixteenth-century German Lutheranism was associated with a new belief in the supremacy of the Prince."[80] Also, he added, "the Protestant prince exercised legislative, administrative, and judicial powers over the temporal affairs of the church in his territory. Lutheranism thus strengthened the authority of the prince—not only in Germany but also in other parts of Europe to which it penetrated."[81] What is more, said Berman, "Lutheran support for the authority of the prince was not merely a matter of political strategy. It was a matter of theology as well."[82] In a premonition of Sir Robert Filmer's patriarchal argument for the Divine Right of Kings in the seventeenth century, Luther, according to Berman, held that "the citizen owes the same duty of obedience to the prince that the child owes to a father."[83]

In abolishing canon law, Luther destroyed the source from which the constitutional principles and practices of the Middle Ages had emerged (as we saw in chapter 2). It was a commonplace in the Middle Ages that the natural law included the equal liberty of all

[77] John Neville Figgis, *The Divine Right of Kings* (New York: Harper and Row, 1965), 91.

[78] Christopher Dawson, *The Dividing of Christendom* (Garden City, N.Y.: Doubleday, 1967), 73; also see Luther's *Address to the Christian Nobility of the German Nation*.

[79] Cited in Harold J. Berman, *Faith and Order: The Reconciliation of Law and Religion* (Atlanta: Scholars Press, 1993), 161.

[80] Berman, *Faith and Order*, 83.

[81] Ibid., 90.

[82] Ibid.

[83] Ibid., 91.

persons. Luther seemed to contest even this, however, and therefore lost all that goes with it. In addressing the claim of the Swabian peasants that "there shall be no serfs, for Christ has made all men free", Luther responded that "this article ... is a piece of robbery by which every man takes from his lord the body, which has become his lord's property.... This article would make all men equal, and turn the spiritual kingdom of Christ into a worldly, external kingdom; and that is impossible."[84] Lutheran scholar Thomas Pearson observes that "from the beginning, classical natural law theory held that all persons were equal on the basis of the 'higher law', and that natural justice required that civil law recognize the fundamental equality of each human being, regardless of the political consequences. Luther disagrees."[85]

Classical natural law was displaced by political theology, drawn from Scripture. Now, pointed out Heinrich Rommen, "the historical concrete state in its constitution must be considered as instituted directly by God without the intervention of free human act based upon natural law."[86] As a consequence, the monarchy becomes theocratic, though the possibility of a republican theocracy also exists (e.g., Cromwell). The dedivinization of the secular ruler achieved by medieval Christianity went into reverse with the resacralization of the prince and the melding of church and state. Disarmament of the Church led to a reenchantment of secular rulers such as they had not enjoyed since ancient times. "Luther", wrote Joseph Costanzo, "restored to the state the sacred rights of the ancient pagan cities."[87] Luther said, "The hand that wields the secular sword is not a human hand but the hand of God. It is God, not man, Who hangs, and brakes on the wheel, and decapitates, and flogs; it is God who wages war."[88]

Sovereignty is no longer vested in the people who, through their consent, transfer it to the prince; it is the prince's directly from God, unmediated by man's consent. The ruler is not inhibited by the notion

---

[84] Martin Luther, *Christian in Society*, vol. 3, *LW*, 46:39, cited in Thomas Pearson, "Luther on Natural Law".

[85] Pearson, "Luther on Natural Law".

[86] Rommen, *The State in Catholic Thought*, 108.

[87] Joseph F. Costanzo, S.J., *Political and Legal Studies* (West Hanover, Mass.: Christopher Publishing House, 1982), 120.

[88] Cited in Durant, *The Reformation*, 448.

of a social compact with his people, and their obedience is not conditional on his fulfilling any obligations toward them. Therefore, the people do not possess a right to rebellion even against tyrants. This is completely consistent with the voluntarist view, as it was inconsistent with the entire medieval tradition. The two swords were now held by one hand, but the wielding was no longer constrained by natural law. Figgis noted:

> So long as this belief [in natural law] is held, however inadequate may be the conception as a view of the facts of life, it affords some criterion for submitting the acts of statesmen to the rule of justice, and some check on the rule of pure expediency in internal and of force in external politics. The more law comes to be thought of as merely positive, the command of a lawgiver, the more difficult is it to put any restraints upon the action of the legislator, and in cases of monarchical government to avoid tyranny.... When, however, natural law and its outcome in custom are discarded, it is clear that the ruler must be consciously sovereign in a way he has not been before.[89]

Since the distinction between church and state was the very thing out of which medieval constitutionalism grew, it is not surprising that its diminution foreclosed any further constitutional development or even the maintenance of what had already been achieved (except in England, where common law, rather than Roman law, pertained). Even if this was not the intention of the Reformers, it was the result. French Calvinist historian François Guizot acknowledged that the Reformation "fortified rather than weakened the power of princes. It was more against the free institutions of the Middle Ages than favorable to their development."[90] Lord Acton observed, "The progress of the Constitution, which it was the work of Catholic Ages to build up, was interrupted by the attractions which the growth of absolutism excited and by the Reformation's transferring the ecclesiastical power to the crown."[91]

---

[89] Figgis, *Gerson to Grotius*, 85.

[90] François Guizot, *The History of Civilization in Europe*, trans. William Hazlitt, ed. Larry Siedentop (Indianapolis: Liberty Fund, 2013), 238.

[91] John Emerich Edward Dalberg Acton, *The History of Freedom and Other Essays* (London: Macmillan, 1907), 208.

Legal Positivism—Law as Will

The consequences for the very idea of law were profound. In the absence of canon law, there remained the principle of Roman law, happily embraced by royal authority: *Quod principi placuit, legis vigorem habuit* (What has pleased the prince has the force of law). It is law because it proceeds from the will of the prince, who is responsible to God alone. If God is a positivist, so too is the ruler in his name. Harold Berman summarized:

> The Lutheran reformers ... were skeptical of man's power to create a human law which would reflect the eternal law, and they explicitly denied that it was the task of the church to develop human law. This Lutheran skepticism made possible the emergence of a theory of law—legal positivism—which treats the law of the state as morally neutral, a means and not an end, a device for manifesting the policy of the sovereign and for securing obedience to it.[92]

Divorced from natural and eternal law, legal positivism is anchored in will. Once the state reabsorbs religion and no longer has a moral reference point outside of itself, it becomes pure power. We are getting closer to Machiavelli.

One can imagine that Luther would have been disturbed by the extent to which his teachings strengthened the state. He emphatically believed there were limits beyond which the temporal ruler should not go, for if "given too wide a scope, intolerable and terrible injury follows." Nonetheless, he held that, inasmuch as the invisible church "exists in the visible world, [it] must be the subject of the power of the state".[93] Luther's "two kingdoms" doctrine, set forth in *Temporal Authority: To What Extent It Should Be Obeyed* (1523) and *Whether Soldiers, Too, Can Be Saved* (1526), was formulated to restrict secular power. Luther wrote, "Where the temporal authority presumes to prescribe laws for the soul, it encroaches upon God's government and

---

[92] Harold Berman, *Law and Revolution: The Formation of the Western Legal Tradition* (Cambridge, Mass.: Harvard University Press, 1983), 29.

[93] Cited in J. A. Fernández-Santamaría, *Natural Law, Constitutionalism, Reason of State, and War: Counter-Reformation Spanish Political Thought*, vol. 1 (New York: Peter Lang, 2005), 68.

only misleads souls and destroys them."[94] Thus, civil authority, while a directly divine institution, has limits in theory that Luther spelled out. But the two-kingdoms teaching was not an effective substitution for the two-swords teaching. It existed only as an idea. Luther created no institutional structure to replace the one he had destroyed. And thus, as George Sabine pointed out, "The disruption of the universal church, the suppression of its monastic institutions and ecclesiastical corporations, and the abrogation of the Canon Law, removed the strongest checks upon secular power that had existed in the Middle Ages."[95] The great German biographer of Luther, Heinrich Boehmer, wrote: "The result of these innovations was also a great secularization, principally in favor of the temporal power. The latter, at last, gained full freedom of movement throughout the wide field of secular life; indeed, it soon succeeded in obtaining the direction of all purely spiritual matter, too.... Government, as the holder of the paternal power, claimed authority over *all* departments of social life."[96] It is not hard to see the great attraction of this teaching to German princes. Raymond G. Gettell stated: "By applying these doctrines in practical politics, the Reformation substituted once for all in men's minds the authority of the state for the authority of the Church.... To Luther, the state was essentially holy. Accordingly, he paved the way for the exalted theory of the state held later by Hegel and by recent German theorists."[97]

As holy, the state could not be resisted under any circumstances and is owed at least passive obedience, if not complete submission. In *Medieval Political Theory in the West*, R.W. and A.J. Carlyle remarked, "As far as we have been able to discover, the first writer of

---

[94] Martin Luther, *Temporal Authority: To What Extent It Should Be Obeyed* (1523), in *Selected Writings of Martin Luther*, vol. 2 (1520–1523), ed. Theodore G. Tappert, trans. J.J. Schindel (Minneapolis: Fortress Press, 2007), 295.

[95] George H. Sabine, *A History of Political Theory* (New York: Holt, Rineheart, and Winston, 1961), 362.

[96] Erik von Kuehnelt-Leddihn, *Liberty or Equality: The Challenge of Our Time* (Caldwell, Idaho: Caxton Printers, 1952), 240 (emphasis in the original).

[97] Cited in Schall, "Luther and Political Philosophy", 28. Eric Voegelin went so far as to say that there is "an intelligible line of meaning running from Luther's destruction of ecclesiastical authority ... to the destruction of 'all the gods,' that is of all authoritative order, in Marx." Eric Voegelin, *From Enlightenment to Revolution* (Durham, N.C.: Duke University Press, 1975), 283; see also Eric Voegelin, *History of Political Ideas: Renaissance and Reformation* (Columbia: University of Missouri Press, 1998), 256.

the sixteenth century of whom we can say that he, at one time, held and affirmed the conception that the temporal ruler was in such a sense representative of God that under no circumstances could he be resisted, was Luther."[98] Violence against the ruler was forbidden. If one presupposes that man is fundamentally evil—incapable of keeping his own internal order—it becomes all the more important that the state be strong enough to impose external order. Luther declared, "The princes of this world are gods, the common people are Satan, through whom God sometimes does what at other times he does directly through Satan, that is, makes rebellion as a punishment for the people's sins. I would rather suffer a prince doing wrong than a people doing right."[99] Luther said that, if ordered to do something explicitly against the will of God, the people may resist, but even then only passively. "If wrong is to be suffered", he declared, "it is better to suffer it from the rulers than that the rulers suffer it from their subjects. For the mob has no moderation, and knows none, and in every individual there stick more than five tyrants. Now, it is better to suffer wrong from one tyrant, that is, from the ruler, then from unnumbered tyrants, that is, the mob."[100] As quoted earlier, Luther thought that "the world would be reduced to chaos" without a ruler invested with unquestionable authority.[101] Therefore, contrary to Thomas Aquinas and the entire medieval tradition, Luther wrote that rebellion is never justified: "It is in no wise proper for anyone who would be a Christian to set himself up against his government, whether it act justly or unjustly. There are no better works than to obey and serve all those who are set over us as superiors. For this reason also disobedience is a greater sin than murder, unchastity, theft, and dishonesty, and all that these may include."[102] One should note that Luther modified his position sometime after 1530. (One may presume that, within Luther's perspective, none of the grievances

---

[98] R. W. Carlyle and A. J. Carlyle, *A History of Medieval Political Theory in the West* (London: William Blackwood and Sons, 1950), 272.

[99] Cited in Sabine, *A History of Political Theory*, 361.

[100] Martin Luther, *Whether Soldiers, Too, Can Be Saved*, cited in Strauss and Cropsey, *History of Political Philosophy*, 337.

[101] Gillespie, *The Theological Origins of Modernity*, 122.

[102] Sabine, *A History of Political Theory*, 361.

listed in the Declaration of Independence would have served as sufficient justification for the American Revolution.)[103]

Cambridge scholar G. R. Elton remarked that in general

> all the leading reformers preached non-resistance because kings were kings by right divine, responsible to God and punishable by Him alone, and because resistance meant the dissolution of God's decree for the fallen creation. Just because they saw the kingdoms of this

---

[103] Since the American colonies were almost completely Protestant, one might reasonably ask how it was that the people arrived upon a natural law foundation for the American republic. One possible answer concerns the kinds of changes that had taken place in Calvinism as contrasted to Lutheranism by the late eighteenth century. First, Lutheranism was not a major presence in colonial America. In the 1770s, the estimated percentage of Lutherans was no more than 1.5 percent. (Lyman Stone, "A Very Brief History of American Lutheranism", *In a State of Migration* [blog], March 7, 2018, https://medium.com/migration-issues/a-very -brief-history-of-american-lutheranism-be8b7a26fd59.) Calvinists were far more numerous and influential, particularly as they dominated New England. In *The State in Catholic Thought*, p. 109, Heinrich Rommen offered an intriguing reflection as to why natural law became more compatible with Calvinism than with Lutheranism:

> Luther surrendered the Church rule and morality to the worldly government for which he had little room in his theology.... But Calvin, on the basis of his characteristic unification of *lex naturae* (state) and *lex spiritualis* (ecclesiastical community), erected his theocratic republic.... In the beginning the Old Testament as a statute book of divine law served as the moral code. Later when, through the influence of the milder personal religion of tolerant revivalism and through humanistic Bible criticism, Calvinism lost this austerity, the idea of natural law automatically came into the foreground and made possible a political philosophy and ethics on its basis. On the other hand, once Lutheran theology lost the biblical basis and became liberal theology, it offered no basis for natural law and so its political philosophy became positivist and relativist.

On the other hand, there is the view that, in later Lutheranism, "the tension between reason and revelation, prominent in Luther, was replaced by the insistence on the harmony of the two, with revelation representing the ultimate truth.... Lutheran philosophers and theologians, such as Christian Wolff (1679–1754) and Johann Salomo Semler (1725–1791), defended the notion of the harmony of reason and revelation. In contrast to medieval scholasticism, which advocated the use of reason but emphasized the primacy of revelation, Lutheran theology subordinated revelation and declared reason to be the key to understanding the will of God. This sentiment, known as Neology, dominated Lutheranism in the second half of the 18th century." *Encylopaedia Britannica*, s.v. "Lutheranism", by Hans J. Hillerbrand, accessed June 15, 2019, http://www.britannica.com/EBchecked/topic/352073/Lutheranism.

One must also not discount the contributions of Lutherans such as Peter Muhlenberg (1746–1807), a "fighting parson" during the Revolutionary War who—despite the opposition of his father, Rev. Henry Melchior Muhlenberg—abandoned his ministry to fight in the war and rose to the level of major general. He later served in Congress.

world in so much worse a light, by comparison with the kingdom of God, than had the theorists of the later middle ages, they would not consider the questions of political liberty or limitations upon the powers of the magistrate.... Naturally this suited princes.[104]

Indeed, it did. Christopher Dawson noted that "the establishment of the Lutheran territorial Church under the supervision and control of the prince involved a thoroughgoing reconstruction of society, to the benefit of the prince, who thus acquired a patriarchal religious authority that was almost absolute."[105] The German princes quickly realized the immediate advantages of Luther's teachings: Luther provided the perfect rationalization for seizing Church property. At his urging, Albert of Brandenburg, the Grand Master of the Teutonic Knights in Prussia, "secularized the property of his Order and made himself hereditary Duke of Prussia, thus creating the first Protestant State".[106]

Once churches became "national", Catholic princes did not behave much differently from Protestant ones in respect to their recovered supremacy. After all, as we saw in chapter 2, this is what they exercised before Gregory VII's reforms in the eleventh century. They were only too pleased to wrest it back from a weakened papacy. Francis I reclaimed from Pope Leo X the right to name the bishops, abbots, and abbesses of France.[107] It should be noted that there were also Catholic proponents of absolutism, found particularly in the writings of Frenchman Jean Bodin (1530–1596), who believed that "the sovereign Prince is accountable only to God."

In Protestant countries, as mentioned, the claim of Divine Right also included supreme spiritual power as head of the national church (*summus episcopus*). Reflecting upon this period, Joseph Cardinal Ratzinger said, "What came to pass in the political sphere was quite the contrary of liberation: with the creation of territorial and national churches the power of the secular authority was augmented and consolidated."[108] Heinrich Rommen ironically noted, "All that the pope

[104] Cited in Figgis, *The Divine Right of Kings*, xxiii.

[105] Dawson, *The Dividing of Christendom*, 82.

[106] Ibid., 76.

[107] Rodney Stark, *How the West Won: The Neglected Story of the Triumph of Modernity* (Wilmington, Del.: ISI Books, 2014), 273.

[108] Joseph Cardinal Ratzinger, "Truth and Freedom," *Communio* 23 (Spring 1996): 20.

claimed for the liberty of the Church is now claimed by the absolute king."[109] No doubt, this is what John Neville Figgis had in mind when he said, "Had there been no Luther there could never have been a Louis XIV."[110] This is not to suggest that Luther intended such an outcome—his concerns were primarily theological, not political—but then William of Ockham did not intend Luther either. In both cases, the results flowed from premises taken from one area and applied to another.

Ockham and Luther were not aiming at absolutism; if anything, they were trying to counter what they saw as absolutism in the Church. They did not seem to consider that their undermining of the Church's authority and the abandonment of natural law would ultimately clear the path to political absolutism. With the segregation of religious faith and the obliteration of natural law, the public arena was open not only to Luther's Christian prince but to Machiavelli's amoral one. As faith diminished under the pressures of secularism, it became more Machiavelli's prince than Luther's who prevailed in the public arena.

Charles McCoy observed that, after the Peace of Augsburg (1555) adopted the principle *cuius regio, eius religio* (the religion of the prince determines the religion of the people), "Catholic and Protestant princes alike effected a 'union' of Church and State, of religion and politics precisely as Machiavelli had recommended: Christianity was made a tool in the hands of the political masters."[111] As horrified as Luther would have been by the amoral political principles of Machiavelli, he inadvertently abetted their application. German theologian Ernst Troeltsch pointed out that in Luther's disapproval of revolution and his "glorification" of authority, "there were certain resemblances to the doctrine of Machiavelli."[112] He stated that "by delivering the state from the guidance of the Church as a divinely established society, its effect was such that the principles which Machiavelli ... developed in opposition to the Christian consciousness ... became

---

[109] Rommen, *The State in Catholic Thought*, 560.

[110] Figgis, *Gerson to Grotius*, 62.

[111] Charles Nicholas Reiten McCoy, *On the Intelligibility of Political Philosophy: Essays of Charles N. R. McCoy*, eds. James V. Schall and John J. Schrems (Washington, D.C.: Catholic University of America Press, 1989), 181–82.

[112] Ernest Troeltsch, *The Social Teachings of the Christian Churches*, vol. 2 (Louisville, Ky.: Westminster John Knox Press, 1992), 532.

capable of combining with [that consciousness] and being strengthened by it."[113]

With Machiavelli, there is no nature as a moral standard by which
to guide and judge the life of the polis by what is right and wrong.
This much came from Ockham and Luther. An antiteleological
metaphysics of voluntarism was the perfect support for a Machia-
vellian politics based on the will of the ruler. Just as rationality is
based on irrationality (in voluntarism), so too is morality based on
immorality. Machiavelli, who dispensed with faith altogether, secularized the voluntarist God into the prince whose will and power
now constitute what is just. As he said, "Where there are good arms
there must be good laws." Machiavelli seems to have worked out
in the secular sphere what Luther worked out in the theological
sphere. I do not mean to suggest there was any cross-pollination
between them, even though they were contemporaries for more than
four decades, but they were subject to the same influences and shared
the same view that men, as Machiavelli said, "are, by nature, more
prone to evil than to good".[114] As Luther inadvertently opened the
door to the politicization of religion, Machiavelli walked through
that door, totally subordinating religion to the utility of the state.
Ockham and Luther helped put religion in the power of the state,
and Machiavelli taught the state how to use it.

So long as the will of the ruler was constrained by firm Christian
belief, there were limits to it. When that belief was weakened or removed altogether, however, the exercise of will became unlimited—
as was graphically illustrated in twentieth-century totalitarianism.
Luther did not foresee the consequences of his teaching of *sola fide*
in a world *sine fide*. He could only envisage Christian princes. As the
tide of faith receded, however, the positivistic legal order became
accepted as the *only* "moral" order, whatever it might be. In the absence of both faith and reason, man lost his bearings. This disorientation ineluctably led to Hobbes' *Leviathan* or to the absolutism of the
Divine Right of Kings.

---

[113] Ernst Troeltsch, *Protestantism and Progress: A Historical Study of the Relation of Protestantism to the Modern World* (Boston: Beacon Press, 1958), 107–8.

[114] Niccolò Machiavelli, *Discourses on Livy* 1, 9, Literature Network, http://www.online-literature.com/machiavelli/titus-livius/9/.

In the way of epitaph, Eric Voegelin wrote, "Concretely, in the wake of the Reformation, the taboo had to fall on classic philosophy and scholastic theology; and, since under these two heads came the major and certainly decisive part of Western intellectual culture, this culture was ruined to the extent to which the taboo became effective. In fact, the destruction went so deep that Western society has never completely recovered from the blow."[115] But there was a recovery, without which there would never have been an American Founding. It began in England, as the next chapter tells, with Richard Hooker as a reaction against the irrationality of extreme Puritanism—with a reassertion of the natural law grounds of a rationally ordered creation in a God of reason. This recovery would lay the basis for the opposition to political absolutism.

---

[115] Eric Voegelin, *The New Science of Politics* (Chicago: University of Chicago Press, 1952), 140–41.

5

Richard Hooker: Restoring Natural Law

After the damage of the Reformation, Anglican prelate Richard Hooker's great achievement was to restore the integrity of reason through the recovery of the classical and Christian natural law traditions. He reinstated key constitutional principles from the Middle Ages that had been undermined by the Reformation. As mentioned in the previous chapter, Luther had abandoned the ideas of popular sovereignty, social contract, and the requirement of consent, as they were inconsistent with his voluntarist view of God. To reestablish these, Hooker (1554–1600) first had to reaffirm a God in whom intellect preceded will in the notion of the Divine Logos. Then he could reconnect with medieval natural law and the doctrine of free will. Against the nominalists, Hooker returned to the essences of things, or rather returned to things their essences. By doing so, he restored to, or at least shored up in, Anglican Protestantism the one solid platform from which the secular absolutism of Hobbes and the Divine Right absolutism of James I (and his apologist Sir Robert Filmer), both of which came shortly after him, could be combated.

Hooker was up against the extremes of sixteenth-century English Puritanism. Its excesses would engender strong reactions. As we shall see, Thomas Hobbes (1588–1679) would seek to replace Puritan sacred absolutism with secular absolutism. On the other hand, Richard Hooker endeavored to save the Reformation from itself by restoring essential aspects of pre-Reformation thought. Through his recovery of the realist metaphysics of Aquinas and Aristotle, he concomitantly restored the basis of medieval constitutionalism for a new era. It was his response that formed the foundation for a counterattack against absolutism—in both its sacred and secular iterations—that ultimately reached practical fruition in the American Founding.

The Protestant denigration of reason and the emphasis on *sola scriptura* reached their most radical forms in the theocracy advocated by Puritans. By itself, they claimed, Scripture is a sufficient guide to everything. No outside guidance is required or welcome. Biblical laws would entirely replace the laws of England. In *The First Admonition to Parliament* (1572), the Puritans boldly instructed that "nothing be done in this or any other thing, but that which you have the express warrant of God's Word for."[1] Their own rule was proposed as the "sovereign remedy of all evils". They cloaked their assertion of will in the Word of God, to which they claimed exclusive access stemming from their "nearness to the Spirit". Hooker spoke of their "persuading of men credulous and over-capable of such pleasing errors, that it is the special illumination of the Holy Ghost, whereby they discern those things in the word, which others reading yet discern them not".[2] Those who were moved by the Spirit would rule according to their own lights. All others were in darkness. Reason, after all, was corrupt. Nothing of natural law remained as a brake against Puritanism's extravagant claims.

It was against this deracinated form of Christianity that Hooker arose. In the face of the Puritan onslaught, he sought to restore the integrity of reason and the authority of natural law by reaching back to Aquinas and Aristotle, whom he called "the Arch-Philosopher" and "the mirror of humaine wisdom". Regarding the Puritan condemnation of the "laws of this land", Hooker retorted that these laws were such "as no law of God nor reason of man hath hitherto been alleged of force sufficient to prove they do ill".[3] In fact, he insisted, "Those Laws are investigable by Reason, without the help of Revelation supernatural and divine."[4] Whereas his Puritan opponents were, like Ockham and Luther, voluntarists and nominalists, Hooker was a rationalist and a realist, a man of the *via antiqua*. To refute the Puritans, Hooker penned his magisterial work, *Of the Laws of Ecclesiastical*

---

[1] Cited in Leo Strauss and Joseph Cropsey, eds., *History of Political Philosophy*, 3rd ed. (Chicago: University of Chicago Press, 1987), 356.

[2] Richard Hooker, *Of the Laws of Ecclesiastical Polity*, in *The Works of That Learned and Judicious Divine Mr. Richard Hooker with an Account of His Life and Death by Isaac Walton*, arranged by the Rev. John Keble, M.A., 3 vols., 7th rev. ed. (Oxford: Clarendon Press, 1888), 1:105.

[3] Ibid., 1:127.

[4] Ibid., 1:233.

Polity (1594), one of the great works of the late Elizabethan era. In its opening, he stated that he wrote in order "that posterity may know we have not loosely through silence permitted things to pass away as in a dream".[5]

The vituperative attacks against Hooker disclosed the radical fideist nature of the Puritan opposition. Addressed to Hooker, the *Christian Letter of 1599* said:

> Yet in all your discourse, for the most parte, Aristotle the patriarch of Philosophers (with divers other human writers) and the ingenuous schoolemen, almost in all pointes have some finger; Reason is highlie sett up against holie scripture, and reading against preaching; the church of Rome favourablie admitted to bee of the house of God.... Shall wee doe you wronge to suspect ... that you esteeme ... the bookes of holy scripture to bee at the least of no greater moment then Aristotle and the Schoolemen: Or else doe you meane to bring in a confusion of all thinges, to reconcile heaven and earth, and to make all religions equall: Will you bring us to Atheisme, or to Poperie?[6]

The anonymous writer informed Hooker that his attempt to restore natural law was superfluous because "the unsufficiencie of the light of nature is by the light of scripture so fully and so perfectly herein supplied, that further light than this hath added there doth not neede unto that ende."[7] Later, Presbyterian radical Francis Cheynell proclaimed a similar sentiment to the Long Parliament in a 1645 sermon: "Now grant me but these two Principles; That there is a God, and, That scripture is the Word of God, and my work is at an end."[8]

The *Christian Letter* accused Hooker of promoting "Romishe doctrine" and "the darkenesse of schoole learning", hardly a harmless denunciation at the time. He was guilty as accused. He insisted on the grand synthesis of faith and reason accomplished by Aquinas. At the beginning of the *Summa theologica*, Aquinas had asked, "Whether,

---

[5] Ibid., 1:125.

[6] Cited in W.J. Torrance Kirby, "Richard Hooker's Discourse on Natural Law in the Context of the Magisterial Reformation", *Animus* 3 (1998): 34n24, http://www2.swgc.mun .ca/animus/Articles/Volume%203/kirby3.pdf.

[7] Ibid.

[8] Francis Cheynell, "A Sermon Preached to the Right Honourable the House of Lords, At the Monethly-Fast, March 26. 1645", Early English Books Online, https://quod.lib.umich .edu/e/eebo/A79474.0001.001/1:3?rgn=div1;view=fulltext.

Besides Philosophy, Any Further Doctrine Is Required?"[9] The Reformation posed the opposite question: whether, besides Scripture, any further doctrine is required. To those who claimed the perfect sufficiency of *sola scriptura*, Hooker answered that wisdom's

> maner of teaching is not meerely one and the same. Some things she openeth by the sacred bookes of Scripture; some things by the glorious works of nature: with some things she inspireth them from above by spirituall influence, in some thinges she leadeth and trayneth them onely by worldly experience and practise. We may not so in any one speciall kind admire her that we disgrace her in any other, but let all her wayes be according unto their place and degree adored.[10]

In other words, faith and reason stand separately but together.

According to Hooker, the Puritans had "disgraced" the place of reason. As we have seen, direct divine revelation was their sole source of authority. Hooker explained the peril of this teaching: "By fashioning the very notions and conceits of men's minds in such sort, that when they read the Scripture, they may think that everything soundeth towards the advancement of that [Puritan] discipline, and to the utter disgrace of the contrary."[11] Free of the fetters of reason, the Puritan program quite literally had no reasonable limits. Hooker acerbically pointed out that as "the absolute command of Almighty God, it must be received although the world by receiving it should be clean turned upside down; herein lieth the greatest danger of all."[12] In other words, one could not legitimately ask whether the avowed divine inspiration claimed by the Puritans was *reasonable*. Indeed, said Hooker, "Let any man of contrary opinion open his mouth to persuade them, they close up their ears, his reasons they weight not, all is answered with rehearsal of the words of John: 'we are of God; he that knoweth God heareth us': as for the rest ye are of the world: for this world's pomp and vanity it is that ye speak, and the world, whose ye are, heareth you."[13] Their understanding of Scripture was supposed to end the discussion. In fact, there was no discussion—only a

---

[9] Thomas Aquinas, *Summa theologica* I, qq. 1–27.
[10] Hooker, *Laws*, in *Works of Hooker*, 1:290.
[11] Ibid., 1:147.
[12] Ibid., 1:182.
[13] Ibid., 1:153.

pronouncement. One need not *reason* concerning things since reason has no standing, and God has spoken.

Philosopher Eric Voegelin characterized the Puritan ideology as an effort "to destroy the universe of rational discourse as well as the social function of persuasion".[14] To tackle this danger, Hooker reiterated the Thomist understanding of the complementary relationship between faith and reason in which one is incomplete without the other: "It sufficeth therefore that Nature and Scripture do serve in such full sort, that they both jointly and not severally either of them be so complete, that unto everlasting felicity we need not the knowledge of anything more than these two, may easily furnish our minds on all sides."[15] Again, he stated: "There are but two ways whereby the spirit leadeth men into all truth: one extraordinary, the other common; one belonging but unto some few, the other extending itself unto all that are of God; the one that which we call by a special divine excellency Revelation, the other Reason."[16]

Recovery of Reason

Reason is indispensable, Hooker said, because all creation is rooted in Reason, or Logos, which is the cause of and the order of all things. Reaching back to Anaxagoras, he spoke of reason's discernment of Divine Logos as the ultimate cause of the rational order of things:

> The wise and learned among the very heathens themselves have all acknowledged some First Cause, whereupon originally the being of all things dependeth. Neither have they otherwise spoken of that cause than as an Agent, which knowing *what* and *why* it worketh, observeth in working a most exact *order* or *law*.... All confess therefore in the working of that first cause, that Counsel is used, Reason followed, a Way observed; that is to say, constant Order and Law is kept; whereof itself must needs be author unto itself.[17]

[14] Eric Voegelin, *The New Science of Politics* (Chicago: University of Chicago Press, 1952), 138.
[15] Hooker, *Laws*, in *Works of Hooker*, 1:271.
[16] Ibid., 1:150.
[17] Ibid., 1:201–2.

In further evidence of which Hooker added, "Thus much [was] confest by Anaxagoras and Plato, terming the maker of the world an *intellectual* Worker."[18]

Reason is also imperative, Hooker said, because "there is as yet no way known how to determine of things disputed without the use of natural reason."[19] Reason has separate standing and an essential role in discerning right from wrong.

> The rule to discern when the actions of men are good, when they are such as they ought to be, is more ample and large than the law which God hath set particular down in his holy word; the Scripture is but a part of that rule, as hath been heretofore at large declared. If therefore all things be of God which are well done, and if all things be well done which are according to the rule of well-doing, and if the rule of well-doing be more ample than the Scripture: what necessity is there, that every thing which is of God should be set down in holy Scripture?[20]

There was no necessity whatsoever, Hooker averred, since God has given man the power to know and recognize moral truth through his use of reason. Reason is man's participation in the Divine Logos. To deny this, according to Hooker, is a gross distortion of what a human person is. Such a denial bifurcates man. It invites metaphysical schizophrenia. Thus, it is by the "light of Reason, whereby good may be known from evil, and which discovering the same rightly is termed right".[21] Since the Puritan nominalists vigorously rejected this teaching, as had Luther, Hooker had repeatedly to insist upon the power of reason to apprehend right and wrong: "Wherefore the natural measure whereby to judge your doings, is the sentence of Reason determining and setting down what is good to be done."[22] God imparts to us the fundamental laws of reason, "not revealing by any extraordinary means unto them, but they by natural discourse attaining the knowledge thereof". Such "natural discourse" occurs

---

[18] Ibid. (emphasis in the original).
[19] Ibid., 1:379.
[20] Ibid., 3:212–13.
[21] Ibid., 1:222.
[22] Ibid., 1:232.

first and foremost within the family, for "education and instruction are the means, the one by use, the other by precept, to make our natural faculty of reason both the better and the sooner able to judge rightly between truth and error, [and between] good and evil."[23] Hooker was at such pains to demonstrate the rational apprehension of moral law because of his adherence to the doctrine of free will, as against Puritan predestination. Unless man can apprehend the difference between good and evil, free will makes little sense.

For Hooker, as for Aquinas, will apart from reason will not do. In his work, Hooker annulled the Reformation's divorce of the two. Reason and revelation were once again conjoined. Lee W. Gibbs writes that Hooker "closed the breach opened by the magisterial Reformation and maintained by the disciplinarians between reason and revelation, nature and grace".[24] Nature and grace are back in partnership, the latter perfecting the former, as Aquinas held. Gibbs zeroes in on the crux of the controversy: "Hooker stands predominantly within the medieval rationalist and realist tradition represented by Aquinas, while the magisterial Protestant Reformers and their disciplinarian progeny stand squarely in the camp of the medieval voluntarists and nominalists."[25] That is exactly right: for Hooker, the essence of law is reason; for the Reformers, and especially the Puritans, it is command or will. One view can lead to constitutionalism; the other cannot. It is no exaggeration to say that, had he not "closed the breach" between reason and revelation, there either would have been no American Founding, or its character would have been fundamentally different.

Since reason is available to all men, said Hooker, it is the only shared basis on which truth can be reached, even by those not possessed of revelation. Likewise, it is because reason is held in "common" that a rational politics becomes possible in a *common*wealth—a political community based on the recognition of the reason possessed by all men. Otherwise, force becomes the only instrument left for ordering things according to pure will and power, divine or human.

[23] Ibid., 1:219.
[24] Cited in Kirby, "Richard Hooker's Discourse", 31.
[25] Ibid.

This is precisely the problem Puritanism presented in its advocacy of theocracy and why Hooker so adamantly opposed it.

Though perhaps somewhat obscured for the modern reader by the archaic language of Elizabethan erudition, here is what these extremely vital and important passages accomplish: they fully restore divine intellect to its primacy over will—as against the preceding primacy of will over intellect in the work of the voluntarists and nominalists. It is no exaggeration to say that, as a consequence, the whole order of creation is reinstated upon its proper foundations. In turn, this has political ramifications. It means that man's laws *must* be a reflection of this order. Since in his essence God is Logos, one must have *reasons* for law because law *is* Reason at the very source of creation. Therefore, the constitutive element of law is not will, but reason. Reason is obligatory in man's behavior and in his laws because it exists in nature's order and as the law of God's essence. In other words, there is nothing arbitrary about it. Hooker wrote that "they err therefore who think that the will of God to do this or that, there's no reason besides his will."[26] God's purpose in man's case, said Hooker in a statement that could have come right out of Aristotle's *Nicomachean Ethics* (bk. 10), is that "proceeding in the knowledge of truth and by growing in the exercise of virtue, man amongst the creatures of this inferior world aspireth to the greatest conformity with God."[27] Hooker made clear that "God worketh nothing without cause. All those things which are done by him, have some end for which they are done."[28] God is a teleologist. This is exactly opposite to the Puritan voluntarist understanding of God.

Hooker's grand conception of the order of creation was congruent with constitutional government. He restored what the early Reformation had lost in terms of popular sovereignty, the requirement of consent, and representation. Hooker also related the order of creation to the types of law and their status. Like Aquinas before him, he went down the great chain of being to establish the source and hierarchical order of law: from God's eternal law in his plan of the

---

[26] Hooker, *Laws*, in *Works of Hooker*, 1:203.
[27] Ibid., 1:216.
[28] Ibid., 1:202.

universe, the celestial law of the angels, the natural law for all of the created world, the law of reason governing man, the divine law of revelation, and human law made by men from natural and divine law. For Hooker, natural law is the "Law of Reason": "The general and perpetual voice of men is as the sentence of God Himself. For that which all men have at all times learned Nature herself must needs have taught; and God being the author of Nature, her voice is but His instrument."[29] In turn, "law is man's reason on paper."

Having reinstated the role of reason and natural law, Hooker sought their application to political order. Given the role of natural law in his thinking, his rejection of predestination and his insistence on man's free will, it is no surprise that he should have gone about reestablishing the contours of medieval constitutional thought, most especially regarding its requirements for political legitimacy. Hooker began with the core principle of equality, and on it he developed the requirement of consent. One of the most important laws, love of neighbor, follows from "we all being of one and the same nature" and the "relation of equality between ourselves and them that are as ourselves".[30] Contrary to what Thomas Hobbes would later teach about a lawless state of nature, Hooker insisted that even before men had consented to any human laws, they were nonetheless governed by laws of nature. He wrote, "We see then how Nature itself teacheth Laws and statutes to live by. The Laws, which have been hitherto mentioned, do bind men absolutely, even as they are men, although they have never any settled fellowship, never any solemn agreement amongst themselves what to do, or not to do."[31]

---

[29] Ibid., 1:227. "The law of reason, that which bindeth creatures reasonable in this world, and with which by reason they may most plainly perceive themselves bound; that which bindeth them, and is not known but by special revelation from God, Divine law; human law, that which out of the law either of reason or of God men probably gathering to be expedient, they make it a law. All things therefore, which are as they ought to be, are conformed unto this second law eternal; and even those things which to this eternal law are not conformable, are notwithstanding in some sort ordered by the first eternal law. For what good or evil is there under the sun, what action correspondent or repugnant unto the law which God hath imposed upon his creatures, but in or upon it God doth work according to the law which himself hath eternally purposed to keep; that is to say, the first law eternal? So that a twofold law eternal being thus made, it is not hard to conceive how they both take place in all things." Ibid., 1:205.

[30] Ibid., 1:231.

[31] Ibid., 1:239.

The Requirement of Consent

Following Aristotle, Hooker said that men have a natural sociability:

> We are naturally induced to seek communion and fellowship with others. This was the cause of men's uniting themselves at first in politik Societies, which Societies could not be without government, nor government without a distinct kind of Law from that which hath been already declared. Two foundations there are which bear up public Societies; the one, a natural inclination, whereby all men desire sociable life and fellowship; the other, an order expressly or secretly agreed upon touching the manner of their union in living together. The latter is that which we call the Law of a Commonweal.[32]

As civil society is natural to man, civil government is naturally concomitant to it, because in order "to take away all such mutual grievances, injuries and wrongs there was no way, but only by growing unto composition and agreement amongst themselves by ordaining some kind of government public and by yielding themselves subject thereunto."[33]

The *form* of the civil government could be of several kinds. Which kind is decided by the consent of those in the civil society who give rise to it and who will be ruled by it. "Without which consent", Hooker said, "there were no reason that one man should take upon him to be lord or judge over another."[34] Explaining the transition from "those times wherein there were no civil societies", Hooker spoke of a voluntary compact at the foundation of government, an idea that was to have a profound impact on John Locke and others. He said, "All public regiment of what kind soever seemeth evidently to have risen from deliberate advice, consultation, and composition between men, judging it convenient and behoveful, there being no impossibility in nature considered by itself but that men might have lived without any public regiment."[35] One can see that it is a short step from Hooker to the principles of the Declaration of Independence. This is not unlike the philosophy and natural theology implicit in the Declaration.

---

[32] Ibid.
[33] Ibid., 1:241–42.
[34] Ibid.
[35] Ibid., 1:243.

Hooker also reasserted the notion of popular sovereignty, which has, as a necessary corollary, the requirement of consent:

> The lawful power of making laws to command whole politick societies of men, belongeth so properly unto the same entire societies, that for any prince or potentate of what kind soever upon earth, to exercise the same of himself, and not either by express commission immediately and personally received from God, or else by authority derived, at the first, from their consent, upon whose persons they impose laws, it is no better than mere tyranny. Laws they are not, therefore, which publick approbation hath not made so.[36]

In fact, wrote Hooker, such approbation by the people is required at a king's accession: "Every particular person advanced into such [regal] authority hath at his entrance into his reign the same bestowed on him, as an esstate in condition by the voluntary deed of the people, in whom it doth lie to put by any one and to prefer some other before him, better liked or of judged fitter for the place."[37] He said, "Happier that people whose law is their King in the greatest things, than that whose King is himself the law."[38] Hooker's statement that "Laws human, of what kind soever, are available by consent" was later cited by American Founder James Wilson in his *Lectures on Law*. Consent, taught Hooker, can be expressed through representation: "But approbation not only they give who personally declare their assent, by voice, sign, or act, but also when others do it in their names by right originally at the least derived from them. As in parliaments, councils, and the like assemblies, although we be not personally ourselves present, notwithstanding our assent is by reason of others [*sic*] agents there in our behalf."[39]

Hooker's Influence

The brilliance and profundity of Hooker's work evoked almost universal admiration (except from the Puritans). Izaak Walton's 1665

---

[36] Ibid., 1:245–46.
[37] Ibid., 3:347.
[38] Ibid., 3:352.
[39] Ibid., 1:246.

biography of Hooker (hugely popular until the nineteenth century), *The Life of Mr. Richard Hooker*, quotes King James I as saying, "I observe there is in Mr. Hooker no affected language; but a grave, comprehensive, clear manifestation of reason, and that backed with the authority of the Scriptures, the fathers and schoolmen, and with all law both sacred and civil."[40] Despite Hooker's criticisms of what he took to be the errors of Rome, Clement VIII so admired *Of the Laws of Ecclesiastical Polity* (1594) that he exclaimed of this "poor obscure English priest": "There is no learning that this man hath not searched into. This man indeed deserves the name of an author; his books will get reverence by age, for there is in them such seeds of eternity, that if the rest be like this, they shall last until the last fire shall consume all learning."[41]

Hooker is a vitally important figure in the continuity of medieval constitutional theory, which, through him, had a major impact on Algernon Sidney and John Locke, both of whom profoundly influenced the American Revolution. One need only recall from Locke's *Second Treatise of Civil Government* (1690): "This equality of men by nature, the judicious Hooker looks upon as so evident in itself, and beyond all question, that he makes it the foundation of that obligation to mutual love amongst men, on which he builds the duties they owe one another, and from whence he derives the great maxims of justice and charity."[42] Because he relied so much on Hooker's authority, Locke gave extensive quotations from him sixteen times in the *Second Treatise*. These, in turn, had an impact on John Adams, who quoted from them to Massachusetts governor Thomas Hutchinson in 1773:

> We shall sum up our own Sentiments in the Words of that learned Writer Mr. Hooker, in his Ecclesiastical Policy, as quoted by Mr. Locke, "The lawful Power of making Laws to command whole political Societies of Men, belonging so properly to the same intire Societies, that for any Prince or Potentate of what kind soever, to exercise the same of himself, and not from express Commission immediately and personally received from God, is no better *than mere Tyranny*.

[40] Izaak Walton, "Mr. Richard Hooker,", in *Lives of the Poets* (London: J.M. Dent, 1898), 75.

[41] Cited in Russell Kirk, *The Roots of American Order* (Malibu, Cal.: Pepperdine University Press, 1977), 246.

[42] John Locke, *Second Treatise of Government* 2, 5.

Laws therefore they are not which *publick Approbation* hath not made so, for Laws human of what kind soever are available by Consent." "Since Men naturally have no full and perfect Power to command whole politick Multitudes of Men, therefore, utterly without our Consent we could in such Sort be at no Man's Commandment living. And to be commanded we do not consent when that Society whereof we be a Part, hath at any Time before consented."[43]

We can also see Hooker's direct influence on James Wilson, who signed both the Declaration of Independence and the Constitution, played a major role in the Constitutional Convention, and served as one of the first Supreme Court justices. Wilson quoted extensively from Hooker's *Laws* in his own work *Of the General Principles of Law and Obligation*. Wilson referred to "the judicious Hooker", "the sagacious Hooker", and "the sublime language of the most excellent Hooker". Here is one instance of Wilson's referral to Hooker on the key issues of equality, sovereignty, and consent:

If this superiour cannot rest a title on any inherent qualities; the qualities, which constitute his title, if any title he has, must be such as are derivative. If derivative; they must be derived either from a source that is human or from a source that is divine. "Over a whole grand multitude," says the judicious Hooker, "consisting of any families, impossible it is, that any should have complete lawful power, but by consent of men, or by immediate appointment of God."[44]

Of the Laws of Ecclesiastical Polity became the theological spine of the Anglican Church, which directly conveyed Hooker's teachings to its American branches, which dominated in all but the upper Northeastern colonies. At the time of the Revolution, nine of the thirteen colonies had established churches; six of them were Anglican. Some three-quarters of the signers of the Declaration of Independence

---

[43] "Reply of the House to Hutchinson's Second Message", March 2, 1773, in *Papers of John Adams*, vol. 1, *September 1755–October 1773*, ed. Robert J. Taylor (Cambridge, Mass.: Belknap Press, 1997), Massachusetts Historical Society, https://www.masshist.org/publications/apde2/view?id=ADMS-06-01-02-0097-0004 (emphasis in the original).

[44] James Wilson, *Lectures on Law*, in *The Collected Works of James Wilson*, vol. 1 (Indianapolis: Liberty Fund, 2007), 483, Online Library of Liberty, https://oll.libertyfund.org/titles/2072#Wilson_4140_2166.

were, at least nominally, Anglican. The vast majority of delegates to the Virginia Convention of 1776, which produced the state constitution and the Virginia Declaration of Rights, were vestrymen of the Church of England. More broadly, it would be hard to imagine any educated eighteenth-century American who was unacquainted with Hooker's ideas.

Hooker's enormous contribution is seldom dwelt upon for the simple reason of its success. He won the argument (at least temporarily). Of course, by itself Hooker's thought was not sufficient to prevent either Divine Right absolutism or Hobbes' secular version, but it did provide a solid foundation for the forces that would eventually coalesce against both forms of absolutism. It did this by successfully reasserting the traditional transcendent sources of order. Had Hooker not been there to reconnect the golden cord of medieval constitutional theory in his time, his absence would have been duly noted in the future because, as mentioned earlier, there might well have been an American Founding of a far different character, if one at all. That is a measure of his impact and importance.

6

Thomas Hobbes and the Rise
of Secular Absolutism

Before dealing with the absolutism of the Divine Right of Kings in
the next chapter, we will look at the secular absolutism advanced by
Thomas Hobbes (1588–1679). Hobbes is interesting to consider, not
because he is a link to the American Founding, but because he is not.
He is the path not taken by the Founders. They took the Richard
Hooker path, not the Hobbes one. Therefore, it may be helpful to
examine what they rejected. An understanding of Hobbes is also very
important in locating one of the main origins of the corrosive teachings of modernity that have led to the contemporary moral and cultural decay decried by the critics of the Founding, of whom we spoke
in the introduction. No one would claim that the Divine Right of
Kings produced the American Founding, except in the sense that
the Founding so explicitly rejected it, but some do claim that John
Locke, who certainly did influence the Founding, was simply Hobbes
with a smiley face. Therefore, they conclude, the American Founding was Hobbesian. As we shall see, however, his thought could not
have led to the Founding, which was based on the primacy of reason
and man's free will, the very opposite of Hobbes' primacy of the
will and materialistic determinism.

Fr. James Schall traced the path of the primacy of will over intellect as the foundation of absolutism: "The transition from William
of Occam ... to Hobbes marks the end of medieval thinking. The
divine will, presupposed to nothing but itself, presupposed to no
divine reason in Occam ..., becomes the political will in Hobbes,
again a will presupposed to nothing but itself. In a sense, the late

medieval treatises on the divine will and the early modern treatments of the sovereign are the same treatise."[1]

Once divine voluntarism has been theologically posited, there is a very short bridge to cross to arrive at its human version in political absolutism, whether secular or royal. As I have tried to show, the bridge was built, however unwittingly, by Ockham and Luther. The destination, however, was fashioned partly by Machiavelli and the rest by Hobbes, who exalted the will of the sovereign in exactly Schall's terms—as presupposed to nothing but itself and, therefore, absolute and indivisible.

If one wonders at the extreme and unorthodox nature of Hobbes' teachings, one must keep in mind his single-minded purpose: above all, to avoid civil strife, particularly in light of the internecine religious wars of his time. The people of his era were very much conscious of the devastation to both Great Britain and the Continent brought about by the recent civil wars and were anxious not to repeat them. The question was how. Hobbes thought he had the answer: "that miserable condition of war ... is necessarily consequent ... to the natural passions of men when there is no visible power to keep them in awe."[2] Had there been such a power in England, he said, "the People had never been divided and fallen into this Civil War."[3] He was willing to advocate almost anything to achieve the goal of unified civil government. An undivided "visible Power" could provide the blessings of "peace, security, riches, decency, society, elegancy, sciences, and benevolence".[4] His most famous book, *Leviathan* (1651), provides the prescription for creating it. As we shall see, the establishment of this "visible Power" requires the elimination of any competing authorities, including classical natural law and even God, at least as they had heretofore been understood.

[1] James V. Schall, *The Mind That Is Catholic: Philosophical and Political Essays* (Washington, D.C.: Catholic University of America Press, 2008), 160.

[2] Thomas Hobbes, *Leviathan*, rev. ed. (London: Andrew Crooke, 1651; Hamilton, Ontario: McMaster University Archive of the History of Economic Thought, n.d.), 103, https://socialsciences.mcmaster.ca/econ/ugcm/3ll3/hobbes/Leviathan.pdf.

[3] Ibid., 112.

[4] Thomas Hobbes, *De Cive* 10, 1.

Hobbes versus Hooker

Before getting to his rationale for, and the features of, an absolute state, we need to examine Hobbes' epistemology and his view of reality. He is, first of all, easiest to see in contrast to Richard Hooker and Hooker's two foremost authorities, Aristotle and Aquinas. Very much a man of the *via moderna*, Hobbes was everything Hooker was not—a nominalist and a voluntarist who denied classical natural law. Like Aristotle and Aquinas, Hooker had held that the good was essentially the same for each man. Hobbes denied this. We have seen that Hooker's reaction to Puritan excesses was a profound re-elaboration of the metaphysical and rational sources of order that naturally limit the nature of the political enterprise. Hobbes' reaction to the same excesses was the opposite: the elaboration of a rationale for the unlimited power of the sovereign in order to suppress such excesses. Hooker opposed Puritan extremism on the basis of traditional Christianity and classical philosophy. Hobbes opposed Puritanism on the basis of his denial of both. Hooker corrected the Puritan notion of a totally corrupt nature. Hobbes found no good in nature, only an enemy to be overcome and mastered. To Hobbes, nature was not an order, but a disorder—the opposite of Hooker's position. For Hooker, nature was morally normative. For Hobbes, it was not.

Hooker derived the right to life and liberty from the laws of nature. Hobbes, on the other hand, derived the law of nature from self-preservation, as he found it imperiled in the state of nature. Hooker thought that civil law approximates and draws its authority from natural law and is legitimate only insofar as it reflects natural law. As we shall see, Hobbes thought that civil law *is* natural law and, as such, constitutes its own authority, as nothing is higher than it. He said, "The law of nature and the civil law contain each other and are of equal extent."[5] If this is true, then there obviously is nothing *natural* about civil law: it is completely conventional. The name for this is legal positivism—law as pure will and power, presupposed to nothing but itself (as Fr. Schall would say).

Hooker appealed to a common good based on reason. By its lights, man is capable of ruling himself. Hobbes asserted that no rational

---

[5] Hobbes, *Leviathan*, 164.

common good exists aside from the necessity of survival and that man is incapable of ruling himself. Hooker insisted that law had an ultimately transcendent source that necessarily constrained political power. Hobbes likely held that there is no transcendent and that, in any case, there are no limitations to political power. The way to make men one is not through reason but through dread. The only reliable source of political community is fear of the state, which can deliver violent death to those who oppose it. Political life will no longer be organized around what is highest in man, the *summum bonum*, as Hooker would have it, but around what is lowest, the *summum malum*. It now concerns itself with the avoidance of evil (as Hobbes understood evil), rather than the pursuit of good. Hobbes recognized how unappetizing his premise was in noting that the "first grounds of all science are not only not beautiful, but poor, arid, and in appearance deformed."[6]

For Hobbes, man is not Aristotle's (or Hooker's) political animal endowed with reason to form political communities within which to fulfill his nature. The belief that man is "born fit for society" is, he said, "certainly false, and an error proceeding from our too slight contemplation of human nature".[7] Hobbes' vilification of "the vain Philosophy of Aristotle" rivals Luther's. In *Leviathan*, he wrote, "I believe that scarce anything can be more absurdly said in natural philosophy than that which now is called Aristotle's Metaphysics; nor more repugnant to government than much of that he hath said in his Politics, nor more ignorantly, than a great part of his Ethics."[8] It is Aristotle's teleology that particularly offended Hobbes, who, contrariwise, insisted that "there is no *finis ultimus*, utmost aim, nor *summum bonum*, greatest good, as is spoken of in the books of the old moral philosophers."[9] Scholastic philosophy is likewise characterized by its "frequency of insignificant speech".[10] For both Aristotle and the

---

[6] Thomas Hobbes, *The Elements of Philosophy*, in William Molesworth, ed., *The English Works of Thomas Hobbes*, vol. 1 (London: John Bohn, 1839), 2.

[7] Thomas Hobbes, *Philosophical Rudiments concerning Government* 1, 2, cited in Thomas A. Spragens Jr., *The Politics of Motion: The World of Thomas Hobbes* (Lexington, Ky.: University Press of Kentucky, 1973), 102.

[8] Hobbes, *Leviathan*, 418.

[9] Ibid., 60.

[10] Ibid., 10.

Scholastics, the *summum bonum* is happiness. For Hobbes, it was not, because there is no longer any way to tell what happiness is, other than the absence of strife.

Denial of the Highest Good

A nominalist and a voluntarist, Hobbes rejected the existence of formal and final causality. There exists only material and efficient causality. Things are not ordered to ends in themselves. Nature in the Aristotelian, teleological sense does not exist. (Recall Aristotle's four causes. The material cause is that out of which something is made, i.e., its matter; e.g., wood is the material cause of a table. The form is the shape or design of what it is—in this case, a table. The efficient cause is the thing or agent that brings something about; the carpenter is the efficient cause of the table. The final cause is the purpose or end for which the thing is made; the table is made to dine on, etc.) In this sense, Hobbes' natural law has no nature. The banishment of formal and final causes puts man in a predicament because of his resulting innate purposelessness. The problem is acute. Philosopher Eric Voegelin succinctly diagnosed the difficulty with Hobbesian man:

> If there is no *summum bonum*, however, there is no point of orientation which can endow human action with rationality. Action, then, can only be represented as motivated by passions, above all by the passion of aggression, of the overcoming of one's fellow man.... If men are not moved to live with each other in peace through common love of the divine highest good, then the fear of the *summum malum* of death must force them to live in an orderly society.[11]

Although this situation is dire, the denial of formal and final causality creates an opportunity. Once existence becomes nonteleological, man is left to impose *his own* ends upon it.

If there is no *summum bonum* as a source of rational ethics by which man should direct his actions, there remains, nonetheless, the *summum malum*, expressed as man's fear of violent death. Aquinas'

---

[11] Eric Voegelin, *Science, Politics and Gnosticism* (Chicago: Regnery Gateway, 1968), 102–3.

primary precept that "good is to be sought, evil avoided" is demoted by Hobbes into "survival is to be sought, extinction avoided." This grim situation is actually a net plus for man because it is on the basis of the *summum malum* that he can engineer, with Hobbes' guidance, a political order so as to make it "(excepting by external violence) everlasting".[12] It is only with the truncation of reality, the elimination of the highest good, that Hobbes' political project becomes possible. Its success was completely predicated on leaving things out—i.e., leaving out the teachings of Plato, Aristotle, Cicero, Aquinas, Hooker, and any other significant thinker who held to natural teleology as the source for determining right and wrong. Only with their elimination could Hobbes give a compelling motive for his endeavor: "For want of a right Reason constituted by Nature", man would have to "set up for right Reason, the Reason of some Arbitrator, or Judge".[13] And who might that arbitrator be? Hobbes' answer is the absolute sovereign. The lack of a natural moral order leads ineluctably to this result.

Hobbes' radical moral skepticism serves, and ineluctably eventuates in, tyranny. Msgr. Robert Sokolowski has pointed out that Hobbes' epistemology, from which he derived his moral agnosticism, is not indifferent to his prescribed form of political rule.

> The conjunction between politics and epistemology is not accidental. If human beings are to be made abject subjects of the sovereign, they have to understand themselves in a certain way. Since they will not be permitted to act in the public domain (only the sovereign can carry out public actions), they must take themselves as neither moral agents nor agents of truth. They have to understand their intellect as a mechanical, impersonal process, not a power of disclosure.... The "egocentric predicament" and the reduction of mind to brain, the cancellation of public truth in favor of private relativism, are not just epistemological theories, but also political predispositions.... The understanding of human reason as boxed into the brain [is] an understanding that serves the sovereign state.[14]

---

[12] Hobbes, *Leviathan*, 207.

[13] Thomas Hobbes, *De Cive* 2, 6, 9.

[14] Robert Sokolowski, *Introduction to Phenomenology* (Cambridge: Cambridge University Press, 2000), 205–6.

Man's nonteleological nature *necessitates* an absolute sovereign. Instead of ends ordered by nature, Hobbes discerned in man "a continual progress of the desire, from one object to another; the attaining of the former being still but the way to the latter".[15] There is only ceaseless striving. Satisfying desires only leaves more to be desired: "In the first place, I put for a general inclination of all mankind, a perpetual and restless desire of power after power, that ceaseth only in death."[16] Hobbes compares "the life of man to a race" in which "to forsake the course, is to die."[17] Thus, Hobbes fulfilled Aristotle's prediction that, without "the good", we are "to go on choosing one act for the sake of another, thus landing ourselves in an infinite progression with the result that desire will be frustrated and ineffectual".[18] Hobbes denied Aristotle's "absolutely good" and Aquinas' "perfect good, which lulls the appetite altogether". For him, there was no state of perfection or fulfillment in which nothing else remains to be desired. Hobbes also rejected Aquinas' statement that "the object of the will i.e. of man's appetite is the universal good."[19] Other than self-preservation and those things attendant to it, there is no universal good. The natural law for Hobbes is that there is no natural (moral) law—though he is happy to call "a law of nature" those rules "by which a man is forbidden to do that which is destructive of his life or taketh away the means of preserving the same". For Hobbes, said Harry Jaffa, "men are rational only when they pursue bodily self-preservation in preference to any other goal."[20]

Because of Hobbes's nominalism, there could not be much more to it. What can be universal in its application when the universal has been denied? In what sounds like a line out of Ockham, he proclaimed, "There being nothing in the world Universal but Names; for the things named, are every one of them Individual and Singular."[21] This means, as it did for Ockham, that things have no natures

---

[15] Hobbes, *Leviathan*, 60.

[16] Ibid., 2.

[17] Thomas Hobbes, *The Elements of Law Natural and Politic* (1640), chap. 9, Constitution Society, https://www.constitution.org/th/elements.htm.

[18] Aristotle, *Nicomachean Ethics* 1094a.

[19] Thomas Aquinas, *Summa theologica* I-II, q. 3, a. 7.

[20] Harry V. Jaffa, *Crisis of the Strauss Divided: Essays on Leo Strauss and Straussianism, East and West* (Lanham, Md.: Rowman and Littlefield, 2012), 115.

[21] Hobbes, *Leviathan*, 21.

or essences. The "doctrine of *separated essences*", Hobbes said, was "built on the vain philosophy of Aristotle."[22] Since the universe contains only matter and motion, so-called essences turn out to be "the names of *nothing*". The result, as was the case with Ockham, is that objective morality from natural law becomes an impossibility. As we have seen, the existence of a universal good requires an immutable human nature as a standard by which to know and judge good and evil. Hobbes rejected this explicitly and openly embraced the consequences. Nonteleological nature is *necessarily* amoral. This is why Hobbes stated that "the desires and other passions of man are in themselves no sin. No more are the actions that proceed from those passions, till they know a law that forbids them—which till laws be made they cannot know."[23]

Hobbes' nominalism is likewise explicit when he says:

> But whatsoever is the object of any man's appetite or desire, that is it which he for his part calleth "good"; and the object of his hate and aversion, "evil"; and of his contempt "vile" and "inconsiderable." For these words of good, evil, and contemptible, are ever used with relation to the person that useth them, there being nothing simply and absolutely so; nor any common rule of good and evil, to be taken from the nature of the objects themselves.[24]

Or again, he states, "Good and evil are names that signify our appetites and aversions; which in different tempers, customs, and doctrines of men, are different.... Nay, the same man in diverse times differs from himself, and one time praiseth, that is, calleth good— what another time he dispraiseth, and calleth evil."[25] Also, "insomuch that while every man differeth from other in constitution, they differ also one from another concerning the common distinction of good and evil."[26] Because of the "*inconstant* signification" of moral words used by men, "such names can never be true grounds of any ratiocination."[27] So much for the prospect of moral philosophy.

[22] Ibid., 421.
[23] Ibid., 10.
[24] Ibid., 33.
[25] Ibid., 97–98.
[26] Hobbes, *The Elements of Law*, chap. 7.
[27] Hobbes, *Leviathan*, 26.

Mutable Man

What is more, since "the constitution of man's Body, is in continual mutation, it is impossible that all the same things should always cause in him the same Appetites, and Aversions: much less can all men consent, in the Desire about most any one and the same Object."[28] Of course, if there are no ends in nature, then things *must* be subject to incessant change and be in constant motion because nothing defines or fixes them in place. The continual mutation of man is not an obstacle for Hobbes' project; it is the grounds for it. "Continual mutation" really means that man does not possess an immutable nature in the Aristotelian sense. He changes and therefore can be changed. So long as man is nothing more than the product of his mutable attractions to pleasure and aversions to pain, Hobbes' social engineering scheme becomes practicable.

Hobbes did not flinch from the implications of his teaching—a dog-eat-dog state of nature in which there is nothing morally wrong or right. "To this warre of every man against every man", he wrote, "this is also consequent; that nothing can be Unjust. The notions of Right and Wrong, Justice and Injustice have there no place. Where there is no common Power, there is no Law: where no Law, no Injustice."[29] From where, then, does the standard of right and wrong originate? Hobbes answered that it originates in man's will. What is just is not something to be discovered in nature or the transcendent but is to be *determined* by will. In *De Homine* (1658), he asserted that "politics and ethics (i.e., the sciences of *just* and *unjust*, of *equity* and *inequity*) can be demonstrated *a priori*, because we ourselves make the principles—that is, the causes of justice (namely laws and covenants)—whereby it is known what *justice* and *inequity*, are."[30] Who are "we ourselves" who make the principles of right and wrong? Hobbes answered unequivocally, "It belonged therefore to the sovereign to be judge, and to prescribe the rules of discerning

---

[28] Ibid., 33.

[29] Ibid., 79.

[30] Thomas Hobbes, *De Homine* 10, 5, cited in Paul A. Rahe, *Republics Ancient and Modern*, vol. 2, *New Modes and Orders in Early Modern Political Thought* (Chapel Hill: University of North Carolina Press, 1994), 147.

good and evil: which rules are laws; and therefore in him is the leg-islative Power."[31] The Sovereign does not arise to advance or defend what is just, but to *define for itself* what justice is. As Hobbes said, "The makers of civil laws are not only declarers, but also makers of justice and injustice of actions, there being nothing in men's manners that makes them righteous or unrighteous but their conformity with the law of the sovereign."[32] This makes possible Hobbes' position that "another doctrine repugnant to Civil Society, is that *whatsoever a man does against his Conscience, is Sin.*"[33] For Ockham and Luther, God's might makes right. For Hobbes, the genesis of justice is the *will* of the omnipotent Sovereign; *his* might makes right. The only sin for man is acting against his sovereign's will. This is a modern version of Thrasymachus' right as the rule of the stronger.

Hobbes is Ockham and Luther without the compensation of a redemptive Christ. Or, as Herbert Deane suggested, "The Hobbesian theory or vision of man and society is the Augustinian vision after God and the City of God have been eliminated."[34] Hobbes takes Luther's degraded view of human nature as the sole foundation of his political philosophy. For Hobbes, there is no grace covering the dung heap of mankind like pure, white snow. There is only the dung heap, and from its perspective he sees everything and builds his new, purportedly foolproof political science.

Primacy of Passion and Power

For Hobbes, the motivation for human action is passion or appetite alone. Power is the defining passion because it allows its possessor to suborn others to one's desires. Everything is reducible to power. Hobbes said, "Riches, knowledge and honour are but several sorts of power."[35] Even religion is nothing but a projection of the will to power and the desire to dominate other men by instilling in them

---

[31] Hobbes, *Leviathan*, 127.

[32] Ibid., 350.

[33] Ibid., 198 (emphasis in the original).

[34] Herbert A. Deane, *The Political and Social Ideas of St. Augustine* (New York: Columbia University Press, 1963), 236.

[35] Hobbes, *Leviathan*, 45.

fear of phantoms.[36] In a preview of David Hume's infamous statement that reason is but a slave to the passions,[37] Hobbes wrote that "the thoughts are to the desires as scouts and spies to range abroad and find the way to the things desired."[38] From this perspective, it is easy to see why Hobbes held the view that reasoning is computation. Reason does not seek truth. It only figures out how to satisfy the passions; this is what it computes. Thus, in Hobbes' world, the high can be understood only in terms of the low. If all of man's "higher" aspirations are really nothing but masks for the imposition of the *libido dominandi*, then those "higher" things need be dealt with only as excrescences of the passions. In no sense did Hobbes think that man could rise above his passions—certainly not with his reason. Reason, after all, is based on unreason.[39] The advantage of bringing everything down to the same appetitive level is that it makes things more manageable, as we shall see.

The War of All against All

Here is how Hobbes defined the political problem that he set out to solve. Man, a creature dominated by his limitless desires, constantly

[36] "And they that make little or no inquiry into the natural causes of things, yet from the fear that proceeds from the ignorance itself of what it is that hath the power to do them much good or harm are inclined to suppose, and feign unto themselves, several kinds of powers invisible, and to stand in awe of their own imaginations, and in time of distress to invoke them; as also in the time of an expected good success, to give them thanks, making the creatures of their own fancy their gods. By which means it hath come to pass that from the innumerable variety of fancy, men have created in the world innumerable sorts of gods. And this fear of things invisible is the natural seed of that which every one in himself calleth religion; and in them that worship or fear that power otherwise than they do, superstition. And this seed of religion, having been observed by many, some of those that have observed it have been inclined thereby to nourish, dress, and form it into laws; and to add to it, of their own invention, any opinion of the causes of future events by which they thought they should best be able to govern others and make unto themselves the greatest use of their powers." Hobbes, *Leviathan*, 65.

[37] In *A Treatise of Human Nature* (1738), Hume wrote: "Reason is, and ought only to be, the slave of the passions and can never pretend to any other office than to serve and obey them."

[38] Hobbes, *Leviathan*, 46.

[39] Gregory of Nyssa wrote, "Whenever a man ... forces his reason to become the servant of his passions, there takes place a sort of conversion of the good stamp [of the Divine] in him into the irrational image, his whole nature being traced anew after that design, as his reason, so to say, cultivates the beginnings of his passions, and gradually multiplies them; for once it lends its cooperation to passion, it produces a plenteous and abundant crop of evils." Gregory of Nyssa, *A Select Library of Nicene and Post-Nicene Fathers of the Christian Church*, vol. 5, ed. Philip Schaff and Henry Wace (New York: Christian Literature, 1893), 48.

seeks their fulfillment at the expense of other men, who likewise seek fulfillment of their unlimited desires. In *The Elements of Law*, he explained: "Men from their very birth, and naturally, scramble for every thing they covet, and would have all the world, if they could, to fear and obey them."[40] He described the "natural state" as a place where "all things were in common, for which reason all sexual unions were licit"; where "it was a state of war, hence licit to kill"; and where "the only definitions were those of each man's own judgement."[41] Therefore, men are naturally at odds with one another. Defined in this way, it is easy to see that every person's self-interest is necessarily at odds with every other person's self-interest. Or, as Hobbes wrote, "Man is a wolf to Man."[42] This is the basis of the war of all against all that Hobbes described as the state of nature, and why life in it is "solitary, poor, nasty, brutish and short".[43] It is through this unremitting competition and the threat or use of violence to succeed that man is thus possessed of the "continual fear and danger of violent death".[44]

What can be done about this war of all against all? Hobbes' aim was to transform a Jurassic world into a Jurassic park, or a dog-eat-dog world into a kennel—all under the supervision of an all-powerful dogcatcher and keeper. Through the application of force or the threat of its use, citizens would be trained much as dogs are.[45] Enforced discipline eventually transforms into habitual obedience. How this was to be achieved and in what form (so long as it was with the original consent of the participants), was less important to Hobbes than that it *be* achieved, for his highest goal was civic peace. By finding the one thing common in men—fear of a violent death—Hobbes thought that he had discovered the Philosopher's Stone with which to conjure a durable, perhaps eternal political order impervious to the terrible internecine religious strife that he had seen (from his safe distance in exile) in the English Civil Wars. Hobbes declared, "For every man is desirous of what is good for him, and shuns what is evil, but chiefly

---

[40] Cited in Rahe, *Republics Ancient and Modern*, 2:145.

[41] Thomas Hobbes, *On the Citizen* (Cambridge: Cambridge University Press, 1998), 158.

[42] Ibid., 3.

[43] Hobbes, *Leviathan*, 78.

[44] Ibid.

[45] Bertrand de Jouvenal, *Sovereignty: An Inquiry into the Political Good* (Chicago: University of Chicago Press, 1957), 242.

the chiefest of natural evils, which is death."[46] If man is incapable of rising above his passions, he must be ruled by his strongest passion: fear of losing his life. Death is the greatest "evil" because, if one is no longer alive, one can no longer satisfy one's passions. Therefore, self-preservation is not *a* good; it is *the* good. This is the only reason the other passions are, or should be, subordinate to it.

This scenario is what Hobbes, in an act of semantic infiltration, called natural law. Though he obliterated the idea of essences, he nonetheless appropriated natural law language so he could change its meaning and turn it to his own purposes. For him, natural law is autonomous; it no longer exists as a link in the great chain of being. It is not related to eternal or divine law, as it was for Hooker and Aquinas. By redefining natural law, Hobbes hoped to overthrow the meaning that it had from Aristotle to Hooker. As seen earlier, the laws of nature are those rules of action prescribed by the ends toward which man is ordered by the constitution of his being and by which he must abide for his fulfillment. For Hobbes, the laws of nature meant those things that are "binding only to the extent to which their performance does not endanger our self-preservation". For such laws "are but conclusions or theorems concerning what conduceth to the conservation and defense" of man over against other men.[47]

How does Hobbes' scenario work? "This perpetual fear", he said, inspires man to bring himself out of the state of nature through a contract or covenant in which he voluntarily surrenders his right to beat, rob, or kill his fellow man, so long as his fellow man gives up his right to beat, rob, or kill him—a kind of nonaggression pact that, obviously, requires the consent of its members. It cannot be emphasized enough that, aside from the right to self-defense, any other presumed "rights" that man enjoys are the product of this contract and of nothing else. They do not preexist the contract as inherent in man's nature. Moreover, such are the passions of man that this contract can be enforced only *by force* because, as Hobbes explained, "Covenants, being but words and breath have no force to oblige, contain, constrain, or protect any man but what it has from the public

---

[46] Hobbes, *De Cive* 1, 7.
[47] Hobbes, *Leviathan*, 98.

sword, that is from the untied hands of that man or assembly of men that hath the sovereignty."[48] He repeated for emphasis that contracts "without the sword, are but words and of no strength to secure a man at all ... if there be no power erected, or not great enough for our security".[49]

All-Powerful Leviathan

How great must this power be? Hobbes said that the sovereign "hath the use of so much power and strength conferred on him, that by terror thereof, he is enabled to form the wills of them all."[50] In other words, it must be absolute and indivisible. Otherwise, how could it instill the fear necessary to curtail the unrestrained passions of man? Therefore, men must "confer all their power and strength upon one man, or upon one assembly of men, that may reduce all their wills by plurality of voices unto one will."[51] As Hobbes explained, "This is the Generation of that great LEVIATHAN, or rather (to speak more reverently) of that *Mortal God*" whose power must be such that it is beyond challenge.[52] If it is subject to challenge, then it is obviously not powerful enough. Hobbes wrote that "whoever, thinking sovereign power too great, will seek to make it less, must subject himself to a power that can limit it, that is to say, to a much greater."[53] Hobbes created what seems to be a secular parody of Anselm's ontological argument—that God *must* exist, since he is the greatest and nothing greater can be thought of than he—and applied it to the state instead. Thus, the "Mortal God" *must* exist.

What about the *immortal* God, though? Does he not present a challenge to the fearful loyalty to Leviathan? Can Hobbes' system work if man finds a cause worth giving his life for even in violent death? As French scholar Rémi Brague said, "If we accept Hobbes's thesis that the city of men is founded on the fear of death, religion is intrinsically

[48] Ibid., 108.
[49] Ibid., 103.
[50] Ibid., 106.
[51] Ibid.
[52] Ibid. (emphasis in the original).
[53] Ibid., 128.

dangerous."[54] Hobbes recognized this obvious danger. In fact, it was the one he principally intended to address, since it seemed to be the source of the English Civil Wars and the religious wars on the Continent. He did so by removing the immortal God from competition with the "Mortal God". The Christian distinction between "temporal and spiritual government", Hobbes said, in total rejection of Gelasius' two-swords teaching, "are but two words brought into the world to make men see double and mistake their lawful sovereign".[55] Therefore, he dispensed with the division altogether: "For this distinction of temporal and spiritual power is but words."[56] There was no longer one truth and two swords (the Middle Ages), or two truths and one sword (the Reformation), but one sword and one truth: the Leviathan's. On the frontispiece of *Leviathan*, the "Mortal God" is depicted holding the scepter in one hand and the crozier in the other, making it graphically clear that both powers reside indistinguishably in the same person. In effect, Hobbes eradicated the distinction between the sacred and the secular, the very basis on which constitutional government first developed. There *must* be only one sword, the temporal one, so concomitantly there can only be one "truth". In fact, the power of the sword *constitutes* the truth and, therefore, also the law. Hobbes' dictum was *Auctoritas, non veritas facit legem* (Authority, not truth, decides the law). It is as succinct a summation of legal positivism as has ever been penned. In his argument against Bellarmine's defense of papal authority, Hobbes stated, "From this consolidation of the right politic and ecclesiastic in Christian sovereigns, it is evident that they have all manner of power over their subjects ... both in policy and religion ... for both State and Church are the same men."[57] Hobbes sought to subvert anything that would "serve to lessen the dependence of Subjects on the Sovereign Power of their Country".[58] He therefore espoused the subordination of religion to

[54] Rémi Brague, interview by Christophe Cervellon and Kristell Trego, in Rémi Brague, *The Legend of the Middle Ages: Philosophical Explorations of Medieval Christianity, Judaism, and Islam* (Chicago: University of Chicago Press, 2009), 14, University of Chicago Press, https://www.press.uchicago.edu/Misc/Chicago/070803.html.

[55] Hobbes, *Leviathan*, 289.

[56] Ibid., 359–60.

[57] Ibid., 342.

[58] Ibid., 422.

the state, as had been the case in the Roman state and in the ancient Greek city-states.

Over Leviathan's crowned head in the frontispiece appears an inscription from the book of Job: "Non est potestas Super Terram quae Comparetur ei. Iob. 41. 24" (There is no power on earth to be compared to him [Job 41:24]). Individuals are depicted only as constituent parts of Leviathan's body below his neck. All of them are faced into Leviathan, gazing upward at his visage. We see only people's backs. They possess no individuality. Nothing, and no one, exists apart from Leviathan. As Charles McCoy wrote:

> Hobbes' citizen is defined in relation to the ruler as Aristotle's natural slave was defined in relation to the master: as *"alterius"*, belonging to another as of natural right. But there is an important difference, a difference which is to the advantage of Aristotle's slave: for *he* was described as a "man" and a "separate" instrument, whereas Hobbes' citizen is an integral part of his master, and achieves his humanity in and through the sovereign's power.[59]

Saint Paul spoke of "one body and one Spirit" in Christ (Eph 4:4). Leviathan's one body seems a grotesque parody or profane substitute for the Mystical Body of Christ that Paul described. What is more, said Paul, Christ "will change our lowly body to be like his glorious body, by the power which enables him even to subject all things to himself" (Phil 3:21). Through his absolute power, Leviathan likewise subjects all things to himself and incorporates all the bodies of his subjects, not to glorify them, but to conform them to, and glorify, the "Mortal God". Leviathan's one body, however, can exist only insofar as Christ's Mystical Body does not and is banished from men's minds. Otherwise, men will "see double", and their allegiance to the sovereign will not be absolute.

Hobbes went so far as to insist that "it is impossible [that] a Commonwealth should stand where any other than the sovereign hath a power of giving greater rewards than life; and of inflicting greater punishments than death."[60] He was referring, of course, to God's

---

[59] Charles N. R. McCoy, *The Structure of Political Thought: A Study in the History of Political Ideas* (New York: McGraw-Hill, 1963), 202.

[60] Hobbes, *Leviathan*, 275.

power to give the reward of heaven or the punishment of hell. To overcome this threat to Leviathan, Hobbes transposed the future state of rewards and punishments from the next world to this one. Since he was living in a Christian society, he had to do this through the Bible, which required extraordinary feats of biblical exegesis on his part; this included denials of the existence of spirits, the Trinity, purgatory, and hell. Lord Clarendon (1609–1674) referred to Hobbes' biblical interpretation as an "insult upon the Scripture, by perverting, and applying it to unnatural significations, which never occurred to any man but himself".[61] Benjamin Wiker observes that "through Hobbes' exegetical ministrations, the Bible becomes the political instrument of an absolutist king."[62] In a priceless bit of exegetical legerdemain, Hobbes announced: "CHRIST's law therefore ... commands one to obey the commonwealth alone."[63] Heinrich Rommen sarcastically commented, "It is remarkable that Hobbes, eagerly quoting Scripture in his chapter 43, omits all mention of the famous 'one must obey God rather than men.' Or perhaps it is not remarkable after all, because Hobbes regards the civil sovereign as God, *Deus mortalis*."[64] As brilliantly explicated by Scott Hahn and Wiker, Hobbes transformed the Old and New Testaments into basically secular tracts enjoining the faithful to obey unreservedly their worldly sovereign.[65] Through their obedience, they will come as close as possible to heaven—in fact, to the only possible heaven, which is here on earth. If not, they will be in an earthly hell, which is the *only* hell. There is no such thing as an afterlife with which to frighten people into good behavior or threaten them with damnation. If it can be said to exist, the soul is, like everything else, material. Therefore, it ends when man ends. Man does not have an immortal soul. For Hobbes, this solves the problem of "double vision".

---

[61] Edward, Earl of Clarendon, *A Brief View and Survey of the Dangerous and Pernicious Errors to Church and State in Mr. Hobbes's Book Entitled Leviathan*, pt. 4, Survey of Chapter 44, 285, Early English Books, https://quod.lib.umich.edu/e/eebo/A33236.0001.001/1:8?rgn=div1;view=fulltext.

[62] Benjamin Wiker, *The Reformation 500 Years Later: Twelve Things You Need to Know* (Washington, D.C.: Regnery, 2017), 143.

[63] Thomas Hobbes, *De Cive*, 17, 10.

[64] Heinrich A. Rommen, *The State in Catholic Thought* (St. Louis: B. Herder, 1945), 399n25.

[65] See Scott W. Hahn and Benjamin Wiker, *Politicizing the Bible* (New York: Crossroad, 2013).

On its own terms, Hobbes' project requires for its realization an all-material world. Therefore, he posited:

> The world (I mean not the earth only, that denominates the lovers of it "worldly men," but the universe, that is, the whole mass of all things that are) is corporeal, that is to say, body; and hath the dimensions of magnitude, namely, length, breadth, and depth: also every part of body is likewise body, and hath the like dimensions; and consequently every part of the universe is body, and that which is not body is no part of the universe: and because the universe is all, that which is no part of it, is nothing, and consequently nowhere.[66]

Since it does not exist, the spiritual cannot possibly conflict with the material. In fact, in what seems a reversion to the pagan pantheism of Epicurus or Lucretuis, for Hobbes the material *is* God or, perhaps more accurately, God is material. In his *Answer to Bishop Bramhall*, Hobbes described God as a "corporeal spirit".[67] As far as he was concerned, divine will and material causality are the same thing. They are indistinguishable. Hobbes combined Reformation predestination with materialism to provide man with an understanding of how a corporeal God determines everything through material, mechanical causality.

Dispositive Despotism

According to Hobbes, like everything else in the universe, man is amoral matter in motion. He saw all things in a state of constant alteration. The proper study of bodies in motion is the subject of physics. Thus Hobbes considered political science as a kind of physics. He reduced politics to a form of arithmetic or a geometrical arrangement of atoms bumping into and bouncing off one another. As mentioned, this reductive view had advantages for Hobbes. Without the order of essences, reality is malleable and can

---

[66] Hobbes, *Leviathan*, 420.

[67] Thomas Hobbes, *An Answer to Bishop Bramhall's Book, Called "The Catching of the Leviathan"*, in William Molesworth, ed., *The English Works of Thomas Hobbes*, vol. 4 (London: John Bohn, 1840), 306.

be reconstituted so long as one can control efficient causality. This is precisely what science seemed to promise—the power to achieve that end. The new science of politics is a physical science of material and efficient causes. Therefore, its success is measured in purely quantitative terms. By the power he gains through science, man can become the source of his secular self-redemption. The goal of Hobbes' science, Michael Gillespie points out, is "to understand the causal power of God himself and use this power to reconstruct the world in ways that will facilitate human thriving".[68] To improve his estate, man must step in and do what Providence will not. For Hobbes, "the end of knowledge is power"—the power to achieve precisely the construction of reality according to his schema. The absolute Leviathan is logically the proper political order because it will "keep [people] in such motion as not to hurt themselves by their own impetuous desires, rashness or indiscretion".[69] Hobbes becomes the master political scientist who arranges the atoms so as to minimize their collisions.[70] This relatively frictionless state provides the new definition of peace and the substitute understanding of justice. Hobbes' metaphysics makes despotism dispositive.

The devastation from Hobbes' view of reality is considerable, as it undoes the achievements of Jerusalem, Athens, and Rome. Hobbes subverted Greek philosophy by erasing the distinction between nature and convention. In a way, he dragged man back into the prephilosophical mind—except, man was now worse off. One can get from the prephilosophical to the philosophical, but it is almost impossible to get from the postphilosophical back again because all the signposts have been destroyed (thus our present predicament). By materializing the transcendent Yahweh of the Jews, Hobbes reintroduced pantheism into a world that had been freed from it. He sabotaged the Christian distinction between the sacred and the secular with a redeification of the state. Overall, he removed the foundations necessary for the development of constitutional government, certainly of the kind that the American Founders conceived. On top of this, his

---

[68] Michael Allen Gillespie, *The Theological Origins of Modernity* (Chicago: University of Chicago Press, 2008), 234.

[69] Hobbes, *Leviathan*, 213.

[70] See Gillespie, *The Theological Origins of Modernity*, 231; Thomas Hobbes, *De Corpore* 1, 6–7.

epistemological nominalism led necessarily to radical individualism, because the individual is all that is left in its wake of destruction. There is no common good other than survival, or rather peace; all other "goods" are private and personal. Thus, the realm of public life, as it had been understood prior to Hobbes, is demoted to the level of the private, overseen by Leviathan.

The Reaction

Leviathan pleased almost no one. Hobbes was called "the beast of Malmesbury". An early reader, Anglican theologian Henry Hammond, noted that the book "destroyed Trinity, Heaven, Hell", and found it "a farrago of Christian atheism".[71] In 1683, "the thinkeing men of Oxford" held a book burning to incinerate *Leviathan*, among other works. In a declaration of July 21, the university condemned propositions from his works, and from works by other authors, as "false, seditious and impious; and ... also heretical and blasphemous, infamous to Christian religion, and destructive of all government and church and state".[72] While the book was professedly a defense of Divine Right monarchy, the royalist exiles in France were appalled. Sir Edward Nicholas referred to Hobbes in 1652 as "that grand Atheist" and "that father of atheists".[73] Those influenced most by Richard Hooker, the Earl of Clarendon among them, found the most to dislike. Clarendon said that he "had ... some hand in the discountenancing"[74] that led to Hobbes' removal from the exiled Stuart court in 1652. In later years, he wrote in his scathing critique of *Leviathan*, "I would make no scruple to declare, that I have never read any Book that contains in it so much Sedition, Treason, and Impiety as this Leviathan; and therefore it is unfit to be read, taught, or sold, as dissolving all the ligaments of Government, and undermining all

---

[71] Cited in Rahe, *Republics Ancient and Modern*, 2:153–54.

[72] Robert Wodrow, *The History of the Sufferings of the Church of Scotland: From the Restoration to the Revolution*, vol. 3 (Glasgow: Blackie and Son, 1836), 506, cited in Rahe, *Republics Ancient and Modern*, 2:177.

[73] George F. Warner, ed., *The Nicholas Papers: Correspondence of Sir Edward Nicholas, Secretary of State* (Westminster: Nichols and Sons, 1886–1867), 284.

[74] Cited in Rahe, *Republics Ancient and Modern*, 2:153–54.

principles of Religion."[75] He sarcastically added that Hobbes would "erect an engine of Government by the rules of Geometry, more infallible than Experience can ever find out". Richard Cumberland, bishop of Peterborough, wrote *De Legibus Naturae* (1672) to refute Hobbes, whom he criticized for having "assign'd no *larger* Bounds to *Right* and the *Laws of Nature*, than the Preservation of this frail *Life*; as if Men, like Swine, had Souls given them only, instead of Salt, to preserve the Body from Putrefaction".[76] Like others, he found Hobbes' teaching destructive of religion, morality, and civil society.

Does Hobbes sound like the intellectual foundation of the American republic, or like something alien to it? Is a notion of mutable man possessed by his passions, incapable of ruling himself, requiring an absolute sovereign to hold his desires in harness compatible with that of immutable man under the reign of his reason, capable of ruling himself through constitutional, representative government requiring his consent? Needless to say, Hobbes' teaching was as antithetical to the Founders' thinking as Hooker's was congenial to it. In a letter to Francis W. Gilmer, dated June 7, 1816, Thomas Jefferson wrote that "the principles of Hobbes [are a] humiliation to human nature; that the sense of justice and injustice is not derived from our natural organization, but founded on convention only." In a letter to his son John Quincy Adams in 1777, John Adams warned him that Hobbes' works contain "a great deal of mischievous Philosophy"—with the word "mischievous" meaning something far more serious than it does today.[77] In 1810, he wrote to Benjamin Rush that "Hobbes calumniated the classics because they filled young men's heads with ideas of liberty and excited them to rebellion against Leviathan."[78] In *The Farmer Refuted*, Alexander Hamilton also vigorously attacked Hobbes:

> Moral obligation, according to [Hobbes], is derived from the introduction of civil society; and there is no virtue but what is purely artificial, the mere contrivance of politicians, for the maintenance of

[75] Edward, Earl of Clarendon, *Brief View*, 319.

[76] Cited in Paul Rahe, *Republics Ancient and Modern*, 2:217.

[77] John Adams to John Quincy Adams, August 11, 1777, Founders Online, National Archives, https://founders.archives.gov/documents/Adams/04-02-02-0247.

[78] Cited in Ellis Sandoz, *Republicanism, Religion, and the Soul of America* (Columbia: University of Missouri Press, 2006), 93.

social intercourse. But the reason he ran into this absurd and impious doctrine was that he disbelieved the existence of an intelligent superintending principle, who is the governor and will be the final judge of the universe. To grant that there is a supreme intelligence who rules the world and has established laws to regulate the actions of his creatures; and still to assert that man, in a state of nature, may be considered as perfectly free from all restraints of law and government, appears to a common understanding altogether irreconcilable. Good and wise men, in all ages, have embraced a very dissimilar theory. They have supposed that the deity, from the relations we stand in to himself and to each other, has constituted an eternal and immutable law, which is indispensably obligatory upon all mankind, prior to any human institution whatever. This is what is called the law of nature. Upon this law depend the natural rights of mankind.[79]

There were other such expressions of repugnance. As Paul Downes writes, "Hobbes, if he was mentioned at all in polite company in the 1770s and 1780s, was immediately repudiated as the philosopher of everything the American Revolution sought to eradicate, including monarchism, absolutism, and an epicurean or atheistical refusal to believe in mankind's natural propensity for goodness."[80]

Paul Samuel Reinsch pointed out that in the eighteenth-century American colonies, "the analytical theory of Hobbes, making positive law independent of moral considerations and basing it on a sovereign will, was not accepted at that time. The law of God, the law of nature, was looked upon as the true law, and all temporal legislation was considered to be binding only in so far as it was an expression of this natural law."[81]

It has been necessary to show in some detail what exactly Hobbes' endeavor entails, so we are ready, when the time comes, to address the charge mentioned at the beginning of this chapter: that Locke was simply Hobbes with a smiley face and that, therefore, Locke's influence demonstrates that the American republic was a Hobbesian

---

[79] Alexander Hamilton, "The Farmer Refuted, &c." (February 23, 1775), Founders Online, National Archives, https://founders.archives.gov/documents/Hamilton/01-01-02-0057.

[80] Paul Downes, *Hobbes, Sovereignty, and Early American Literature* (New York: Cambridge University Press, 2015), 83.

[81] Paul Samuel Reinsch, *English Common Law in the Early American Colonies* (1899; repr. New York: Da Capo Press, 1970), 56.

enterprise. This is the strategy—sometimes explicit, other times implicit—behind the attacks on the Founding mentioned at the beginning of this book. Political philosopher Harry Jaffa succinctly described the deleterious significance of Hobbes' influence in a way that brings things around full circle to the quotation from Fr. James Schall at the beginning of this chapter:

> Hobbes was the precursor of modern scientific positivism, which regards all knowledge as essentially hypothetical and experimental. Its core conviction is that we know only what we make. And constructing a world from hypotheses, we ourselves are the source of all creativity: there is neither need nor room for God. And constructing a world from hypotheses, we have a priori perfect knowledge of that world: there is neither need nor room for philosophy. Since there is no a priori knowledge in nature or of nature (no "self-evident" truths) to guide the human will, the human will must itself be the a priori source of all knowledge. Unfettered will is the ground, then, of all morality.[82]

For a closing summary of what Hobbes looks like, we turn to one of his followers, twentieth-century German political and legal theorist Carl Schmitt (known as the Crown Jurist of the Third Reich), who also demonstrates Hobbes' contemporary relevance:

> Hobbes's *Leviathan*, a combination of God and man, animal and machine, is the mortal god who brings to man peace and security. Because of this—and not on account of the "divine right of kings"— his Leviathan demands unconditional obedience. There exists no right of resistance to him, neither by invoking a higher nor a different right, nor by invoking religious reasons and arguments. He alone punishes and rewards. Based on his sovereign power, he alone determines by law, in questions of justice, what is right and proper and, in matters pertaining to religious beliefs, what is truth and error.... But even much more: The sovereign state power alone, on the basis of its sovereignty, determines what subjects of the state have to believe to be a miracle.[83]

---

[82] Edward J. Erler and Ken Masugi, eds., *The Rediscovery of America: Essays by Harry V. Jaffa on the New Birth of Politics* (Lanham, Md.: Rowman and Littlefield, 2019), 134–35.

[83] Carl Schmitt, *The Leviathan in the State Theory of Thomas Hobbes* (Chicago: University of Chicago Press, 2008), 53.

This is the basis of Hobbes' creation of an absolute secular right of sovereigns. In the words of Heinrich Rommen, "The absolute power of God in Occam's doctrine became at the hands of Thomas Hobbes the absolute sovereignty of the king."[84] Thus, the immortal God transmogrified into the "Mortal God". All of this, remarked Fr. Schall, "was a working out of the consequences of the denial [begun with Machiavelli] of any higher judgment on politics other than politics itself. The absolute states of the sixteenth and seventeenth centuries were the empirical products of this belief."[85] We now turn to the Divine Right iteration of this absolutism, which bore more directly on the American Founding.

---

[84] Heinrich A. Rommen, *The Natural Law: A Study in Legal and Social History and Philosophy* (Indianapolis: Liberty Fund, 1998), 54–55.

[85] James V. Schall, *The Politics of Heaven and Hell* (Lanham, Md.: University Press of America, 1987), 288.

7

The Divine Right of Kings and Its Enemies

In the late sixteenth century, another form of absolutism arose that was as foreign to medieval tradition as was Hobbes—the Divine Right of Kings. It was looked upon favorably by many, because it took religion seriously and was decidedly not materialistic. But in reality, the distance between absolutism's two forms—secular and sacred—was not so great. Consider the praise for Hobbes from Sir Robert Filmer (1588–1653), a Divine Right proponent, in his 1652 pamphlet *Observations concerning the Original of Government*: "With no small content, I read Mr. Hobbes's book *De Cive*, and his *Leviathan*, about the rights of sovereignty, which no man, that I know, hath so amply and judiciously handled. I consent with him about the rights of exercising government." Indeed, the two absolutisms shared the idea of will as the source of law (although Filmer criticized Hobbes in other respects).

The Divine Right doctrine fits comfortably within the voluntarist perspective of the primacy of will. If God, as the primary cause, acts without intermediaries, then he may constitute political authority the same way. Kingship is the immediate and unmediated result of the Creator's will. It is miraculous. No acts of rational free will or consent by the members of the political community are required for its institution or justification. This concept frees the monarch from constitutional limitations and the natural law's rational constraints. Just as God's will reigns, so does the king's. Divine Right is the antithesis of medieval popular sovereignty.

Perhaps its most extreme exponent was James I of England (1566–1625).[1] In a way, he represented a return to the era of sacred kingship,

---

[1] As James VI of Scotland, he inherited the English throne upon the death of Elizabeth I.

prior to Pope Gregory VII's eleventh-century "papal revolution", which claimed that the royal ruler was *rex et sacerdos* (king and priest). This time, however, the assertion came without even nominal acknowledgment of papal authority—indeed, it was made in direct defiance of it. Divine Right was a product of the Reformation, seeking to substitute royal for papal spiritual authority (though Catholic monarchs, especially in France and Spain, were only too happy to join in).[2] As churches became national, kings became absolute. Thus, James collapsed the distinction between spiritual and temporal powers, investing both in his person (as had Henry VIII and Elizabeth I to some degree before him). He said, "The royal dignity is at once civil and ecclesiastical."[3] There could be no claim of authority, temporal or spiritual, superseding his. The king can do no wrong. His power is also indefeasible and irresistible. No rightful heir, defined by primogeniture in the legitimate line, can be justifiably dispossessed under any circumstances.

We shall briefly examine James I's teachings, as well as those of Sir Robert Filmer, and then the most prominent reactions against them. Filmer was James' principal Divine Right apologist. He became notable for his enemies. His claims on behalf of the Stuarts incited John Locke (1632–1704) to write the first of his *Two Treatises of Government*, with the revealing subtitle *The False Principles, and Foundation of Sir Robert Filmer, and His Followers, Are Detected and Overthrown*. Also rebutting Filmer was Algernon Sidney's *Discourses concerning Government*. The criticisms of Divine Right by Locke and Sidney, however, had been preceded by those of Italian Jesuit Robert Cardinal Bellarmine (1542–1621) and Spanish Jesuit Francisco Suárez (1548–1617)—two of the most powerful thinkers of the late sixteenth and early seventeenth centuries. Filmer thought it was his principal duty to refute them, as they had adduced the strongest arguments against James' teaching. The two Jesuits demonstrated that the natural

---

[2] "The royal throne is not the throne of a man but of God himself", wrote the French bishop Jacques-Bénigne Bossuet in *Politics Drawn from the Very Words of Holy Scripture* (1679, published 1709). George H. Sabine, *A History of Political Theory* (New York: Holt, Rineheart, and Winston, 1961), 543.

[3] James I, *Basilikon Doron* (The King's Gift) (1603), cited in Rev. John Clement Rager, *The Political Philosophy of St. Robert Bellarmine* (Spokane, Wash.: Apostolate of Our Lady of Siluva, 1995), 79.

law spine of Christian political tradition, however bent by Ockham, Machiavelli, Luther, and others, had not been broken. While it is notable (and contrary to popular belief) that the strongest critiques of Divine Right came from Catholic priests, some of the same arguments were voiced by Protestants, such as Algernon Sidney, who, under Richard Hooker's influence, had not forsaken the Christian medieval natural law heritage. Bellarmine and Suárez, however, were so prominent that there was hardly a defense of Divine Right that did not have to confront their arguments against it. Anglican prelate John Neville Figgis wrote, "It is only necessary to take up at random any tract or pamphlet on behalf of royal rights written during the seventeenth century. In all probability the name of . . . Bellarmine will be prominent on the first page."[4] He noted: "The original sovereignty of the people is a cardinal doctrine of Jesuit thinkers."[5]

Bellarmine and Suárez

Because they spoke from the heart of the Western tradition, much of what Bellarmine and Suárez wrote will sound familiar from the preceding chapters, especially those on the Middle Ages and on Richard Hooker. Nonetheless, due to their influence in restoring the relevance of these ideas to the early modern period, we need to hear directly from them on the abiding principles of natural law. Bellarmine and Suárez are crucial links in the lineage of popular sovereignty and constitutional limits reaching from the Middle Ages to the birth of America (as indirect as their influence may at first seem). They not only conveyed but also developed traditional teachings to such a point that their articulations of them sound startlingly similar to those of the American Founders. How many would suppose that an Italian Jesuit in the late sixteenth century said, "All men are born naturally free and equal" and that these words were not first spoken by John Locke in the seventeenth century or Thomas Jefferson in the eighteenth? The similarity is not accidental. According to scholar Paul

---

[4] John Neville Figgis, *The Divine Right of Kings* (New York: Harper and Row, 1965), 179.
[5] John Neville Figgis, *Political Thought from Gerson to Grotius: 1414–1625* (New York: Harper and Brothers, 1960), 155.

Sigmund, "John Locke, who based political authority on the consent of the people, knew Bellarmine's arguments seeing as he wrote his *Two Treatises on Civil Government* in order to refute the defense of divine right that Filmer had made against Bellarmine's attack."[6] Sigmund could have said the same of Suárez, whom Filmer had also tried to refute in *Patriarcha*. From his critique of Filmer, it is clear that Sidney was equally aware of Bellarmine and Suárez, and for the same reasons. "Locke and Sidney", Figgis wrote, "if they do not take their political faith bodily from Suárez or Bellarmine, managed in a remarkable degree to conceal the difference between the two.... Their theory of natural rights, of an original compact, and of a utilitarian basis to the State, differs but little from Jesuit doctrines."[7]

Citing Bellarmine and Suárez is not meant to insinuate that America's origins were Catholic. Most of the Founders were Protestant, after all, but the provenance of their ideas was ultimately Catholic in that they invoked natural law and natural rights to justify their cause. And to that extent, it was a shared heritage. Bellarmine's and Suárez's arguments against Divine Right were just as pertinent to Americans when they rejected Parliament's absolutist claims over colonies in the 1766 Declaratory Act. Their relevance is immediately apparent in their repeated emphasis on the indispensability of consent, as derived from man's equality.

Medieval constitutionalism (chapter 2) arose upon the distinction between church and state. Reflecting this tradition, the two Jesuits severely criticized Divine Right's conflation of spiritual and temporal power and insisted on a separate spiritual sovereignty—a position the Church had upheld at least since Pope Gelasius. Bellarmine even quoted Gelasius to James I to remind the king of this fact. While they wrote in defense of papal spiritual power, they also wished to protect popular sovereignty against claims of absolute power by a temporal ruler. Their argument, they said, was based on principles that were discoverable by "natural reason"—the same foundation on which

[6] Paul E. Sigmund, "Natural Law, Consent, and Equality: William of Ockham to Richard Hooker", Natural Law, Natural Rights, and American Constitutionalism, http://www.nlnrac.org/classical/late-medieval-transformations.

[7] John Neville Figgis, "On Some Political Theories of the Early Jesuits", *Transactions of the Royal Historical Society* 11 (December 1897): 94, Cambridge Core, https://doi.org/10.2307/3678216.

constitutional principles were developed during the Middle Ages. There was, therefore, a catholicity to their thinking (i.e., in its very *reasonableness*), which explains why Bellarmine attracted Catholic *and* Protestant audiences in the thousands to his lectures at the University of Louvain, and why Suárez's *Metaphysical Disputations* and *De Legibus* were texts even in some Lutheran universities.[8] Frederick Copleston remarked that *Metaphysical Disputations* was studied in the Protestant universities of Germany by "those who preferred Melanchthon's attitude toward philosophy to that of Luther".[9]

James I's Divine Right

So effective were Bellarmine's arguments that James I, under a nom de plume, felt compelled to answer him in *Triplici nodo, triplex cuneus* (1608). The cardinal fired back in *Responsio*, also under a pseudonym. Then, in a highly unusual step for a reigning monarch, James took up the pen in his own name to attack Bellarmine, a commoner, in *Premonition to Christian Princes*. In 1609, Bellarmine responded in kind under his own name in *Apologia*.[10] With some wit, he addressed the morganatic nature of their exchange: "I cannot see the necessity, in a theological discussion, of one side's having as many titled uncles as the other, so long as both possess equal knowledge."[11] At the same time, James was so infuriated by Suárez's *Defensio fidei catholicae* that he had the hangman burn the book in London at Saint Paul's Cross on November 21, 1613.

While king of Scotland but not yet on the English throne, James set forth his doctrine in *The Trew Law of Free Monarchies* (1598), republished in England in the year of his accession, 1603. He asserted that the king is "maister over every person that inhabiteth the same (countries) having power of life or death over every one of them".[12]

---

[8] Heinrich A. Rommen, "*De Legibus* of Francisco Suárez", *Notre Dame Law Review* 24, no. 1 (October 1948): 71.

[9] Frederick Copleston, S.J., *A History of Philosophy*, vol. 3, *Late Mediaeval and Renaissance Philosophy*, pt. 2, *The Revival of Platonism to Suárez* (Garden City, N.Y.: Image, 1963), 199.

[10] Rager, *Political Philosophy*, 78.

[11] Ibid.

[12] Cited in A.J. Carlyle, *Political Liberty: A History of the Conception in the Middle Ages and Modern Times* (London: Oxford University Press, 1941), 32.

According to James, the king ruled directly by God's authority, accountable only to God. He wrote, "I deny any such contract to be made [between the king and the people]."[13] He was the sole source of law but was not bound by it. "The power flows always from himself", he vouchsafed, "which makes the king to be a speaking law.... The king is above the law, as both the author and giver of strength thereto.... He is not bound thereto but of his own good will, and for good example-giving to his subjects."[14] Reversing the entire medieval tradition, James I declared that "kings were the authors and makers of the laws, and not the laws of the kings."[15] Therefore, "what pleases the Prince has the vigor of law, the Prince is free from the law."[16] He used the epigram *A Deo rex, a rege lex* (The king is from God, the law from the king).[17] The assent of the people, as required by Aquinas and Hooker, was therefore unnecessary.

In 1604, James I expanded upon his patriarchal role: "What God hath joined, then, let no man separate. I am the husband and all the whole isle is my lawful wife. I am the head and it is my body. I am the shepherd and it is my flock."[18] The Christlike allusions here are obvious. Six years later, he proclaimed a gulf between himself and his subjects almost as great as that between them and God:

> The state of monarchy is the supremest thing upon the earth, for kings are not only God's lieutenants upon earth and sit upon God's throne, but even by God himself they are called gods.... Kings are justly called gods, for that they exercise a manner or resemblance of divine power upon earth: for if you will consider the attributes to God, you shall see how they agree in the person of a king. God hath power to create or destroy, make or unmake at his pleasure, to give life or send death, to judge all and to be judged [by] nor accountable to none; to

---

[13] James I, *The Trew Law of Free Monarchies*, in *The Political Works of James I* (Cambridge: Harvard University Press, 1918), 68.

[14] James I, *The True Law of Free Monarchies* (Toronto, Canada: CRRS Publications, 1996), 72; Kate Aughterson, ed., *The English Renaissance: An Anthology of Sources and Documents* (New York: Routledge, 1998), 120.

[15] James I, *Trew Law*, 62.

[16] Rager, *Political Philosophy*, 37.

[17] Ibid., 38.

[18] Cited in E.P. Cheyney, *European Background of American History*, Whitefish, Mont.: Kessinger Publishing, 2018), 146.

raise low things and to make high things low at his pleasure, and to God are both souls and body due. And the like power have kings: they make and unmake their subjects, they have power of raising and casting down, of life and of death, judges over all their subjects and in all causes and yet accountable to none but God only.[19]

Kings, James further wrote, "are breathing images of God upon earth and disobedience to their dictates is disobedience to the God".[20] They are not to be opposed. Nonresistance becomes a *religious* obligation. Gone was the universally held medieval view that the ruler may be lawfully resisted if his commands are contrary to natural law. The sovereign's limited authority and the conditional obedience of his people were replaced by absolute royal authority and the unconditional obedience of his subjects. Lord Acton summarized the new teaching: "That the king is consequently anterior to the people, that he is its maker rather than its handiwork, and reigns independently of consent. Theology followed in the footsteps of the political. In the golden age of religious science, Archbishop Ussher, the most learned of Anglican prelates, and Bossuet, the ablest of the French, declared that resistance to kings is a crime."[21]

Parliament resisted. Its 1604 declaration *Apology of the Commons* said: "The voice of the people, in the things of their knowledge, is as the voice of God."[22] James regarded such statements (though he likely never saw this specific one) as sheer effrontery. In 1610, he chastised Parliament: "You know I can do it without you."[23] Four years later, he remarked that he was surprised his ancestors "should have permitted such an institution [as Parliament] to come into existence.... As to dispute what God may do is blasphemy.... It is sedition in subjects to dispute what a king may do in the height of his

[19] James I, speech proclaiming the Divine Right of Kings, Whitehall Palace, March 21, 1609, in *Works*, 307–8; see "Classic Podium: Kings Are Justly Called Gods", *Independent*, August 29, 1998, https://www.independent.co.uk/arts-entertainment/classic-podium-kings-are-justly-called-gods-1174669.html.

[20] Cited in Sabine, *A History of Political Theory*, 395.

[21] Ibid.

[22] Paul A. Rahe, *Republics Ancient and Modern*, vol. 2, *New Modes and Orders in Early Modern Political Thought* (Chapel Hill: University of North Carolina Press, 1994), 175.

[23] Andrew Thrush and John P. Ferris, eds., *The History of Parliament: The House of Commons 1604–1629* (London: Cambridge University Press, 2010), chap. 13, The History of Parliament, http://www.historyofparliamentonline.org/volume/1604-1629/survey/xiii-management-commons.

power."[24] James advised: "Encroach not upon the prerogative of the crown; if there falls out a question that concerns my prerogative or mystery of state, deal not with it till you consult with the king or his counsel, or both, for they are transcendent matters."[25] By December 1621, he felt compelled to write to Sir Thomas Richardson, speaker of the House of Commons, "These are, therefore, to command you to make known in our name unto the House that none therein shall presume henceforth to meddle with anything concerning our government or deep matters of state." He insisted that "these are unfit things to be handled in Parliament except your king requires it of you."[26]

In 1628, Parliament forced Charles I, James I's son and successor, to accept the Petition of Right, to restore what they saw as ancient rights that had been usurped by the throne:

> Your subjects have inherited this freedom, that they should not be compelled to contribute to any tax ... not set by common consent in Parliament:... that no freeman may be taken or imprisoned or be dipossessed of his freehold or liberties, or his free customs, or be outlawed or exiled; or in any manner destroyed, but by the lawful judgment of his peers, or by the law of the land:... that no man of what estate or condition that he be, should be put out of his land or tenements, nor taken, nor imprisoned, nor disinherited, nor put to death without being brought to answer by due process of law.[27]

An outraged Charles dissolved Parliament the next year, unknowingly sowing the seeds of the English Civil War.

Filmer's Defense of Divine Right

James' Divine Right arguments were championed by Sir Robert Filmer in *Patriarcha: The Naturall Power of Kinges Defended against the*

[24] David Ross, ed., "The Early Stuarts and the English Civil War", Britain Express, http://www.britainexpress.com/History/Early_Stuarts_and_the_Civil_War.htm.

[25] Guy Carleton Lee, *Leading Documents of English History* (New York: Henry Holt, 1900), 336.

[26] Letter of the King to the Speaker of House of Commons, December 3, 1621.

[27] Petition of Right (1628) in Guy Carleton Lee, ed., *Source-Book of English History* (New York: Henry Holt, 1901), 349–50, Liberté, Égalité, Fraternité, http://chnm.gmu.edu/revolution/d/266/.

Unnatural Liberty of the People, by Arguments, Theological, Rational, Historical and Legall. Though likely written before 1632, the book did not appear until 1680. It achieved widespread popularity and renown as the ablest defense of Divine Right. In the course of his defense, Filmer realized that Scripture citations could be quoted by both sides of the argument ad infinitum without a decisive outcome. He did not neglect Scripture, but he also moved the argument onto the grounds of natural right. He wished to base his system not only on theology but also on philosophy. The Bible and natural law spoke of the same thing: the authority of the father as undisputed head of the family. If Filmer could prove that political authority is, in essence, the same as patriarchal, he believed his case conclusive. He put the natural law argument on behalf of Divine Right front and center, while attesting to a genealogy of the Stuart descent all the way from Adam. (John Locke would make great fun of this attempted genealogy.)

His major point was that the king's authority is absolute because the father's authority is absolute, and the king is the father of his country. The state and the family are one and the same entity, the one being a larger version of the other. The king's rights are as inalienable as the father's: "I see not then how the children of Adam, or of any man else, can be free from subjection to their parents. And this subjection of children is the only fountain of all regal authority, by the ordination of God himself."[28] Therefore, one has the same obligation to obey the king as a child does his father. As children have no right to resist their father, subjects have no right to resist the king. People are not born free and equal, any more than children are born equal to their parents. Based on these presuppositions, Filmer concludes that there is no basis for social contract or need for consent and that absolute monarchy is the form of government most natural to man. What is natural is by divine right. Since kingship is natural, it is by divine right.[29] Therefore, it is not to be opposed under any circumstances.

As noted, Filmer's principal targets were Bellarmine, whom he mentions by name sixteen times, and Suárez, who comes in second with ten mentions. Filmer began *Patriarcha* by accurately stating the positions he set out to refute:

---

[28] Cited in Scott W. Hahn and Benjamin Wiker, *Politicizing the Bible* (New York: Crossroad, 2013), 457.

[29] Figgis, *Divine Right*, 155.

Since the time that school divinity began to flourish there hath been a common opinion maintained, as well by divines as by divers other learned men, which affirms: "Mankind is naturally endowed and born with freedom from all subjection, and at liberty to choose what form of government it please, and that the power which any one man hath over others was at first bestowed according to the discretion of the multitude." This tenet was first hatched in the schools, and hath been fostered by all succeeding Papists for good divinity. The divines also of the Reformed Churches have entertained it, and the common people everywhere tenderly embrace it as being most plausible to flesh and blood, for that it prodigally distributes a portion of liberty to the meanest of the multitude, who magnify liberty as if the height of human felicity were only to be found in it, never remembering that the desire of liberty was the cause of the fall of Adam.[30]

Here is Filmer's first quotation from Bellarmine, who insisted that secular or civil authority is instituted by men.

It is in the people unless they bestow it on a prince. This power is immediately in the multitude, as in the subject of it; for this power is in the divine law, but the divine law hath given this power to no particular man.... Power is given by the multitude to one man, or to more, by the same law of nature; for the commonwealth cannot exercise this power, therefore it is bound to bestow it upon some one man or some few. It depends upon the consent of the multitude to ordain over themselves a king, or council, or other magistrates; and if there be a lawful cause, the multitude may change the kingdom into an aristocracy or democracy.[31]

Filmer's answer to Bellarmine was equally forceful:

I see not then how the children of Adam, or of any man else can be free from subjection to their parents: And this subjection of children being the fountain of all regal authority, by the ordination of God himself; it follows that civil power not only in general is by divine institution, but even the assignment of it specifically to the eldest

---

[30] Sir Robert Filmer, *Patriarcha, or the Natural Power of Kings* 1, 1 (London: Richard Chiswell, 1680), Constitution Society, https://www.constitution.org/eng/patriarcha.htm.

[31] Robert Bellarmine, *De Laicis* 3, 4, quoted in Sir Robert Filmer, *Patriarcha* 1, 2.

parents, which quite takes away that new and common distinction which refers only power universal and absolute to God, but power respective in regard of the special form of government to the choice of the people.[32]

Filmer's chapter headings show the regard in which he held the notion of popular sovereignty: the first chapter, "That the First Kings Were Fathers of Families"; the second, "It Is Unnatural for the People to Govern, or Choose Governors; and the third, "Positive Laws Do Not Infringe the Natural and Fatherly Power of Kings."

Bellarmine had contested these points both on their scriptural bases and as natural law:

> God, indeed, made David a king, as he had promised, but by means of the consent of the people. Likewise, God elected Jeroboam king but he finished the appointment by consent of the people, who rebelled against Roboam and constituted Jeroboam king. If, therefore, those whom God himself designates and makes king, He does not so make without the consent of the people, certainly other rulers chosen in other ways, cannot be said to receive their political power immediately from God.[33]

"All power is indeed from God," Bellarmine wrote, "but some power is immediately from God, as that of Moses or of St. Peter, or of St. Paul, and other power comes mediately by the consent of the people, as the power of kings, consuls and tribunes, for as St. Thomas says, 'human dominions and princedoms are by human right, not by divine right.'"[34] Therefore, Bellarmine said, "In temporal governments, supreme power ... is derived from the people and is radically in, and supplied by the kingdom. The people make the king, who otherwise would be a private individual like the rest of men, naturally free and equal. Nor can one man command all others unless they subject themselves to him and concede to him powers over themselves."[35]

---

[32] Filmer, *Patriarcha* 1, 4.

[33] Rager, *Political Philosophy*, 31.

[34] Robert Bellarmine, *De Potestate Papae in Rebus Temporalibus*, chap. 3, obj. 10, cited in Rager, *Political Philosophy*, 32.

[35] Robert Bellarmine, *De Conciliorum Auctoritate* 16, cited in Rager, *Political Philosophy*, 36.

This argument could hardly be more antagonistic to James, who objected that Bellarmine "hath made the people and the subjects of everyone of us our superiors". Indeed, Bellarmine replied, "Kings will profit much to remember that the people over whom they rule are of the same kind and equality as they themselves. It is possible that not a few of their subjects be more prudent, capable, conscientious, and worthy of the crown than they themselves."[36] Also, contrary to James' pretensions, Bellarmine said that "kings, too, are bound by the law." In insisting upon this, Bellarmine was upholding long-established Christian tradition. In the early ninth century, Hincmar, archbishop of Reims, propounded that the sovereign, like his subjects, was under the law. As for those who argued otherwise, "Such language is not that of a Catholic Christian; it is full of blasphemy and the spirit of demons."[37]

Sovereignty of the People

Against arguments in favor of absolute rule, Bellarmine repeatedly defended the sovereignty of the people and the requirement of consent. In *Apologia*, he affirmed:

> The authority of the king descends, not immediately from God nor by divine right, but only by the law of nations. This has been indeed, the common opinion of almost all writers and the general usage and practice of the past. We see, for instance, how kingdoms have been converted into republics and republics into kingdoms, and both rules were regarded as equally just. This could not be so if the authority of kings did not depend on the common consent, but on divine right.[38]

He made the same point in *De Laicis*: "Particular forms of government exist by the law of nations; they are not determined by the Divine Law because it depends on the consent of the multitude to place over itself a king, a counsul, or other magistrates, and for a

---

[36] Robert Bellarmine, *De Officio Principis Christiani* 22, cited in Rager, *Political Philosophy*, 72.

[37] Cited in Larry Siedentop, *Inventing the Individual: The Origins of Western Liberalism* (Cambridge, Mass.: Harvard University Press, 2014), 174.

[38] Robert Bellarmine, *Apologia Pro Juramento Fidelitatis*, cited in Rager, *Political Philosophy*, 32.

legitimate reason, they can change royalty into aristocracy or democracy or vice versa, as it was done in Rome."[39]

Principle of Equality

The requirement of the people's consent was founded upon the principle of equality. In what sounds like a statement out of John Locke, Bellarmine said, "There is no reason why amongst equals one should rule rather than another."[40] This is because "men endowed with human reason are born free and cannot be subjected one to another, except by just title, such as election, succession, or others known to all."[41] As he repeated elsewhere: "In a commonwealth all men are born naturally free and equal."[42]

What does "equality" mean? For Bellarmine, the equality of men is in "their fundamental nature as human beings"; thus, no man has a right to dominate or tyrannize his fellow man. "Man dominates over beasts, he rules the fishes of the sea, the birds of the air, and other animals by despotic rule, but his fellow men he merely governs or directs politically."[43] Political rule is carefully differentiated from tyranny: man cannot be ruled as if he were a beast or a bird. On the other hand, Bellarmine made clear that "to be ruled by a superior is not contrary, however, to human liberty, dignity, and equality. Only the despot offends thus."[44] Therefore, "the servant is ruled for the benefit of the master; the citizen for his own benefit. A political head seeks not his own but the people's good; otherwise, he is a tyrant."[45]

Tyrants can be legitimately overthrown, Bellarmine explained: "A people never transfers its power to a king so completely, but it reserves to itself the right of withdrawing it."[46] On what valid grounds could it be withdrawn? Here Bellarmine cited Aquinas: "If

---

[39] Bellarmine, *De Laicis* 6, cited in Rager, *Political Philosophy*, 64.
[40] Ibid.
[41] Bellarmine, *De Officio* 22, cited in Rager, *Political Philosophy*, 53.
[42] Robert Bellarmine, *De Clericis* 7, cited in Rager, *Political Philosophy*, 89.
[43] Bellarmine, *De Laicis* 7, cited in Rager, *Political Philosophy*, 72.
[44] Ibid.
[45] Bellarmine, *De Officio* 22, cited in Rager, *Political Philosophy*, 73.
[46] Bellarmine, *Apologia* 13, cited in Rager, *Political Philosophy*, 64.

any society of people have the right of choosing a king for itself, it is not unjust if he be deposed by the same, or if his power be curbed, when by a royal tyranny he abuses his power."[47] Recall that Aquinas had said that a tyrant may be overthrown if he "has violently seized power against the will of his subjects, or has forced them to consent". Indeed, "he who kills a tyrant to free his country is to be praised and rewarded."[48]

If tyranny is clearly against the principles of equality and consent, what forms of political rule are congruent with natural law? Like Aquinas, Bellarmine acknowledged monarchy, aristocracy, and democracy as being equally valid so long as they served the common good. Like Aquinas, and Aristotle before him, he also said that the rule of a wise king would ideally be best. But it is unlikely that one wise king would follow another, or even that the one would stay wise for long. "Kings often succeed their fathers, and it is not rare that unworthy sons follow worthy fathers; a foolish son, a prudent father."[49] Therefore, Bellarmine favored a mixed regime, as Aristotle and Aquinas had. "On account of the corruption of human nature," Bellarmine wrote, "we consider as more useful for men at this time a monarchy tempered with aristocracy and democracy rather than simple monarchy."[50]

The reason for the democratic elements, Bellarmine said, is that "all love that form of government best in which they can participate."[51] Democracy's role in a mixed regime is this: "If the supreme head and the minor heads acquire office not by hereditary succession but by consent of the people, then democracy, too, has found its representation in this mixed form of government."[52] Bellarmine counseled, "In an election, reason, age, knowledge, prudence, and the best moral qualifications are considered in the choice." He added, "Such a mixed and more useful government would therefore ... contain such democratic elements as should reasonably ensure the Commonwealth

---

[47] Thomas Aquinas, *De Regno ad Regem Cypri* 7, 49.

[48] Thomas Aquinas, *Commentary on the Sentences of Peter Lombard* 44, 2, 2.

[49] Bellarmine, *De Officio* 22, cited in Rager, *Political Philosophy*, 32.

[50] Robert Bellarmine, *De Ecclesiastica Monarchia*, cited in Rager, *Political Philosophy*, 19.

[51] Robert Bellarmine, *De Romani Pontificis Ecclesiastica Monarchia* 3, cited in Rager, *Political Philosophy*, 36.

[52] Bellarmine, *De Ecclesiastica Monarchia*, cited in Rager, *Political Philosophy*, 22–23.

against incompetent rulers and secure the highest degree of popular right, liberty, approval, self-expression, participation, and welfare."[53]

In his analysis of governments, Bellermine explained the relationship between freedom and law. "Human liberty really consists in this," he said, "that one is free to choose the good and reject the evil. The law is manifestly not repugnant to true liberty; for its purpose is not to impede the choosing of good and the rejection of evil but to promote the exercise and enjoyment of liberty. The law can rightly be said to be the opponent of servitude and the protector of liberty."[54] Concomitantly, Bellarmine, echoing Cicero and Aquinas, said: "A bad law is not a valid law. Good laws are not a curtailment of liberty, but a charter of every man's right. When laws do not protect men's rights, but infringe upon them, when laws are an impediment to the community's development and welfare, they are not good laws and they are therefore not valid laws."[55]

Francisco Suárez

There are strong similarities between Bellarmine and his contemporary Suárez because they drew from the same sources and upheld the same principles. Given the strength and the persistence of his arguments, however, it is worth the risk of repetition to hear from Suárez directly. The Spanish Jesuit declared Divine Right to be "new and singular, invented to exaggerate the temporal and to minimize the spiritual power".[56] Bellarmine's position, he said, was "the ancient, commonly accepted, and true teaching". Suárez objected that "King James is of the opinion that political authority issues immediately from God."[57] Not so, he responded: "No king has ever held or now holds political power immediately of God."[58] Suárez agreed that political

---

[53] Bellarmine, *De Ecclesiastica Monarchia*, cited in Rager, *Political Philosophy*, 23.

[54] Bellarmine, *De Laicis* 10, cited in Rager, *Political Philosophy*, 73.

[55] Bellarmine, *De Laicis* 10, cited in Rager, *Political Philosophy*, 38–39.

[56] Cited in John A. Ryan and Francis J. Boland, *Catholic Principles of Politics* (New York: Macmillan, 1952), 79.

[57] Francisco Suárez, *Defensio fidei catholicae* 3, 2, 1, cited in J. A. Fernández-Santamaría, *Natural Law, Constitutionalism, Reason of State, and War: Counter-Reformation Spanish Political Thought*, vol. 1 (New York: Peter Lang, 2005), 206.

[58] Suárez, *Defensio* 3, 2, 10, cited in Fernández-Santamaría, *Natural Law*, 215.

authority comes from God, but how is it conveyed? Like Bellarmine, he explained that "natural reason only proves that political power is necessary in the whole community, not in a single person or group. Therefore, in so far as political power comes immediately from God it is to be understood that it lies with the whole community and not all with any of its parts." Thus, "natural reason does not offer any grounds to assume that political authority rests with one person more than with another ...; consequently, *potestas* immediately rests with the whole commonwealth alone."[59]

Suárez's *De Legibus* further fortified this point, much as Bellarmine had done, with the underlying principles of man's equality and freedom: "In the nature of things all men are born free; so that, consequently, no person has political jurisdiction over another person."[60] While Suárez maintained that "man is by his nature free and subject to no one, save only to the Creator",[61] he realized that power must be vested in one or some individuals because "nobody can be preserved unless there exists some principle whose function is to provide for and seek its common good."[62] But the natural sovereignty of the people remains inalienable, since "after that power has been transferred to some individual person, even if it has been passed on to a number of people through various successions or elections, it is still always regarded as possessed immediately by the community."[63]

Suárez noted that it was a teaching of the Church Fathers that "man was created by God noble and free."[64] He has an "intrinsic right of liberty".[65] Therefore,

inasmuch as the [community] is immediately ruled by God through natural law, it is free and its own master; a freedom, however, that does not exclude—on the contrary, it includes it—the power to rule

---

[59] Suárez, *Defensio* 3, 2, 7, 10, cited in Fernández-Santamaría, *Natural Law*, 208.

[60] Francisco Suárez, *De Legibus* 3, 2, 3, cited in Augustin Fagothey, *Right and Reason: Ethics in Theory and Practice* (Charlotte, N.C.: TAN Books, 2000), 400.

[61] Francisco Suárez, *De Legibus* 3, 1, 1.

[62] Suárez, *De Legibus* 3, 1, 4–5.

[63] Suárez, *De Legibus* 3, 4, 8.

[64] Suárez, *Defensio* 3, 2, 11, cited in Fernández-Santamaría, *Natural Law*, 215.

[65] Cited in Stephen J. Brust, "Retrieving a Catholic Tradition of Subjective Natural Rights from the Late Scholastic Francisco Suárez, S.J.", *Ave Maria Law Review* 10, no. 2 (Spring 2012): 349.

itself and its members. What it does exclude, in so far as natural law
is concerned, is the subjection of the community to another man;
because to no man did God grant such power until such time when it
shall be transferred by human *institutio* or election.[66]

What Suárez means by natural law is the moral law "which dwells
within the human mind, in order that the righteous may be distinguished from the evil".[67] "True law", he said, manifests itself
through the "dictates of natural reason".[68] Therefore, the powers
of kings and any obligations to them "have their foundation in a
human social pact and consequently are not the result of a divine
immediate arrangement, because all human pacts are contracted by
the human will."[69] For sovereignty to be vested in any given individual, "it must necessarily be bestowed upon him by the consent of
the community."[70]

What are the limits of this bestowed power? Suárez answered that
rulers may make laws "as long as they are not repugnant to reason
and they are subject to the proviso that they should reflect man's
free will".[71] The limits also depend on the nature of the pact that the
king agreed to upon accepting the original grant of power, though
any such pact *necessarily* includes that he should govern in accord
with the common good. In other words, the transfer of power is
conditional on the king's fulfilling the pact. A prince who failed to
promote the public interest could be deposed by the people because
"the state, when it granted him his power, is held to have granted
it upon these conditions: that he should govern in accord with the
public weal, and not tyrannically; and that if he did not govern thus,
he might be deposed from that position of power."[72] The king maintains his power "unless perchance he lapses into tyranny, on which

---

[66] Suárez, *Defensio* 3, 2, 11, cited in Fernández-Santamaría, *Natural Law*, 215.

[67] Francisco Suarez, *Selections from Three Works* (Indianapolis: Liberty Fund, 2015), 43, cited
in Robert John Araujo, S.J., "The Catholic Neo-Scholastic Contribution to Human Rights:
The Natural Law Foundation", *Ave Maria Law Review* 1, no. 1 (Spring 2003): 168.

[68] Cited in Araujo, "Catholic Neo-Scholastic Contribution", 168.

[69] Cited in Fernández-Santamaría, *Natural Law*, 215.

[70] Suárez, *De Legibus* 3, 4, 2, cited in Copleston, *A History of Philosophy*, vol. 3, 219.

[71] Suárez, *De Legibus* 3, 2, 18, cited in Fernández-Santamaría, *Natural Law*, 217.

[72] Francisco Suárez, *De Bello* 8, 2, cited in J.P. Somerville, "From Suárez to Filmer: A
Reappraisal", *Historical Journal* 25, no. 23 (1982): 534.

ground the kingdom may wage just war against him".[73] Suárez said that "this action is sanctioned by the law of nature, which always allows us to repel force by force, as well as by the terms of the original contract under which the first king accepted sovereignty from the people."[74]

Relying on the same such thinking, Suárez's fellow Jesuit, the Englishman John Floyd, published a tract in 1620 claiming, more than two centuries before the abolition of slavery in Great Britain, that every person possessed certain inalienable rights, stating that "slaves, (to speak nothing of humane lawes that have appointed limits to their miseries) have some rightes and liberties by the law of nature inviolable, which (if they be able) they may defend by force against even their owne Maisters."[75]

In case of any suspicion that Bellarmine and Suárez were outliers, Irish scholar Alfred O'Rahilly, one-time president of University College, Cork, stated: "I have made the laborious investigation of every accessible Catholic philosopher and theologian from the 13th to the 19th century and here is the significant result: Fifty-two writers prior to Suárez and eighty-seven after him, uphold the principle that government is based upon the consent of the governed; Sixty-five do not discuss the subject at all, and only seven Gallicans of very doubtful orthodoxy, reject the principle."[76] He furthermore stated:

> The Scholastic theory may now be fairly summarized as follows. Sovereignty is an essential attribute of the people, as constituting a corporate entity; it is radically and fundamentally inalienable, but for convenience and efficiency it may be transferred, by and with the consent of the community, for such time and under such conditions as the people deem expedient for the public good. The ultimate test of the juridical validity of any system of government is the consent of the governed.[77]

[73] Suárez, *De Legibus* 3, 4, 6, cited in Copleston, *A History of Philosophy*, vol. 3, 220.

[74] Cited in Bishop John Ireland, "The Catholic Church in Civil Society", 48; Third Plenary Council of Baltimore (1884).

[75] Somerville, "From Suárez to Filmer", 535.

[76] Alfred O'Rahilly, "Theology on Tyranny", *Irish Theological Quarterly* (January 1921), cited in Rager, *Political Philosophy*, 84.

[77] Alfred O'Rahilly, "The Sovereignty of the People", *Studies* 10, no. 37 (March 1921): 49.

It should be evident from the above that Bellarmine and Suárez were restoring the central truths at the heart of the Christian-Aristotelian political tradition after the absolutist attacks against them.

A Catholic Founding?

By applying these truths to the conditions of their day, these men brought them to such a state of maturity that they could have been more or less directly transferred to the America's Founding. For the most part, they were conveyed indirectly (though Charles Carroll, Jesuit-educated in France, would have been thoroughly familiar with Bellarmine and Suárez). For example, Thomas Jefferson had to have been aware of Bellarmine's and Suárez's teaching because he had a copy, notated and underlined in pencil, of Filmer's *Patriarcha*. The point here is not to make a silly sectarian claim that Jefferson was a covert Catholic, but to demonstrate through the startling similarities of their words the common world of discourse that they shared. When Jefferson referred to the sources upon which the Declaration of Independence drew, he emphasized the aim "to place before mankind the common sense of the subject". It was the "common sense of the subject" of which Sidney spoke when he said Bellarmine "seems to have laid the foundation of his discourses in such common notions as were assented to by all mankind".[78] Bellarmine himself said that he expressed "the common opinion of almost all writers and the general usage and practice of the past". And Suárez spoke of Bellarmine's views as being "the ancient, commonly accepted, and true teaching". In other words, it was a *common patrimony* that Bellarmine and Suárez helped to restore for everyone's benefit—because its source was in natural law, accessible to all by right reason. What Jefferson would call "the harmonizing sentiments of the day" that made the Declaration of Independence possible were themselves made possible by the restoration of this lineage. This illustrates the strength of the medieval legacy in both Catholic and Protestant political thought, conjoined in such a way that both Thomas Jefferson and Charles Carroll could

[78] Algernon Sidney, *Discourses concerning Government* (1698), ed. Thomas G. West (Indianapolis: Liberty Fund, 1996), 19.

embrace the same principles. Catholic and Protestant opponents to absolutism called upon the same constitutional traditions to defend representative government. The examples of Bellarmine and Suárez also show that the fundamental principles of constitutional rule are not somehow fatally dependent on Enlightenment notions that are alien to them, since they preceded the Enlightenment.

How influential were the ideas of Bellarmine and Suárez on the American Revolution? What follows is a comparison of their writings in the early 1600s to George Mason's Virginia Declaration of Rights (VDR) and to the Declaration of Independence (DI), written principally by Thomas Jefferson. The comparison relies on the parallels with Bellarmine that Fr. John Rager offered in *The Political Philosophy of Blessed Robert Bellarmine*, published in 1923. I have amended these and added the parallels with Suárez.

On the Source of Political Power

Bellarmine: "Political power emanates from God. Government was introduced by divine law but the divine law has given this power to no particular man.... There is no good reason why, in a multitude of equals, one rather than another should dominate. Therefore, power belongs to the collective body."[79]

Suárez: "Everything that is of natural law flows from God as Creator of nature; but political authority is of natural law and it therefore issues from God as nature's author."[80]

"If this power does not reside in any specific individual, it must necessarily exist in the community as a whole.... Because inasmuch as [the community] is immediately ruled by God through natural law, it is free and its own master; a freedom, however, that does not exclude—on the contrary, it includes it—the power to rule itself and its members."[81]

VDR: "That power is by GOD and NATURE vested in the people."

DI: "They [the people] are endowed by their Creator with certain unalienable rights."

---

[79] Bellarmine, *De Laicis* 3, 6.
[80] Fernández-Santamaría, *Natural Law*, 196.
[81] Suárez, *De Legibus* 3, 2, 4.

216

On the Origin of Government

Bellarmine: "Men must be governed by some one, lest they be willing to perish. It is impossible for men to live together without some one to care for the common good. Society must have power to protect and preserve itself."[82]

Suárez: "Nobody can be preserved unless there exists some principle whose function is to provide for and seek its common good."[83]

VDR: "Government is or ought to be instituted for the common benefit, protection, and security of the people, nation, or community."

DI: "To secure these rights [Life, Liberty, and the Pursuit of Happiness] governments are instituted among men."

On the Power of the People and the Requirement of Consent

Bellarmine: "The people themselves, immediately and directly, hold political power so long as they have not transferred this power to a king or ruler."[84] "It depends upon the consent of men to place over themselves a king, counsel, or magistrate."[85]

Suárez: "After that power has been transferred to some individual person, even if it has been passed on to a number of people through various successions or elections, it is still always regarded as possessed immediately by the community."[86] "It must necessarily be bestowed upon him [the ruler] by the consent of the community."[87]

VDR: "All power belongs to the people."

DI: "Governments are instituted among men, deriving their powers from the consent of the governed."

On the Freedom and Equality of All Men

Bellarmine: "In the commonwealth, all men are born naturally free and equal."[88] "There is no reason why amongst equals one should rule rather than another."[89]

[82] Bellarmine, *De Laicis* 6.
[83] Suárez, *De Legibus* 3, 1, 4–5.
[84] Bellarmine, *De Clericis* 7.
[85] Bellarmine, *De Laicis* 3, 4.
[86] Suárez, *De Legibus* 3, 4, 8.
[87] Suárez, *De Legibus*, 3, 4, 2, cited in Copleston, *A History of Philosophy*, vol. 3, 219.
[88] Bellarmine, *De Clericis* 7.
[89] Bellarmine, *De Laicis* 6.

Suárez: "In the nature of things all men are born free."[90]
VDR: "All men are by nature equally free and independent."
DI: "All men are created equal."

On the Right to Revolution and Self-Determination

Bellarmine: "For legitimate reason the people can change the government to an aristocracy or a democracy or vice versa."[91]

Suárez: "The state as a whole, is superior to the king, for the state, when it granted him his power, is held to have granted it upon these conditions: that he should govern in accord with the public weal, and not tyrannically; and that if he did not govern thus, he might be deposed from that position of power."[92]

VDR: "When government fails to confer common benefit, a majority of the people have a right to change it."

DI: "Whenever any form of government becomes destructive of these ends, it is the Right of the People to alter or abolish it, and to institute a new government."

These comparisons constitute a prima facie case that Bellarmine's and Suárez's influence was felt in eighteenth-century America. It may not have had their names on it, but much of the intellectual substance was the same. In any case, they illustrate the striking compatibility of their thought with the principles of the Declaration of Independence. To demonstrate that there was a pre-Enlightenment version of the principles essential to the American independence is not to suggest that the Founding was unaffected by the Enlightenment. But all too often it has been taken to be the sole property of eighteenth-century *philosophes*. It would be odd to think that the classically educated Christian gentleman of colonial America had John Locke and Enlightenment thinkers as his only reference for the ideas of popular sovereignty, the rule of law, equality, representation, consent, and the right to resist tyranny. It is commonplace to hear the American Founding referred to as almost exclusively Lockean (though the origins of its principles predate Locke). Perhaps one could refer to Locke as Bellarminian or Suárezian.

---

[90] Suárez, *De Legibus* 3, 2.
[91] Bellarmine, *De Laicis* 6 cited in Rager, *Political Philosophy*, 64.
[92] Suárez, *De Bello* 8, 2, cited in Somerville, "From Suárez to Filmer", 534.

Algernon Sidney

As stated earlier, Bellarmine's and Suárez's influence was mostly indirect. Sidney's however, was direct and substantial. In the American colonies, he was widely revered as a republican hero and martyr. Prominent eighteenth-century Boston clergyman Andrew Eliot's remark that Sidney was "the first who taught me to form any just sentiments on government"[93] was not atypical. Copies of *Discourses concerning Government*, which Sidney wrote in refutation of Filmer's *Patriarcha*, were present in nearly every large colonial library of the time. Sidney's work was so important that Jefferson regarded it as "probably the best elementary book of the principles of government, as founded in natural right which has ever been published in any language: and it is much to be desired in such a government as ours that it should be put into the hands of our youth as soon as their minds are sufficiently matured for that branch of study."[94] Dr. Bradley Birzer points out that "not just Thomas Jefferson, but men as diverse as Josiah Quincy, John Adams, Jonathan Mayhew, and John Taylor of Caroline revered Sidney and his *Discourses*"[95]—as did prominent Virginia politician Arthur Lee. Such was Sidney's renown at the time of the Revolution that distinguished Virginians, including Patrick Henry, founded Hampden–Sydney College in 1776 in his (and John Hampden's) honor. And in 1825, as a founder of the University of Virginia, Thomas Jefferson issued this statement with James Madison and others: "Resolved, that it is the opinion of this Board that as to the general principles of liberty and the rights of man, in nature and in society, the doctrines of Locke, in his 'Essay concerning the true original extent and end of civil government,' and of Sidney in his 'Discourses on government,' may be considered as those generally approved by our fellow citizens of this, and of the United States."[96]

[93] Alice M. Baldwin, *The New England Clergy and the American Revolution* (Durham, N.C.: Duke University Publications, 2016), 11.

[94] Thomas Jefferson to John Trumbull, January 18, 1789, Founders Online, National Archives, https://founders.archives.gov/documents/Jefferson/01-14-02-0239.

[95] Bradley J. Birzer, "Algernon Sidney and Yet One More Beautiful Founding Complication", *Imaginative Conservative*, March 24, 2014, https://theimaginativeconservative.org/2014/03/algernon-sidney-yet-one-beautiful-founding-complication.html.

[96] Thomas Jefferson, "Meeting Minutes of University of Virginia Board of Visitors, 4–5 Mar. 1825, 4 March 1825", in *Thomas Jefferson: Writings*, ed. Merrill Peterson (New York: Library of America, 1984), 479, Founders Early Access, http://rotunda.upress.virginia.edu/founders/default.xqy?keys=FOEA-print-04-02-02-5019.

James Madison included *Discourses* in his 1783 "list of books proper for the use of Congress".

What remains to be seen is how closely Sidney's ideas align with those of Bellarmine and Suárez. As mentioned earlier, Sidney was well aware of, and influenced by, them. "What is surprising", Dr. Birzer remarks, "is how much Sidney relies upon the arguments of the greatest of neo-Thomist Jesuits—especially the Italian so hated in Britain, Roberto Bellermino. Indeed, his own understanding of a state of nature, of Divine grace, and of human liberty is much more closely related to Thomas and his followers than it is to Hobbes, Locke, and their respective followers."[97] The extent of their influence will become clear from Sidney's own words, though he, as a Protestant, could be tetchy about his indebtedness to the thought of Catholic prelates. Sidney objected that Filmer "absurdly imputes to the School Divines that which was taken up by them as a common notion, written in the heart of every man, denied by none, but such as were degenerated into beasts".[98] He said that "the common Notions of Liberty are not from School Divines, but from Nature"—a remark with which School divines Bellarmine and Suárez would no doubt have agreed. Sensitive to the similarities of his arguments with Bellarmine's, Sidney complained:

> I do not find any great matters in the passages taken out of Bellarmine, which our author [Filmer] says, comprehend the strength of all that ever he had heard, read, or seen produced for the natural liberty of the subject ...; however there is certainly nothing new in them: We see the same, as to the substance, in those who wrote many ages before him, as well as in many that have lived since his time, who neither minded him, nor what he had written.... He seems to have laid the foundation of his discourses in such common notions as were assented to by all mankind.[99]

But Sidney admitted that "the school men could not lay more approved foundations than that man is naturally free; that he cannot justly be deprived of that liberty without cause; that only those

---

[97] Birzer, "Algernon Sidney".
[98] Sidney, *Discourses*, 43.
[99] Ibid., 52.

governments can be called Just which are established by the consent of nations."[100]

Sidney was far more comfortable quoting fellow Anglican Richard Hooker as a source in attacking Filmer, but the principles he cited are the same as Bellarmine's and Suárez's. Hooker did not directly critique the Divine Right doctrine. He was dead before James I ascended to the throne, but the publication of the eighth book of his *Laws of Ecclesiastical Polity*, forty-eight years after his death, was most likely withheld because of its openly constitutional stance. Though Hooker's attention was mainly directed against the Puritans, his political philosophy had clear implications against absolutism, royal or otherwise. "Happier that people whose law is their King in the greatest things", wrote Hooker, "than that whose King is himself the law."[101] (Certainly that is how John Locke read him, when he liberally drew upon Hooker in his own attacks against the Divine Right theory.) As was seen in chapter 5, Hooker required the people's consent for the sovereign power's legitimacy.

After a series of lengthy quotations from Hooker, Sidney said, "If he [Hooker] be in the right, the choice and constitution of government, the making of laws, coronation, inauguration, and all that belongs to the chusing and making of kings, or other magistrates, is merely from the people; and that all power exercised over them, which is not so, is usurpation and tyranny, unless it be by an immediate commission from God."[102] This point is completely congruent with Bellarmine and Suárez, as is the next one Sidney takes and develops from Hooker:

> The opinions of Hooker, *That all publick regiment, of what kind soever, ariseth from the deliberate advice of men seeking their own good, and that all other is mere tyranny*, are not *untrue and unnatural conceits set abroad* by the seedsmen of *rebellion*; but real truths grounded upon the laws of God and nature, acknowledged and practiced by mankind. And no nation being justly subject to any, but such as they set up, nor in any other

---

[100] Ibid., 43.

[101] Richard Hooker, *Of the Laws of Ecclesiastical Polity*, in *The Works of That Learned and Judicious Divine Mr. Richard Hooker with an Account of His Life and Death by Isaac Walton*, arranged by the Rev. John Keble, M.A., 3 vols., 7th rev. ed. (Oxford: Clarendon Press, 1888), 3:352.

[102] Sidney, *Discourses*, 126.

manner than according to such laws as they ordain, the right of chusing and making those that are to govern them, must wholly depend
upon their will.[103]

Sidney used his central point as the title of chapter 31: "The Liberties of Nations Are from God and Nature, Not from Kings." Should
people be subject to tyranny, they have the right to resist. In the title
of chapter 36, he declared: "The General Revolt of a Nation Cannot
Be Called a Rebellion."[104] The reason for this, he said, is that "all
laws must fall, human societies that subsist by them must be dissolved,
and all innocent persons be exposed to the violence of most wicked,
if men might not justly defend themselves against injustice by their
own natural right, when the ways prescribed by public authority cannot be taken."[105] Here again we see the consistent strain of thought
moving from the Middle Ages and Aquinas through Hooker, Bellarmine, and Suárez to Sidney, and thence to the American Founders.

Like his progenitors, Sidney saw the essential significance of equality as the foundation for all else. "And that liberty, for which we contend as the gift of God and nature, remains equally to them all."[106]
Sectarian sensitivities aside, Sidney supported Bellarmine's positions
and admitted, "I take Bellarmine's first argument ['because by nature
all men are equal; therefore he hath given power to the people or
multitude'] to be strong."[107] It is therefore "hard to comprehend
how one man can come to be master of many, equal to himself in
right, unless it be by consent or by force.... No right can come by
conquest, unless there were a right of making that conquest."[108] In
summary, he understood that "to depend upon the will of a man
is slavery."[109]

Strongly reminiscent of Bellarmine, Sidney wrote as the title of section 6: "God Leaves to Man the Choice of Forms in Government; and
Those Who Constitute One Form, May Abrogate It."[110] He said:

---

[103] Sidney, *Discourses*, 127 (emphasis in original).
[104] Ibid., 438.
[105] Ibid., 298.
[106] Ibid., 475.
[107] Ibid., 55.
[108] Ibid., 64.
[109] Ibid., 51.
[110] Ibid., 54.

Laws and constitutions ought to be weighed, and whilst all due reverence is paid to such as are good, every nation may not only retain
in itself a power of changing or abolishing all such as are not so, but
ought to exercise that power according to the best of their understanding, and in the place of what was either at first mistaken or afterwards corrupted, to constitute that which is most conducing to the
establishment of justice and liberty.[111]

Like Hooker, Bellarmine, and Suárez, he thought that "the best governments of the world have been composed of monarchy, aristocracy, and democracy."[112]

Not surprisingly, Sidney's view of law was also consonant with
Bellarmine's: "If all princes are obliged by the law of nature to preserve the lands, goods, lives and liberties of their subjects, those subjects have by the law of nature a right to their liberties, lands, goods,
&c. and cannot depend upon the will of any man, for that dependence destroys liberty, &c."[113] Echoing Cicero, Aquinas, Suárez, and
Bellarmine, Sidney said, "That which is not just, is not Law; and that
which is not Law, ought not to be obeyed."[114] Furthermore, "there
can be no peace, where there is no justice; nor any justice, if the government instituted for the good of a nation be turned to its ruin."[115]

On a diplomatic mission to Sweden in 1659, Sidney signed the
visitor's book, *The Book of Mottoes*, at the University of Copenhagen
thus: PHILIPPUS SIDNEY MANUS HAEC INIMICA TYRAN-
NIS ENSE PETIT PLACIDAM CUM LIBERTATE QUIETEM
(This hand, enemy to tyrants, by the sword seeks peace with liberty).
The second line of this inscription—"Ense petit placidam sub libertate quietem" (By the sword we seek peace, but peace only under
liberty)—was adopted as the motto of Massachusetts and emblazoned
on its state seal in 1780 by an act of legislature. Sidney's sarcastic summation of Filmer's defense of Divine Right is that God "caused some
to be born with crowns upon their heads, and all others with saddles
upon their backs".[116] This quip found a powerful echo in Jefferson's

[111] Ibid., 392–93.
[112] Ibid., 169.
[113] Ibid., 350
[114] Ibid., 330.
[115] Ibid., 55.
[116] Ibid., 431.

famous line in his last letter, written a few days before his death: "The mass of mankind has not been born with saddles on their backs, nor a favored few booted and spurred, ready to ride them legitimately, by the grace of God."[117]

Sidney's work conveyed influences from the Middle Ages through Hooker, Bellarmine, and Suárez on the subjects of equality, popular sovereignty, the requirement of consent, the rule of law, and the right to revolution directly to the American colonies. These same influences did not leave his contemporary John Locke untouched, though Locke introduced a new element, as we shall see. Michael Novak remarked that

> the founders often paired together Algernon Sidney and John Locke, although they more often cite Locke. Sidney is religiously more orthodox than Locke, and closer to the traditions of Aristotle and Cicero in defining liberty and linking it to certain indispensable virtues. Both authors were, in their respective masterpieces, commenting on the same work of Filmer. However, Sidney gives a larger role to virtue in the definition of liberty; Locke tends to stress the natural equality of all and thus to see individuals as "equal," that is, denuded of the virtues that characterize them differentially. In this, Sidney is closer to the ancients, and Locke to the tendencies of modernity. On *these* matters (not all) Sidney is a better guide to what the founders actually said and did than Locke.[118]

Locke scholar Peter Laslett provides an interesting but controversial claim about Locke's *Two Treatises of Government*. The book, he wrote, "was not the most sought after by the colonists, and it is now known that other 'classics of liberal revolutionism' were in greater demand. Sidney, it appears, did more to legitimate the American revolution than ever Locke did, and *Two Treatises* were used in favour of the Royal regime as established in North America as well as against it."[119] In his famous *The Ideological Origins of the American Revolution*,

---

[117] Thomas Jefferson to Roger Weightman, June 24, 1826, Thomas Jefferson exhibit, Library of Congress, https://www.loc.gov/exhibits/jefferson/214.html.

[118] Michael Novak, *On Two Wings* (San Francisco: Encounter Books, 2002), 198 (emphasis in the original).

[119] John Locke, *Two Treatises of Government*, ed. Peter Laslett (New York: Cambridge University Press, 1988), 14.

Bernard Bailyn pointed to evidence for the latter contention[120] and, in terms of the former, said that "above all, they [the American Revolutionary writers] referred to the doctrines of Algernon Sidney, that 'martyr to civil liberty' whose *Discourses Concerning Government* (1698) became, in Caroline Robbins's phrase, a 'textbook of revolution in America.'"[121]

Regardless of the controversy over who had the greater effect, we have seen how closely aligned the Declaration of Independence and the Virginia Declaration of Rights are to the sources so far outlined. But it is to Locke we now turn to test his teachings against these traditions and consider how he was understood by the Americans whom he so greatly influenced.

[120] Bernard Bailyn, *The Ideological Origins of the American Revolution* (Cambridge, Mass.: Belknap Press, 1967), 28–29.
[121] Ibid., 34–35.

8

John Locke: Problem or Solution?

We have endeavored to show that there is a lineage from Aristotle, Aquinas, Hooker, and Sidney, influenced to a degree by Bellarmine and Suárez, from which the American Founders' thoughts developed, heavily weighted toward the primacy of reason. Where does John Locke fit within this tradition? This is an important question because of his considerable influence on them. Some critics rest their case against the goodness of the Founding's principles largely on Locke, whom they see as a thinly disguised version of Thomas Hobbes. Therefore, we need to take a careful look at Locke's teachings. As we saw in chapter 6, Hobbes was clearly alien to the aforementioned lineage. Did the influence of Hobbes, through Locke's thinking, derail the American Founding from the Christian and natural law tradition by steering it toward radical individualism and materialism? To put the question another way: Was Locke a nominalist and a voluntarist, or was he a natural law realist? The stakes here are high, because, as we saw in earlier chapters, nominalism and voluntarism are the philosophical foundations for the primacy of will over reason—in other words, the will to power—which translates politically as tyranny. Did a Locke-influenced Founding enthrone human will as the untethered supreme power in these United States—thus leading to our current moral and cultural catastrophe?

Locke's standing is a difficult and somewhat contentious matter because, as we shall see, there are ways in which Locke was in continuity with the tradition, and other ways in which he was not. The first part of this chapter will examine the continuity, and the latter half will deal with the controversy over Locke as a Hobbesian Trojan Horse. There is no attempt here to resolve the Locke quandary—which by itself would require a lifetime of scholarship—nor is any resolution necessary. The question at issue is not whether his teachings could be put to disparate uses, but rather to what use the Founders put them. What matters is how the Founders understood him and to what purposes they applied their understanding. What attracted them to Locke, and why was he so frequently quoted from the pulpits of New England divines in the colonial period? This question is answerable.

The Founders took Locke to be in the tradition of Richard Hooker. It was reasonable for them to do so. The continuity in Locke's thinking is easy to detect from his many citations of Hooker in the *Treatises* (sixteen quotations) and elsewhere. Locke frequently called upon Hooker as an authority because he relied on the classical natural law tradition to shore up his arguments. This was not necessarily disingenuous—a screen behind which to hide his more radical thinking. As the early *Essays on the Law of Nature* demonstrate, he genuinely admired Hooker and was steeped in his thinking. James O. Hancey claims, "Essentially, the law of nature for Locke is the same universal law of reason valid for all men because of their human nature, which can be traced to the Stoics, through the Roman lawyers, the Christian era ... and ultimately through the 'judicious' Hooker."[1] Later in life, Locke compiled a reading list for gentlemen. Under the subject of "politics", he recommended his own *Two Treatises*, but also Hooker's *Laws* (as well as Sidney's *Discourses*).

From Locke's writings we will extract statements that parallel those of Bellarmine, Suárez, and Sidney, as set forth in chapter 7, regarding the principles of human equality, popular sovereignty, the requirement of consent, representation, and the moral right to revolution against tyranny. As the reader will see, the statements from all four sources are so similar that they could well be paraphrases of each other. Locke *inherited* the ideas he passed on so persuasively in his writings. One can argue that the basis on which Locke made such statements had changed, but we shall see that the substance nevertheless largely remained the same. Furthermore, we will observe the same close coincidence of Locke's statements with the words of the Declaration of Independence and the Virginia

---

[1] James O. Hancey, "John Locke and the Law of Nature", *Political Theory* 4, no. 4 (November 1976): 440.

Declaration of Rights, as were seen in the three other thinkers. Of course, in Locke's case, this is hardly strange, since certain lines in those documents, such as the "pursuit of happiness", are thought to have come more or less straight from him (though the prior chapter showed from where else they might have come). In any case, the following citations are well within the tradition we have been tracing and show why the American Founders saw Locke as part of it.

In concert with the lineage above, Locke especially espoused the rule of law as based on reason, not on the arbitrariness of will. His attack on Sir Robert Filmer's *Patriarcha* demonstrated that he was a lethal opponent of the Divine Right of Kings or any other form of political absolutism. "Freedom", wrote Locke, "is not what Sir Robert Filmer tells us: 'A liberty for every one to do what he lists, to live as he pleases, and not to be tied by any laws'; but freedom of men under government is to have a standing rule to live by, common to every one of that society, and made by the legislative power erected in it."[2] The objective, he said, is "not to be subject to the inconstant, uncertain, unknown, arbitrary will of another man".[3] He wrote that "freedom from absolute, arbitrary power is so necessary to, and closely joined with, a man's preservation that he cannot part with it, but by what forfeits his preservation and life together."[4] Thus, "reason bids me look on him, as an enemy to my preservation, who would take that freedom away."[5] So great is Locke's repugnance for those who do not recognize, or will not abide by, the rule of reason that such a person may be destroyed by anyone "for the same reason that he may kill a wolf or a lion, because they are not under the ties of the common law of reason, have no other rule but that of force and violence, and so may be treated as a beast of prey, those dangerous and noxious creatures that will be sure to destroy him whenever he falls into their power".[6]

In the *First Treatise*, Locke repeatedly cited the Genesis account of man made in "the image of God" to make the point against Filmer that *all* men are so made, and not Adam exclusively.

[2] John Locke, *Second Treatise of Government* 4, 21.
[3] Ibid.
[4] Locke, *Second Treatise* 4, 22.
[5] Ibid., 3, 18.
[6] Locke, *Second Treatise* 3, 16.

Therefore, Adam was not possessed of a patriarchal Divine Right to rule, passed on to his eldest male heirs down to the present day. In the *Second Treatise*, Locke uses the imago Dei without recourse to Scripture, but to the same effect: to demonstrate the inviolability of the human person as God's property. "For men being all the workmanship of one omnipotent and infinitely wise Maker; all the servants of one sovereign Master, sent into the world by His order and about His business; they are His property, whose workmanship they are, made to last during His, not one another's pleasure."[7] Like his predecessors, Locke believed that human life is sacrosanct because of its provenance. In fact, this provenance is the foundation of his entire political philosophy, which stands or falls on it alone. He warned: "The taking away of God, even if only in thought, dissolves all."[8] Obviously, man's life cannot be sacred unless there is a God to sanctify it, which is why Locke was so adamantly insistent on God's existence.

This also helps explain Locke's revulsion at atheism: "Those are not at all to be tolerated who deny the being of God. Promises, covenants, and oaths, which are the bonds of human society, can have no hold upon or sanctity for an atheist."[9] Locke maintained that "the belief of a deity is not to be reckoned amongst purely speculative opinions, for it being the foundation of all morality, and that which influences the whole life and actions of man, without which a man is to be counted no other than one of the most dangerous sorts of wild beasts and so incapable of all society."[10] The "infinitely wise Maker" is also the guarantor of man's equality, as no one is any less the workmanship of God than anyone else. This is the sacred basis of equality. If we are all God's property, we cannot be each other's property; we cannot own what properly belongs to God. Therefore, man "cannot take away his own life, cannot give another power over it".[11] Thus, declared Locke, "the State of Nature [into which man is born] has a law of Nature to govern it, which obliges everyone,

---

[7] Locke, *Second Treatise* 2, 6.

[8] John Locke, *A Letter concerning Toleration* (Buffalo, N.Y.: Broadview Editions, 2013), 81.

[9] Ibid.

[10] John Locke, "Essay on Toleration", in *Political Essays*, ed. Mark Goldie (New York: Cambridge University Press, 1997), 137.

[11] Locke, *Second Treatise* 4, 22.

and reason, which is that law, teaches all mankind, who will but consult it, that being *all equal* and independent, no one ought to harm another in his life, health, liberty, or possessions."[12] Beyond that, "every one, as he is bound to preserve himself, and not to quit his station wilfully, so by the like reason, when his own preservation comes not in competition, ought he as much as he can to preserve the rest of mankind."[13] The state of nature is imperfect, however, in not having a means of enforcement for the law of nature. Therefore, men are naturally driven to form a polity by means of which it can be enforced.

Being subject to the law of nature, the laws of this polity must be in conformity with it: "Thus the Law of Nature stands as an Eternal Rule to all Men, *Legislators* as well as others. The *Rules* that they make for other Men's actions must ... be conformable to the Law of Nature, i.e., to the will of God."[14] He repeated: "The law of Nature ... [is] as intelligible and plain to a rational creature, and a studier of that law, as the positive laws of commonwealths; nay, possibly plainer.... The municipal laws of countries ... are only so far right, as they are founded on the law of Nature, by which they are to be regulated and interpreted."[15] What is emphatically clear is that, unlike Hobbes, Locke held that moral rights and duties exist in the state of nature and *precede* the formation of government and the formulation of human laws. Government obtains its legitimacy through its foundation on the laws of nature, which it cannot subsequently transgress. It is held to account by these laws, which are an expression of God's law. First among these laws is man's equality.

Equality and Consent

Equality means that no one has the *natural* right to rule another: "A state [all men are naturally in] ... of equality, wherein all the power and jurisdiction is reciprocal, no one having more than another,

---

[12] Locke, *Second Treatise* 2, 6 (my emphasis).
[13] Ibid.
[14] Locke, *Second Treatise* 11, 135.
[15] Locke, *Second Treatise* 2, 12.

there being nothing more evident than that creatures of the same species and rank, promiscuously born to all the same advantages of Nature, and the use of the same faculties, should also be equal one amongst another, without subordination or subjection."[16] This statement is followed by an extensive citation from Hooker to the effect, as Locke says in his own words, that "this *equality* of Men by Nature" supplies "the Foundation of that Obligation to mutual Love amongst Men, on which he Builds the Duties they owe one another, and from whence he derives the great Maxims *of Justice* and *Charity*." As both Hooker and Locke make clear, equality is a *moral* principle.

As Hooker, Bellarmine, and Suárez had said, equality *requires* consent in being ruled. Locke strongly reiterated this: "MEN being, as has been said, by nature, all free, equal, and independent, no one can be put out of this estate, and subjected to the political power of another, without his own consent. The only way whereby any one divests himself of his natural liberty, and puts on the bonds of civil society, is by agreeing with other men to join and unite into a community."[17] Locke said, "The liberty of man, in society, is to be under no other legislative power, but that established, by consent, in the commonwealth; nor under the dominion of any will, or restraint of any law, but what that legislative shall enact, according to the trust put in it."[18]

Once having consented, the people yet preserve sovereignty and therefore may hold accountable those who rule them: "The community perpetually retains a supreme power of saving themselves from the attempts and designs of anybody, even of their legislators, whenever they shall be so foolish or so wicked as to lay and carry on designs against the liberties and properties of the subject."[19] Locke insisted that governments are limited by the purpose for which they were founded, the good of the people.[20] Or again, he stated that "there remains still in the people a supreme power to remove or alter

---

[16] Locke, *Second Treatise* 2, 4.

[17] Locke, *Second Treatise* 8. 95.

[18] Locke, *Second Treatise* 4, 21.

[19] Locke, *Second Treatise* 13, 149.

[20] Steven M. Dworelz, *The Unvarnished Doctrine: Locke, Liberalism, and the American Revolution* (Durham, N.C.: Duke University Press, 1990), 153.

the legislative, when they find the legislative act contrary to the trust reposed in them."[21]

The Right to Revolution

This standard gives the people the right to revolution, and it made Locke especially attractive to Americans. What might constitute so grave a breach in trust between the people and their government as to warrant a revolution? "Whenever the legislators endeavor to take away and destroy the property of the people", said Locke, "or to reduce them to slavery under arbitrary power, they put themselves into a state of war with the people, who are thereupon absolved from any further obedience, and are left to the common refuge which God hath provided for all men against force and violence."[22] Locke repeated this point to make sure it was understood: "He who attempts to get another man into his absolute power, does thereby put himself into a state of war with him; it being to be understood as a declaration of a design upon his life." He added, "He who would get me into his power without my consent, would use me as he pleased when he had got me there ... unless it be to compel me by force to that which is against the right of my freedom, i.e. make me a slave."[23] In 1770, the Massachusetts Assembly responded to a speech of Lt. Gov. Thomas Hutchinson by invoking Locke: "We beg leave to recite to your honor what the great Mr. Locke has advanced in his treatise of civil government." They repeated Locke's argument that if the government seeks to "enslave or destroy" the people, they have no other remedy "but to appeal to Heaven" for the justified use of violence.[24]

Applying this principle to his own time, Locke found James II at fault for "actually putting himself in a State of War with his People", just as the Colonial Congress would later find George III had done

---

[21] Locke, *Second Treatise* 13, 149.

[22] Locke, *Second Treatise* 19, 222.

[23] Locke, *Second Treatise* 3, 17.

[24] *Speeches of the Governors of Massachusetts from 1765–1775* (Boston: Russell and Gardner, 1818), 242, in cited in Thomas G. West, *The Political Theory of the American Founding: Natural Rights, Public Policy, and the Moral Conditions of Freedom* (New York: Cambridge University Press, 2017), 56.

in respect to the American people. Locke stated: "If a long train of abuses, prevarications, and artifices, all tending the same way, make the design [of tyranny] visible to the people, and they cannot but feel what they lie under, and see whither they are going, it is not to be wondered that they should then rouse themselves, and endeavour to put the rule into such hands which may secure to them the ends for which government was at first erected."[25] The Declaration of Independence echoed this pronouncement very closely: "When a long train of abuses and usurpations, pursuing invariably the same Object evinces a design to reduce them under absolute Despotism, it is their right, it is their duty, to throw off such Government, and to provide new Guards for their future security."

Locke and the Founders

The American Founders clearly saw Locke in the tradition we have been delineating. Jefferson and Adams explicitly placed him there. In an 1825 letter to Henry Lee about the Declaration of Independence, Jefferson wrote: "All its authority rests on the harmonizing sentiments of the day, whether expressed in conversation, in letters, in printed essays, or the elementary books of public right, as Aristotle, Cicero, Locke, Sidney, etc."[26] Closer to the time of the Revolution, John Adams said something similar: "These are what are called revolution principles. They are the principles of Aristotle and Plato, of Livy and Cicero, of Sydney, Harrington and Locke; the principles of nature and eternal reason."[27]

Locke is the only one in these groupings who could possibly be read as undermining classical natural law teleology due to his empiricist epistemology in the *Essay concerning Human Understanding*. Since the other thinkers embraced a more teleological understanding of

---

[25] Locke, *Second Treatise* 19, 225.

[26] Thomas Jefferson to Henry Lee, May 8, 1825, Founders Online, National Archives, https://founders.archives.gov/documents/Jefferson/98-01-02-5212.

[27] John Adams, *The Letters of Novanglus*, no. 1, January 23, 1775, in *Papers of John Adams*, vol. 2, *December 1773–April 1775*, ed. Robert. J. Taylor (Cambridge, Mass.: Belknap Press, 1977), Massachusetts Historical Society, http://www.masshist.org/publications/adams -papers/view?&id=PJA02dg5.

nature, one can assume that Jefferson and Adams did not read Locke in this way. Otherwise, his presence in their groupings would be completely incongruous. Jefferson could hardly have claimed that the "harmonizing sentiments of the day" included them all together, as they would not have harmonized.

When one sets Locke's empiricist epistemology from the *Essay* aside and focuses on the subject of what Jefferson called "public right", the problem goes away and the sentence makes sense. The modern way of reading Locke, strongly influenced by Leo Strauss' *Natural Right and History*, is to extract the radical epistemology from the *Essay* and then use it to elicit esoteric teachings from the rest of Locke, including from his earlier writings on natural law. There is certainly a modern element in Locke, but it is not the only element and it is not what appealed to the Founders. They did not read Locke and then decide to start a revolution. They took from Locke what was useful to them in their revolution, and not necessarily his epistemology. Jefferson rejected the Lockean notion that there are no innate ideas. As we shall see, James Wilson was overtly critical of Locke's epistemology. Michael Novak mused: "If it is legitimate to argue [as some followers of Leo Strauss do] that Locke used Christian terms to subvert Christian premises, it is equally legitimate to hypothesize that many in the founding generation used Lockean terms for Christian purposes."[28] John Adams mocked Locke's legislative acumen. In *A Defence of the Constitutions of Governments of the United States*, he spoke of the "signal absurdity" that Locke produced: "Mr. Locke, in 1663, was employed to trace out a plan of legislation for Carolina; and he gave the whole authority, executive and legislative, to the eight proprietors.... Who did this legislator think would live under his government? He should have first created a new species of beings to govern, before he instituted such a government."[29] Speaking of Locke's analysis of moral law and its enforcement in his *Essay*, scholar Thomas West says, "I know of no evidence that the founders knew of Locke's analysis, although some were familiar with the *Essay*."[30] Indeed, it was irrelevant to their endeavors.

---

[28] Michael Novak, *On Two Wings* (San Francisco: Encounter Books, 2002), 198n34.

[29] Cited in ibid., 87–88.

[30] West, *Political Theory*, 188–89.

In any case, we will contend that the attempt to portray Locke as an epigone of Hobbes for the purpose of imputing modern America's faults to the Founding will not stand up to scrutiny. Since so much in the contemporary attacks on the Founding depends on the characterization of Locke as Hobbes with a smiley face, it is necessary to address the charge. The argument can be reduced to a simple syllogism:

> Hobbes and Locke are the same;
> the American Founding is Lockean;
> ergo, the American Founding is Hobbesian.

The first part of the syllogism is on ample display in the writings of scholars such as Patrick Deneen and Michael Hanby, who typically refer to "Hobbes' philosophical successor John Locke". In their work, Locke's name rarely appears unless it is paired with Hobbes'—as in "Hobbes and Locke", repeated over and over again. But do they really belong together?

For all the influence Hobbes is supposed to have had on Locke, Locke scholar Peter Laslett points out that, in the voluminous body of Locke's private notebooks, which consist largely of citations from the books of others, "it is a most remarkable fact that it has not been possible to find a single referenced extract from the works of Hobbes in the whole Lockeian corpus."[31] In his other writings, Locke only referred to Hobbes several times, always disparagingly, as in Hobbes' "justly decried" name.[32] A staunch believer in free will, Locke spoke of "the religion of Hobbes and Spinoza ... resolving all ... into an irresistible fatal necessity".[33] In another unfavorable reference, he wrote: "If a Christian ... be asked why a man must keep his word, he will give this as a reason: because God, who has the power of eternal life and death, requires it of us. But if an Hobbist be asked why; he will answer: because the public requires it, and the Leviathan will punish you, if you do not."[34] More importantly, if Hobbes

---

[31] *Locke: Two Treatises of Government*, ed. Peter Laslett (New York: Cambridge University Press, 1988), 74.

[32] Ibid.

[33] Locke, *Political Essays*, 214n1.

[34] John Locke, *An Essay concerning Human Understanding* 3, 5.

and Locke shared the same premises, as scholars such as Deneen and Hanby allege, how is it that they reached opposite conclusions, one in favor of absolutism and the other against it? In what might be read as a rebuke to Hobbes, Locke wrote, "He that thinks absolute power purifies men's bloods, and corrects the baseness of human nature, need read but the history of this or any other age to be convinced of the contrary."[35]

A Two-Faced Janus?

Nonetheless, let us briefly review the controversy over Locke's thinking that helped give rise to the impression of him as a covert clone of Hobbes. One thing on which we can rely is the complexity of Locke's thought. There seems to be a profound ambiguity in it. Some scholars, such as George Sabine, think that there are really two Lockes and they cannot ultimately be reconciled with each other. This problem did not go unobserved at the time at which Locke wrote or later in the American colonial era. Founder James Wilson, for instance, said:

> I am ... far from believing that Mr. Locke was a friend to infidelity. But yet it is unquestionable, that the writings of Mr. Locke have facilitated the progress, and have given strength to the effects of scepticism. The high reputation, which he deservedly acquired for his enlightened attachment to the mild and tolerating doctrines of christianity, secured to him the esteem and confidence of those, who were its friends. The same high and deserved reputation inspired others of very different views and characters, with a design to avail themselves of its splendour, and, by that means, to diffuse a fascinating kind of lustre over their own tenets of a dark and sable hue.[36]

Legal scholar Harold Berman wryly observed that "the surprising fact that both sides in this great religious-philosophical and political-legal debate could appeal to the writings of John Locke is due to the

---

[35] Locke, *Second Treatise* 7, 92.

[36] *Collected Works of James Wilson*, ed. Kermit L. Hall and Mark David Hall, vol. 1 (Indianapolis: Liberty Fund, 2007), 472–73.

greatly neglected fact that those writings could be construed either as a justification of the aristocratic, traditionalist, and communitarian English Revolution, or as a foundation of the democratic, rationalist, and individualist program eventually embodied in the French Revolution."[37]

How is it that Locke could be read in two such opposing ways? A great deal depends on the context in which he is placed, because, to a certain degree, the context decides the content. *Philosophes* such as Helvétius and Condorcet put Locke in the framework of French Enlightenment thinking and radicalized his empiricism and sensationalist psychology to materialist ends of which he no doubt would have disapproved—since they resulted in the proto-totalitarian Jacobin state of the French Revolution.[38] They did this at the expense of his sincere Christian beliefs and his aversion to extremism. Wilson himself protested that "the writings of Mr. Locke, one of the most able, most sincere, and most amiable assertors of christianity and true philosophy, have been perverted to purposes, which he would have deprecated and prevented, had he discovered or foreseen them."[39] Modern detractors of Locke assert that he had foreseen such purposes and intended them, or else that his premises and method invariably produced such ill effects, despite his intentions.

The susceptibility of Locke's writings to "perversion" may have come from the empirical perspective he brought to things. From his medical training, Locke may have been predisposed toward empiricism. Sensory experience, he thought, is impressed upon the tabulae rasae of our minds, which contain no innate ideas. Our only knowledge comes from reflection upon these experiences. Locke insisted on starting with the particular, as only the particular comes through the senses, and then carefully exploring what can be generally postulated.

---

[37] Harold J. Berman, "The Impact of the Enlightenment on American Constitutional Law", *Yale Journal of Law and the Humanities* 4, no. 2 (January 1992): 324.

[38] Note: Thomas Jefferson reviled Helvétius: "What other motive than self-interest could determine a man to generous action? It is as impossible for him [Helvétius] to love what is good for the sake of good, as to love evil for the sake of evil." Cited in Deal W. Hudson, *Happiness and the Limits of Satisfaction* (Lanham, Md.: Rowman and Littlefield, 1996), 86.

[39] Wilson, *Collected Works*, 473.

Locke was attempting to use the scientific approach of Sir Isaac Newton as a foundation for constitutional government's resistance to absolutism. Much of his work is really an exploration of how well empiricism could be used to undergird a constitutional edifice that defended the very same principles Sidney, Hooker, and his other predecessors espoused. He wanted to get to the same destination by other means. The advantage the empirical approach would provide, thought Locke, was one of certainty, though he recognized that empiricism carried with it an element of probability. If it worked, he would have proofs of almost mathematical indisputability for things that were thought to be known only theoretically. Empirical assessments would strip away the dross and reveal the real fundamentals and reliable knowledge of morality on which all else could be built. And so, Locke made the remarkable statement: "Morality is capable of demonstration, as well as mathematics; since the precise real essence of things moral words stand for may be perfectly known, and so the congruity or incongruity of the things themselves can be certainly discovered, in which consists perfect knowledge."[40]

In addition, as a Protestant, Locke was affected to some degree by the nominalism and voluntarism of the Reformation, which itself also ineluctably led to empiricism, as indicated in chapter 4. Things are the way they are because the strongest will—God's—commanded that they be so. Locke said natural law is "a law enacted by a superior power"; "for, in the first place, it is a decree of a superior will".[41] Law as will is the essence of voluntarism, which, in turn, undermines the foundation of nature as intrinsic in things (nominalism), as we saw in chapter 3. These two Protestant (and Ockhamist) trends may also have driven Locke in the direction of empiricism, though his grounding in Hooker saved him from their full implications (e.g., the results of voluntarism and nominalism seen in Luther in chapter 4). In fact, James O. Hancey observes that "Locke brings to natural law a rationalist position and, like Aquinas, achieves one of the more curious unions in the history of philosophical thought, that of the rationalist and the fideistic positions."[42] Locke also clearly saw

---

[40] Locke, *Essay concerning Human Understanding* 3, 11, 16.
[41] Locke, *Political Essays*, 83.
[42] Hancey, "John Locke", 440.

that something else was necessary to reach his goal of constraining arbitrary rule. In fact, he came to conclusions opposite to Luther's and embraced the constitutional principles that Luther jettisoned.

Despite the tinge of voluntarism and nominalism in his thinking, Locke believed that God's divine intellect was rational. Contrary to the impression of voluntarism in the statements above, Locke wrote that natural law

> does not depend on an unstable and changeable will, but on the eternal order of things. For it seems to me that certain essential features of things are immutable, and that certain duties arise out of necessity and cannot be other than they are.... Since man has been made such as he is, equipped with reason, and his other faculties ... there necessarily result from his inborn constitution some definite duties for him which cannot be other than they are.... For according to His infinite and eternal wisdom, [God] has made man such that these duties of his necessarily follow from his very nature.[43]

This affirmation provides theological support for natural law. Thus, reason retains its integrity in its capacity to apprehend the order of creation, which is rationally discernible and morally compelling. Locke referred to reason as "our only star and compass".[44] What is more, Locke's statement regarding a "superior will" should not be misunderstood as meaning a superior *force*. Power in this sense does not bestow moral legitimacy. To the contrary, Locke asserted, "A man can never be obliged in conscience to submit to any power, unless he can be satisfied who is the person who has a *right* to exercise that power over him. If this were not so, there would be no distinction between pirates and lawful princes, he that has force is without any more ado to be obeyed, and crowns and scepters would become the inheritance of violence and rapine."[45] As far as Locke's alleged nominalism, it did not extend to the absurdities of the fourteenth-century English nominalists examined in chapter 3. Locke said, "If anyone pretends to be so skeptical as to deny his own existence (for

[43] Locke, *Political Essays*, 125.
[44] John Locke, *First Treatise of Government* 1, 58.
[45] Locke, *First Treatise* 9, 81 (my emphasis).

really to doubt of it is manifestly impossible) let him for me enjoy his beloved happiness of being nothing, until hunger, or some other pain, convince him of the contrary."[46]

Locke's rather restrictive epistemology, however, considerably reduced what man could know with full confidence—thus the charge of skepticism—while concomitantly expanding the realm of what he must therefore accept provisionally. While there might be great certainty about a few things, there would be less certainty about many. This had the effect of deflating competing claims to surety. There was an advantage to this. It minimized differences or, more accurately, minimized the importance of those differences. In doing so, Locke was not driven by a radical skepticism (of the kind seen later in David Hume) but by a desire for civic peace. With so much reduced to mere probability, men would have less to fight over and more reason to behave moderately. Why kill each other over a mere probability? The lack of certainty would promote toleration—something Locke saw as sorely needed after the slaughters of the English Civil Wars. Locke scholar Greg Forster explains that "this minimal-content approach allowed Locke to build consensus across the lines of religious belief."[47] Grounding man's obligations only in religion no longer worked in regard to civil order because it was religious dissension that most threatened that order. The universality of the Church had made a single Christian commonwealth conceivable. The common faith that had been the glue of medieval society no longer existed—torn asunder by the Reformation. There was no longer a shared agreement as to *how* to know what true Christianity is. As Locke said, "everyone is orthodox to himself",[48] but not necessarily to others. Religious uniformity could no longer be a desideratum of civil order because it was precisely this requirement that was tearing society apart by transforming politics into a form of spiritual warfare. Religious toleration became, if for no other reason, a political necessity. Therefore, said Locke (sounding like Gelasius), "I esteem it above all things necessary to distinguish exactly the business of civil

---

[46] Locke, *An Essay concerning Human Understanding* 10, 2.

[47] Greg Forster, *Starting with Locke* (New York: Continuum International, 2011), 140.

[48] John Locke, *A Letter concerning Toleration* (1689), trans. William Popple, Constitution Society, http://www.constitution.org/jl/tolerati.htm.

government from that of religion and to settle the just bounds that lie between the one and the other."[49]

The State of Nature

A new basis for civil order had to be provided, grounded in reason yet retaining a transcendent dimension of authority as its foundation. Reason, backed by generic, nonsectarian Christianity, is Locke's solution to the dissolution of Christendom. What could provide a national basis for a return to some kind of civil comity? The answer came in the form of "the state of nature", applying to all, regardless of religious sect. According to Harry Jaffa, "The theory of the state of nature—whose law is reason—as the ground of political obligation, emancipates church and state to pursue their proper goals in a manner both complementary and harmonious."[50] Thomas West writes that Locke's "overall argument gave to political obligation a new basis consistent with Christianity's universal claim but independent of any particular religious sect."[51] That new basis was the law of nature, in light of which a confessional state was no longer a necessity.

He was everywhere trying to reduce the sources of faction. George Sabine said, "Locke's political philosophy was an effort to combine past and present and also to find a nucleus of agreement for reasonable men of all parties."[52] One must also keep in mind that Locke, as Sabine said, was "an empiricist but with a large residue of philosophical rationalism and a firm belief in self-evident principles of right and wrong".[53] Indeed, it was only outside his empirical methodology that Locke found justification for the divinely endowed right to life, liberty, and estate that was the bedrock of his political philosophy. Locke was not *only* an empiricist. Reducing his thought to just that is

[49] Ibid.

[50] Edward J. Erler and Ken Masugi, eds., *The Rediscovery of America: Essays by Harry V. Jaffa on the New Birth of Politics* (Lanham, Md.: Rowman and Littlefield, 2019), 45.

[51] Thomas G. West, introduction to Algernon Sidney, *Discourses concerning Government*, ed. Thomas G. West (Indianapolis: Liberty Fund, 1996), xxii.

[52] George H. Sabine, *A History of Political Theory* (New York: Holt, Rineheart, and Winston, 1961), 537.

[53] Ibid., 519.

what allowed it to be "perverted to purposes, which he would have deprecated and prevented", as James Wilson said.[54]

Happiness or Hedonism?

We will briefly examine some statements by Locke that led to his having been taken as a radical individualist. Locke shared with Aristotle the notion that human action was directed by nature to the ultimate end of human happiness. As Aristotle said in book 10 of *The Ethics*, "We choose everything for the sake of something else— except happiness; for happiness is an end." Locke agreed that *"all desire happiness."*[55] In fact, he declaimed: "God Almighty himself is under the necessity of being happy."[56] Locke seemed to differ substantially from Aristotle, however, on what constitutes happiness. He wrote: "Happiness then in its full extent is the utmost Pleasure we are capable of, and Misery the utmost pain."[57] He said, "Happiness and misery seem to me wholly to consist in the pleasure and pain of the mind."[58]

Some critics have claimed that in these and other remarks, Locke reduced morality to a subjective pleasure-pain mechanism and that this hedonism is what the American Founding ingested through his influence. They believe that Locke's teaching is one of self-centered felicific calculation: to each his own good, and who is to say what that good is? It is all relative to an individual's desires. One thinks of Callicles, who, in Plato's *Gorgias*, asserted that "luxury and licentiousness and self-indulgence, if they have the support of force, are virtue and happiness." Yet Locke is not so far from Plato's view as expressed in his *Laws* (1, 636): "Pleasure and Pain are two fountains set flowing by nature, and according to the degree of prudence and moderation with which men draw from them, men are happy or otherwise." In *Essays on the Law of Nature*, Locke emphatically stated that "each man's personal interest is not the basis of natural law." In

---

[54] See footnote 36.

[55] John Locke, *An Essay concerning Human Understanding* 21, 42.

[56] Ibid., 21, 51.

[57] Ibid., 21, 43.

[58] John Locke, *Essays on the Law of Nature* (Oxford: Oxford University Press, 1988), 268.

what could serve as a rebuttal to the charges of hedonism, he asserted that "in fact, a great number of virtues, and the best of them, consist in this: that we do good to others at our own loss."[59] Further, he said:

> We do deny that each person is at liberty to do what he himself, according to the circumstances, judges to be of advantage to him. You have certainly no reason for holding that each person's own interest is the standard of what is just and right.... Hence the point of the question is precisely this: is it true that what each individual in the circumstances judges to be of advantage to himself and his affairs is in accordance with natural law, and on that account is not only lawful for him but also unavoidable, and that nothing in nature is binding except so far as it carries with it some immediate personal advantage? It is this we deny.[60]

Locke made clear that happiness is not whatever man says it is, but only what will truly make him happy. "The highest perfection of intellectual nature", wrote Locke, "lies in a careful and constant pursuit of true and solid happiness; so the care of ourselves, that we mistake not imaginary for real happiness, is the necessary foundation of our liberty."[61] He warned that "I must have a care I mistake not, for if I prefer a short pleasure to a lasting one, 'tis plain I cross my own happiness."[62] In fact, in *Some Thoughts on Education*, he stated, "The principle of all virtue lies in a power of denying ourselves the satisfaction of our own desires, where reason does not authorize them."[63] He advised that "he that has not a mastery over his inclinations, he that knows not how to resist the importunity of present pleasure or pain, for the sake of what reason tells him is fit to be done, wants the true principle of virtue and industry, and is in danger never to be good for any thing." Young gentleman, he said, should be taught to "be in love with all the ways of virtue".[64]

What is "fit to be done" is what it is reasonable, and therefore moral, to do. In the *Letter on Toleration*, Locke used explicitly moral

---

[59] Locke, *Political Essays*, 129.
[60] Ibid.
[61] Locke, *An Essay concerning Human Understanding* 21, 52.
[62] Locke, *Political Essays*, 296.
[63] Cited in Dworetz, *The Unvarnished Doctrine*, xiii.
[64] John Locke, *Some Thoughts concerning Education* 58.

language in referring to "the wickedness of human beings ... such that most prefer to enjoy the fruits of other men's labor rather than work to provide for themselves".[65] Locke spoke of "covetousness and the desire of having in our possession and under our dominion more than we have need of, being the root of all evil, should be early and carefully weeded out and the contrary quality of a readiness to impart to others implanted."[66] He warned, " 'Twould always be a sin in any man of estate, to let his brother perish for want of affording him relief out of his plenty."[67] In the *Second Treatise*, as quoted earlier, he said, "Freedom, then, is not what Sir Robert Filmer tells us: 'A liberty for every one to do what he lists, to live as he pleases, and not to be tied by any laws.' "[68] Indeed, wrote Locke, if men's appetites "were left to their full swing they would carry men to the overturning of all morality. Moral laws are set as a curb and restraint to these exorbitant desires."[69] In *A Letter concerning Toleration*, Locke said that a true Christian would exercise charity, meekness, and goodwill in general toward all mankind; even to those that are not Christians.[70] He added, "Nay, we must not content ourselves with the narrow measures of bare justice: charity, bounty, and liberality must be added to it. This the Gospel enjoins, this reason directs, and this that natural fellowship we are born into requires of us."[71]

It should be clear from these and other statements that, for Locke, happiness is the quality of a *morally* good life, which is mandatory for man to seek by his nature. It is a moral end that must be pursued rationally. "The freedom then of man and liberty of acting according to his own will is grounded on his having reason, which is able to instruct him in that law he is to govern himself by, and make him know how far he is left to the freedom of his own will."[72]

---

[65] Locke, *A Letter concerning Toleration*, 125.

[66] Locke, *Some Thoughts concerning Education* 110.

[67] Locke, *First Treatise* 4, 42.

[68] Locke, *Second Treatise* 4, 21.

[69] Locke, *An Essay concerning Human Understanding* 3, 13.

[70] John Locke, *A Letter concerning Toleration* (1689), Classic Liberals, http://classicliberal .tripod.com/locke/toleration1.html.

[71] Ibid.

[72] Locke, *Second Treatise* 6, 63.

Rational means are not, as they were for Hobbes, simply "Scouts, and Spies, to range abroad, and find a way to the things Desired". For Locke, happiness is never divorced from virtue. In a fragment written in 1670, Locke said, "Morality is the rule of man's actions for the obtaining of happiness." Elswhere, he added that the virtuous life is to be preferred although "the virtuous life here had nothing but pain, and the vicious continual pleasure." Wicked men, however, "all things rightly considred, have, I think, even the worst part here".[73] This is not far removed from Aristotle's statement that "the happy life is regarded as a life in conformity with virtue."[74] What is more, said Locke, God has "by an inseparable connection joined virtue and public happiness together; and made the practice thereof, necessary to the preservation of society, and visibly beneficial to all, with whom the virtuous man has to do; it is no wonder, that every man should, not only allow, but recommend and magnify those rules to others."[75] In his *Letter on Toleration*, Locke also made clear that this teaching bears upon the proper character of political order: "Rectitude of morals ... concerns political life, and in it is involved the safety ... of the commonwealth; moral actions, therefore ... are subject to the government.... No doctrines adverse ... to the good morals that are necessary to the preservation of civil society are to be tolerated by the government."[76] As Locke scholar Dr. Thomas G. West says: "Someone will object that for Locke, morality is not the purpose of government. That is incorrect. The law of nature is a moral law, and government's main task is to enforce that law."[77]

Locke reviled the very kind of hedonism that he is sometimes accused of advocating. He criticized those "who, giving way to their own desires, making themselves their own god and their own end, will not hearken to any of the truths of natural or revealed religion.... They seek it not for that end for which God designed it, which is not as improvement of our parts and speculations, but of our love of Him and charity to our neighbor, and that increase of our

---

[73] Locke, *An Essay concerning Human Understanding* 2, 70.

[74] Aristotle, *Ethics* 10, 1177a.

[75] Locke, *An Essay concerning Human Understanding* 3, 6.

[76] Cited in West, *Political Theory*, 174.

[77] Thomas West, "Locke's Neglected Teaching", *Social Science and Modern Society* 50, no. 5 (September–October 2013), 475.

knowledge should make our lives better."[78] To those not cognizant of "the greatest absent good", by which Locke meant heaven, because of their "pursuit of nearer satisfactions", he exhorted:

> To him, I say, who hath a prospect of the different state of perfect happiness or misery that attends all men after this life, depending on their behaviour here, the measures of good and evil that govern his choice, are mightily changed. For since nothing of pleasure or pain in this life can bear any proportion to the endless happiness, or exquisite misery, of an immortal soul hereafter, actions in his power will have their preference, not according to the transient pleasure or pain that accompanies or follows them here, but as they serve to secure that perfect durable happiness thereafter.[79]

Locke seemed to live by this creed himself. As he lay dying in 1704, he asked to be remembered in evening prayer. He said that, as he was departing, what remained for him to do here was to thank God. While grateful, he said that this life appeared to him as "pure vanity". Then he told Lady Damaris Masham, "Regard this world only as a stage of preparation for a better one." The last thing he heard and asked to hear were the psalms, read to him by Lady Masham.[80] This touching scene gives further force to Oxford's Jeremy Waldron's statement that he doubts "one can even make sense of a position like Locke's ... apart from the specifically biblical and Christian teaching that he associated with it."[81]

Locke versus Hobbes

The purpose here has not been to deny that there are other readings of Locke but only to emphasize that there is ample reason for the

---

[78] Cited in David Walsh, *The Growth of the Liberal Soul* (Columbia: University of Missouri Press, 1997), 158–59.

[79] Locke, *An Essay concerning Human Understanding* 21, 60.

[80] Jean Le Clerc, *Bibliothèque Choisie, pour servir de suite à la Bibliothèque Universelle*, vol. 6 (Amsterdam: Henry Schelte, 1705), 400.

[81] Jeremy Waldron, *God, Locke and Equality: Christian Foundations of John Locke's Political Thought* (Cambridge: Cambridge University Press, 2002), 13, cited in Donald Devine, "The Real John Locke—and Why He Matters," Law and Liberty, May 21, 2014, http://www.libertylawsite.org/2014/05/21/the-real-john-locke-and-why-he-matters/.

Founders to have seen him within the tradition of the other thinkers whom they embraced, such as Aristotle, Cicero, Hooker, and Sidney. In any case, the argument for Locke as a Hobbesian would have to deal with these essential—I think insurmountable—differences:

- Hobbes used his transmogrification of natural law theory to defend absolutism. Locke used natural law teaching against absolutism and as the basis for limited, representative government.
- Locke asserted the right, indeed the duty, to revolt again tyranny; Hobbes denied any such right.
- Hobbes denied the existence of any moral law in the state of nature. Locke said the moral law of nature existed in the state of nature.
- Locke taught that man is naturally moral; Hobbes asserted that man is only conventionally moral, i.e., made so artificially by society's rules.
- Locke said that the law of nature was the "eternal, immutable standard of right"; Hobbes held that the will of the sovereign was the only standard of right.
- Hobbes said man was presocial in the state of nature. Locke said he was social in that condition.
- For Hobbes, nature was the enemy; for Locke, it was the guide and friend.
- Hobbes said the sovereign was unaccountable; Locke, that he was accountable to the people.
- Locke believed men could be self-governing; Hobbes did not.
- Hobbes was a materialist; Locke was not.

Most importantly, for the success of Hobbes' endeavor, as we saw in chapter 6, it was necessary that there be no eternal rewards or punishments, only temporal ones that Leviathan could deliver. A transcendent God's everlasting judgment in sending souls to heaven or hell according to their just deserts, however, was fundamentally necessary for the success of Locke's. From the former, you get tyranny. From the latter, you can get constitutional government.

In sum, the Founders' detestation of Hobbes, outlined at the end of chapter 9, and their concomitant embrace of Locke suggest that they emphatically did not understand Locke in terms of Hobbes but took him in concert with the classical and Christian lineage that had preceded him. Thus, that lineage, as far as the Founders were concerned, was unbroken—but for the secular and Divine Right absolutists against whom they reacted with words and by force of arms, as we shall see in the next chapter.

9

A Restorative Founding on Reason

We have attempted to trace the genealogy of the ideas without which the United States would not have come into existence. We have emphasized that liberty and constitutional order are not the products of just any conception of the universe, but of only one—that of the Judeo-Christian and natural law tradition. And so we come around at last to *what* this genealogy made possible. The Founders not only declared the *inherited* principles of human equality, popular sovereignty, the requirement of consent, and the moral right to revolution that we have been following since the Middle Ages but, *for the first time in history*, instantiated them, put them into practice, producing a constitutional republic that was the product of deliberation and free choice. The eighteenth-century American historian David Ramsay wrote:

> In no age before, and in no other country, did man ever possess an election of the kind of government under which he would choose to live. The constituent parts of the ancient free governments were thrown together by accident. The freedom of modern European governments was, for the most part, obtained by the concessions or liberality of monarchs or military leaders. In America alone, reason and liberty concurred in the formation of constitutions.[1]

The Founders accomplished this in the form of an extended federal republic the likes of which the world had never seen. This is why the Great Seal of the United States proclaims, borrowing from

---

[1] David Ramsay, *History of the American Revolution* (Philadelphia: R. Aitken and Son, 1789), cited in Bernard Bailyn, *The Ideological Origins of the American Revolution* (Cambridge, Mass.: Belknap Press, 1967), 273n39. This quotation provides one of the often overlooked meanings of the frequently misunderstood term "American exceptionalism".

Virgil, "Novus Ordo Seclorum"—a new order of the ages, meaning the beginning of the new American era. That is certainly how the Founders saw its significance. They did not mean a "new world order", much less a utopia or a perfect polity, but a new hope for mankind in how it could order political life in conformity with human nature, if it chose to do so. America would choose only for itself, not for anyone else.

In this chapter, we will see how the Founders talked—how they presented their grievances and justified independence from Great Britain—and how their actions comported with their words. But the treatment of the Founding itself will be brief, as the subject matter is extremely well-trodden ground, and this book is less about the Founding than about its intellectual provenance.

As we have already seen in chapters 7 and 8, and will see in what follows, the Founders used the *same* language as Hooker, Bellarmine, Suárez, Sidney, and Locke—in other words, of the natural law tradition reaching back to Aquinas, Cicero, and Aristotle. From it, they wove a coherent case for independence and self-rule at the levels of both principle (the Declaration of Independence) and practice (the Constitution). The evidence is overwhelming that they expressed themselves in terms of this tradition and meant the same thing by it. To understand them in a way other than they understood themselves would mean they were in the grip of forces beyond their own comprehension. The last chapter will show why such a proposition is not feasible.

The focus on intellectual lineage is not meant to deny that the Founders accomplished something new—because, as noted above, they did—but to show that their accomplishment neither sprang from nowhere nor was a radical break from or betrayal of the ancient heritage to which they appealed. As mentioned in earlier chapters, both John Adams and Thomas Jefferson explicitly referred to the genealogy of the Founding. Their statements bear repeating here.

Speaking from the heart of this heritage, Adams said:

> They [the revolutionaries] begin by reminding the people of the elevated rank they hold in the universe, as men; that all men by nature are equal; that kings are but the ministers of the people; that their authority is delegated to them by the people for their good; and that

they have a right to resume it, and place it in other hands, or keep
it themselves, whenever it is made use of to oppress them.... These
are what are called revolution principles. They are the principles of
Aristotle and Plato, of Livy and Cicero, and Sidney, Harrington, and
Locke; the principles of nature and eternal reason; the principles on
which the whole government over us now stands.[2]

Commenting elsewhere on what he states as Rousseau's claim that
"the Science of the Rights of Man is a new science. The Americans
have invented it", Adams retorted: "The Americans did not invent this
foundation of Society. They found it in their religion."[3] In the introduction to *Defense of the Constitution* (1787–1788), Adams cited Saint
Augustine's paraphrase of Cicero: "Where there is no justice there can
be no right ... denying the definition commonly given by those who
misconceived the matter, that right is what is useful to the stronger."[4]
Later he quoted Cicero directly on the rule of law as "those laws,
which are right reason, derived from the Divinity." One sees the line
from Cicero through Augustine to Adams. The lineage is clear.

Some years after Adams' statements, Jefferson confirmed:

This was the object of the Declaration of Independence. Not to find
out new principles, or new arguments, never before thought of, not
merely to say things which had never been said before ... neither aiming at originality of principle or sentiment, nor yet copied from any
particular and previous writing, it was intended to be an expression
of the American mind, and to give to that expression the proper tone
and spirit called for by the occasion. All its authority rests then on the
harmonizing sentiments of the day, whether expressed in conversation, in letters, printed essays, or in the elementary books of public
right, as Aristotle, Cicero, Locke, Sidney, &c.[5]

[2] John Adams, *The Letters of Novanglus*, no. 1, January 23, 1775, in *Papers of John Adams*,
vol. 2, *December 1773–April 1775*, ed. Robert. J. Taylor (Cambridge, Mass.: Belknap Press,
1977), Massachusetts Historical Society, http://www.masshist.org/publications/adams-papers
/view?&id=PJA02dg5.

[3] John Adams to Thomas Boylston Adams, March 19, 1794, cited in James Hutson, *Forgotten Features of the Founding: The Recovery of Religious Themes in the Early American Republic*
(Lanham, Md.: Lexington Books, 2003), 100.

[4] Augustine, *The City of God* 19, 21.

[5] Thomas Jefferson to Henry Lee, May 8, 1825, Founders Online, National Archives,
https://founders.archives.gov/documents/Jefferson/98-01-02-5212.

In 1823, Jefferson stressed that, when writing the Declaration, "I did not consider it as any part of my charge to invent new ideas altogether & to offer no sentiment which had ever been expressed before."[6] Indeed, it has been the endeavor of this book to give at least some idea of how often they had been expressed before.

Scholar Donald S. Lutz mapped other strands of America's DNA in his study of the references cited by the Founding Fathers from 1760 to 1805. Of 3,154 items surveyed, 34 percent came from the Bible. Nine percent were from such classical authors as Cicero, Plutarch, Livy, and Plato. Thus, 1,356 citations came from the Bible and the classics, comprising 43 percent of the citations. The Founders knew their classics in the original languages—Greek and Latin. Some also knew Hebrew. Additionally, 18 percent were from Whig writers, 11 percent derived from English common law, and 18 percent from so-called Enlightenment thinkers. Of these, Montesquieu, the author of *The Spirit of the Laws*, was most frequently cited.[7]

War of Ideas

Intellectual pedigree is important because wars begin in the minds of men well before the shooting starts. John Adams rightly pointed to the conflict of ideas that preceded the Revolution. In an 1818 letter to publisher Hezekiah Niles, Adams wrote, "The Revolution was effected before the War commenced. The Revolution was in the Minds and Hearts of the People.... *This radical Change in the Principles, Opinions Sentiments and Affection of the People, was the real American Revolution*."[8] What was in the minds of the Founders was in part absorbed in colonial colleges. Half of the signers of the Declaration of Independence were college graduates. Those who attended were largely educated in the Scholastic tradition—the trivium and the quadrivium. They needed to know Latin in order to get in, as

---

[6] Thomas Jefferson to James Madison, August 30, 1823, Founders Online, National Archives, https://founders.archives.gov/documents/Jefferson/98-01-02-3728.

[7] Donald S. Lutz, "The Relative Importance of European Writers on Late Eighteenth Century American Political Thought", *American Political Science Review* 189 (1984), 189–97.

[8] John Adams to Hezekiah Niles, February 13, 1818, Founders Online, National Archives, https://Founders.archives.gov/documents/Adams/99-02-02-6854 (emphasis in the original).

entrance exams required applicants to translate passages from Cicero and Virgil. In *The Education of the Founding Fathers of the Republic*, James Walsh stated that "the metaphysics and ethics as taught by the college presidents and tutors, were a direct heritage from the Scholastic philosophy of the medieval universities."[9]

Examining the commencement theses at colonial colleges gives an idea of what formed the American mind. At Princeton in 1750, two government theses were: "In the state of nature with the exception of certain individual qualities men are equal so far as government is concerned" and "The right of kings had its original foundation from popular compact." A 1765 Harvard ethics thesis contended that "Absolute monarchy tends to the destruction of the happiness of the human race."[10] Sounding as if it were straight out of the Middle Ages (or Cicero), a 1778 Harvard thesis defended the proposition that "no civil law is just unless it agrees with the principles of the natural law."[11] A 1769 thesis at Brown held that "to reduce Africans into perpetual servitude does not agree with divine or human law." In the same year, a Brown proposition defended the medieval principle of *Quod omnes tangit ab omnibus approbari*—What touches all must be approved by all. It held that "all power of making laws and penalties is derived from the people and therefore, For a Senate to impose taxes upon people who are not represented in that Senate (legislative body) is not just."[12] At Brown in 1770, a proposition in an ethics thesis asserted that "to all men by nature liberty belongs equally; therefore, every civil power owes its origins the consent of the people." A 1772 thesis at the same institution proposed that "the best form of democracy is that which comes from their own delegates chosen by popular suffrage."[13] It is not hard to see from where these came or to what they were leading.

Regardless of academic grounding, most Americans had *experience* in self-government. In his draft of the Declaration of Independence, Jefferson spoke of the Americans as "a people fostered and fixed in the principles of liberty". The fostering had taken place during the

---

[9] James J. Walsh, *The Education of the Founding Fathers of the Republic* (New York: Fordham University Press, 1935), 11.

[10] Ibid., 118.

[11] Ibid., 119.

[12] Ibid., 258.

[13] Ibid., 119.

preceding century and a half, when, for the most part, colonial Americans were left on their own through the benign neglect, or lack of reach, of the British Empire. By necessity, if for no other reason, they acclimated to self-rule. Early on, Americans became used to making their own laws. In terms of internal governance, their daily lives were their own. They were also the natural inheritors of the principles of British constitutionalism and common law. The experience of self-rule is what they wished to continue as free Englishmen if that was still possible.

As late as the "Declaration and Resolves on Colonial Rights of the First Continental Congress" in 1774, the colonists were still thinking of themselves as Englishmen. They insisted that, like their ancestors, they were "entitled to all the rights, liberties, and immunities of free and natural-born subjects, within the realm of England" and "that the respective colonies are entitled to the common law of England". After all, they had been promised as much in early colonial charters. The first charter of Virginia (1606), for example, stated that its residents "shall have and enjoy all Liberties, Franchises and Immunities ... as if they had been abiding and born within this our Realm of England".[14] Therefore, it was hardly odd that Samuel Adams would write: "British Rights are in great measure, inalienably, the Rights of the colonists."[15] "We wish not for independence", said Pastor Daniel Stillman of Boston's First Baptist Church, "but we have too great of a Sense of the Privileges of Englishmen ... to consent to be Slaves."[16] For the most part, the colonists wished only to be restored to their prior state before the late usurpations of Parliament.

Parliament's Violation of the Right of Consent

In 1765, Parliament had passed the Stamp Act, which required Americans to pay a tax on almost every piece of printed paper—legal documents, newspapers, pamphlets, court documents licenses, playing cards, and so forth. Of course, Parliament did not contain any

---

[14] Cited in Bernhard Knollenberg, *Origin of the American Revolution: 1759–1766* (New York: Crowell-Collier, 1961), 152.

[15] Rod Gragg, *The Declaration of Independence: The Story behind America's Founding Document and the Men Who Created It* (Nashville: Rutledge Hill Press, 2005), 18.

[16] Ibid., 19.

representatives from the American colonies, thus giving rise to the famous cry—so redolent of *Quod omnes tangit ab omnibus approbari*— "No taxation without representation" and to a boycott of British imports. The Virginia House of Burgesses responded by passing Patrick Henry's Stamp Act Resolutions, which declared that Virginians were "entitled to all the Liberties, Privileges and Immunities that have at any time been held, enjoyed, and possessed by the people of Great Britain" and that these included the "inestimable Right of being governed by such Laws respecting their Internal Policy and Taxation as are derived from their own Consent".[17] In "An Address to Friends and Countrymen on the Stamp Act" (November 1765), John Dickinson also emphasized the necessity for consent: "Men cannot be happy, without Freedom; nor free, without Security of Property; nor so secure, unless the sole Power to dispose of it be lodged in themselves; therefore no People can be free, but where Taxes are imposed on them with their own Consent, given personally, or by their Representatives."[18]

In March 1766, for prudential reasons, Parliament repealed the Stamp Act. Rubbing salt in the wound, however, it simultaneously passed the Declaratory Act, which asserted in principle that Parliament "had, hath, and of right ought to have, full power and authority to make laws and statutes of sufficient force and vitality to bind the colonies and people of America ... *in all cases whatsoever*".[19] In this sweeping assertion, Parliament assumed powers over the colonies as absolute as James I had claimed over England. The Divine Right of Kings had become the divine right of Parliament. The colonial grievance against this claim would be forthrightly expressed in the Declaration of Causes and Necessity of Taking Up Arms issued by the Continental Congress on July 6, 1775:

---

[17] Virginia Stamp Act Resolutions (1775), USHistory.org, http://www.ushistory.org /declaration/related/vsa65.html, cited inKnollenberg, *Origin of the American Revolution*, 210.

[18] John Dickinson, *The Writings of John Dickinson*, vol. 1, *Political Writings, 1764–1774* (Philadelphia: Historical Society of Pennsylvania, 1895), 202, cited in John S. Schmeeckle, "Prelude to the Declaration of Independence: The Congressional Resolution of May 10 and 15, 1776", 9, Academia, https://www.academia.edu/1479704/Safety_and_Happiness_The _American_Revolutionary_Standard_for_Governmental_Legitimacy.

[19] Bailyn, *Ideological Origins*, 202 (my emphasis).

If it was possible for men, who exercise their reason to believe, that the divine Author of our existence intended a part of the human race to hold an absolute property in, and an unbounded power over others, marked out by his infinite goodness and wisdom, as the objects of a legal domination never rightfully resistible, however severe and oppressive, the inhabitants of these colonies might at least require from the parliament of Great-Britain some evidence, that this dreadful authority over them, has been granted to that body.[20]

Exercising these absolute powers, Parliament then passed a series of four acts, together known as the Townshend Acts (1767), which contained provisions for the collection of import duties, again, without the consent of the colonists, who responded with another boycott of British goods. Parliament repealed the Acts in 1770.

Violating the "Law of Nature" and "Natural Right"

By the mid-1770s, the colonial language of appeal had changed from the rights of Englishmen to the rights of mankind. In his talk on "The Jubilee of the Constitution" in 1839, John Quincy Adams reminisced that "English liberties had failed them. From the omnipotence of Parliament [claimed in the Declaratory Act] the colonists appealed to the rights of man and the omnipotence of the God of battles." The intellectual preparation for this change was already apparent in some of the rhetoric of the 1760s. In *The Rights of the British Colonies Asserted and Proved* (1764), James Otis wrote that, "The Colonists being ... entitled to all the rights of nature ... are not to be restrained in the exercise of any of these rights, but for the evident good sense of the whole community ... and if [natural liberty is] taken from them without their consent, they are so far enslaved."[21] Otis said: "There can be no

---

[20] *A Declaration by the Representatives of the United Colonies of North-America, Now Met in Congress at Philadelphia, Setting Forth the Causes and Necessity of Their Taking Up Arms*, in *Documents Illustrative of the Formation of the Union of the American States* (Washington, D.C.: Government Printing Office, 1927), Avalon Project, Yale Law School Lillian Goldman Law Library, http://avalon.law.yale.edu/18th_century/arms.asp.

[21] James Otis, *The Rights of the British Colonies Asserted and Proved* (1763), Online Library of Liberty, https://oll.libertyfund.org/pages/1763-otis-rights-of-british-colonies-asserted-pamphlet.

prescription old enough to supersede the law of nature and the grant of
God Almighty, who has given to all men a natural right to be free."[22]

Since this book is about the contest between the primacy of reason
and the primacy of will, it is worth pausing to view the remarkable
statements by Otis that display with such clarity that these are precisely the terms in which the American colonists saw the issue. Otis
was reacting to the assertions of absolute parliamentary sovereignty
when he said:

> To say Parliament is absolute and arbitrary is a contradiction. The
> Parliament cannot make 2 and 2, 5: omnipotency cannot do it....
> Parliaments are in all cases to *declare* what is for the good of the whole;
> but it is not the *declaration* of Parliament that makes it so. There must
> be in every instance a higher authority, viz., GOD. Should an act
> of Parliament be against any of *his* natural laws, which are *immutably*
> true, *their* declaration would be contrary to eternal truth, equity, and
> justice, and consequently void.[23]

It would be difficult to imagine in so few sentences a more eloquent
denunciation of voluntarism or a more powerful defense of reason
(natural law).

A year later, in the *Resolutions of the Massachusetts House of Representatives*, October 29, 1765, Samuel Adams wrote, "There are certain
essential rights of the British Constitution of government, which are
founded in the law of God and nature and are common rights of
mankind. No law of society can, consistent with the law of God and
nature, take those rights away."[24] In the same year, John Adams said
that "liberty must at all hazards be supported. We have a right to it,
derived from our Maker.... Let it be known, that British liberties are
not the grants of princes or parliaments, but original rights ...; that
many of our rights are inherent and essential, agreed on as maxims,
and established as preliminaries, even before a parliament existed."[25]

---

[22] Ibid.

[23] Ibid. (emphasis in the original).

[24] Cited in Rousas J. Rushdoony, *This Independent Republic* (Nutley, N.J.: Craig Press,
1964), 37–38.

[25] John Adams, *A Dissertation on the Canon and Feudal Law* (1765), Teaching American
History, http://teachingamericanhistory.org/library/document/a-dissertation-on-the-canon
-and-feudal-law/.

Rights, he said, are "derived from the great Legislator of the Universe" and "cannot be repealed or restrained by human laws".[26] Like his natural law predecessors, Adams thought that "a manifest design in the Prince, to annul the contract on his part, will annul it on the part of the people. A settled plan to deprive the people of all the benefits, blessings and ends of the contract, to subvert the fundamentals of the constitution, to deprive them of all share in making and executing laws, will justify a revolution."[27] In 1772, before the General Court of Virginia, James Mason, speaking firmly within the tradition developed from the Middle Ages, argued:

All acts of legislature apparently contrary to natural right and justice are, in our laws, and must be in the nature of things, considered as void. The laws of nature are the laws of God, whose authority can be superseded by no power on earth. A legislature must not obstruct our obedience to Him from whose punishments they cannot protect us. All human constitutions which contradict His (God's) laws, we are in conscience bound to disobey.[28]

In early 1775, Benevolus (a pseudonym) wrote to the New Jersey Assembly, advising it to drop altogether any appeal to the rights of Englishmen: "It has mortified me to hear our warmest advocates for liberty (tho' with the best design) recurring to doubtful constitutions, charters, acts of Parliament, and public faith, as a foundation of our reasonable and rightful claims—These, at best, can be but declaratory of those rights—The true foundation of American liberty, is in human nature."[29] In *The Farmer Refuted*, Alexander Hamilton said something similar: "The sacred rights of mankind are not to be rummaged for among old parchments or musty records. They are written, as with a sunbeam, in the whole volume of human nature, by

---

[26] Ibid.

[27] Adams, *Novanglus*.

[28] Robin v. Hardaway, I Jefferson 109, 114, 1 Va. Reports Ann. 58, 61 (1772) aff'd; Gregory v. Baugh, 29 Va. 681, 29 Thomas Jefferson, *Reports of Cases Determined in the General Court of Virginia* (Charlottesville: F. Carr, 1829), 114.

[29] Cited in Clinton Rossiter, *Seedtime of the Republic: The Origin of the American Tradition of Political Liberty* (New York: Harcourt, Brace, 1953), 352.

the hand of the Divinity itself, and can never be erased or obscured by mortal power."[30]

James Wilson and Natural Law

Another powerful voice was raised in 1774, but the words it spoke had been composed six years earlier—making them all the more prescient. They were those of James Wilson, who was in many ways the quintessential Founder in combining such a complete understanding of the Christian and natural law traditions. In 1768, friends persuaded Wilson (one of only six men to sign both the Declaration of Independence and the Constitution) that publication of his pamphlet *Considerations on the Nature and Extent of the Legislative Authority of the British Parliament* at that time would have been injudicious and likely hazardous to his health. When the work finally appeared, Thomas Jefferson was so taken with it that he transcribed various paragraphs into his commonplace book. Wilson's words bear a striking resemblance to the language of the Declaration and are as clearly expressive of the core ideas of the Christian and natural law heritage that made it possible. The objective for the colonies, he said, was to recover "the enjoyment of those rights, to which we are entitled by the supreme and uncontrollable laws of nature".[31] Or as the Declaration later put it, "to which the Laws of Nature and of Nature's God entitle them". Wilson stated: "All men are, by nature, equal and free.... All lawful government is founded on the consent of those who are subject to it: such consent was given with a view to ensure and to increase the happiness of the governed."[32] This tracks closely with the Declaration's expressions that "all men are created equal", with governments "deriving their just powers from the consent of the governed", and in

---

[30] Alexander Hamilton, "The Farmer Refuted, &c.", February 23, 1775, Founders Online, National Archives, https://founders.archives.gov/documents/Hamilton/01-01-02-0057, cited in Daniel L. Dreisbach, Mark David Hall, and Mark A. Noll, eds., *The Forgotten Founders on Religion and Public Life* (Notre Dame, Ind.: University of Notre Dame Press, 2009), 113.

[31] James Wilson, *Nature and Extent of the Legislative Authority of the British Parliament*, Constitution Society, https://www.constitution.org/jwilson/legislative_authority_british _parliament.html.

[32] Ibid.

line with the inalienable right to "the pursuit of Happiness". Wilson reinforced the traditional natural law view that in constitutional government, "the first maxims of jurisprudence are ever kept in view— that all power is derived from the people—that their happiness is the end of government."[33] This language is not far removed from the Declaration's "Right of the People to institute new Government, laying its foundation on such principles and organizing its powers in such form, as to them shall seem most likely to effect their Safety and Happiness." Jefferson also noted the beginning of Wilson's fifth paragraph: "Will it ensure and increase the happiness of the American colonies, that the parliament of Great Britain should possess a supreme, irresistible, uncontrolled authority over them?" In such a case, Wilson said, all men "are, every moment, exposed to slavery", or, as the Declaration stated, to "absolute Despotism" or "absolute Tyranny". Wilson's list of grievances against Great Britain also closely track those enumerated in the Declaration.[34]

The purpose of pointing to these parallels is not to deprive Jefferson of originality for, as seen, he eschewed any such claim, but to show how really "harmonizing", as Jefferson called them, the sentiments of the day were and how congruent with the natural law lineage.[35] Wilson was solidly grounded in the tradition of Hooker, Aquinas, Cicero (whom he cites more often than any other classical author), and Aristotle. Not surprisingly, he stated the necessity of "the consent of those whose obedience the law requires. This I conceive to be the true origin of the obligation of human laws."[36] He was probably the greatest exponent of classical natural law teaching in the American Founding, though he was not alone—for example, see Nathaniel Chipman, senator from Vermont and chief justice of the Vermont Supreme Court, and his *Sketches of the Principles of Government* (1793).

[33] Ibid.

[34] See Nicholas Pederson, "The Lost Founder: James Wilson in American Memory", *Yale Journal of Law and the Humanities* 22, no. 2 (January 2010): 263n24, https://digitalcommons .law.yale.edu/yjlh/vol22/iss2/3.

[35] It is worth noting, however, that Wilson's intellectual pedigree, unlike Jefferson's, did not include Locke. As we saw in the last chapter, he was quite critical of Locke's epistemology

[36] *Collected Works of James Wilson*, ed. Kermit L. Hall and Mark David Hall, vol. 1 (Indianapolis: Liberty Fund, 2007), 494, Online Library of Liberty, https://oll.libertyfund.org /titles/2072#Wilson_4140_2309.

(These thinkers are exactly, precisely, the "continuation of premodern natural law thinking" that critics such as Patrick Deneen so adamantly deny existed in the American Founding.)

Like Aquinas and Hooker, Wilson was a metaphysical realist and was avidly against the voluntarist idea of God, finding repugnant the notion that God is arbitrary pure will and power. He held that "the law of nature and the law of revelation are both divine: they flow, though in different channels, from the same adorable source. It is, indeed, preposterous to separate them from each other. The object of both is—to discover the will of God—and both are necessary for the accomplishment of that end." Wilson wrote: "The great and incomprehensible Author, and Preserver, and Ruler of all things—he himself works not without an eternal decree."[37] God is ordered within himself, which is why his creation is ordered. He "is the promulgator as well as the author of natural law", which man perceives "by reason and conscience, the divine monitors within us". He saw that constitutional rule of law required theological underpinning in a God who is wisdom and will conjoined. God's, said Wilson, is "a law more distinguished by the *goodness*, than by the *power* of its all gracious Author".[38] Just as Aquinas held that the divine intellect precedes the divine will, so Wilson held that God's goodness precedes his power.

Wilson also showed his deep grounding in medieval roots by employing the all-important *quod omnes tangit* principle treated in chapter 2 (and echoed in the 1769 Brown student thesis): "Let us next pay the respect, which is due to the celebrated sentiment of the English Justinian, [King] Edward the first. 'Lex justissima, ut quod omnes tangit, ab omnibus approbetur.' It is a most just law that what affects all should be approved by all." Wilson then called upon Lord Chancellor Fortescue, who "in his most excellent tractate concerning the English laws, informs his royal pupil, that the statutes of England are framed, not by the will of the prince, but by that and by the assent of the whole kingdom".[39]

---

[37] James Wilson, *Lectures on Law*, in *The Collected Works of James Wilson*, vol. 1 (Indianapolis: Liberty Fund, 2007), 464, Online Library of Liberty, https://oll.libertyfund.org/titles/wilson-collected-works-of-james-wilson-vol-1.

[38] Ibid., 471 (my emphasis).

[39] Ibid., 565. It is curious that critics such as Deneen and Hanby insist on seeing the Founding as a breach with the natural law heritage rather than something in continuity with it. They need to explain Wilson, and much else.

Whatever his sway on the Declaration of Independence may have been, Wilson's influence on the writing of the Constitution was second only to Madison's. Its first drafts were in his hand, and he spoke more frequently at the Constitutional Convention than anyone but Gouverneur Morris.

The Revolution Arrives

From these various statements, it is easy to see what was coming, from where it came, and why. Both education and experience had inoculated American colonists against arbitrary rule, particularly taxation without their consent. This is what so roiled them regarding Parliament's presumptions and practices. Very briefly—since it is a well told tale elsewhere—here is what sent them over the edge into armed rebellion. In his parliamentary "Speech on American Taxation" (1774), Edmund Burke predicted the consequences: "From the unlimited and illimitable nature of supreme sovereignty, you will teach them [the American colonists] by these means to call that sovereignty itself in question. When you drive him hard, the boar will surely turn upon the hunters. If that sovereignty and their freedom cannot be reconciled, which will they take? They will cast your sovereignty in your face. Nobody will be argued into slavery."[40]

In 1773, Parliament passed the Tea Act, a bill designed to save the faltering East India Company by granting it a monopoly on the American tea trade. Citizens of Massachusetts famously answered with the Boston Tea Party and other acts of defiance. The colonists were rubbed raw by the rhetoric of British leaders such as Lord North, who declared in respect to the revocation of most of the Townshend duties: "I'm against repealing the last act of Parliament, securing to us a revenue out of America; I will never think of repealing it [the tea duty] until I see America prostrate at my feet." Lord Hillsborough, the British secretary of state for America, displayed a similar attitude and promised that "we will grant nothing to the Americans except what they may ask with a halter round their necks."[41] Though not a

---

[40] *Speech of Edmund Burke on Conciliation with the Colonies* (New York: Globe School Book, 1900), 128.

[41] Cited in Gragg, *Declaration of Independence*, 13.

member of Parliament, the renowned Samuel Johnson purportedly opined that "they are a race of convicted felons and they ought to be thankful for anything we allow them short of hanging."[42] In 1775, American colonists reciprocated his ill feelings and burned Johnson in effigy in Massachusetts for his pamphlet *Taxation No Tyranny*.

In 1774 Lord North and Parliament responded to the Boston Tea Party with the Restraining Acts, which closed Boston's harbor until restitution for the destroyed tea was made, abrogated Massachusetts' 1691 charter (dissolving representative provincial government), removed British officials charged with capital crimes from the jurisdiction of colonial courts, and requisitioned unoccupied buildings for the housing of British troops. These "Intolerable Acts", as they were known in the colonies, were meant to chastise Massachusetts, but they only intensified opposition to Great Britain in all thirteen colonies and led to the convening of the First Continental Congress on September 5, 1774.

Several days later, on September 9, delegates from nineteen Suffolk County towns met in Milton, Massachusetts, and passed the Suffolk Resolves, which capture the tenor of colonial grievance and determination:

> If we nobly defeat that fatal edict which proclaims a power to frame laws for us in all cases whatsoever, thereby entailing the endless and numberless curses of slavery upon us, our heirs and their heirs forever; if we successfully resist that unparalleled usurpation of unconstitutional power, whereby our capital is robbed of the means of life; whereby the streets of Boston are thronged with military executioners; whereby our coasts are lined and harbours crouded with ships of war; whereby the charter of the colony, that sacred barrier against the encroachments of tyranny, is mutilated and, in effect, annihilated;... whereby the unalienable and inestimable inheritance, which we derived from nature, the constitution of Britain, and the privileges warranted to us in the charter of the province, is totally wrecked, annulled, and vacated, posterity will acknowledge that virtue which preserved them free and happy.[43]

---

[42] Sarah L. Stocking, *Columbian Entertainments* (Peoria, Ill.: J. W. Franks and Sons, 1892), 108.
[43] Joseph Warren, Suffolk Resolves (1774), America's Homepage, https://ahp.gatech.edu /suffolk_resolves_1774.html.

Carried to Philadelphia by Paul Revere, the Suffolk Resolves were unanimously endorsed by the Continental Congress on September 17. The starting gun had been fired. Ecstatic, John Adams recorded in his diary, "This was one of the happiest Days of my Life. In Congress We had generous, noble Sentiments, and manly Eloquence. This Day convinced me that America will support the [sic] Massachusetts or perish with her."[44]

Declaration of Independence

Less than two years later, the colonists formally broke with Great Britain. On July 4, 1776, the United States first addressed itself to the world concerning its "purpose". We could do no better than consider the terms of the original introduction to see whether they comport with the moral truths about man, or if, as some critics charge, they are based on profound anthropological and metaphysical errors.[45]

The first thing to consider is why the representatives of the thirteen colonies thought their grievances deserved the attention of the world, which they addressed out of "a decent respect to the opinions of mankind". Politics is rooted in the particular, as we know from the long list of specific grievances against Great Britain itemized in the Declaration, among which was "imposing Taxes on us without our Consent". Why not simply secure independence and have done with it? The answer is that the standard of justice to which the Founders appealed was, according to them, universal—true for everyone, everywhere, at all times. If it were not true for everyone, then it was not true for them either, and they had no moral basis for their revolution.

Therefore, the Declaration is not addressed specifically to Christians because men do not possess their inalienable rights by virtue

---

[44] Diary of John Adams, September 17, 1774, Founders Online, National Archives, https://Founders.archives.gov/documents/Adams/01-02-02-0004-0006#DJA02d157n1.

[45] One should keep in mind that the American Founding was a political act, not a philosophical dissertation, though it obviously drew on philosophical principles for its justification. The Founders are best understood as statesmen, or perhaps as philosophical statesmen, not as philosophers, though they were deeply read in philosophy. Therefore, one should not read the Declaration of Independence as if one were reading Locke or Spinoza.

of their Christianity but on account of their common humanity. Harry V. Jaffa made the point that the Founders' "assumptions about Equality—which include assumptions about the subhuman and superhuman—are independent of the validity of any particular religious beliefs." Indeed, they are, insofar as they can be philosophically ascertained. But by reason alone are we able to arrive at all the necessary presuppositions for democratic, constitutional order? One can point to Plato, Aristotle, and Cicero, as among those who approached the necessary truths through unassisted reason but were unable to grasp them in their fullness. It took the assistance of a certain revelation to do that.

The Theology of the Founding

Religious beliefs are not indifferent to the "assumptions about equality", nor are these assumptions indifferent to religious beliefs. Man has worshipped many gods and has lived in many different political orders, most of them tyrannical. Not just any god will do as the ultimate source of constitutional order: neither Moloch, nor Baal, nor Thor, nor Quetzalcoatl, nor Kali. It is only within a form of worship that can accommodate or, even better, mandate a concept of ordered liberty in which the individual is inviolable that this can happen and historically has happened. The primacy of the person defines the very order of the Constitution and ultimately needs theological support for its sustenance. This it finds in the imago Dei. Iranian philosopher Abdolkarim Soroush stated something that has universal applicability: "You need some philosophical underpinning, even theological underpinning in order to have a real democratic system. Your God cannot be a despotic God anymore. A despotic God would not be compatible with a democratic rule, with the idea of rights. So you even have to change your idea of God."[46]

The "Nature's God" of which the Declaration speaks is the Judeo-Christian God for the simple reason that there is no other revelation (or cult, if you will) at the base of a *cult*ure that supports the

---

[46] Abdolkarim Soroush, on receipt of the Erasmus Prize, April 14, 2004, posted on the website of Abdolkarim Soroush, http://www.drsoroush.com/PDF/E-CMB-20041113-%20 Rationalist_Traditions_in_Islam-Soroush_in_Heidelberg.pdf.

Declaration's principles to the extent that they could have *originated* within it. This is not to say that another culture could not support these principles *after* their origination. But it seems that only upon reconsideration of the basic insights of Plato, Aristotle, and Cicero in light of Judeo-Christian revelation was the base secured for the development of democratic constitutional order. The Founding principle "that all men are created equal" arose, and could have arisen only, in a culture thoroughly saturated with the teaching of the imago Dei. John Adams went so far as to say: "The doctrine of human equality is founded entirely in the Christian doctrine that we are all children of the same Father, all accountable to Him for our conduct to one another, all equally bound to respect each other's love."[47] So, while one might say that the Declaration and the Constitution are not explicitly Christian, they are nonetheless Christian products. By this I mean, as Adams most likely did, that the thinking about political first principles that produced them took place in a world profoundly formed and affected by that revelation. The proof for this thesis, however, is somewhat indirect, because there are no Christian principles per se embedded in the Constitution; rather, the Constitution is embedded in Christianity. I think this is what Jacques Maritain meant when he said, "This Constitution can be described as an outstanding lay Christian document.... The spirit and inspiration of this great political Christian document is basically repugnant to the idea of making human society stand aloof from God and from any religious faith."[48]

The Declaration contains an idea of God exactly compatible with democratic constitutional rule but had to state its self-evident truths—especially the truth of the equality of all men—as closely as possible in nonsectarian terms in order for them to be "independent of the validity of any particular religious beliefs". This is neither legerdemain nor deceit but simply returning to the philosophical level insights attained—or reinforced—at the theological level, so that their universality would be more readily recognized and acknowledged. The Declaration fuses the God of natural religion, "Nature's God", reachable by reason alone, with the God of revelation—Creator, Supreme Judge, and Providence. The colonists, who were overwhelmingly Christian,

---

[47] David McCullough, *John Adams* (New York: Simon and Schuster, 2001), 619.
[48] Jacques Maritain, *Man and State* (Chicago: University of Chicago Press, 1951), 184.

could make their philosophical appeals knowing full well that they were vindicated by and sustained by the God who reveals himself as the divine Logos. A small example suffices to illustrate this point. On the occasion of the inauguration of the Massachusetts government under its new constitution (1780), the Rev. Samuel Cooper preached:

> We want not indeed, a special revelation from heaven to teach us that men are born equal and free; that no man has a natural claim of dominion over his neighbors.... These are the plain dictates of that reason and common sense with which the common parent of man has informed the human bosom. It is, however, a satisfaction to observe such everlasting maxims of equity confirmed, and impressed upon the consciences of men, by the instructions, precepts, and examples given us in the sacred oracles; one internal mark of their divine original, and that they come from him "who hath made of one blood all nations to dwell upon the face of the earth" [Acts 17:26].[49]

Benedict XVI eloquently expressed this same point: "Strictly speaking, these human rights are not truths of faith, even though they are discoverable—and indeed come to full light—in the message of Christ who 'reveals man to man himself' (*Gaudium et Spes*, 22)."[50] Benedict further said, "The transcendent dignity of the person is an essential value of Judeo-Christian wisdom, yet thanks to the use of reason, it can be recognized by all."[51] This is the recognition contained in the Declaration.

"All Men Are Created Equal"

The Declaration's proclamation of equality takes it beyond what any previous political document had proposed, as did its call to found

---

[49] Ellis Sandoz, ed., *Political Sermons of the American Founding Era: 1730–1805* (Indianapolis: Liberty Press, 1990), 637.

[50] Benedict XVI, Address to Participants in the Fifteenth Plenary Session of the Pontifical Academy of Social Sciences, May 4, 2009, Vatican website, http://www.vatican.va/holy_father/benedict_xvi/speeches/2009/may/documents/hf_ben-xvi_spe_20090504_social-sciences_en.html.

[51] Benedict XVI, Message for the celebration of the World Day of Peace, January 1, 2011, Vatican website, http://w2.vatican.va/content/benedict-xvi/en/messages/peace/documents/hf_ben-xvi_mes_20101208_xliv-world-day-peace.html.

a regime on this principle. *All* people must be treated as beings of intrinsic worth, and not as the means of some despotic design. This is because the Creator endows man with inalienable rights, among which are "Life, Liberty and the pursuit of Happiness". Man does not get to invent these rights; they are given to him. They have meaning only in reference to their Author. As Harry Jaffa pointed out: "When the Signers of the Declaration appealed to the 'supreme judge of the world' for the 'rectitude of [their] intentions' they acknowledged the divine government of the world as the framework within which their rights might be exercised."[52] The source of man's dignity is secure only in the transcendent, which is what makes it irrevocable. All of the principles in the Declaration and its references to God as Creator, Supreme Judge, and Divine Providence presume the truth of man made in his image. Constitutional, democratic government is unthinkable without the presupposition of God as the source of rights, but also because, without him, there is no basis for the restraint that is the essence of such government. Thomas Jefferson wondered whether "the liberties of a nation [can] be thought secure when we have removed their only firm basis, a conviction in the minds of the people that these liberties are the gift of God."[53]

That "all men are created equal" means that it is unjust to treat a man as if he were an animal or to behave toward him as if one were God, in other words, tyrannically. Treating a man as if he were a dog is manifestly unjust to anyone who knows the distinction between the two, as it is equally unjust to behave toward a man as if one were God. By virtue of this principle, the Declaration accused George III of committing acts "totally unworthy of the Head of a *civilized* nation" (my emphasis), meaning exactly that the King had withdrawn his recognition of American colonists as fellow human beings—the very definition of barbarism.[54] Great Britain had behaved in a way that

---

[52] Edward J. Erler and Ken Masugi, eds., *The Rediscovery of America: Essays by Harry V. Jaffa on the New Birth of Politics* (Lanham, Md.: Rowman and Littlefield, 2019), 271.

[53] Thomas Jefferson, *Notes on the State of Virginia*, Query 18: Manners (1781), Teaching American History, http://teachingamericanhistory.org/library/document/notes-on-the-state-of-virginia-query-xviii-manners/.

[54] It should be noted that it was when George III conformed his will to Parliament's that the colonies felt their bonds with him were broken. As Jefferson expressed it in his autobiography, the debate in the Continental Congress in June 1776 held "that as to the king, we had been bound to him by allegiance, but that this bond was now dissolved by his assent to the late act of parliament".

violated their integrity as human beings—in other words, unjustly. It did this precisely by denying the citizens of the colonies their right as rational creatures to consent in their own rule.

The Relationship between Liberty and Happiness

The Declaration shares in the conviction of the entire tradition to which we have alluded that the good is not whatever we say it is, in other words, something we get to make up; it is embedded in our very being as the end to which we are ineluctably ordered. Freedom is first of all a function of man's *moral* condition. Liberty is demanded by the principle of equality, which Lincoln called "the father of all moral principle". To be fully human, one must be free. This is why Jefferson said that "the God who gave us life, gave us liberty at the same time."[55] If freedom is God's intention for man, then the ground of freedom must be virtue, so as to prevent enslavement by vice. One is not given something for its use outside of the purposes for which it is given. The purpose of freedom is not the pursuit of vice. This means that freedom is intended to be used in certain ways, and in only those ways can it bring happiness. What does the Declaration mean by "happiness"? In *Thoughts on Government,* John Adams could have spoken for all the Founders when he wrote: "Upon this point all speculative politicians will agree, that the happiness of society is the end of government, as all divines and moral philosophers will agree that the happiness of the individual is the end of man.... All sober inquirers after truth, ancient and modern, pagan and Christian, have declared that the happiness of man, as well as his dignity, consists in *virtue.*"[56] Jefferson pereceived "the order of nature to be that individual happiness shall be inseparable from the practice of virtue."[57] In his presidential inaugural address, George Washington proclaimed

---

[55] Thomas Jefferson, *Rights of British America* (1774), in *The Papers of Thomas Jefferson,* ed. Julian P Boyd et al., 33 vols. (Princeton: Princeton University Press, 1950–), 1:135.

[56] John Adams, *Thoughts on Government,* chap. 4, doc. 5 in *The Founders' Constitution,* vol. 1 (Chicago: University of Chicago Press, n.d.), http://press-pubs.uchicago.edu/founders/documents/v1ch4s5.html (my emphasis).

[57] Thomas Jefferson to José Corrêa da Serra, April 19, 1814, Founders Online, National Archives, https://founders.archives.gov/documents/Jefferson/03-07-02-0216.

that "there is no truth more thoroughly established than that there exists in the economy and course of nature an indissoluble union between virtue and happiness."[58] None of the Declaration's signers would have disagreed with these statements.

It should be clear enough from the foregoing that the Founders did not consider happiness apart from virtue. It certainly could not be constituted by the fulfillment of narrow self-interest. In a letter to James Monroe, Madison made this explicit:

> There is no maxim in my opinion which is more liable to be misapplied, and which therefore more needs elucidation than the current one that the interest of the majority is the political standard of right and wrong. Taking the word "interest" as synonymous with "ultimate happiness," in which sense it is qualified with every necessary moral ingredient, the proposition is no doubt true. But taking it in the popular sense, as referring to immediate augmentation of property and wealth, nothing can be more false. In the latter sense it would be the interest of the majority in every community to despoil & enslave the minority of individuals; and in a federal community to make a similar sacrifice of the minority of the component States. In fact it is only re-establishing under another name and a more specious form, force as the measure of right.[59]

In word and deed, the American Founding was a refutation of "force as the measure of right", of the primacy of will over reason.

The Constitution

As we have seen in the previous chapters, a cascade of ancillary rights naturally flows from the principle of equality. That man must be ruled with his consent is a corollary to it. The condition of man's free consent is, in turn, his freedom of conscience, without which consent

[58] George Washington, Inaugural Address, April 30, 1789, American Presidency Project, https://www.presidency.ucsb.edu/documents/inaugural-address-16.

[59] James Madison to James Monroe, October 5, 1786, James Madison Papers, 1723–1859, Library of Congress, https://www.loc.gov/resource/mjm.02_0756_0758/?st=text. Madison's statement makes all the more inexplicable the voluntarist views Patrick Deneen assigns to Madison, as we will see in chapter 11.

would be constrained. The external expression of freedom of conscience is freedom of speech, without which freedom of conscience would be mute. Freedom of conscience also inheres in the right to religious freedom. George Weigel writes, "It turns out that religious freedom is not an inert doctrine; it has dramatic consequences. If there is a sanctuary of conscience inside every human person where no earthly power can legitimately tread, then the state is, by definition, a limited state."[60] Today, freedom of conscience is often distorted. It does not mean that whatever you think is right *is* right. It means, above all, the obligation to conform your mind to the truth of reality—which is the natural law—and thereby be prepared to exercise informed moral judgment.

If this, then, is who man is, he ought to govern himself through rational deliberation and free choice, rather than be subject to accident and force. Constitutional government is exactly the form of government that attempts to direct people to behave reasonably and can exist only to the extent that they do.

The political result of the principle of equality, correctly understood, is precisely limited government. The need for limited government gives rise to constitutionalism, which enshrines the rule of law. The rule of law derives directly from the principle of equality and requires that all persons be equal before the law. The rule of law is the necessary condition not only of liberty, but also of excellence, because by removing the artificial constraints upon man, it leaves, as Lincoln said, "an open field and a fair chance for [man's] industry, enterprise and intelligence". The U.S. Constitution endeavored to embody this understanding of things.

A close reading of the Constitution leads to the conclusion that, divorced from natural law and Christian principles, the Constitution would be incomprehensible—devoid of compelling moral vision or unifying principles. (One would do well to remember that it was ratified by an overwhelmingly Christian citizenry in each of the thirteen states.) As mentioned earlier, however, the proof for this thesis is indirect because there are no Christian principles per se implanted in the Constitution. The Constitution does not declare principles; it provides for their implementation. It considers the

---

[60] Cited in Erler and Masugi, *The Rediscovery of America*, 185.

principles on which America is founded so self-evident that it does not even name, much less defend, them. In its short preamble, the Constitution briefly mentions, without defining, justice, general welfare, and the blessings of liberty, clearly indicating that these are commonly accepted ends.

In fact, what is not in the Constitution is, in some ways, more interesting than what is. More interesting still are the presuppositions that these omissions suggest. I do not mean things already contained in the Declaration of Independence, but those that are not mentioned at all, things that might be considered truisms. But the problem with truisms, as G. K. Chesterton once quipped, is that people forget that they are true. So, the truisms that the Constitution omits because it takes them for granted can tell us much more about what the Founding Fathers intended than we might think.

The Founders had a keen appreciation of the ill effects of Original Sin both in individuals and in groups. Moreover, they realized that any document describing how men should govern and be governed must make ample provision for man's basically flawed nature and his unfortunate propensities. The Constitution implicitly recognizes this flawed nature and these propensities when it advocates the separation of powers. Because of man's imperfections and inclinations to evil, constitutional order must be arranged so as to prevent a concentration of power—legislative, executive, and judicial—from falling into the hands of a single individual or group of individuals who could then misuse it. "Concentrating these in the same hands is precisely the definition of despotic government", warned Jefferson.[61] He was of one mind with John Adams, who wrote to him: "The fundamental Article of my political Creed is, that Despotism, or unlimited Sovereignty, or absolute Power is the same in a Majority of a popular Assembly, and Aristocratical Counsel, an Oligarchical Junto and a Single Emperor. Equally arbitrary cruel bloody and in every respect, diabolical."[62] In *Federalist* 47, James Madison echoed Jefferson: "The accumulation of all powers, legislative, executive, and

---

[61] Thomas Jefferson, *Notes on the State of Virginia*, Query 13 (1782), Teaching American History, https://teachingamericanhistory.org/library/document/notes-on-the-state-of-viriginia -query-xiii/.

[62] John Adams to Thomas Jefferson, November 13, 1815, National Archives, Founders Online, https://founders.archives.gov/documents/Adams/99-02-02-6539.

judiciary, in the same hands, whether of one, a few, or many, and whether hereditary, self-appointed, or elective, may justly be pronounced the very definition of tyranny." The holders of such power could rule over other men as if they, the rulers, were gods. It mattered not if it were an "elective despotism", for a despotism it would remain. The constitutional division of the government into the three branches—executive, legislative, and judicial—and the checks and balances set up among them were emplaced to prevent such a concentration from occurring. Furthermore, the Constitution implicitly acknowledges Original Sin and its baneful effects in that, as we have mentioned, it does not offer any solution to the problem of evil. The notion of Original Sin protects government from undertaking something of which it is incapable. The Founding Fathers clearly considered a solution to evil beyond the realm of politics and beyond their own individual competence, which is why they necessarily limited government. But this does not mean that they did not think that a solution had been provided. Indeed, they believed that the "solution"—in the form of Christianity—was so widely known and accepted by them and their fellow countrymen that there was no need to make it explicit.

Limited government does not—and due to its limited nature cannot—usurp man's destiny or grant itself salvific aims. It implicitly acknowledges the need for salvation and its own impotence before this need. Politics cannot meet the demands of the human soul, for it cannot achieve perfect justice. The Founders realized that one must look beyond politics for the spiritual fulfillment for which man hungers. To repeat, Socrates showed that any attempt to fulfill the soul's ultimate desire through politics—by trying to achieve perfect justice here—would transform the state into a totalitarian enterprise. The Founders knew this.

Without this limiting view of politics, constitutional thinking is not possible. Only such a vision as this supports the effort to restrain political power. (It is also this view that should restrain any impulses to democratic millenarianism.) If man has no transcendent end, politics will consume him completely in some form of totalitarianism. The proper role of government is to maintain a temporal order sufficient for the pursuit of man's higher ends, especially by securing man's fundamental rights.

One of those rights, which it is the role of government to secure, is the right to property—so often thought to be simply a matter of economic efficiency or, worse, a spur to materialism. It is exactly the right to private property that insulates the individual from the caprices of state power and creates a protected legal and material space within which he can exercise his freedom.[63] The right to private property stems directly from, and is a requirement of, the *spiritual* inviolability of the human person. Without this right, man is naked before the state. Without economic freedom, there is no political freedom. What can happen under these conditions was made horrifically clear by the depredations of the totalitarian regimes in the twentieth century, which denied this right and imprisoned or slaughtered their defenseless subjects in the scores of millions.

In fact, the profound implications of the other propositions mentioned above, all of which flow from the Declaration, can also be illustrated by examining the consequences of their opposites. If, for instance, man is not a political creature endowed with reason, why attempt to order political life based on deliberation and representation? Likewise, if man does not have free will, deliberating over what he ought to do is superfluous. If reason is incapable of discerning good from evil, then deliberations are meaningless. Freedom, obviously, is a hollow idea if free will and reason do not exist. These faculties themselves make sense only in an order of nature that directs man toward ends that make him fully human. This is the perspective that formed the Founders and that infuses the Declaration of Independence, the Constitution, and the Founding Fathers' ancillary writings with moral purpose. The American Constitution makes no sense divorced from these presuppositions. As such, anything that undermines these premises ultimately undermines the Founding.

---

[63] Cicero's *De officiis* (*On Duties*, 44 B.C.), a work well known to the Founders, stated: "The chief purpose in the establishment of states and constitutional orders was that individual property rights might be secured.... For, as I said above, it is the peculiar function of state and city to guarantee to every man the free and undisturbed control of his own property" (1, 21, 73; 1, 22, 78).

10

The Antipodes: The American Revolution versus the French Revolution

From the preceding chapter, it should be clear that the American Revolution was not an exclusive product of the Enlightenment but had its roots in the deeper natural law and natural rights tradition. This becomes even clearer in contrast to the real product of the radical Enlightenment—the French Revolution, which was rootless regarding that same tradition. It was everything that the Deneen and Hanby school of critics mistakenly claims the American Revolution to have been. (Had they been writing about the former, there would have been little with which to disagree.) For confirmation, one need only look briefly at several luminaries of the French Revolution: Abbé Sieyès, the Marquis de Condorcet, the Marquis de Sade, and Louis de Saint-Just. We will counterpoise their statements with those of several American Founders. I do not deal with the full spectrum of the French Revolutionary parties, but only with the most radical elements, for the simple reason that they took over from all the others.

French Enlightenment Ideologues

Abbé Sieyès, one of the authors of the Declaration of the Rights of Man and of the Citizen, announced the foundational principle of the new French state: "The nation is prior to everything. It is the source of everything. Its will is always legal.... The manner in which the nation exercises its will does not matter; the point is that it does exercise it; any procedure is adequate, and its will is always the supreme law."[1] Thus, Rousseau's *volonté générale*—the general will—becomes

---

[1] Cited in Roger Scruton, "The Case for Nations", *Wall Street Journal*, June 3–4, 2017, C3.

the all in all. As George Makari notes, the general will was "a term once used by Pascal to refer to the will of God, but which Jean-Jacques considered the will of the people".[2] The French Declaration proclaimed that "the origin of all sovereignty resides essentially in the nation" and that "the law is the expression of the general will", not of "the Laws of Nature and of Nature's God". Thus, "no body or individual may exercise any authority which does not proceed directly from the nation." According to R. L. Bruckberger, the French Convention inscribed a sentence on the wall as a preamble to the French Declaration: "The citizen is born, lives, and dies for his country."[3] The nation assumes the attributes of divinity—omnipotence and infallibility. These pronouncements were as clearly voluntaristic in their perspective—asserting the primacy of will—as the pronouncements of the American Founders were not.

For instance, compare Sieyès' notion of unlimited sovereignty with John Quincy Adams' condemnation of the same, which he grounded in natural law:

> This principle, that a whole nation has a right to do whatever it pleases, cannot in any sense whatever be admitted as true. The eternal and immutable laws of justice and morality are paramount to all human legislation. The violation of those laws is certainly within the power of a nation, but it is not among the rights of nations.... If, therefore, a majority thus constituted are bound by no law human or divine, and have no other rule but their sovereign will and pleasure to direct them, what possible security can any citizen of the nation have for the protection of his inalienable rights?[4]

The Marquis de Condorcet wrote *The Progress of the Human Mind*, in which he epitomizes the ambition of the French Enlightenment: "My work will prove, by fact and reasoning, that no bounds have been fixed to the improvement of the human faculties; that *the*

---

[2] George Makari, *Soul Machine: The Invention of the Modern Mind* (New York: W. W. Norton, 2015), 336.

[3] R. L. Bruckberger, *Image of America*, trans. C. G. Paulding and Virgilia Peterson (New York: Viking Press, 1959), 86.

[4] *An Answer to Pain's Rights of Man*, in *Writings of John Quincy Adams*, vol. 1 (New York: Macmillan, 1913), 70.

perfectibility of man is truly limitless."[5] This is simply a follow-up to Rousseau's yearning to "change human nature".[6] Man's perfectible future "has no other limit than the duration of the globe on which nature has placed us", Condorcet wrote. What's more, "someday no time limit will be assignable to the average human life."[7] He went on to argue that the state provides the vehicle for organizing and implementing man's self-perfection. Alexis de Tocqueville would write that the men of the Revolution "had a robust faith in man's perfectibility and power.... They had no doubt but that they were appointed to transform the human race. These sentiments and passions had become a sort of new religion."[8] The contrast with the American Revolution could not be greater. While the French Revolution was intoxicated with the prospect of man's perfectibility, the American Revolution kept a sober appreciation of human imperfectibility.

The transformation of mankind and the conquest of death are, properly speaking, not political goals, but metaphysical ones—to remove man from contingency; to restart, if not end, history; to make man completely at home in the world by transforming him into God and his world into paradise through the total transformation of, and total revolution against, reality as it is. This enterprise would place within man's grasp the complete means to his own happiness. Man's aspiration for the divine is for something within *himself* that needs only to be unlocked to be realized. The French Revolution was the key. Its ambition to begin *de novo* (anew) was based on the assumption that Eric Voegelin characterized as "a change in the order of being ... in the realm of human action, that this salvational act is possible through man's own effort".[9] This is what the claim to unlimitedness means. British statesman Edmund Burke knew what this thinking

---

[5] Zoltán Haraszti, *John Adams and the Prophets of Progress* (Cambridge, Mass.: Harvard University Press, 1952), 242 (emphasis in the original).

[6] Jean-Jacques Rousseau, *The Social Contract* 2, 7.

[7] Haraszti, *John Adams*, 239–40.

[8] Alexis de Tocqueville, *The Old Regime and the Revolution* (New York: Harper and Brothers, 1856), 190.

[9] *The Collected Works of Eric Voegelin.* Vol. 5, *Modernity without Constraint: The Political Religions, the New Science of Politics, and Science, Politics, and Gnosticism.* Edited by Ellis Sandoz (Columbia: University of Missouri Press, 2000), 298.

foreshadowed: "In the groves of their academy, at the end of every vista, you see nothing but the gallows."[10]

If Condorcet was the movement's metaphysician, the Marquis de Sade was its theologian, or rather its antitheologian. Sade was liberated by the Revolution from his imprisonment for rape and other outrages. He was promoted to a government commission, though he was later incarcerated again, this time by Robespierre. (The newly minted "Citizen Sade" was not the only released pornographer to play a role; Mirabeau, author of *Erotika Biblion* and *Ma Conversion, ou le libertin de qualité*, became a major figure in the Assembly.) In *The Philosophy of the Boudoir*, de Sade wrote that the murder of King Louis XVI was insufficient to bring about the desired revolutionary freedom. The morality of the social and political order had survived the king's beheading. How could it finally be destroyed? In the first known use of the phrase, Sade wrote that the murder of the king must be followed by the "murder of God". Only when the morality represented by Divine Kingship was abolished could man express himself in the fullness of his pornographic existence. Sade said, "The idea of God is the sole wrong for which I cannot forgive mankind."[11] As Sade was not to be constrained by God, neither was he to be limited by natural law, which he avowed not to exist. Sounding very much like Callicles and Hobbes, he declared, "Nature has elaborated no statutes, instituted no code; her single law is writ deep in every man's heart: it is to satisfy himself, deny his passions nothing, and this regardless of the cost to others."[12] From this premise, Sade quite logically concluded: "Cruelty is simply the energy in a man that civilisation has not yet altogether corrupted."[13]

Louis de Saint-Just, one of the key figures of the Reign of Terror and a member of the Committee of Public Safety, was a close

---

[10] Edmund Burke, *Reflections on the Revolution in France* (1790; New York: P. F. Collier and Son, 1909), par. 130.

[11] Annie Le Brun, "Sade: Attacking the Sun" (Paris: Musée d'Orsay exhibition catalogue, 2014), 7, https://www.musee-orsay.fr/en/events/exhibitions/archives/exhibitions-archives/browse/4/page/0/article/sade-41230.html?tx_ttnews%5BbackPid%5D=252&cHash=288d0923f2.

[12] Cited in Khalil Habib, "Seven Shades of Gray", review of *Seven Types of Atheism*, by John Gray, *Claremont Review of Books* 19, no. 1 (Winter 2018–2019): 93.

[13] Le Brun, "Sade", 1.

colleague of Maximilien Robespierre, to whom he had written by way of introduction: "You whom I know only, as I know God, by his miracles".[14] Saint-Just was a radical ideologue for whom the achievement of a perfect society justified the elimination of all opposition. He said, "What makes a Republic is the total destruction of whatever stands in its way."[15] This included Louis XVI, whose execution Saint-Just eloquently advocated. He declared that "a government has for principle either virtue or Terror. What do they want, who want neither virtue nor Terror?"[16] He added that "nothing so resembles virtue as a great crime."[17]

Murder in the name of virtue became the prototype for subsequent totalitarian revolutions and regimes. Saint-Just predicted: "It is in the nature of things for our economic affairs to become more and more embroiled until the Republic, once established, takes over all operations, all interests, all rights, all obligations, and imposes a common pattern on all parts of the State."[18] Power is to reside in the laws "which take the place of God".[19] Dubbed by later writers the "Angel of Death", Saint-Just was overheard to say that "a nation can regenerate itself only upon mounds of corpses."[20] He proclaimed, "We must not only punish traitors, but all people who are not enthusiastic. There are only two kinds of citizens: the good and the bad. The Republic owes to the good its protection. To the bad it owes only death."[21] He advised the Convention: "The vessel of the Revolution can arrive in port only on a sea reddened with torrents of blood."[22] He went with Robespierre to his death by guillotine on July 28, 1794.

During the short span from September 5, 1793, to July 27, 1794, some three hundred thousand French suspects were arrested, and

---

[14] Marisa Linton, "The French Revolution's Angel of Death", *History Today*, March 27, 2018, https://www.historytoday.com/marisa-linton/french-revolutions-angel-death.

[15] Cited in Bruckberger, *Image of America*, 65.

[16] Ibid., 66.

[17] Ibid., 69.

[18] Ibid.,72.

[19] Ibid.

[20] Ibid., 64–65.

[21] *Encyclopedia Britannica Online*, s.v. "Louis de Saint-Just", accessed June 24, 2019, https://www.britannica.com/biography/Louis-de-Saint- Just.

[22] Ibid.

tens of thousands were executed or died in prison.[23] More victims fell in the Vendée after the brutal suppression of the peasant uprising there, which included the execution of hundreds of children. French general François Joseph Westermann, known as "the Butcher of the Vendée", wrote to the Committee of Public Safety in Paris: "There is no more Vendée.... According to the orders that you gave me, I crushed the children under the feet of the horses, massacred the women who, at least for these, will not give birth to any more brigands. I do not have a prisoner to reproach me. I have exterminated all."[24]

Sir Roger Scruton, characterizing Joseph de Maistre's reaction to the Revolution, sees the Terror as the predictable unfolding of a spritiual disease:

> The violence of the Revolution was entirely what must be expected when people attempt to deny the reality of original sin and to take their destiny into their own hands. The events of the Terror were literally satanic, re-enacting the revolt of the fallen angels, and displaying what ensues when human beings reject the idea of authority, and imagine themselves capable of discovering a new form of government in the freedom from government.[25]

[23] *Encyclopaedia Britannica Online*, s.v. "Counterrevolution, Regicide, and the Reign of Terror", accessed June 24, 2109, https://www.britannica.com/event/French-Revolution/Counterrevolution-regicide-and-the-Reign-of-Terror#ref177643.

[24] Henry Samuel, "Vendée French Call for Revolution Massacre to Be Termed 'Genocide' ", *Telegraph*, December 26, 2008, https://www.telegraph.co.uk/news/worldnews/europe/france/3964724/Vende-French-call-for-revolution-massacre-to-be-termed-genocide.html; fuller original French text: "Il n'y a plus de Vendée, citoyens républicains. Elle est morte sous notre sabre libre, avec ses femmes et ses enfants. Je viens de l'enterrer dans les marais et dans les bois de Savenay. Suivant les ordres que vous m'avez donnés, j'ai écrasé les enfants sous les pieds des chevaux, massacré des femmes, qui, au moins pur celles-là, n'enfanteront plus de brigands. Je n'ai pas un prisonnier à me reprocher. J'ai tout exterminé. Mon ami, je t'annonce avec plaisir que les brigands sont bien détruits. Le nombre qu'on en amène ici depuis huit jours est incalculable. Il en arrive à tout moment. Comme en les fusillant c'est trop long et qu'on use de la poudre et des balles, on a pris le parti d'en mettre un certain nombre dans de grands bateaux, de les conduire au milieu de la rivière, à une demi-lieue de la ville et là on coule le bateau à fond. Cette opération se fait journellement." Documents sur le génocide vendéen, website of Jean-Baptiste Noé, June 17, 2013, http://www.jbnoe.fr/Documents-sur-le-genocide-vendeen.

[25] Roger Scruton, *Conservatism: An Invitation to the Great Tradition* (New York: St. Martin's Press, 2018).

The Assault on Christianity

The French Revolution attempted a total break with the past by destroying it. The American Revolution sought a fulfillment of the past by preserving and improving upon it. It is telling that while the American Founders dated the U.S. Constitution "in the Year of our Lord", the French Revolutionary government considered the inception of the French Republic as the year zero of a new world. It adopted a calendar to begin time anew with 1792 as the first year of the "era of liberty". Sundays were eliminated as part of the dechristianization campaign that instituted a new ten-day week. On the other hand, the U.S. Constitution implicitly recognized the sanctity of Sunday in article 1, section 7, as James H. Hutson pointed out, "by excluding it from the 10 days in which a president was obliged to return a bill to Congress".[26] "Sundays excepted" reads section 7.

To understand the essential difference between the American and French Revolutions, one need only realize that a dechristianization campaign in the American Revolution would have been unthinkable. In *Democracy in America*, Alexis de Tocqueville observed: "Anglo-American civilization ... is the result ... of two distinct elements, which in other places have been in frequent disagreement, but which the Americans have succeeded in incorporating, to some extent, one with the other and combining admirably. I allude to the *spirit of religion* and the *spirit of liberty*."[27] The disagreement between the two "distinct elements" in France was extreme; they were at war. Rousseau proclaimed that "Christianity preaches only servitude and dependence.... True Christians are made to be slaves."[28] Voltaire had said, "Every sensible man, every honorable man must hold the Christian religion in horror."[29] Therefore, he famously urged, "Écrasez l'infâme", and they did.

---

[26] James H. Hutson, *Religion and the Founding of the American Republic* (Washington D.C.: Library of Congress, 1998), 75.

[27] Alexis de Tocqueville, *Democracy in America*, vol. 1 (New York: Vintage Books, 1991), 43.

[28] Jean-Jacques Rousseau, *The Social Contract* 4, 8.

[29] Cited in Alberto M. Piedra, "The Dechristianization of France during the French Revolution", Institute of World Politics, January 12, 2018, https://www.iwp.edu/news _publications/detail/the-dechristianization-of-france-during-the-french-revolution.

In one act of the Enlightenment in 1793, the French revolutionaries broke into the church of Saint-Étienne-du-Mont near the Pantheon, the burial site of Genevieve, the patron saint of Paris. They desecrated her grave, took the remains, and burned them at the Place de Grève. On November 10, 1793, they proceeded to the Cathedral of Notre Dame, transformed into the Temple of Reason, where they constructed a huge mound of earth on which they enthroned the Goddess of Liberty, a voluptuous opera singer. One of the key coordinators of the event, Jacques Hébert, reported: "What a spectacle to see all the children of liberty rushing into the former cathedral to purify the temple of all the absurdity and to dedicate it to truth and reason!"[30] An altar to Truth supported effigies of Voltaire and Rousseau, among others.[31] The organizer of the event, Pierre-Gaspard Chaumette, was so ashamed of his Christian name that he changed it to Anaxagoras— chosen, no doubt, because of the latter's alleged atheism, for which he was indicted in fifth-century-B.C. Athens.[32] Condorcet celebrated that "the delirium of a supernatural faith disappeared from society, as it has disappeared from philosophy."[33] Citizen Sade told the Convention: "Reason is replacing Mary in our temples and the incense that used to burn at the knees of an adulterous woman will from now on be kindled only at the feet of the goddess who broke our chains."[34]

By late October 1789, new religious vows were forbidden. On November 2, Church property was confiscated and declared the state's possession.[35] Churches were closed or converted into temples of reason, their bells melted down for bullets or coinage. Christian symbols were removed. Crosses were taken from graveyards. The anthropocentric Cult of Reason reigned. Under it, there would be, according to Anacharsis Cloots, "one God only, *Le Peuple*".[36] In his

---

[30] Cited in Shane H. Hockin, *Les Hommes sans Dieu: Atheism, Religion, and Politics during the French Revolution* (Tallahassee: Florida State University Libraries, 2014), 182, https://fsu.digital.flvc.org/islandora/object/fsu:185261/datastream/PDF/view.

[31] Makari, *Soul Machine*, 349.

[32] Ibid.

[33] Cited in Eric Voegelin, *From Enlightenment to Revolution* (Durham, N.C.: Duke University Press, 1975), 126.

[34] Cited in E. Michael Jones, *Libido Dominandi: Sexual Liberation and Political Control* (South Bend, Ind.: St. Augustine's Press, 2000), 50.

[35] William Bush, *To Quell the Terror* (Washington, D.C.: ICS Publications, 1999), xviii.

[36] Thomas Carlyle, *The French Revolution: A History*, vol. 2, Everyman's Library (New York: E. P. Dutton, 1916), 310.

address to the National Convention (November 17, 1793), Cloots, who was later guillotined, proclaimed: "Citizens, religion is the greatest obstacle to my utopia."[37] The dechristianization campaign led to persecution of Christians and, in some cases, the murder of clergy; 25,000 priests fled the country.[38] They didn't all make it. On September 2, 1792, writes E. Michael Jones, "wagons carrying 115 defenseless priests bound for deportation were diverted by an enraged mob to the Abbaye and a Carmelite convent."[39] Citizen Sade reported: "All of the refractory priests had their throats cut in the churches where they were being held, among them the Archbishop of Arles, the most virtuous and respectable of men."[40] A month earlier, on August 2, a decree ordered the closure of all convents. One of the most infamous episodes during the Terror was the execution of the Carmelite nuns of Compiègne. Declared enemies of the state for secretly practicing their vows, the sixteen nuns sang psalms as they were marched to the scaffold and guillotined on July 17, 1794.

Adams and Hamilton React

The French Revolution appalled many of America's Founders, especially John Adams and Alexander Hamilton, who are worth hearing from at length. Before doing so, however, it should be noted that Thomas Jefferson, residing in France as the American minister to the Court of Versailles, was an early enthusiast of the French Revolution, hoping it would replicate America's struggle to found a republic. In a July 1789 letter to James Madison, he expressed the hope that the French were "advancing to a limited, moderate government, in which the people will have a good share".[41] Jefferson, however, left France before September 1789, and he never witnessed the Terror. Later he regretted the lack of moderation that could have

[37] Anacharsis Cloots, "Religion is the Greatest Obstacle". Marxists.org, https://www.marxists.org/history/france/revolution/cloots/1793/religion.htm.

[38] J. M. Thompson, *Robespierre and the French Revolution* (New York: Collier Books, 1973), 111.

[39] Jones, *Libido Dominandi*, 32.

[40] Ibid.

[41] Thomas Jefferson to James Madison, July 31, 1788, Founders Online, National Archives, https://founders.archives.gov/documents/Jefferson/01-13-02-0335.

avoided "those enormities which demoralised the nations of the world, and destroyed, and is yet to destroy millions and millions of its inhabitants".[42]

John Adams was suspicious of the provenance of the French Revolution's animating ideas from nearly the outset. He wrote to a friend in 1790, "I know that the encyclopedists and economists, Diderot and D'Alembert, Voltaire and Rousseau, have contributed to this great event more than Sidney, Locke, or Hoadley, perhaps more than the American revolution; and I own to you, I know not what to make of a republic of 30 million atheists."[43] In a letter to Samuel Adams the same year, Adams forecast the troubles to come: "Everything will be pulled down. So much seems certain. But what will be built up? Are there any principles of political architecture? What are they? Were Voltaire and Rousseau masters of them?... Will the struggle in Europe be any thing other than a change in impostors?"[44]

Adams' habit of annotating the books he read made for a living dialogue. In the case of Condorcet's *The Progress of the Human Mind*, it also gives a key to his reaction to the ideology of the French Revolution. The margins are full of his comments on and to the author, whom he had met in Paris in 1778. As one would expect, Condorcet, like Voltaire and Cloots, attacked organized religion, claiming that priests had become dupes of their own fables and that kings and priests waged a continual war against the truth. In the margin by that statement, Adams wrote, "Just as you and yours have become the dupes of your own atheism and profligacy, your nonsensical notions of liberty, equality, and fraternity.... Your philosophy, Condorcet, has waged a more cruel war against truth than was ever attempted by king or priest."[45] When the Marquis complained that true genius had been suppressed by organized religion, Adams retorted, "But was there no genius among the Hebrews? None among the Christians ...? I understand you, Condorcet, it is atheistical genius alone that you would honor or tolerate."[46] And when the Marquis insisted on

[42] Thomas Jefferson, *Autobiography*, January 6–July 29, 1821, January 6, 1821, Founders Online, National Archives, https://founders.archives.gov/documents/Jefferson/98-01-02-1756.

[43] Cited in Henry F. May, *The Enlightenment in America* (New York: Oxford University Press, 1976), 285.

[44] *The Works of John Adams*, 6:411–12.

[45] Haraszti, *John Adams*, 245–46.

[46] Ibid., 250.

the natural equality of mankind as the foundation of morality, Adams responded, "There is no such thing without a supposition of a God. There is no right or wrong in the universe without the supposition of a moral government and an intellectual and moral governor."[47] Adams sarcastically lamented: "What a pity that this man of genius cannot be king and priest for the whole human race!"[48] Elsewhere in his correspondence, Adams admonished, "Statesmen my dear Sir, may plan and speculate for Liberty, but it is Religion and Morality alone, which can establish the Principles upon which Freedom can securely stand."[49]

In another bit of marginalia, Adams wrote:

> It is to Ideology, to that obscure metaphysics, which searching with subtlety after first causes, wishes to found upon them the legislation of nations, instead of adapting their laws to the knowledge of the human heart and to the lessons of history, that we are to attribute all of the calamities that our beloved France has experienced.... The political and literary world are much indebted for the invention of the new word IDEOLOGY. Our English words Ideocy or Ideotism, express not the force or meaning of it. It is presumed its proper definition is the science of ideocy.[50]

Adams identified and expressed his detestation of this ideology: "Rousseau says the first man who fenced the cabbage garden ought to have been put to death. Diderot says the first man who suggested the idea of a god ought to have been treated as an enemy of the human race."[51] He cautioned:

> If a new order of things has commenced, it behooves us to be cautious, that it may not be for the worse. If the abuse of Christianity

[47] Ibid., 252.

[48] Daniel J. Boorstin, *The Americas: The Colonial Experience* (New York: Vintage Books, 1958), 153

[49] John Adams to Zabdiel Adams, June 21, 1776, Founders Online, National Archives, https://founders.archives.gov/documents/Adams/04-02-02-0011.

[50] Cited in Ellis Sandoz, *Republicanism, Religion, and the Soul of America* (Columbia: University of Missouri Press, 2006), 38–39.

[51] Cited in Richard Samuelson, "Jefferson, Adams, and the American Future", *Claremont Review of Books* 11, nos. 1–2 (Winter–Spring 2010), https://www.claremont.org/crb/article/jefferson-adams-and-the-american-future/.

can be annihilated or diminished, and a more equitable enjoyment of the right of conscience introduced, it will be well; but this will not be accomplished by the abolition of Christianity and the introduction of the Grecian mythology, or the worship of modern heroes or heroines, by erecting statues of idolatry to reason or virtue, to beauty or to taste. It is a serious problem to resolve, whether all the abuses of Christianity even in the darkest ages, when the Pope deposed princes and laid nations under his interdict, were ever so bloody and cruel, ever bore down the independence of the human mind with such terror and intolerance, or taught doctrines which required such implicit credulity to believe, as the present reign of pretended philosophy in France.[52]

At his vituperative best, Adams expressed to a friend that "Helvetius and Rousseau preached to the French Nation Liberty, till they made them the most mechanical Slaves; *equality* till they destroyed all Equity; *humanity* till they became Weasels, and African Panthers; and *Fraternity* till they cut one another's throats like the Roman Gladiators."[53]

Alexander Hamilton was disturbed by and vigorously objected to those who found a resemblance between the American and the French Revolutions. In a May 18, 1793, memorandum to President Washington, he wrote:

The cause of France is compared with that of America during its late revolution. Would to Heaven that the comparison were just. Would to Heaven that we could discern in the mirror of French affairs, the same humanity, the same decorum, the same gravity, the same order, the same dignity, the same solemnity, which distinguished the course of the American Revolution. Clouds and darkness would not then rest upon the issue as they now do. I own, I do not like the comparison. When I contemplate the horrid and systematic massacres of the 2d. & 3d. of September; When I observe that a Marat and a Robespierre, the notorious prompters of those bloody scenes, reign triumphantly in

[52] John Adams to the Grand Jurors of the Hampshire County Massachusetts, October 3, 1798, in *The Works of John Adams: Second President of the United States*, 10 vols. (Boston: Charles C. Little and James Brown, 1850–1856), 9:227.

[53] John Adams to Benjamin Waterhouse, May 21, 1821, Founders Online, National Archives, https://founders.archives.gov/documents/Adams/99-02-02-7496.

the Convention and take a conspicuous part in its measures ...; When I find the doctrines of Atheism openly advanced in the Convention and heard with loud applauses; When I see the sword of fanaticism extended to force a political creed upon citizens who were invited to submit to the arms of France as the harbingers of Liberty; When I behold the hand of Rapacity outstreched to prostrate and ravish the monuments of religious worship erected by those citizens and their ancestors; When I perceive passion tumult and violence usurping those seats, where reason and cool deliberation ought to preside—I acknowledge that I am glad to believe there is no real resemblance between what was the cause of America and what is the cause of France—that the difference is no less great than that between Liberty and Licentiousness. I regret whatever has a tendency to confound them, and I feel anxious, as an American, that the [agitations] of inconsiderate men may not tend to involve our Reputation in the issue.[54]

France missed the opportunity of a constitutional monarchy (which Jefferson had suggested) and went almost straight from Divine Right absolutism to secular absolutism—the same thing but in disguise. In 1770, Abbé Raynal had written, "No divine right but that of the weal of the Republic."[55] And so it sadly was. Tocqueville noted that, as much as they might seem opposed to each other, there was a logical trajectory from the one kind of absolutism to the other. While the American Revolution produced federalism, the French Revolution increased the centralization of the state. Professor Will Morrisey points out:

> In 1789 the French monarchy controlled a fairly large state, by the standards of the day: 50,000 men staffed Louis XVI's bureaucracy. By 1796, French bureaucrats numbered nearly 250,000—most of them appointed during the period of the Terror, in 1792–93. This apparatus has endured throughout the many changes of regime subsequent to 1796.... While the French Revolution continued the monarchic state-building project under several regimes, ending with that of Napoleon, the American Revolution ended such a project.[56]

---

[54] Alexander Hamilton to ———, May 18, 1793, Founders Online, National Archives, https://founders.archives.gov/documents/Hamilton/01-14-02-0312.

[55] Cited in Voegelin, *From Enlightenment to Revolution*, 172.

[56] Will Morrisey, "The French and American Revolutions Compared", Will Morrisey Reviews, April 25, 2018, http://www.willmorriseyreviews.com/?s=By+1796%2C+French +bureaucrats+numbered+nearly+250%2C000.

In other words, the American Revolution ended any further attempt by Great Britain to subordinate the colonies under the control of the king's bureaucratic state.

The French Enlightenment views briefly dealt with here were inimical to those of Adams, Hamilton, and most of the other Founding Fathers. One would be at a loss to find in them anything comparable to the statements quoted above.[57] What Clinton Rossiter wrote specifically of Rousseau, whose *Social Contract* was always at Robespierre's bedside, was generally true of the French Revolutionary ideology in relation to American ideas: "Rousseau's whole approach to man, society, and government ran counter to the basic principles of American Revolutionary thought."[58] Indeed, whereas American political thought was premised on the necessary limits of the political, French Revolutionary thought presumed the absence of such limits.

Contrary principles produced opposite results. Not only were the revolutions different, but the one could be more properly understood as an inversion of the other. British historian Paul Johnson wrote: "The American Revolution in its origins was a religious event,

---

[57] Those who contest this point often rely on Thomas Paine, who arrived in America at the end of 1774, a date far too late to have affected the intellectual formation of the Founders, nor could he possibly be considered one himself. There is no doubt that with the publication of *Common Sense* in 1776, he became a powerful propagandist for independence, and his other writings were important in maintaining the morale of the Continental Army. He later went to France to join its revolution and was given a seat in the National Convention in 1792. When he was arrested by Robespierre, the United States did nothing to obtain his release. His book *The Rights of Man* alienated many of his former American supporters (but not Thomas Jefferson), who considered it atheistic. He became a figure of opprobrium. After Paine returned to the United States to live on his farm in New York State, an election inspector of New Rochelle denied him the right to vote in the 1806 election on the basis that he was no longer an American citizen. Paine apparently sued the election inspectors but lost the case. Only six people attended his funeral in 1809. John Adams expressed his detestation of Paine, particularly for his appropriation of the word "reason" in the title of his book, *The Age of Reason*: "Call it then the Age of Paine. He deserves it much more, than the Courtezan who was consecrated to represent the Goddess in the Temple at Paris, and whose name, Tom has given to the Age. The real intellectual faculty has nothing to do with the Age the Strumpet or Tom." John Adams to Benjamin Waterhouse, October 29, 1805, Founders Online, National Archives, https://founders.archives.gov/documents/Adams/99-02-02-5107.

[58] Clinton Rossiter, *Seedtime of the Republic: The Origins of the American Tradition of Political Liberty* (New York: Harcourt, Brace, 1953), 359. As an illustration of this statement, see Rousseau's *Social Contract* (4, 8): "I am mistaken in speaking of a Christian republic; the terms are mutually exclusive. Christianity preaches only servitude and dependence. Its spirit is so favorable to tyranny that it always profits by such a régime. True Christians are made to be slaves, and they know it and do not much mind." This is antithetical to what the Founders believed.

whereas the French Revolution was an anti-religious event. That fact was to shape ... the nature of the independent state it brought into being."[59] Although Tory loyalists were not treated with kid gloves, there was no Reign of Terror in the American Revolution. No churches were transformed into temples of reason; no crosses were removed from cemeteries; and no clergy were executed. The differences can be defined by the primacy of reason in the one and the primacy of will in the other, which led the American revolutionaries to behave on the whole *reasonably* and the French revolutionaries to behave on the whole *unreasonably*. What the latter left in their wake was political instability in France that persists to this day, while in the United States the Founders left what has become the world's longest-lived constitution.

---

[59] Cited in Bill Flax, "Was America Founded as a Christian Nation?", *Forbes*, September 25, 2012; https://www.forbes.com/sites/billflax/2012/09/25/was-america-founded-as-a-christian -nation/.

11

Critiquing the Critics: Why They Go Wrong about What Was Right

We now return to the poison-pill thesis with which this book began—the question of whether the Founding is at fault for today's deleterious developments. To recapitulate the issue briefly: What did it mean to be constituted as a people in order to "secure these rights", as the Declaration of Independence announced, of "Life, Liberty and the pursuit of Happiness"? Were these "rights" ordered to any natural end, or were they autonomous, to be exercised at the will and complete discretion of their possessor? In other words, was the enterprise primarily an exercise of pure *will*, or was it grounded in *reason*? Critics such as Patrick Deneen and Michael Hanby say it was will—that these "rights" were fatally infected with a notion of radical individualism and that it was only a matter of time till their ill effects were felt in the moral degeneration from which we suffer today. The weight of evidence already seen (and forthcoming), however, makes it well nigh incontrovertible that the Founders held that these inalienable rights were morally ordered to, and could be exercised only within, the very "Laws of Nature and of Nature's God" that bestowed them. The "self-evident" truths of the Declaration were intelligible only within the natural law context in which they were spoken and from which they arose. If that standard of rightness is lost, then all is lost.

The purpose here is not to single out Deneen and Hanby as individuals, but to use their critiques as general stand-ins for those who hold the same or closely similar views. They are specifically addressed only because they express these representative positions so clearly.[1]

---

[1] Despite my criticisms, I should make clear that I find their analysis of the current cultural decay penetrating and profound. They are very good at describing how bad things are, why they are bad, and to where they are leading. Both need to be read for an appreciation of the true precariousness of our situation.

As mentioned in the introduction, their perspective is not unique. I cited the thought of John A. Gueguen as an example. Also, around the time of the bicentennial of the Constitution, a vigorous debate took place between Walter Berns (on the side of Hobbes' influence on the Founding) and Harry Jaffa (on the opposing side). Years before, Herbert J. Storing spoke of "the tendency, under the principles of the Declaration of Independence, for justice to be reduced to self-preservation, for self-preservation to be defined as self-interest, and for self-interest to be defined as what is convenient and achievable".[2] One might also mention Thomas Pangle as a representative of this point of view. We will examine where Deneen and Hanby attempt to locate the presence of the radical autonomy that they claim is in the American Founding. We will see that their evidence for it is negligible.

Scorning America

Deneen asserts that the Founding was based on "a relativistic philosophy". Otherwise, he asks, "if we are to believe that the American Founding represents the culmination of a long and unbroken tradition that stretches back to Plato, Aristotle, Cicero, and Aquinas, then how did that tradition disintegrate so quickly?"[3] First of all, as set forth in chapters 6 and 7, the tradition had *already* been broken by the forces of absolutism well before the American Revolution, which then *restored* it to its rightful place. This is why that tradition did not disintegrate so quickly in the United States, as Deneen would have us believe.

Around the time of John Courtney Murray's book, Leo Strauss pointed out that "unqualified relativism" was characteristic of "Western thought *in general*" (emphasis added), which makes it difficult to attribute it to the American Founding. Indeed, no Catholic country has withstood the forces of relativism and most of them, such as Italy

---

[2] Joseph M. Bessette, ed., *Toward a More Perfect Union: Writings of Herbert J. Storing* (Washington, D.C.: AEI Press, 1995), 143.

[3] Patrick Deneen, "Liberalism's Logic and America's Challenge: A Reply to Schlueter and Muñoz", *Public Discourse*, March 6, 2013, https://www.thepublicdiscourse.com/2013/03/9458/.

and Spain, are in worse shape than the United States. Why has America proven more stalwart? Why was it the principal redoubt against Nazi Germany and the Soviet Union, both of which embodied the voluntarism that Murray decried? And why does America today remain by far the strongest force against the contemporary expression of voluntarism in Islam, as well as the only power capable of defending Europe? Though the United States is obviously not incapable of wholesale defection from the "Laws of Nature", its greatest chance of recovery lies in returning to its principles, not in jettisoning them.

But Deneen claims that "we have today more the country that springs from our political DNA than one that doesn't." That DNA is primarily Lockean, he says, which accounts for the perverted "autonomy of self" we see around us. In his *First Things* article "Moral Minority", Deneen asserts that the practical consequences of the Founders' definition of liberty "were long obscured by the fact that Americans had a rich and sustaining Christian culture that was older and deeper than the political structure.... Over time, our political order would shape our culture, or more accurately, it would eliminate traditional culture in favor of a liberal anti-culture." Thus, Deneen does not speak of "the betrayal of our political origins, but the fulfillment of [their] logic".[4]

The New Abolitionism

This indictment leads Deneen to question the very basis of American republicanism: "To have allegiance even to this mixed Constitutional Founding is ultimately to declare allegiance to the trajectory of radical autonomy and individualism." Can a Christian give such allegiance? If the American Proposition is not only hostile to Christianity but, in fact, the product of its denial, he cannot. Abortionists, pornographers, and same-sex "marriage" proponents can legitimately claim, if Deneen is correct, that "the Founding made me do it." On this basis, they can *require* our approval of their behavior, the legal enforcement of which has been working its way through the court system.

[4] Patrick J. Deneen, "Moral Minority", *First Things* (April 2017), https://www.firstthings.com/article/2017/04/moral-minority.

Therefore, says Deneen, "I increasingly fear that Americans will have to break with America, and seek to re-found the nation on better truths—ones that have perhaps never been self-evident, but rather hard-won, and which are far better than our philosophy and increasingly better than ourselves."[5] In his book *Conserving America?*, he states that these better truths must be "explicitly in departure from the philosophic principles that animated its liberal Founding ... to build a new civilization worthy of preservation".[6] Is there not anything worth saving in the American Founding? Deneen conveys how comprehensively he scorns America by proffering this parallel: "[Václav] Havel did not appeal to the better version of the Communist regime in Czechoslovakia or seek to reform it from within, but to 'expose its unstable foundations' by refusing to pretend that its lies were true."[7] Deneen is the Václav Havel of America, exposing its unstable foundations and refusing to accept its self-evident truths as anything but lies. Just as there could not be a "better" version of communism for Havel, so there can be no "better" version of America for Deneen.

Deneen's views recall William Lloyd Garrison, the abolitionist who believed that the U.S. Constitution was a "covenant with Death, an Agreement with Hell". For Garrison, solving the problem of slavery required eliminating the Constitution, copies of which he publicly burned. To cure today's ills, Deneen calls for replacing, not improving, the American Founding—though he never says what exactly should supplant it, a crippling omission. Both Garrison and Deneen fail to understand that the Founding principles are themselves the strongest case against public moral corruptions such as slavery and abortion.

Misquoting Madison

Where in the Founding *itself* can Deneen and like-minded critics locate the malign principles that render it unworthy of preservation?

---

[5] Patrick J. Deneen, "Better Than Our Philosophy: A Response to Muñoz", *Public Discourse*, November 29, 2012, https://www.thepublicdiscourse.com/2012/11/7156/.

[6] Patrick J. Deneen, *Conserving America? Essays on Present Discontents* (South Bend, Ind.: St. Augustine's Press, 2016), 1.

[7] Deneen, "Moral Minority".

Deneen repeatedly cites James Madison in *Federalist* No. 10 as evidence that the American regime is based on a notion of radical individual autonomy. *Conserving America?* states, "'The first object of government,' writes Madison in *Federalist* 10, 'is the protection of the diversity in the faculties of men.'" From this, Deneen attempts his own paraphrase of Madison and concludes:

> The *first object of government* enshrined in our Constitutional order is the protection of private differences, primarily distinctions that are manifest in different economic attainments, but further, whatever differences that are understood to arise from our "diversity of faculties." Our regime enshrines the priority of inviolable private difference lodged in our "faculties," and is thus designed to shape a polity and the society that removes all potential obstacles to the realization of those private differences.[8]

If the American regime is designed to remove "*all* potential obstacles to the realization of those private differences" (my emphasis), it must include moral ones as well. As skewed as this reading is, it does comport perfectly with Supreme Court Justice Anthony Kennedy's understanding of the Constitution. He and his confrères certainly hold that the purpose of the Constitution is found in "the priority of inviolable private differences". As the late Peter Lawler wrote in 2014:

> If Patrick [Deneen] is right, and the core of America is nothing more than Lockean individualism working itself out by emptying us out over time, then he has to agree, as a matter of Constitutional law, with the opinions of the Court in *Roe* and *Lawrence*. As a Catholic he can object, but he can't deny that the Court has grabbed on to the nerve of our Lockean Constitution in its doctrine of freedom as autonomy unfolding generation by generation.[9]

One must go further and say that Deneen, contra Justices Scalia, Roberts, Alito, and Thomas, must agree even more heartily with

---

[8] Deneen, *Conserving America?*, 5.

[9] Peter Lawler, "Catholic and American (and Quirky about It)", *First Things*, February 8, 2014, https://www.firstthings.com/blogs/firstthoughts/2014/02/catholic-and-american-and-quirky-about-it.

Justice Kennedy on the *Obergefell* decision legitimizing homosexual "marriage". Kennedy had to evoke the mysterious muse of History to justify his mangling of the Constitution. Deneen could have told him that the premise for such radical individualism was there right from the start in *Federalist* 10.

Deneen later continues:

> The political order exists to permit, even positively encourage, humans to differentiate themselves by their choices with near infinite variety, unfettered by limitations of family circumstance, geographic accident, undesired citizenship, unwanted religious identity, and increasingly—as we now see—even gender or any other form of identity that would suggest some form of external limitation on our shaping of selfhood.[10]

That certainly loads a great deal on Madison's shoulders—even transgenderism! What's more, "only when individuals are rootless, culture-less, history-less and context-less—depersonalized and abstracted—do we realize the ends prescribed by our regime. And yet we don't realize that we have been shaped in just this way because we understand our condition to be that of freedom ... while the invisible architecture of the regime continues to exert its shaping force." Shaped by this invisible architecture, "the citizenry increasingly conforms to the stated aims of the Constitutional order, its first object being the protection and encouragement of the 'diversity of faculties.'"[11] Deneen relies very heavily on his Madison quotation for a definitive expression of "the ends prescribed by our regime". So it must be closely examined along with the conclusions that Deneen thinks it supports.

The major problem is that Madison did *not* say: "The first object of government is the protection of the diversity in the faculties of men." Deneen accidentally cobbled together parts of two sentences and created this new one that supports his critique, erecting a Madisonian straw man to indict the Founding. In *Federalist* 10, Madison is talking about minimizing the problems of faction, especially majority

---

[10] Deneen, *Conserving America?*, 200.
[11] Ibid., 7.

factions, in order to preserve the United States. This is a major challenge because, as Madison said, "the latent causes of faction are sown into the nature of man." Just after saying that one insuperable problem leading to faction is the connection between man's "reason and his self-love", he added, "The diversity in the faculties of men, from which the rights of property originate, is not less an insuperable obstacle to a uniformity of interests." In other words, "diversity", a simple fact of nature in men's diverse talents, is in the first place a *problem*, not a solution or a goal. What Madison focused on in *Federalist* 10 is the political problem that arises from the wide disparities that differing abilities, especially in acquiring property, produce. The objective is "to adjust these clashing interests and render them all subservient to the public good". He concluded that the best way to avoid the formation of a tyrannical majority faction that would dispossess the minority of its rights and property is through the form of an enlarged representative republic.

Deneen's reading of *Federalist* 10 mistakes Madison's *prudential* argument as a statement of *principle* about the American regime as dedicated to maximizing human diversity. With this misinterpretation, Deneen thinks he can vindicate his view of the American Founding as a moral poison pill of radical individualism. Madison, however, never says that diversity is something government should positively encourage, as Deneen suggests. A multiplicity of interests (not of factions) can be useful in helping to prevent the formation of a tyrannical majority, Madison emphasized. But the whole point of the *Federalist* is to foster consensus out of diversity: *E pluribus unum*. It is Madison's next sentence that declares, "The protection of these faculties is the first object of government." It is the protection of the *faculties* themselves, not of diversity, that is the government's object. By this, Madison meant that government protects the free exercise of an individual's abilities.

But Deneen might respond that since people's faculties are, in fact, diverse, is not Madison, in effect, calling for the protection of diversity? This objection would be mistaking essence and accident. For instance, men have reason by their nature; in other words, reason is *essential* to them as human beings. Different men, however, have different capacities to reason and differing levels of intelligence. The differences, no matter how great—as between a child and an adult—are *accidental.* No one is less human because of a lesser or impaired capacity to reason or because of different levels of intelligence. What the government guarantees is the free exercise of intelligence. As a result of this freedom, one may expect different outcomes—for example, a wide variance in test scores. What the government is protecting as its first object is not the wide variance, which may cause frictions or envious factions, but the same freedom to think, to speak, and to learn. In other words, the protection of the free exercise of unequal faculties is a function of the protection of equal rights. Equality of rights *necessitates* this protection in somewhat the same way as the rules of a fair race necessitate the different outcomes from it.[12] The sole alternative would be the protection of only the *same* abilities, which would subvert equality of rights and produce a version of Kurt Vonnegut Jr.'s satirical world, in which, thanks to "the unceasing vigilance of agents of the United States Handicapper General", "nobody was smarter than anybody else. Nobody was better looking than anybody else. Nobody was stronger or quicker than anybody else."[13]

Deneen's line of thought mistakes the result for the cause. Madison makes the object of government the protection of something essential (man's faculties and the free exercise thereof), not of something accidental (the diversity of faculties or what results from them). This is the reason Madison *never* uses the phrase "the protection of the diversity in the faculties of men". Deneen inadvertently creates this phrase and then uses it to read back into *Federalist* 10 Justice Kennedy's views of radical individual autonomy—thus implying a straight line from the Founding to today's LGBT rights. Deneen uses this sentence frequently to prove his position.[14]

---

[12] Edward J. Erler and Ken Masugi, eds., *The Rediscovery of America: Essays by Harry V. Jaffa on the New Birth of Politics* (Lanham, Md.: Rowman and Littlefield, 2019), 208.

[13] Kurt Vonnegut Jr., *Welcome to the Monkey House* (New York: Dial Press, 1998), 7.

[14] Here is how Deneen has referred to the key line in *Federalist* 10. In 2012 at *Public Discourse*, in his article "Beyond Wishful Thinking: A Response to Schlueter", Deneen stated: "In the course of *Federalist* 10, Madison makes the matter plain: 'the [protection of the] diversity in the faculties of men, from which the rights of property originate ... is the first object of government.'" In the 2014 Holmer Lecture, from which chapter 12 of *Conserving America?* is drawn, he wrote: "'The first object of government,' writes Madison in *Federalist* 10, 'is the protection of the diversity in the faculties of men.'" (This is the accidental misquotation Deneen admitted to in his reply to me at *Public Discourse*. See Patrick Deneen, "Corrupting the Youth? A Response to Reilly", *Public Discourse*, September 19, 2017, https://www

In 2012, he employed it against the idea that the Founding was in any way a continuation of premodern natural law thinking. He wrote: "We need only look at their words, most obviously the Lockean basis of the Declaration ... but so too to the justifications they offered for the Constitution. In the course of *Federalist* 10, Madison makes the matter plain: 'the [protection of the] diversity in the faculties of men, from which the rights of property originate ... is the first object of government.'"[15] Here again he mistakes what Madison said. It is very hard to "look at their words" if you get their words wrong. Misquotations breed misinterpretations, as when Deneen says, "The pursuit of appetites, in the form of accumulation of property, is understood to be the main activity of individuals, requiring the protection of the government—indeed, forming the 'first object' of government." But Madison does not say that the "pursuit of appetites" forms the first object of government. In fact, in *Federalist* No. 45, Madison asserts it is not the private, but "the public good, the real welfare of the great body of the people [that] is the supreme object to be pursued." Also, in *Federalist* No. 43, he invokes "the transcendent law of nature and of nature's God, which declares that the safety and happiness of society are the objects at which all political institutions aim". In *Federalist* No. 51, Madison proclaims, "Justice is the end of government. It is the end of civil society. It ever has been and ever will be pursued until it be obtained, or until liberty be lost in the pursuit." One simply cannot seek these things—i.e., justice, safety, and happiness—*and* "the pursuit of appetites" at the same time, as they are inimical to each other. Someone is clearly caught in a contradiction, and it is not Madison.

.thepublicdiscourse.com/2017/09/20087/.) In the book's introduction (page 5), written in 2016, he refers to the same Madison passage this way: "As set forth at the birth of the republic by James Madison, one of its main architects, the 'first object of government' is protection of the 'diversity in the faculties of men.'" In these three instances, I see consistency over a substantial period of time. In fact, he added a fourth in his reply to me ("Corrupting the Youth?"): "I contend that Madison's argument in *Federalist* 10 holds that 'the first object of government' is protection of the 'diversity in the faculties of men.'" Then, in an October 2018 speech at Notre Dame University, he again misquoted *Federalist* 10 that the first object of government "is the protection of the diversity of faculties". Patrick Deneen, "Is Liberalism Failing?" Notre Dame University, October 11, 2018, https://www.youtube.com/watch?v=uqhvQckzxvY.

[15] Patrick J. Deneen, "Beyond Wishful Thinking: A Response to Schlueter", *Public Discourse*, December 14, 2012, https://www.thepublicdiscourse.com/2012/12/7411/.

America Devoted to Diversity?

Deneen's emphasis on the maximization of "private differences" as the goal of the Founders is what got us from "diversity of faculties" then to gender diversity now. The sort of diversity that Deneen describes as Madison's goal would mean that there are no common moral precepts because there would be no way of judging whether a certain diverse desire is any better or worse than any other desire. If, as Deneen says, this is the goal, why would there need to be a constitution to guarantee it? Would not the lack of a constitution more likely promote the diversity of desires? The political medium for this kind of moral anarchy is tyranny, for which constitutions are not required. The tyrant is the *most* diverse of men in terms of his desires. As Callicles tells Socrates in Plato's *Gorgias*, the strong man should "let his desires be as strong as possible" and be able to "satisfy each appetite in turn with what it desires". Or, if some sort of constitution is needed for "liberating humanity from the constraints of nature", why would it look anything like the U.S. Constitution, which contains multiple constraints on power according to the external authority of an objective moral standard to which it holds itself obliged? As Madison said, "A Constitution being derived from a superior authority, is to be expounded and obeyed, not countrouled or varied by the subordinate authority of the legislature."[16] These are definitely diversity inhibitors. What is more, Madison asserted that "the sovereignty of the society as invested in and exercisable by the majority, may do anything that could be *rightfully* done."[17] And what might be the standard of judging what could be "rightfully done" as opposed to wrongfully? Harry Jaffa explained that the rights set forth in the Declaration of Independence "are rights under the 'laws of nature and of nature's God.' They are not rights authorizing actions which, by those laws, are wrongs." In other words, they did not include the parade of moral perversities that Deneen would include under "diversity". For instance, the laws of nature exclude the *un*natural.

[16] James Madison to Charles Ingersoll, June 25, 1831, Constitution Society, https://www.constitution.org/rf/jm_18310625.htm.

[17] James Madison, *Essay on Sovereignty*, December 1835, Founders Early Access, https://rotunda.upress.virginia.edu/founders/default.xqy?keys=FOEA-print-02-02-02-3188.

Deneen never explains why Madison supposedly thought diversity is "good" in and of itself, so much so that it defines the ends of the American regime. The reason for this omission is that there is no evidence that Madison thought such a thing. Deneen seems to confound the espousal of liberty with that of diversity for its own sake. Ordered liberty does not leave one free to redefine the purpose or end of human existence, but it does leave one free to choose the *means* by which to reach that end. In this sense, it allows for diversity, but not in the sense that Deneen uses—the choice of "ends" incompatible with the purpose of human existence, for example, homosexual "marriage" or surgically turning oneself into a hermaphrodite. The latter kind of diversity as the end of government would have required the presence of Justice Anthony Kennedy at the Constitutional Convention in 1787, but not James Madison. Kennedy's jurisprudence is based on the primacy of desire and appetite, Madison's on the primacy of reason. You cannot get from the one to the other, try as Deneen might to impute a causal relationship between *Federalist* 10 and *Obergefell*.

To support Deneen's broad contention that the first object of government in the Constitution is "the greatest possible differentiation and development of those 'diverse faculties'", to include "whatever differences" might exist, the first thing we would have to dismiss is what the Constitution itself says it is for. Did it "form a more perfect Union" for the purpose of disunion? Did *E pluribus unum*—"out of many, one"—actually mean "out of one, many"? Was its underlying conception of the common good that there is no common good? Does everyone get to do his own thing, based on "whatever differences" there may be? If American origins were Hobbesian, this would certainly be true. But the Constitution's preamble announces that its purpose is to "establish Justice, insure domestic Tranquility, provide for the common defense, promote the general Welfare, and secure the Blessings of Liberty to ourselves and our posterity". This emphatically does not mean the dissolution of the common good.

Nonetheless, this is a familiar criticism: the American Founding sponsored the privatization of the public good and was therefore a meaner thing than the ancient polis, which promoted virtue, albeit of a martial nature. Deneen, for example, says that "the American Founders rejected the polis as a model", thus implying that they also turned from virtue.[18] "They adopted instead", states Deneen, "the contemporary ideals of Enlightenment freedom, the idea that liberty is the absence of obstacles."[19] What the Founders did, however, in turning from the model of the polis was not so much a product of Enlightenment ideals as it was a reflection of what Fr. James Schall called "the consequences from the proposition that the 'good life,' that search which began political philosophy in the first place with Plato, does not ultimately reside in the human *polis*. This is the conclusion Saint Augustine drew forcefully from all authentically Christian reflection on classical theory."[20] The fact that they rejected the polis as a model did not mean they had abandoned virtue. As Christians, they had a *higher* model than the polis. In light of this, it might be more accurate to call the Founders Augustinian, rather than Hobbesian, or to say that their lower aim was the result of a higher one.

Harry Jaffa expressed this matter in another way: "The American Founding limited the ends of government. It did not limit the ends of man. The ends of the regime, considered as ends of government, were lowered. But the ends both of reason and revelation served by the regime, in and through the limitations on government, were understood to enhance, not to diminish, the intrinsic possibility of human excellence."[21]

Nevertheless, Deneen would have us believe that Madison is making the object of the regime the very thing that Madison knows threatens its success. Madison, like almost all of the Founders, makes explicit that the principal condition for the success of the republic is *virtue*. In *Federalist* No. 55, he states: "As there is a degree of depravity in mankind which requires a certain degree of circumspection and distrust, so there are other qualities in human nature which justify a certain portion of esteem and confidence. Republican government presupposes the existence of these qualities in a higher degree than any other form." Without the exercise of those qualities, said Madison, "the inference would be that there is not sufficient virtue among men for self-government; and that nothing less than the

---

[18] Deneen, "Moral Minority".

[19] Ibid.

[20] James V. Schall, *The Politics of Heaven and Hell* (Lanham, Md.: University Press of America, 1987), xiv.

[21] Erler and Masugi, *The Rediscovery of America*, 136.

chains of despotism can restrain them from destroying and devouring one another." Ironically, it is precisely the chains of despotism that Deneen suggests the Founders forged in creating a Hobbesian regime, the very thing Madison is rejecting here.

As Thomas G. West points out in *The Political Theory of the American Founding*, the Founders' "concern with natural rights and their concern with virtue did not belong to distinct categories of thought. Instead they thought of virtue as a condition of freedom and a requirement of the laws of nature. In the Virginia Bill of Rights, as elsewhere, we are told that 'no free government, or the blessings of liberty, can be preserved ... but by a firm adherence to ... virtue.' "[22] The reason is that the key to republican government is not merely free choice. As we know from the Weimar Republic, people can freely choose anything, even Hitler.

The key, as the Founding Fathers knew, is virtue. This theme is repeated again and again throughout the Founding era by both its leaders and clergymen. They taught that freedom is not divorced from nature; it is rooted in and limited by nature. Virtue is conformity with what is naturally good. That is why freedom, rightly understood, is freedom to choose the good. It is not license or licentiousness, which is unnatural and unreasonable, in other words, against nature. Only a virtuous person is capable of rational consent, because only a virtuous person's reason is unclouded by the habitual rationalizations of vice. Vice inevitably infects the faculty of judgment. No matter how democratic their institutions, morally enervated people cannot be free. And people who are enslaved to their passions inevitably become slaves to tyrants. Thus, the Founders predicated the success of the republic on the virtue of the American people. If there is any one thing on which the Founding generation agreed, it was this. Without it, the republic would fail, and it is why it is failing now—not because of the Founding but despite it.

This is about as far as one can get from a regime, à la Callicles, whose purpose is the advancement and unshackling of private passions, which is exactly what creating the greatest differences in "diversity" would mean. To suppose that the Founders set up a republic to

---

[22] Thomas G. West, *The Political Theory of the American Founding: Natural Rights, Public Policy, and the Moral Conditions of Freedom* (New York: Cambridge University Press, 2017), 169.

vitiate the virtue on which its existence depended requires the belief that they were either stupid (by creating a Hobbesian regime and not noticing) or immoral (by doing it, but also cleverly disguising what they were doing). Detesting Hobbes, the Founders were nonetheless somehow hoodwinked into creating a Hobbesian regime? Were they fools or scoundrels?

Misunderstanding the Declaration

Nevertheless, Deneen draws the conclusion that "their [the Founders'] liberal logic, making protection of sovereign choice and individual appetite the main object of government, leads with nearly inexorable certainty to an outcome such as that we now witness today."[23] This conclusion represents the opposite of the Founders' logic, since it follows from a travesty rather than a fair representation of the Founding. In the absence of "Founders' explicit statements" in support of his argument, Deneen turns to "most obviously the Lockean basis of the Declaration". Deneen's misreading of Madison is typical of his overall misunderstanding of the American Founding, but most especially of the Declaration. One startling example is his misinterpretation of its last words: "We mutually pledge to each other our Lives, our Fortunes and our sacred Honor." Deneen responds by calling this closing "a bit mysterious and incomprehensible". The "willingness to pledge their lives for the sake of independence", he says, "is remarkable especially because the first part of the document is based extensively on the political philosophy of John Locke."[24]

---

[23] Deneen, "Beyond Wishful Thinking".

[24] Deneen, *Conserving America?*, 56–57. Deneen is not alone in finding Locke's influence to be problematic, although others approach it from a different perspective. Ofir Haivry and Yoram Hazony, for instance, also do not like the preamble to the Declaration of Independence and imply that it has some dangerous similarities with the French Revolution's Declaration of the Rights of Man and of the Citizen—an odd insinuation, as it is the preamble that is most at odds with the French Declaration. They prefer what they call "Historical Empiricism", which "entails a skeptical standpoint with regard to the divine right of the rulers, the universal rights of man, or any other abstract, universal systems". Yet, as Christopher Dawson pointed out, "The political rights of democracy presuppose the moral rights of humanity." Christopher Dawson, "Democracy," *The Modern Dilemma: The Problem of European Unity* (London: Sheed and Ward, 1933), 56. In other words, there are no "rights of man" *unless* they are universal. This is why Lincoln referred to the Declaration's proposition that "all men

More specifically, he says, "Social Contract theory is based on the premise that we value, above all, *self-preservation*—even more than we value our total liberty."[25]

For Deneen, the pledge of "our sacred Honor" is especially incomprehensible since he thinks it is precisely "what they are willing to give up". The words do not mean, however, that they are willing to *lose* their sacred honor, but that they promise *not* to lose it, as it can be lost only by acting dishonorably. Honor guarantees the pledge only if it is *not* sacrificed. Deneen thinks the signers are putting their prestige at risk, which they will forfeit if the British win, as victors are in charge of reputations. What is at stake in *sacred* honor, however, is the loss of their very souls, their very selves—something beyond time and space that the British cannot control. At all costs, they refuse to lie about who man is and how he ought to live, in other words, in freedom rather than servility. As a political philosopher Paul Eidelberg explains, "To pledge one's sacred honor is to affirm, in a most emphatic way, allegiance to one's publicly proclaimed moral principles."[26] Since it is "for the support of this Declaration" that they make their pledge, we may be sure these principles are those spelled out in the first part of the Declaration—the part that Deneen so seriously misreads because he thinks it is really about the Hobbesian social contract. He consequently finds the Founders' willingness to stake

---

are created equal" as "an abstract truth, applicable to all men and all times". It is either that or nothing. Haivry and Hazony, however, have a gripe against universals—which ultimately means against natural law. Natural law, as so eloquently articulated in the preamble to the Declaration, is exactly the most powerful argument against "the divine right of rulers", not historical empiricism. The latter seems to mean custom and, in their case, specifically British custom. But who is to say which customs are good and which are bad? They can say that they *prefer* British constitutionalism, or they can say that it is in accord with Mosaic Law. But they cannot really say much more unless they admit to a stronger case for natural law than their hero John Selden, who shrank natural law precisely to the Mosaic Law. Instead of calling for prudence in the application of universal truths, they promote a pragmatism that undermines such truths. As Gratian wrote in 1140, "The natural law prevails over custom and legislation in dignity. Anything that is accepted by custom or included in legislation which is against natural law is to be considered null and void." The strength of the preamble to the Declaration of Independence goes back to this principle. Ofir Haivry and Yoram Hazony, "What Is Conservatism?" *American Affairs* 1, no. 2 (Summer 2017), https://americanaffairsjournal .org/2017/05/what-is-conservatism/.

[25] Deneen, *Conserving America?*, 54.

[26] Paul Eidelberg, *On the Silence of the Declaration of Independence* (Amherst, Mass.: University of Massachusetts Press, 1976), 22.

their sacred honor "unfathomable". It is unfathomable unless one understands that the Declaration's claims are those of *moral* worth, not mere "self-preservation".

It is, however, surprising that Deneen failed to see the obvious contradiction in which he was caught. As Dennis Teti points out, "No one pledges 'sacred honor' if he *doesn't* believe in 'sacred honor'—unless he is a liar through and through. A Hobbesian does not believe in 'honor' at all—honor is vain pride, according to Hobbes—and thus he cannot pledge what he believes no man truly has."[27] What is more, a Hobbesian regime is based on fear of a violent death. Why would a Hobbesian sacrifice his life? The plain answer is: he would not. Therefore, one must be impelled to conclude that the signers were *not* Hobbesians. Deneen's failure to arrive at the simple logic of this led him to create contradictions where none exist and to make the easily fathomable, unfathomable.

Here is another example of the distortions that occur when one views things through the wrong lens. If the Founding was materialistic (Hobbesian), as Deneen seems to believe, it must have been mechanistic, as well. This assumption leads him into the error of ascribing to the Founders the words that the Constitution would be "a machine that would go of itself".[28] This is an opprobrious phrase from James Russell Lowell in 1888, not from the Founders. In later spoken remarks, Deneen claimed that Benjamin Rush said it with only this slight variation: "a machine that goes of itself".[29] Rush, however, never said it either. In 1786, he did say that "it is possible to convert men into republican machines. This must be done if we expect them to perform their parts in the great machine of the government of the state."[30] Rush, however, did not mean creating automatons. In his "Of the Mode of Education Proper in a Republic", these sentences are the only ones using the machine analogy. The whole point of the essay was that the republic *does not* go of itself but requires something else to make it go, in other words, education,

---

[27] Dennis Teti, private correspondence with the author, February 27, 2019.

[28] Patrick J. Deneen, *Why Liberalism Failed* (New Haven, Conn.: Yale University Press, 2018), 4.

[29] Deneen, "Is Liberalism Failing?"

[30] Benjamin Rush, "Of the Mode of Education Proper in a Republic" (1798), in Dagobert D. Runes, ed., *The Selected Writings of Benjamin Rush*, vol. 1 (New York: Philosophical Library, 1947), 686, http://press-pubs.uchicago.edu/founders/documents/v1ch18s30.html.

"laying the foundations for nurseries of *wise and good* men" (emphasis added) so as to get republican men. This is another example of Deneen's reading back into statements or places ideas and words that are not there.

Misunderstanding Massachusetts

This skewed vision also prevents Deneen from properly understanding other basic documents of the early republic, such as the preamble to the Massachusetts Constitution of 1780, which states: "The body-politic is formed by a voluntary association of individuals: it is a social compact, by which the whole people covenants with each citizen, and each citizen with the whole people, that all shall be governed by certain laws for the common good." Deneen says, "What this sentence shows is that this, along with many invocations of 'common good' in the founding documents, cannot be understood to derive from the pre-modern natural-law sense of 'common good.'" In fact, says Deneen, "the phrase takes on a utilitarian cast, departing from its classical meaning of an objective human good, and replaced by its widespread modern meaning of 'mutual advantage.'"[31]

The plain language, however, shows no such thing. Deneen's denial depends on making words mean something other than what they say. He writes:

> Instead, the idea of "natural law" by this time had been considerably re-defined by the very social contract thinkers whose arguments these passages reflect. The meaning of "natural law"—called by Locke "the Law of Nature"—had been fundamentally changed from its medieval understanding in order to support the individualistic premises of social contract theory. For Locke, as well as Hobbes, the "Law of Nature" is primarily a law of self-preservation.[32]

Therefore, "we are by nature rational calculators of individual advantage."[33] Once again, this is certainly true of Hobbes, but Deneen must import Hobbes into both Locke and Massachusetts at a time when

[31] Deneen, "Liberalism's Logic".
[32] Ibid.
[33] Ibid.

Hobbes was not mentionable in polite company and make him the controlling authority on interpreting the Massachusetts Constitution.

How does Deneen's reading comport with this statement, also from the preamble?

> We, therefore, the people of Massachusetts, acknowledging, with grateful hearts, the goodness of the great Legislator of the universe, in affording us, in the course of His providence, an opportunity, deliberately and peaceably, without fraud, violence, or surprise, of entering into an original, explicit, and solemn compact with each other, and of forming a new constitution of civil government for ourselves and posterity.

Deneen should recall Aristotle's statement that "he who first framed the political community was a cause of the greatest goods."[34] What were Americans supposed to do after the dissolution of their former colonial governments due to the success of the American Revolution? They had to *found* new ones, although they incorporated most of the old. Classical scholar Ernest Barker, reflecting on the passage from Aristotle above, said, "Aristotle here concedes, and indeed argues, that in saying that the state is natural he does not mean that it 'grows' naturally, without human volition and action. There is art as well as nature, and art co-operates with nature: the volition and action of human agents 'construct' the state in co-operation with a natural immanent impulse."[35] This is exactly what the colonists of Massachusetts were doing in the Aristotelian sense of framing or forming a new political community, except doing so uniquely through deliberation and choice. It is very clear from reading the full preamble to the Massachusetts Constitution that this is what they understood themselves to be doing in establishing a new Constitution. As such, they were bestowing one of the "greatest goods"—except in Deneen's opinion. Such a new political community has to be agreed upon by its constituent members for it to exist. How else could it come into being— except by consent? (The only other alternatives are force and fraud.) Yet Deneen insists that this reflects some kind of radical individualism.

[34] Aristotle, *Politics* 1253a30–31.

[35] *The Politics of Aristotle*, ed. and trans. Ernest Barker (New York: Oxford University Press, 1962), 6–7.

Deneen seems to think the term "self-preservation" is a dead give-away that the Massachusetts enterprise is Hobbesian. Here, again, one should recall that both Aristotle and Thomas Aquinas begin with self-preservation as an essential goal of government. To prove that the legislators of Massachusetts were Hobbesian, Deneen would have to show that they had abridged government to this element alone—thus reducing the "common good" to a matter of mere utility. Further examination of the Constitution, however, demonstrates the implausibility of this thesis. The document concerns not mere existence, but political existence—one clearly ordered to much more than self-preservation.

Consider, for example, article 2 of the Constitution, which states, "It is the right as well as the duty of all men in society, publicly, and at stated seasons, to worship the SUPREME BEING, the great creator and preserver of the universe." Furthermore, article 3 stipulates that "the happiness of a people, and the good order and preservation of civil government, essentially depend upon piety, religion and morality; and ... these cannot be generally diffused through a community, but by the institution of the public worship of GOD, and of public instructions in piety, religion and morality." Since the end of government is expressed as the "happiness" of the people, it cannot be reduced to an exercise in mere self-preservation. How can the Massachusetts legislators say publicly the very opposite of what Hobbes (who disavowed happiness as the end of government) said, but at the same time build America according to his "invisible architecture"? Or was the architecture invisible even to the builders? If so, who exactly put it there?

Retrofitting the American Founding

Michael Hanby's articles in *Communio* magazine and *First Things* share Deneen's view of the Founding but more explicitly spell out the metaphysics he sees underlying its faulty structure. The "Founders built worse than they intended",[36] he thinks. In fact, he questions

---

[36] Michael Hanby, "The Civic Project of American Christianity", *First Things* (February 2015), https://www.firstthings.com/article/2015/02/the-civic-project-of-american-christianity.

"whether the Founders adequately understood the nature of their own deed". What did they not correctly understand? Hanby says, "American constitutional democracy codifies for all eternity the metaphysical and anthropological assumptions of eighteenth century political thought, assumptions that are premised upon the seventeenth century conflation of nature and art which provide the ontological foundation for the separation of freedom and truth."

The key to understanding Hanby's accusation that the Founding separated *freedom* from *truth* is to grasp that the "conflation of nature and art" means the removal of formal and final causality from metaphysics—leaving only material and efficient causality, in other words, material cause and effect.[37] The truth of things was always thought to be defined precisely by their formal and final causes, which let us know what they really *are*. Aristotle explained that the final cause is "the reason for the existence of the thing" in the first place. The "reason" or truth of an oak tree is not to be confused with the truth of a toad. A man is not a dog, and so forth. Each also has its own form. It is very hard to know *what* a formless mass is exactly because it has no form. It is like a lump of Play-Doh. To put this another way, if there is no nature in Aristotle's teleological sense, meaning things are without ends, then man gets to fill the vacuum by giving them whatever ends he chooses. He gets to form the Play-Doh. Things are what *he* makes them to be through his art or artifice—so everything becomes *artificial*; nothing remains natural—thus, Hanby's "conflation of nature and art" and the consequent "separation of freedom and truth". Man is free in this willful way *at the expense of the truth* of things—which is wrong precisely because reality is not a giant lump of Play-Doh. It comes as already given, as *what is*. Man does not, Aristotle taught, *make* himself to be man. He is already made.

Another way to state the Play-Doh thesis, as put by Fr. James Schall, is that there is "nothing other than human intellect in being. This meant that the final causes were thought of as replaceable by human forms imposed on an infinitely malleable nature, including,

---

[37] Recall Aristotle's four causes. The material cause is that out of which something is made; e.g., wood is the material cause of a table. The form is the shape or design of what it is; e.g., a table. The efficient cause is the agent that brings it about, as the carpenter is the efficient cause of the table. The final cause is the purpose or end for which the thing is made, e.g., to dine on.

eventually, human nature."[38] Rightly, Hanby understands the Play-Doh perspective as the ontological foundation of radical modern thought—the metaphysical premise for accepting as real only those things that man can change—through the instrument of modern science. According to its own methods, modern science can comprehend *only* material and efficient causality—basically, matter in motion. It cannot comprehend formal or final causality. If the entire view of reality is collapsed to fit within this limited scope, then there will be perpetual revolution of one kind or another, because nothing in nature could direct anything toward its end or telos. Therefore, the modern enterprise is *necessarily* unlimited, its goals prescribed by will rather than by reason.

Cogs in the Machine

That view, however, has no connection with what the Founders said or did. They based their claim to freedom on the Declaration's "self-evident" truths, which they considered transcendent. Does Hanby show that they were kidding themselves? Like Deneen, he does not think he needs to. He rests his case almost solely on the evidence of Locke's influence on the Declaration. Hanby contends that seventeenth- and eighteenth-century philosophy was materialistic, mechanistic, and voluntarist, and so, therefore, was the Founding. It is a kind of post hoc, ergo propter hoc argument, a logical fallacy. Edward Erler characterized this perspective thus: "Since the American Founding was post-Machiavellian it was, in the orthodox Straussian schema of ancients and moderns, a radically modern regime."[39]

Deneen, Hanby, and their sympathizers attempt to fit the Founding onto the Procrustean bed of the Straussian critique of modernity. If it does not fit, it does not matter. They will retrofit it. The attempt, of course, negates anything that the Founders *themselves* said about the meaning of the words they used or the actions they took. The

---

[38] Schall, *The Politics of Heaven and Hell*, 258.

[39] Edward Erler, "Natural Right in the American Founding: Harry Jaffa's Legacy" (lecture presented at the American Political Science Association Meeting, San Francisco, California, September 5, 2015), 2, http://contemporarythinkers.org/harry-jaffa/files/2015/09/Erler_Jaffa_APSA2015.pdf.

"Declaration's specification of those rights, its treatment of the end of government, and its justification for dissolving political bonds with England are all recognizably Lockean", according to Hanby, *irre-spective of the Founders' private predilections about the nature of liberty, virtue, and self-governance.*"[40] He adds that "what the founders may have *meant* is less significant than what they actually gave us and how that gift was destined to be received in an emerging culture infused with voluntaristic, nominalist, and mechanistic assumptions about God and nature."[41]

For Hanby, the Founders' "predilections" do not matter so much because the underlying metaphysics had changed—which, in turn, changed the meaning of everything. In other words, what the Founders founded was the result of a fate over which they had no control. Therefore, what they really thought is as irrelevant as the grunts of the Frankenstein monster were to the intentions of Dr. Franken-stein. If one wished to discover those, one would not discuss them with the monster but with Dr. Frankenstein. This is why Hanby spends his time talking about the metaphysics of modernity (the Founding's Dr. Frankenstein), and not the Founders, who played the role of monster to the new metaphysics. What they said did not matter any more than what the monster grunted. Their world was imbued with, and determined by, the new metaphysics, whether or not they realized or admitted that fact. This view, of course, neglects the possibility that the change in metaphysics altered the meaning of things *only* for those who accepted the new metaphysics, and not for those who did not.

For their critique to stand, Hanby and Deneen would have to prove that the Founders held a nonteleological or antiteleologi-cal view of nature along the lines of Hobbes'. But then why did the Founders execrate Hobbes? If the American Founding was inspired by Hobbesian ontology, why did it not look like it? The denial of formal and final causality defines Hobbes' thought and his *unlimited* Leviathan. If they shared in a similar metaphysical rejec-tion, why did the Founders not replicate a Leviathan state? Their

---

[40] Michael Hanby, "Letters", *First Things* (April 2015), https://www.firstthings.com/article/2015/04/letters (emphasis added).

[41] Ibid. (emphasis in the original).

government was *limited* precisely because they did not dismiss either formal or final causality, which they acknowledged in "the Laws of Nature".

Deneen claims that the Constitution perversely "establishes a modern republic, shaped in the wake of the philosophy of Machiavelli, Hobbes and Locke, and informed by the goal of human liberation that requires the accumulation of power toward the end of liberating humanity from the constraints of nature".[42] Why would the Founders seek to subvert the constraints of the very "Laws of Nature" on which their endeavor depends? They would not and did not. The contradiction is only in Deneen. He cannot possibly square his claim with John Adams' statement: "Our Constitution was made only for a moral and religious people." But, as we have seen, the Founders were simply cogs in the wheels of the new ontology. Deneen and Hanby remove from them what Blaise Pascal called "the dignity of causality". Otherwise, they could have seen the disaster coming. Smuggle historicism and relativism back into the Founding, and then wonder why the Founders did not see this "tragic flaw". Thus, although the Founders may have believed they were appealing to transcendent truths, like it or not, they were imprisoned in an eighteenth-century mind-set that denied those truths. They may not have thought of themselves as being mentally incarcerated, but Hanby and Deneen have discovered that they were, by seeing above or beyond the confines of their eighteenth-century prison yard. *They*, not the Founders, see it as it truly was.

The notion of a new ontology controlling and transforming everything, however, has more than a touch of Hegel's historical determinism about it, which is how Hanby can assert that the Founders did not adequately understand "the nature of their own deed". That is why the Founders need to be understood *better* than they understood themselves. We now know where Deneen's "invisible architecture of the regime" came from and who put it there: not the Founders, but the forces of History. The Founders thought *they* were choosing, but, unbeknownst to them, the choice had already been

---

[42] Patrick Deneen, "The Conservative Case against the Constitution" (paper delivered at Princeton University, March 10, 2011), https://jmp.Princeton.edu/events/conservative-case -against-constitution.

made. History, in other words, was acting quite apart from the intentions of the actors.

Ironically, the progressive Left dismisses the Founders on the same grounds, as products of History. The Left is just as happy as Hanby to say that the Founders did not know what they were doing, which is why they "built worse than they intended". The difference is that the Left embraces the new ontology, while Hanby execrates it. The Left has its hands full as a result, while Hanby's are empty. The Left can say, "You are right that the Founders were historically determined by a new ontology, just as we are determined by the same ontology. The difference is that the Founders were largely unconscious of what they were acting out, while we are fully conscious of it—which is why we are another step forward in the progress of History. You, Hanby, standing athwart History, are every bit as much its creature, as you acknowledge the Founders were."

Hanby is caught in a contradiction as profound as Deneen's. As Dennis Teti points out: "In simple terms, Hanby cannot both believe that freedom and truth are united *and* believe that what the Founders said they were doing is irrelevant because they are cogs in the machinery of the new ontology."[43] This is because, as Teti explains, "historical determinism is a form of the conflation of nature and art. If freedom and truth are united (are, strictly speaking, one), if formal and final causes are real, there is no Historicism. Reality is eternal truth, not a gradual unfolding process reaching toward an unknown goal."[44] This is why the signers of the Declaration appealed to the "Supreme Judge of the World" for the rectitude of their intentions, not to the forces of History. Hanby and Deneen, in effect, appeal to History to undermine the Founders' rectitude. Their argument rests on the very determinism they condemn.

Against Hanby's and Deneen's thesis is the fact that nothing like the Declaration and the Constitution could have issued from the irresistible eighteenth-century worldview they depict. They seem unable to realize that, as Ellis Sandoz puts it, "the thought of the Founders sought its headwaters in the oldest traditions of the civilization and partook in no essential way of the currents of radical secularist

[43] Personal e-mail to the author.
[44] Ibid.

modernity already swirling around them."[45] Instead, they make what the Founders said, sacrificed, and did unintelligible. The men who formed America would not recognize or comprehend the choice that Deneen and Hanby see them as having made: to found a regime on moral relativism and radical individual autonomy. The Founders repeatedly described these concepts as repugnant. Moreover, the view of man as radically autonomous, unburdened by "the laws of Nature and of Nature's God", writes Sandoz, "do not reflect the intellectual horizon of any significant segment of the thinking public at the time [of the American Founding]".[46] Hanby and Deneen's attempted retrofitting of the Founding does not fit the facts.

Indeed, the Founders unanimously rejected the voluntarist theology of a capricious God unbound by anything. As we have seen, this was the theology behind tyranny and, not coincidentally, behind radical individualism as well. The Founders, on the other hand, embraced the theology of a providential God whose Word was reliable and whose creation possessed an inherently rational order directed at an ultimately divine purpose. This is how it came to be that natural law was preached from pulpits before and during the American Revolution and how resistance to tyranny became a *sacred* duty. For instance, the Presbyterian Rev. Robert Smith expressed popular beliefs when he preached in Philadelphia that "the great object and contest is whether our essential and unalienable rights and privileges, *as well civil as sacred*, shall be in our own power, or at the sovereign will of tyrants."[47] The United States bears the political imprint of theological ideas—ones incompatible with the radical individualism that some critics purport to find in its establishment. Miss those ideas, and you miss the meaning of the Founding.

Where Deneen and Hanby see a breach, others can see continuity with the Christian and natural law tradition. For instance, Saint John Paul II said:

---

[45] Ellis Sandoz, "Classical and Christian Dimensions of American Political Thought", *Modern Age* (Winter 1981): 15.

[46] Ellis Sandoz, "Philosophical and Religious Dimensions of the American Founding", *Intercollegiate Review* (Spring 1995), https://home.isi.org/philosophical-and-religious-dimensions-american-founding.

[47] Cited in Rod Gragg, *By the Hand of Providence: How Faith Shaped the American Revolution* (New York: Simon and Schuster, 2011), 190 (emphasis added).

The United States possesses a safeguard, a great bulwark, against [moral skepticism]. I speak of your founding documents: the Declaration of Independence, the Constitution, the Bill of Rights. These documents are grounded in and embody unchanging principles of the natural law whose permanent truth and validity can be known by reason, for it is the law written by God in human hearts (cf. Rom. 2:25). At the center of the moral vision of your founding documents is the recognition of the rights of the human person, and especially respect for the dignity and sanctity of human life in all conditions and at all stages of development.[48]

Also, Benedict XVI, like John Courtney Murray, perceives a profound compatibility between the American Proposition and the Catholic tradition:

American Catholics have absorbed the free church traditions on the relationship between the Church and politics, believing that a Church that is separate from the state better guarantees the moral foundation as a whole. Hence the promotion of the democratic ideal is seen as a moral duty that is in profound compliance with the faith. In this position we can rightly see a continuation, adapted to the times, of the model of Pope Gelasius described earlier.[49]

It is safe to assume that Benedict would see a recovery of Christianity in the United States as more than compatible with a restoration of democratic constitutional rule. Deneen, on the other hand, considers the recovery of the one as being contrary to the interests of the other. Therefore, he and others think that a repudiation of the Founding principles of the United States is a necessary condition for Christianity's revival, if not survival.

It should be noted that current Catholic discomfort with the Founding was not shared by Catholics at the time of its establishment. Fr. John Carroll, cousin of Charles Carroll, signer of both the Declaration of Independence and the Constitution, wrote to Fr. Charles

[48] John Paul II, Address, Baltimore, Maryland, October 8, 1995, Vatican website, https://w2.vatican.va/content/john-paul-ii/en/speeches/1995/october/documents/hf_jp-ii_spe_19951008_congedo-usa.html.

[49] Joseph Ratzinger and Marcello Pera, *Without Roots: The West, Relativism, Christianity, Islam* (New York: Basic Books, 2007) 69.

Plowden in England in February 1779: "I am glad ... to inform you that the fullest and largest system of toleration is adopted in almost all the American states; public protection and encouragement are extended alike to all denominations, and Roman Catholics are members of Congress, assemblies, and hold civil and military posts, as well as others."[50] In 1783, he wrote to Rome:

> You are not ignorant that in these United States our Religious system has undergone a revolution, if possible, more extraordinary than our political one. In all of them, free toleration is allowed to Christians of every denomination, and particularly in the States of Pennsylvania, Delaware, Maryland, and Virginia, a communication of Civil rights, without distinction or diminution, is extended to those of our Religion. This is a blessing and advantage, which it is our duty to preserve and improve with the utmost prudence by demeaning ourselves on all occasions as subjects zealously attached to our government.[51]

Fr. Carroll also said, "Thanks to the genuine spirit of Christianity, the United States have banished intolerance from their systems of government", and he spoke of "the luminous principles on which the rights of conscience and liberty of religion depend".[52] Thinking it would please Pope Pius VI because Catholics now had religious liberty, Jefferson purportedly sent him a copy of the Virginia Statute of Religious Freedom.

It is also worth noting how scrupulously the early American republic observed its side of Gelasius' distinction of the respective roles of church and state. In 1806, Fr. Carroll, now a bishop, inquired of President Jefferson: "Would it be Satisfactory to the Executive of the U.S. to recommend a native of France, who has long resided amongst us, and is desirous of continuing under this government to

[50] Peter Guilday, *The Life and Times of John Carroll* (New York: Encyclopedia Press, 1922), 110.

[51] John Gilmary Shea, *Life and Times of the Most Rev. John Carroll* (New York: Edward O. Jenkins' Sons, 1888), 211, cited in Leonard P. Liggio, "Catholicism in the Era of American Independence", *Catholic Dossier* (1999): 14, https://leonardliggio.org/wp-content/uploads/downloads/2011/10/CATHOLICISM%20IN%20THE%20ERA%20OF%20AMERICAN%20INDEPENDENCE.pdf.

[52] John Carroll, "To John Fenno of the Gazette of the United States", June 10, 1789, Founding.com, http://founding.com/founders-library/preachers-pen/john-carroll-to-john-fenno-of-the-gazette-of-the-united-states-june-10-1789/.

be the bishop of New Orleans?"[53] Secretary of State James Madison replied that "the delicacy towards the public authority and the laudable object which led to the enquiries you are pleased to make, are appreciated by the President in the manner which they so justly merit. But as the case is entirely ecclesiastical, it is deemed most congenial with the scrupulous policy of the Constitution in guarding against a political interference with religious affairs, to decline" giving an opinion on the matter.[54]

George Washington's adopted son, George Washington Custis, wrote of the esteem in which the first president held Bishop Carroll. In a letter to the Rev. Charles White, he said:

> You are pleased to ask me whether the late Dr. Carroll was an intimate acquaintance of Washington. He was more, sir. From his exalted worth as a minister of God, his stainless character as a man and above all his distinguished services as a patriot of the Revolution, Dr. Carroll stood high, very high in the esteem and affection of the Pater Familias.... The Catholic priesthood of the olden or of the present time had a great moral as well as religious influence over their flocks; to direct their influence in favour of the cause of American Liberty formed the untiring and patriotic labours of Dr. Carroll from the commencement of the troubles between the Mother Country and the colonies. And nobly did he succeed, Catholic Maryland responded to the call of the Patriot and the Priest and many a gallant Catholic grasped his arms and fought for the civil and Religious Liberty of generations yet unborn.[55]

Suicidal Blunder

Deneen and Hanby offer a slow motion verion of *The Invasion of the Body Snatchers*, with Hobbesian pod people laid aside the original Founders. Slowly the Hobbes pods assume the features of their hosts until they exactly resemble and then replace them. Thus Deneen and

---

[53] John Caroll to James Madison, November 17, 1806, Founders Early Access, http://rotunda.upress.virginia.edu/founders/default.xqy?keys=FOEA-print-02-01-02-1087.

[54] James Madison to John Carroll, November 20, 1806, Founders Online, National Archives, https://founders.archives.gov/documents/Madison/99-01-02-1094.

[55] *The American Catholic Historical Researches*, vols. 15–17 (Philadephia: Martin I.J. Griffin, 1898), 49–50.

Hanby hold that the Founders produced a Hobbesian state; it just took some two hundred years for the replicants to take over. They claim that the success of America's Founding principles is measured by today's depravity. This is like blaming adultery on marriage. In the end, they can do no more than leap to the conclusion that Hobbesian results *must* have come from Hobbesian premises in the (Lockean) American Founding, especially since today's radical individualism is justified in terms of its principles. (See an alternative explanation in the epilogue that follows.)

There is, however, no guarantee that an originally sound polity may not turn against its founding principles, debauch itself, and then try to rationalize its debauchery by a different set of principles, all the while retaining the same vocabulary—just as Hobbes kept the language of natural law while eviscerating its content. As soon as one moves from the rational "Laws of Nature and of Nature's God" as the standard of justice to one making human will that standard, one is headed for Leviathan. We are now enduring such a transformation of the United States, where political rule is becoming increasingly arbitrary. This is happening under the cloak of "natural rights", understood in the Hobbesian way as validating one's "right" to have or do whatever one desires. But it is entirely wrong to say that this turning away is the result of the principles it turns away from, when it is precisely the denial of them. Something cannot be what it is and also its opposite.

Deneen and Hanby confuse the cure for the disease. To the extent to which it is accepted, their misdiagnosis demoralizes our youth and disarms us in the face of our enemies, who are further empowered by the disavowal of the country's Founding principles. This school of thought has penetrated higher education. Courses on American political thought at some Catholic and other universities are imbued with it, causing real, deleterious consequences. In one instance of which I know, a professor prevailed in convincing the majority of his students that the Founding principles were morally compromised. Their reaction was captured in a question: "Okay, you've convinced us, but what are we supposed to do now?" Students feel they no longer have a country they can love and should wish to serve. Deneen complains, "Today ... too often, who we are accords with our philosophy— evinced, for instance, in the example of today's liberals being unlikely to serve in the military."[56] But what is his teaching's effect on those who *are* willing to serve? Since he thinks the regime is only about self-preservation and the promotion of private differences, why should *anyone* serve it?

It is a suicidal blunder to denigrate the Founding in this way. Those who do so automatically exclude themselves from the public arena by conceding it to their opponents, thereby accelerating the very decline they decry. They should heed Gerhart Niemeyer's warning: "The critic who forgets that he is a citizen produces not a changed order but sheer disorder."[57] They also ought to consider the words of President Calvin Coolidge. In his oration on the 150th anniversary of the Declaration of Independence in 1926, he said:

> It is often asserted that the world has made a great deal of progress since 1776, that we have had new thoughts and new experiences which have given us a great advance over the people of that day, and that we may therefore very well discard their conclusion for something more modern. But that reasoning can not be applied to this great charter. If all men are created equal, that is final. If governments derive their just power from the consent of the governed, that is final. No advance, no progress can be made beyond these propositions. If anyone wishes to deny their truth or their soundness, the only direction in which he can proceed historically is not forward, but backward.... In its main features the Declaration of Independence is a great spiritual document. It is a declaration not of material but of spiritual conceptions.

He concluded that "the things of the spirit come first.... If we are to maintain the great heritage which has been bequeathed to us, we must be like-minded as the fathers who created it.... We must cultivate the reverence which they had for the things that are holy. We must follow the spiritual and moral leadership which they showed."[58] Coolidge warned: "We can not continue to enjoy the

---

[56] Deneen, "Corrupting the Youth?"

[57] Gerhart Niemeyer, *Between Nothingness and Paradise* (Baton Rouge: Louisiana State University Press, 1971), 206.

[58] Calvin Coolidge, Speech on the 150th Anniversary of the Declaration of Independence, July 5, 1926, Teaching American History, http://teachingamericanhistory.org/library/document/speech-on-the-occasion-of-the-one-hundred-and-fiftieth-anniversary-of-the-declaration-of-independence/.

result, if we neglect and abandon the cause."[59] In other words, the fault is not in our Founding principles, but in ourselves—in our neglect or outright disavowal of them. We have not remained true to the Founding. As John Courtney Murray might say, the Founding is not the problem; it is the solution. We had best return to its principles before it is too late.

[59] Ibid.

EPILOGUE

If the Founding Was Good, Why Did Things Go Bad?

If the Founders are not responsible for the moral malaise afflicting America today, who or what is? This subject would require another book, so I will not offer more than a suggestion of a reply here. But the short-form answer is: German historicism. Before explaining this cryptic response, I note briefly that the Founders themselves predicted our decline if we could not sustain our moral character. Here are just a few of their warnings.

> In 1776, Samuel Adams counseled that "the diminution of publick Virtue is usually attended with that of publick Happiness, and the publick Liberty will not long survive the total Extinction of Morals."[1] He warned that "if we are universally vicious and debauched in our manners, though the form of our Constitution carries the face of the most exalted freedom, we shall in reality be the most abject of slaves."[2]

> His cousin John Adams agreed: "We have no government, armed with power, capable of contending with human passions, unbridled by morality and religion. Avarice, ambition, revenge and licentiousness would break the strongest cords of our Constitution, as a whale goes through a net."[3]

> Charles Carroll cautioned: "Without morals a republic cannot subsist any length of time; they therefore who are decrying the Christian religion, whose morality is so sublime and pure ... are

---

[1] Samuel Adams to John Scollay, April 30, 1776, Federalist Papers, https://thefederalist papers.org/founders/samuel-adams/samuel-adams-to-john-scollay-april-30-1776.

[2] William Vincent Wells, *The Life and Public Services of Samuel Adams* (Boston: Little, Brown, 1865), 23.

[3] John Adams to Massachusetts Militia, October 11, 1798, Founders Online, National Archives, https://founders.archives.gov/documents/Adams/99-02-02-3102.

undermining the solid foundation of morals, the best security for
the duration of free governments."[4]

Such remonstrations from the Founders are too numerous to
count. As they predicted, we are in trouble because the virtue needed
to sustain the republic is fast disappearing, close to the point of irre-
trievability. We won the American Revolution but lost the sexual
revolution—with all its attendant debasement (pornography, sexual
perversity, homosexual "marriage", abortion, infidelity, the destruction of the family, the general coarsening of culture, etc.). So can
we write all this off as due to Original Sin? Well, yes, in a way, but
it is not as simple as that. Something else has been at work. The loss
of virtue *always* requires a rationalization to justify it. Anyone who
chooses an evil act must present it to himself as good; otherwise, as
Aristotle taught, he would be incapable of choosing it. And here is
where German historicism comes in.

In *Natural Right and History*, Leo Strauss spoke about "the historical
sense" in German thought, which by "abandoning the idea of natural
right" eventuates in "unqualified relativism". He said: "It would not
be the first time that a nation, defeated on the battlefield and, as it
were, annihilated as a political being, has deprived its conquerors of
the most sublime fruit of victory by imposing on them the yoke of its
own thought."[5] Strauss was speaking of the import of German historicism into America. Historicism is not a plant native to this country.
Who let it past U.S. Customs?

It first came in the baggage train of American graduate students
who went to Germany to obtain advanced degrees and then returned
home to spread the new gospel. Or it came in the valises of German professors who came here to teach. As Dr. Ronald J. Pestritto
explains,

The influence of German political philosophy is evident ... from the
historical pedigree of the most influential progressive thinkers. Almost
all of them were either educated in Germany in the nineteenth century

[4]Charles Carroll to James McHenry, November 4, 1800, Federalist Papers, https://
thefederalistpapers.org/founders/charles-carroll/charles-carroll-letter-to-james-mchenry-of
-november-4-1800.

[5]Leo Strauss, *Natural Right and History* (Chicago: University Press of Chicago, 1971), 1–2.

or had as teachers those who were. This fact reflects the sea change that had occurred in American higher education in the second half of the nineteenth century, a time when most Americans who wanted an advanced degree went to Europe to get one. By 1900, the faculties of American colleges and universities had become populated with European PhDs, and the historical thinking that dominated Europe (especially Germany) in the nineteenth century came to permeate American higher education.[6]

What does "historical thinking" refer to? It means the essential historicity of truth—that is, that claims to truth can be explained as products of their time and place, and nothing more. Historicism teaches that as historical circumstances change, so do the meanings of words, as well as of right and wrong. Everything is contingent on History. Everything goes with the flow. We are now in different times at a different place with different "truths". Nothing transcends History; there are no unchanging trans-historical truths rooted in the transcendent. Everything is *intra*historical—meaning there is nothing *outside* History immune to its alterations. Historicism erases the moral authority of Nature—taken as a reflection of God's reason—of which the Declaration of Independence was an explicit expression, and replaces it with relativism. Gone are the tenets that Nature and reason are *not* temporal and that they supply truths which are right everywhere and always.

Twentieth-century French theologian Réginald Garrigou-Lagrange captured the essence of the change brought by historicism: the movement from truth as a philosophy of *being* to truth as a philosophy of *action*. In the former, being is an object of contemplation by the intellect, from which it comes to know *what is*; in the latter, truth as action is a *product* of the human will, in other words, something it makes and therefore can change. What goes around comes around. We see here the results of Ockham's transposition of the relationship in God: from the primacy of the divine intellect over the divine will (Aquinas) to the primacy of the will over the divine intellect. Transposed down to the human level, this

[6] Ronald J. Pestritto, "Progressivism and America's Tradition of Natural Law and Natural Rights", Natural Law, Natural Rights, and American Constitutionalism, http://www.nlnrac .org/critics/american-progressivism#_ednref7.

means the very thing that defines modernity's essence: human voluntarism. It is a singular achievement of modernity to have given us a world without ends—which has created the opportunity for the triumph of the will.

It is a short leap from historicism to what Strauss called "unqualified relativism". Relativism is the dogmatic assertion of the incapability of knowing what is intrinsically good or evil in an objective way. It logically leads from the possibility that man can know unchanging moral truths about reality to the denial that he can access such truths, which are now transformed into mere subjective preferences. In *The Abolition of Man*, C. S. Lewis said, "A dogmatic belief in objective value is necessary to the very idea of the rule which is not tyranny or an obedience which is not slavery." Moral subjectivism, he warned, "must be the destruction of the society which accepts it". By denying objective truth and morality, moral subjectivism undermines democracy in the worst way. It not only neglects the cultivation of virtue in the young but, worse still, tells them there is no such thing as virtue. Thus, it is doubly culpable for eroding both the practical and theoretical foundations of free government.

The same perspective diminishes democratic government to the study of who gets what, where, when, and how. There is no common good; everything is reduced to self-interest and power. The high-sounding words of the Declaration of Independence and the Constitution are just cloaks for the self-aggrandizement of individuals who benefit most from the "system". In fact, this prevalent school of thought teaches Americans that *all* "systems" can be understood in exactly the same way. We can point to different means of distribution in each, but we have no rational means to make any fundamental moral distinctions among them. In effect, this view denies that democratic freedom is intrinsically superior to nonfreedom.

Once ingested, German historicism produced not only relativism, but progressivism, which regards the Founding principles as the main obstacle to its project for improvement. The idea that the forces of History are marching onward and upward has Hegelian roots. If only one can get astride the spirit of History, which is immanent in all things, one can ride it, maybe even steer it. One must absolutely not stand athwart it, as that would be to hinder "progress"—which becomes *the* remaining moral imperative.

One of the most notable American products of German historicism was President Woodrow Wilson (1856–1924). When addressing the Jefferson Club of Los Angeles (May 12, 1911), he ironically advised that "if you want to understand the real Declaration of Independence, do not repeat the preface", written by Jefferson. Since the preface contains the principles, it was logical for Wilson to conclude: "We are not bound to adhere to the doctrines held by the signers of the Declaration of Independence."[7] Why not? In 1912, Wilson said that government is subject to evolution and "is accountable to Darwin, not Newton. It is modified by its environment, necessitated by its tasks, shaped to its functions by the sheer pressure of life. No living thing can have its organs offset against each other as checks and live." In other words, Wilson discounted not only the Declaration's principles but also the Constitution's checks and balances, because "living political constitutions must be Darwinian in structure and in practice." He said, "All that progressives ask or desire is permission—in an era when 'development,' 'evolution,' is the scientific word—to interpret the Constitution according to the Darwinian principle."[8]

What did this mean? Its political import was suggested by Wilson in an essay written earlier on the subject of "Socialism and Democracy": "Men as communities are supreme over men as individuals. Limits of wisdom and convenience to the public control there may be: limits of principle there are, upon strict analysis, none." In light of the challenges of the day, Wilson asks rhetorically, "Must not government lay aside all timid scruple and boldly make itself an agency for social reform as well as for political control?"[9] This control was to be exercised by the bureaucratic state as the supreme instrument of Hegelian progress.

Wilson's contemporary, the highly influential philosopher and educational reformer John Dewey, (1859–1952) was even more

[7] Woodrow Wilson, "An Address to the Jefferson Club of Los Angeles", May 12, 1911, in Arthur S. Link, ed., *The Papers of Woodrow Wilson*, 69 vols. (Princeton: Princeton University Press, 1966–1993), 23:34.

[8] Woodrow Wilson, *The Essential Political Writings* (Lanham, Md.: Lexington Books, 2001), 121; see also Woodrow Wilson, "What Is Progress?" (1913), Teaching American History, http://teachingamericanhistory.org/library/document/what-is-progress/.

[9] Wilson, *Essential Political Writings*, 79; Woodrow Wilson, "Socialism and Democracy", August 22, 1887, Teaching American History, http://teachingamericanhistory.org/library/document/socialism-and-democracy/.

explicit than Wilson about progressivism's underlying tenets, which included the rejection of formal and final causality. He claimed that man's nature is to have no nature, as human beings are "nothing in themselves". Rather, it is "social arrangements, laws, institutions" that "are means of *creating* individuals".[10] He looked forward to a time when schools would be "managed on the psychological basis as great factories are run on the basis of chemical and physical sciences".[11] Obviously, those with their hands on the levers of these means will decide what kind of individuals to create. A courageous humanity should "press forward ... until we have a control of human nature comparable to our control of physical nature".[12]

This was not the American Founders' view. "The real difficulty", Dewey said, was their notion that "the individual is regarded as something *given*, something already there." The "natural rights and natural liberties" of which the Founders spoke, he said, along with the utilitarian thinker Jeremy Bentham, "exist only in the kingdom of mythological social zoology". Nonetheless, they still cause great harm because they establish "the primacy of the individual over the state not only in time but in moral authority". This is a problem, Dewey said, because "ideas that at one time are means of producing social change assume another guise when they are used as means of preventing further social change. This fact is itself an illustration of historic relativity, and an evidence of the evil that lay in the assertion by earlier liberalism of the immutable and eternal character of their ideas."[13]

The Founders' appeal to transcendent truths, Dewey claimed, "blinded the eyes of liberals to the fact that their own special interpretations of liberty, individuality and intelligence were themselves historically conditioned, and were relevant only to their own time. They put forward their ideas as immutable truths good at all times and places; they had no idea of historic relativity, either in general or in its application to themselves."[14] The imperious nature of progressivism

[10] John Dewey, *Reconstruction in Philosophy* (New York: Henry Holt, 1920), 194 (emphasis in the original).

[11] Cited in E. Michael Jones, *Libido Dominandi: Sexual Liberation and Political Control* (South Bend, Ind.: St. Augustine's Press, 2000), 105.

[12] Cited in ibid., 152.

[13] John Dewey, *Problems of Men* (New York: Philosophical Library, 1940), 135–36.

[14] John Dewey, *Liberalism and Social Action* (Amherst, N.Y.: Prometheus Books, 2000), 40–41.

is reflected in Dewey's remark that "changes in knowledge have *out-lawed* the signification of the words they commonly used" (emphasis added). This means that what the Founders actually meant is forbidden from consideration. Nevertheless, because of its harmful residue, Dewey said, "there still lingers in the minds of some the notion that there are two different 'spheres' of action and of rightful claims; that of political society, and that of the individual, and that in the interest of the latter the former must be as contracted as possible."[15] This is clearly mistaken, because in progressivism, Dewey proclaimed, democracy becomes "that form of social organization, extending to *all* areas and ways of living, in which the powers of individuals shall ... be fed, sustained and directed".[16] As with Wilson, so with Dewey, the instrument of the total direction of life is the bureaucratic state.

Joseph Cardinal Ratzinger trenchantly addressed the underlying problem of the progressivist view: "The concept of truth has been virtually given up and replaced by the concept of progress. Progress itself 'is' truth. But through this seeming exaltation, progress loses its direction and becomes nullified. For if no direction exists, everything can just as well be regress as progress."[17]

Where, then, does this leave us? We are left with some sort of positivism, which states that "truth" is basically what "we" say it is, and all we can know is what "we" say. There is no metaphysical point of reference that can substantiate truth or falsehood. By positing it, we *make* it true. Truth becomes the object of the will, rather than of reason. In *The Audacity of Hope*, President Barack Obama, in the progressivist Wilsonian tradition, said: "Implicit in [the Constitution's] structure, in the very idea of ordered liberty, was a rejection of absolute truth, the infallibility of any idea or ideology or theology or 'ism', and any tyrannical consistency that might lock future generations into a single, unalterable course."[18] In other words, the truth does not set you free; the truth enslaves you. Therefore, freedom requires the rejection of objective truth, which gets us to where we are today.

---

[15] John Dewey, *Liberalism and Social Action* (1935), Teaching American History, http://teachingamericanhistory.org/library/document/excerpts-from-liberalism-and-social-action/.

[16] Ibid. (italics added).

[17] Joseph Cardinal Ratzinger, "Conscience and Truth" (presented at the Tenth Workshop for Bishops, Dallas, Texas, February 1991), EWTN, http://www.ewtn.com/library/conscience-and-truth-2468.

[18] Barack Obama, *The Audacity of Hope* (New York: Crown Publishers, 2006), 93.

The denial of the truth of natural law leads to the "tyranny of unreason", according to Joseph Cardinal Ratzinger. It lays the ground floor for what John Paul II called "totalitarian democracy", which may seem a contradiction in terms. When its context in "the Laws of Nature and of Nature's God" is removed, however, democracy loses its authority in higher law and becomes simply another vehicle for the expression of the primacy of will. What one wills (voluntarism), not what one reasons, is paramount. Force, not free will, is the means. Whether it is the force of the majority or of the minority matters not. This is the basis of democratic totalitarianism—all done in the name of "human rights". The problem, of course, involves the question as to whether nominalism is the basis for modern human rights. If the human will, rather than Nature, is their source, then rights become both mutable and illimitable. They are no longer tethered to the laws of Nature. They are no longer discovered, but invented. Therefore, they can be extended as far as appetite and will can reach. They can also be annulled.

Political philosopher Harry Jaffa put in a succinct paragraph why we are in the shape we are today:

Atheistic nihilism transforms the "bourgeois" and highly moral individualism of the American Revolution into something entirely different. That older individualism was based on the idea of unalienable rights endowed by man's Creator. Such rights were not unconditional. They were to be exercised only in accordance with the laws of nature and of nature's God, which were moral laws. Rights and duties were in a reciprocal relationship. But the nature revealed by modern science—the unconditional basis of the belief in Progress— was that of mindless matter, a source of power to be commanded, not a source of morality to be obeyed. From here on, "rights" would be understood as the unconditional empowerment of the individual to do as he pleased. Self-realization became the code word for the new morality. The human self, however, was no longer understood to be made in the image of God, since God was dead. Self-realization was in fact only the correlate of the new atheism. As there could no longer be any distinction between man and God, which distinction is as fundamental to the Declaration of Independence as to the Bible, there could be no distinction between base and noble desires. All desires were understood to be created equal, since all desires were seen as originating in that highest of all authorities, the self-creating self. Each human being was to be his own God, obeying only those restrictions that were enforced upon him by the fact that he was not yet himself the universal tyrant. In time, however, Science would enable everyone to act as if he were the universal tyrant.[19]

Ironically enough, this kind of radical modernity is a creature of Christianity in that it is an inversion of it—and this is a cause for optimism. Even the most extreme perversions found in modern ideologies are dependent on the very things they deny in Christianity. They become comprehensible only in opposition to them. To play off the slogan taken from the work of Eric Voegelin, one cannot "immanentize the eschaton", unless there is an eschaton to immanentize in the first place.

In an interview with an agnostic journalist, the late Jean-Marie Cardinal Lustiger of Paris remarked that "modern civilization is inescapably marked by the encounter with the true God." That encounter is the Incarnation. "Whether you like it or not", he told his interlocutor, "atheistic society is Christian society."[20] This is true not only in the mirror-image sense that a negative is formed from a positive, but also in another way. The Incarnation is the promise of love fulfilled by Love itself, which turns out to be not a Platonic ideal, but a Child in a manger. It is a revelation beyond man's imagination and has changed the world even for those who know nothing of it. It can be denied, but it is impossible to forget or to ignore. Once made, the claim that there is a Savior and he has come resonates throughout the world and haunts it. The hole in the soul is larger after the Incarnation for those who reject it, because of the enormity of what is missing. Blaise Pascal cried out: "This infinite abyss can be filled only with an infinite and immutable object; in other words by God himself."[21] What can replace him? The frenzy of the search for a substitute is at the heart of the modern project.

If there is no God, in Christ, "reconciling the world to himself" (2 Cor 5:19), "by the blood of his cross" (Col 1:20), then man

[19] Harry V. Jaffa, *A New Birth of Freedom: Abraham Lincoln and the Coming of the Civil War* (Lanham, Md.: Rowman and Littlefield, 2000), 95–96.

[20] Jean-Louis Missika and Dominique Wolton, eds., *Choosing God—Chosen by God: Conversations with Cardinal Jean-Marie Lustiger* (San Francisco: Ignatius Press, 1991), 171.

[21] Blaise Pascal, *Pensées* (London: Penguin Books, 1995), 45.

undertakes to reconcile the world to *himself*, invariably using the blood of other men. "My kingdom is not of this world" (see Jn 18:36) becomes "My kingdom *is* of this world." Instead of God become man, it is man become God. Millenarian ideology attempts, in its clumsy and destructive way, to ape the redemptive action of Christianity. During the Reign of Terror, Jean-Pierre-André Amar, a deputy to the French National Convention, spoke enthusiastically of the "red Mass" celebrated at the "great altar" of the "holy guillotine". Every historical substitution for Christianity replaces its basic elements: mimics it with an ersatz paradise from which man fell, an ersatz origin of the Fall as the source of evil, and an ersatz plan for salvation. This is, in effect, why modern ideology can be accurately understood only as a pseudo-religion for the transformation of the world without grace.

The attempt to create an intra-historical eschatology, to put man's end in his own hands, to solve the problem of evil without God, defines the perversity of the enterprise. In short, it is an attempt to deny the transcendent—to secularize Christianity and achieve an intra-historical perfectibility. From it a perverted version of equality grew as the basis for the transformation of politics into an engine of salvation with man as his own savior. As the then Cardinal Ratzinger said in respect to Marxism, though it is equally applicable to other strains of modern thought: "[It] even came to be seen as the power by which the Christian doctrine of redemption could finally be transformed into a realistic praxis of liberation—as the power whereby the kingdom of God could be concretely realized as the true kingdom of man."[22]

The "gnosis of pragmatism and positivism" denounced by John A. Gueguen in a quote at the beginning of this book grew out of this ideology, not out of the Christian and natural law principles of the Founding. While the equality of the Founding is grounded in Genesis, the Gospels, and natural law, the distorted version of equality developed a leveling ideology with the ambition of taking history to the next, perhaps final, phase of "progress", no longer under an external Divine Providence, but under man's total internal control. In the natural law, equality is the metaphysical basis of freedom: it

---

[22] Joseph Cardinal Ratzinger, "Truth and Freedom", *Communio* 23 (Spring 1996): 18.

preexists freedom and is the condition for it. It is at the beginning, not the end. In modern ideology, equality does not yet exist; it is at the end, not the beginning. It is man who will metaphysically transform reality in order to establish equality, which then leads to total freedom. This kind of equality is man's project, not God's. It is a process of self-deification rather than receiving divine life as a gift from God. One cannot pretend that these two notions of equality are the same, when, in fact, they are antithetical to each other. Therefore, the charge that one "grew out" of the other is not sustainable (unless one has bought the German historicist logic that A equals non-A—dialectical opposites come together to form a new and higher historical synthesis of B). Recognition of this difference is the very essence of the fight against modern ideology. Otherwise, without it, one ends up confusing one's natural allies with one's enemies—in the very way in which Deneen and Hanby do.

As grim as this all might seem, one should recognize that failure is written into the DNA of the modern project because it cannot withstand the loss of the thing of which it is a distortion. Radical modernity is parasitic. It will fail to the extent to which it succeeds. It cannot survive its own erasure of natural law and Christianity. Paradoxically, the loss of faith and reason is a cause for hope. It proved the downfall of the Soviet Empire, which imploded from its own hollowness. The West's moral, social, and political implosion proceeds apace for similar reasons. Yet we can avoid the cataclysm anytime we choose to, by returning to reality, to reason, to "the Laws of Nature and of Nature's God". Reality is resilient because, as Plato said, it is *what is*—not whatever one fancies. *Logos* wins in the end.

SELECTED BIBLIOGRAPHY

Acton, John Emerich Edward Dalberg. *The History of Freedom and Other Essays*. London: McMillan, 1907.

Adams, John. *The Letters of Novanglus*. No. 1. January 23, 1775. In *Papers of John Adams*. Vol. 2, *December 1773–April 1775*. Edited by Robert. J. Taylor. Cambridge, Mass.: Belknap Press, 1977. Massachusetts Historical Society. http://www.masshist.org/publications/adams-papers/view?&id=PJA02dg5.

———. "Reply of the House to Hutchinson's Second Message", March 2, 1773. In *Papers of John Adams*. Vol. 1, *September 1755–October 1773*. Edited by Robert J. Taylor. Cambridge, Mass.: Belknap Press, 1997. Massachusetts Historical Society. https://www.masshist.org/publications/apde2/view?id=ADMS-06-01-02-0097-0004.

———. *Thoughts on Government*. Chap. 4, doc. 5 in *The Founders' Constitution*. Vol. 1. Chicago: University of Chicago Press, n.d. http://press-pubs.uchicago.edu/founders/documents/v1ch4s5.html.

———. *The Works of John Adams: Second President of the United States*. 10 vols. Boston: Charles C. Little and James Brown, 1850–1856.

Adams, John Quincy. "The Jubilee of the Constitution: A Discourse (1839)". Lonang Institute. https://lonang.com/library/reference/jqadams-jubilee-constitution-1839/.

Adams, Samuel. *The Writings of Samuel Adams: 1770–1773*. New York: G.P. Putnam's Sons, 1906.

Aquinas, Thomas. *On Kingship: To the King of Cyprus*. Translated by Gerald B. Phelan. New York: Sheed and Ward, 1938.

———. *Summa contra gentiles*. Cincinnati, Ohio: Benziger Brothers, 1928.

———. *Summa theologica*. Cincinnati, Ohio: Benziger Brothers, 1947.

Araujo, Robert John, S.J. "The Catholic Neo-Scholastic Contribution to Human Rights: The Natural Law Foundation". *Ave Maria Law Review* 1, no. 1 (Spring 2003): 159–74.

Aristotle. *The Art of Rhetoric*. Translated by Robin Waterfield. Oxford: Oxford University Press, 2018.

———. *Generation of Animals*. Translated by Arthur Platt. Oxford: Clarendon Press, 1910.

———. *Metaphysics*. Translated by C.D.C. Reeve. Indianapolis: Hackett Publishing Company, 2016.

————. *Nicomachean Ethics*. Edited and translated by Roger Crisp. Cambridge: Cambridge University Press, 2014.

————. *The Politics of Aristotle*. Edited and translated by Ernest Barker. New York: Oxford University Press, 1962.

Augustine. *The City of God*. Translated by Henry Bettenson. New York: Penguin Books, 1972.

————. *Confessions*. Translated by John K. Ryan. Garden City, N.Y.: Image Books, 1960.

————. *Earlier Writings*. Louisville, Ky.: Westminster John Knox Press, 2006.

Averroes. *Averroes' Tahafut al-Tahafut (The Incoherence of the Incoherence)*. Translated by Simon Van Den Bergh. Cambridge: Gibb Memorial Trust, 2008.

Bailyn, Bernard. *The Ideological Origins of the American Revolution*. Cambridge, Mass.: Belknap Press, 1967.

Baldwin, Alice M. *The New England Clergy and the American Revolution*. Durham, N.C.: Duke University Publications, 2016.

Beer, Samuel H. *To Make a Nation: The Rediscovery of American Federalism*. Cambridge, Mass.: Belknap Press, 1993.

Bellarmine, Robert. *On Temporal and Spiritual Authority*. Edited by Stefania Tutino. Indianapolis: Liberty Fund, 2012.

Benedict XVI. Address to participants in the Fifteenth Plenary Session of the Pontifical Academy of Social Sciences, May 4, 2009. Vatican website. http://www.vatican.va/holy_father/benedict_xvi/speeches/2009/may /documents/hf_ben-xvi_spe_20090504_social-sciences_en.html.

————. Encyclical Letter on Christian Hope *Spe Salvi* (November 30, 2007).

————. *Faith and Politics*. San Francisco: Ignatius Press, 2018.

————. Lecture at a meeting with the representatives of science, Regensberg, Germany, September 12, 2006. Vatican website. http://w2.vatican .va/content/benedict-xvi/en/speeches/2006/september/documents/hf _ben-xvi_spe_20060912_university-regensburg.html.

Berman, Harold J. *Faith and Order: The Reconciliation of Law and Religion*. Atlanta: Scholars Press, 1993.

————. "The Impact of the Enlightenment on American Constitutional Law". *Yale Journal of Law and the Humanities* 4, no. 2 (January 1992): 311–34.

————. *Law and Revolution: The Formation of the Western Legal Tradition*. Cambridge, Mass.: Harvard University Press, 1983.

Brague, Rémi. Interview by Christophe Cervellon and Kristell Trego. In *The Legend of the Middle Ages: Philosophical Explorations of Medieval Christianity, Judaism, and Islam*, by Rémi Brague, 1–22. Chicago: University

of Chicago Press, 2009. University of Chicago Press. https://www.press.
uchicago.edu/Misc/Chicago/070803.html.

———. *The Law of God: The Philosophical History of an Idea*. Translated by
Lydia G. Cochrane. Chicago: University of Chicago Press, 2007.

———. *The Wisdom of the World: The Human Experience of the Universe in
Western Thought*. Translated by Teresa Lavender Fagan. Chicago: University of Chicago Press, 2003.

Brann, Eva. "Plato's 'Republic': Impossible Polity". *Imaginative Conservative*,
July 23, 2018. http://www.theimaginativeconservative.org/2018/07/platos
-republic-impossible-polity-eva-brann.html?mc_cid=d8a48ab415&mc
_eid=89abaa241c.

———. "The Roots of Modernity in Perversions of Christianity". *Imaginative Conservative*, September 17, 2018. http://www.theimaginative
conservative.org/2018/09/the-roots-of-modernity-in-perversions-
christianity-eva-brann.html?mc_cid=1c76c2c21d&mc_eid=89abaa241c.

Brust, Stephen J. "Retrieving a Catholic Tradition of Subjective Natural
Rights from the Late Scholastic Francisco Suárez, S.J." *Ave Maria Law
Review* 10, no. 2 (Spring 2012): 343–63.

Burke, Edmund. *Reflections on the Revolution in France*. New York: P.F.
Collier and Son, 1909. First published 1790.

Carey, George W., and James V. Schall, S.J., eds. *Essays on Christianity and
Political Philosophy*. Lanham, Md.: University Press of America, 1984.

Carlyle, A.J. *Political Liberty: A History of the Conception in the Middle Ages and
Modern Times*. London: Oxford University Press, 1941.

Carlyle, R.W., and A.J. Carlyle. *A History of Medieval Political Theory in the
West*. London: William Blackwood and Sons, 1950.

Carlyle, Thomas. *The French Revolution: A History*. Vol. 2. Everyman's
Library. New York: E.P. Dutton, 1916.

Chipman, Nathaniel. *Sketches of the Principles of Government*. Rutland, Vt.: J.
Lyon, 1793. Evans Early American Imprint Collection. https://quod.lib
.umich.edu/cgi/t/text/text-idx?cc=evans;c=evans;idno=N19425.0001
.001;view=text;rgn=div1;node=N19425.0001.001%3A8.

Cicero. *De Officiis*. Translated by Walter Miller. Cambridge, Mass.: Harvard
University Press, 1913.

———. *On the Commonwealth and On the Laws*. Translated by James E.G.
Zetzel. Cambridge: Cambridge University Press, 2017.

Clement of Alexandria. *The Sacred Writings of Clement of Alexandria*. Vol. 1.
Translated by Philip Schaff and William Wilson. Altenmünster, Germany: Jazzybee Verlag, 2017.

Coolidge, Calvin. Speech on the 150th Anniversary of the Declaration of
Independence, July 5, 1926. Teaching American History. http://teaching

americanhistory.org/library/document/speech-on-the-occasion-of
-the-one-hundred-and-fiftieth-anniversary-of-the-declaration-of
-independence/.

Copleston, Frederick, S.J., *A History of Philosophy*. Vol. 3, *Late Mediaeval and Renaissance Philosophy*. Pt. 1, *Ockham to the Speculative Mystics*. Garden City, N.Y.: Image, 1963.

———. *A History of Philosophy*. Vol. 3, *Late Mediaeval and Renaissance Philosophy*. Pt. 2, *The Revival of Platonism to Suárez*. Garden City, NY: Image, 1963.

———. *A History of Philosophy*. Vol. 6, *Modern Philosophy*. Pt. 1, *The French Enlightenment to Kant*. Garden City, N.Y.: Image, 1960.

———. *Medieval Philosophy*. New York: Harper and Row, 1961.

"Correspondence and Other Writings of Six Major Shapers of the United States". Founders Online. National Archives. https://founders.archives.gov/.

Costanzo, Joseph F., S.J. "Catholic Politeia I". *Fordham Law Review* 21, no. 2 (June 1952): 91–155.

———. "Juridic Origins of Representation II". *Fordham Law Review* 23, no. 3 (1954): 296–322.

———. *This Nation under God: Church, State and Schools in America*. New York: Herder and Herder, 1964.

———. *Political and Legal Studies*. West Hanover, Mass.: Christopher Publishing House, 1982.

Dawson, Christopher. *The Dividing of Christendom*. Garden City, N.Y.: Doubleday, 1967.

———. *The Dynamics of World History*. New York: New American Library, 1956.

———. "Democracy". In *The Modern Dilemma: The Problem of European Unity*. London: Sheed and Ward, 1933.

Deane, Herbert A. *The Political and Social Ideas of St. Augustine*. New York: Columbia University Press, 1963.

DeHart, Paul R. *Uncovering the Constitution's Moral Design*. Columbia, Mo.: University of Missouri Press, 2007.

D'Elia, Donald J., and Stephen M. Krason, eds. *We Hold These Truths and More: Further Catholic Reflections on the American Proposition: The Thought of Fr. John Courtney Murray, S.J., and Its Relevance Today* Steubenville, Ohio: Franciscan University Press, 1993.

Deneen, Patrick J. "Better Than Our Philosophy: A Response to Muñoz". *Public Discourse*, November 29, 2012. https://www.thepublicdiscourse.com/2012/11/7156/.

———. "Beyond Wishful Thinking: A Response to Schlueter". *Public Discourse*, December 14, 2012. https://www.thepublicdiscourse.com/2012/12/7411/.

————. "The Conservative Case against the Constitution". Paper delivered at Princeton University, March 10, 2011. https://jmp.Princeton.edu/events/conservative-case-against-constitution.

————. *Conserving America? Essays on Present Discontents*. South Bend, Ind.: St. Augustine's Press, 2016.

————. "Corrupting the Youth? A Response to Reilly". *Public Discourse*, September 19, 2017. https://www.thepublicdiscourse.com/2017/09/20087/.

————. "Moral Minority". *First Things* (April 2017). https://www.firstthings.com/article/2017/04/moral-minority.

————. *Why Liberalism Failed*. New Haven, Conn.: Yale University Press, 2018.

Devine, Donald. "The Real John Locke—and Why He Matters". Law and Liberty, May 21, 2014. http://www.libertylawsite.org/2014/05/21/the-real-john-locke-and-why-he-matters/.

Dickinson, John. *The Writings of John Dickinson*. Vol. 1, *Political Writings, 1764–1774*. Philadelphia: Historical Society of Pennsylvania, 1895.

Downes, Paul. *Hobbes, Sovereignty, and Early American Literature*. New York: Cambridge University Press, 2015.

Dreisbach, Daniel L., Mark David Hall, and Mark A. Noll, eds. *The Forgotten Founders on Religion and Public Life*. Notre Dame, Ind.: University of Notre Dame Press, 2009.

Durant, Will. *The Reformation*. New York: Simon and Schuster, 1957.

Dworetz, Steven M. *The Unvarnished Doctrine: Locke, Liberalism, and the American Revolution*. Durham, N.C.: Duke University Press, 1990.

Edward, Earl of Clarendon. *A Brief View and Survey of the Dangerous and Pernicious Errors to Church and State in Mr. Hobbes's Book Entitled Leviathan*. Early English Books. https://quod.lib.umich.edu/e/eebo/A33236.0001.001/1:8?rgn=div1;view=fulltext.

Eidelberg, Paul. *On the Silence of the Declaration of Independence*. Amherst, Mass.: University of Massachusetts Press, 1976.

Erler, Edward. "Natural Right in the American Founding: Harry Jaffa's Legacy". Lecture presented at the American Political Science Association Meeting, San Francisco, California, September 5, 2015. http://contemporarythinkers.org/harry-jaffa/files/2015/09/Erler_Jaffa_APSA2015.pdf.

Erler, Edward J., and Ken Masugi, eds. *The Rediscovery of America: Essays by Harry V. Jaffa on the New Birth of Politics*. Lanham, Md.: Rowman and Littlefield, 2019.

Evans, M. Stanton. *The Theme Is Freedom*. Washington D.C.: Regnery Publishing, 1994.

Fernández-Santamaría, J. A. *Natural Law, Constitutionalism, Reason of State, and War: Counter-Reformation Spanish Political Thought*. Vol. 1. New York: Peter Lang, 2005.

Feser, Edward. *Aquinas: A Beginner's Guide*. Oxford, England: Oneworld Publications, 2009.

————. *The Last Superstition: A Refutation of the New Atheism*. South Bend, Ind.: St. Augustine's Press, 2008.

————. *Locke*. Oxford, England: Oneworld Publications, 2007.

————. *Scholastic Metaphysics: A Contemporary Introduction*. Heusenstamm, Germany: Editiones Scholasticae, 2014.

Figgis, John Neville. *The Divine Right of Kings*. New York: Harper and Row, 1965.

————. "On Some Political Theories of the Early Jesuits". *Transactions of the Royal Historical Society* 11 (December 1897): 89–112. Cambridge Core. https://doi.org/10.2307/3678216.

————. *Political Thought from Gerson to Grotius: 1414–1625*. New York: Harper and Brothers, 1960.

Filmer, Sir Robert. *Patriarcha, or the Natural Power of Kings*. London: Richard Chiswell, 1680.Online Library of Liberty. https://oll.libertyfund.org /titles/filmer-patriarcha-or-the-natural-power-of-kings#lfo140_label _006.

Forster, Greg. *Starting with Locke*. New York: Continuum International, 2011.

Fustel de Coulanges, Numa Denis. *The Ancient City*. Kitchener, Ontario: Batoche Books, 2001.

Gierke, Otto. *Political Theories of the Middle Ages*. Cambridge: Cambridge University Press, 1900.

Gillespie, Michael Allen. *The Theological Origins of Modernity*. Chicago: University of Chicago Press, 2008.

Gilson, Etienne. *Being and Some Philosophers*. Toronto, Canada: Pontifical Institute of Mediaeval Studies, 1952.

————. *The Spirit of Medieval Philosophy*. New York: Charles Scribner's Sons, 1940.

————. *The Spirit of Thomism*. New York: Harper and Row, 1966.

————. *The Unity of Philosophical Experience*. New York: Charles Scribner's Sons, 1965.

Gragg, Rod. *By the Hand of Providence: How Faith Shaped the American Revolution*. New York: Simon and Schuster, 2011.

Gregory, Brad S. *The Unintended Reformation: How a Religious Revolution Secularized Society*. Cambridge, Mass.: Belknap Press, 2012.

Guardini, Romano. *The End of the Modern World*. Wilmington, Del.: Intercollegiate Studies Institute, 2001.

Guizot, François. *The History of Civilization in Europe*. Translated by William Hazlitt. Edited by Larry Siedentop. Indianapolis: Liberty Fund, 2013.

Hamilton, Alexander, John Jay, and James Madison. *The Federalist Papers.* New York: Signet Classics, 2003.

Hannan, Daniel. *Inventing Freedom, How the English-Speaking Peoples Made the Modern World.* New York: HarperCollins, 2013.

Haraszti, Zoltán. *John Adams and the Prophets of Progress.* Cambridge, Mass.: Harvard University Press, 1952.

Hittinger, Russell. *The First Grace: Rediscovering the Natural Law in a Post-Christian World.* Wilmington, Del.: ISI Books, 2003.

Hobbes, Thomas. *An Answer to Bishop Bramhall's Book, Called "The Catching of the Leviathan".* In vol. 4 of *The English Works of Thomas Hobbes,* edited by Williams Molesworth, 279–384. London: John Bohn, 1840.

———. *The Elements of Law Natural and Politic* (1640). Constitution Society. https://www.constitution.org/th/elements.htm.

———. *The Elements of Philosophy.* In vol. 1 of *The English Works of Thomas Hobbes,* edited by William Molesworth. London: John Bohn, 1839.

———. *Leviathan.* London: Andrew Crooke, 1651. Reprinted with modernized English spelling, capitalization, and punctuation by Rod Hay. Hamilton, Ontario: McMaster University, n.d. https://socialsciences.mcmaster.ca/econ/ugcm/3ll3/hobbes/Leviathan.pdf.

———. *Leviathan.* Edited by C.B. MacPherson. New York: Penguin Books, 1968.

———. *On the Citizen.* Cambridge: Cambridge University Press, 1998.

Hooker, Richard. *Of the Laws of Ecclesiastical Polity.* In *The Works of that Learned and Judicious Divine Mr. Richard Hooker with an Account of His Life and Death by Isaac Walton.* Arranged by the Rev. John Keble. 7th edition revised by the Very Rev. R.W. Church and the Rev. F. Paget. 3 vols. Oxford: Clarendon Press, 1883. Online Library of Liberty, 2019. https://oll.libertyfund.org/titles/hooker-the-works-of-that-learned-and-judicious-divine-mr-richard-hooker.

Hutson, James. *Forgotten Features of the Founding: The Recovery of Religious Themes in the Early American Republic.* Lanham, Md.: Lexington Books, 2003.

Hutson, James H. *Religion and the Founding of the American Republic.* Washington D.C.: Library of Congress, 1998.

Jacob, E.F. "Political Thought". In *The Legacy of the Middle Ages,* edited by C.G. Crump and E.F. Jacob. Oxford: Clarendon, 1926.

Jaffa, Harry V. *Crisis of the Strauss Divided: Essays on Leo Strauss and Straussianism, East and West.* Lanham, Md.: Rowman and Littlefield, 2012.

———. *A New Birth of Freedom: Abraham Lincoln and the Coming of the Civil War.* Lanham, Md.: Rowman and Littlefield, 2000.

Jaki, Stanley. *Christ and Science.* New Hope, Ky.: Real View Books, 2000.

James I. *The Political Works of James I*. Cambridge: Harvard University Press, 1918.

———. *The True Law of Free Monarchies*. Toronto, Canada: CRRS Publications, 1996.

Jefferson, Thomas. *Thomas Jefferson: Writings*. Edited by Merrill Peterson. New York: Library of America, 1984. Founders Early Access. http://rotunda.upress.virginia.edu/founders/default.xqy?keys=FOEA-print -04-02-02-5019.

———. *The Papers of Thomas Jefferson*. Edited by Julian P Boyd, Mina R. Bryan, L. H. Butterfield, Charles T. Cullen, John Catanzariti, Barbara Oberg, and James P. McClure. 33 vols. Princeton: Princeton University Press, 1950.

Jouvenal, Bertrand de. *Sovereignty: An Inquiry into the Political Good*. Chicago: University of Chicago Press, 1957.

Kennedy, Leonard A., C.S.B. "Philosophical Skepticism in England in the Fourteenth Century". *Vivarium* 21, no. 1 (1983). https://www.jstor.org /stable/42569749?seq=1#page_scan_tab_contents.

Kerwin, Jerome G. *Catholic Viewpoint on Church and State*. Garden City, N.Y.: Hanover House, 1960.

Kiecker, James G. "The Influence of William of Ockham on Luther's Eucharistic Theology". Wisconsin Lutheran Seminary Digital Library. http://www.wlsessays.net/handle/123456789/2494.

Kirk, Russell. *The Roots of American Order*. Malibu, Cal.: Pepperdine University Press, 1977.

Kloppenberg, James T. *Toward Democracy*. New York: Oxford University Press, 2016.

Knollenberg, Bernhard. *Origin of the American Revolution: 1759–1766*. New York: Crowell-Collier, 1961.

Krason, Stephen M. *The Transformation of the American Democratic Republic*. New Brunswick, N.J.: Transaction Publishers, 2012.

Lewis, C. S. *Mere Christianity*. New York: Macmillan, 1960.

Locke, John. *An Essay concerning Human Understanding*. London: J. M. Dent & Company, 1993.

———. *Essays on the Law of Nature*. Oxford: Oxford University Press, 1988.

———. *A Letter concerning Toleration*. Buffalo, N.Y.: Broadview Editions, 2013.

———. *Political Essays*. Edited by Mark Goldie. New York: Cambridge University Press, 1997.

———. *Two Treatises of Government*. Edited by Peter Laslett. New York: Cambridge University Press, 1988.

Lubac, Henri de. *The Drama of Atheist Humanism*. San Francisco: Ignatius Press, 1995.

Luther, Martin. *The Bondage of the Will*. Grand Rapids: Revell, 1992.

———. *Disputation against Scholastic Theology*. Translated by H.J. Grimm. CheckLuther.com. https://www.checkluther.com/wp-content/uploads /1517-Disputation-against-Scholastic-Theology.pdf.

———. *Luther's Epistle Sermons*. Minneapolis: Luther Press, 1909.

———. *Luther's Works*. Translated by Jaroslav Pelikan. 55 vols. St. Louis: Concordia Publishing House, 1955–1986.

———. *An Open Letter to the Christian Nobility*. In *Works of Martin Luther*. Vol. 2. Edited and translated by Adolph Spaeth, L.D. Reed, Henry Eyster Jacobs, et al. Philadelphia: A.J. Holman, 1915.

———. *Temporal Authority: To What Extent It Should Be Obeyed* (1523), In *Selected Writings of Martin Luther*, vol. 2 (1520–1523), edited by Theodore G. Tappert, translated by J.J. Schindel, Minneapolis: Fortress Press, 2007.

Lutz, Donald S. "The Relative Importance of European Writers on Late Eighteenth Century American Political Thought". *American Political Science Review* 189 (1984): 189–97.

MacIntyre, Alasdair. *Whose Justice? Which Rationality?* Notre Dame, Ind.: University of Notre Dame Press, 1988.

Madison, James. *Essay on Sovereignty*. December 1835. Founders Early Access. https://rotunda.upress.virginia.edu/founders/default.xqy?keys =FOEA-print-02-02-02-3188.

Makari, George. *Soul Machine: The Invention of the Modern Mind*. New York: W.W. Norton, 2015.

Maritain, Jacques. *Man and State*. Chicago: University of Chicago Press, 1951.

———. *A Maritain Reader*. Edited by Donald Gallagher and Idella Gallagher. Garden City, N.Y.: Doubleday and Company, 1966.

———. *Three Reformers*. New Delhi, India: Isha Books, 2013.

Mattson, Brian G. "Double or Nothing: Martin Luther's Doctrine of Predestination". The Highway. https://www.the-highway.com/Luther -on-predestination_Mattson.html.

May, Henry F. *The Enlightenment in America*. New York: Oxford University Press, 1976.

McCoy, Charles N.R. *On the Intelligibility of Political Philosophy: Essays of Charles N.R. McCoy*. Edited by James V. Schall and John J. Schrems. Washington, D.C.: Catholic University of America Press, 1989.

———. *The Structure of Political Thought: A Study in the History of Political Ideas*. New York: McGraw-Hill, 1963.

McIlwain, Charles Howard. *Constitutionalism: Ancient and Modern*. Ithaca, N.Y.: Cornell University Press, 1947.

Murray, John Courtney, S.J. *We Hold These Truths: Catholic Reflections on the American Proposition*. New York: Sheed and Ward, 1960.

Niemeyer, Gerhart. *The Loss and Recovery of Truth*. Edited by Michael Henry. South Bend, Ind.: St. Augustine's Press, 2013.

Novak, Michael. *On Two Wings*. San Francisco: Encounter Books, 2002.

Oakley, Francis. *Natural Law, Laws of Nature, Natural Rights*. New York: Continuum International, 2005.

Otis, James. *The Rights of the British Colonies Asserted and Proved* (1763). Online Library of Liberty. https://oll.libertyfund.org/pages/1763-otis -rights-of-british-colonies-asserted-pamphlet.

Paul III. Encyclical on the Enslavement and Education of Indians *Sublimus Dei* (May 29, 1537). Papal Encyclicals Online. http://www.papalen cyclicals.net/paulo3/p3subli.htm.

Pearson, Thomas D. "Luther on Natural Law". *Journal of Lutheran Ethics* 7, no. 12 (December 2007). https://www.elca.org/JLE/Articles/472.

Pederson, Nicholas. "The Lost Founder: James Wilson in American Memory". *Yale Journal of Law and the Humanities* 22, no. 2 (January 2010): 257–337. https://digitalcommons.law.yale.edu/yjlh/vol22/iss2/3.

Pennington, Kenneth. "Bartolomé de Las Casas and the Tradition of Medieval Law". *Church History* 39 (1970): 149–61. https://scholarship.law .edu/scholar/653/.

————. "Representation in Medieval Canon Law". *Jurist* 64 (2004): 361–83.

Pieper, Josef. *Abuse of Language, Abuse of Power*. San Francisco: Ignatius Press, 1988.

————. *The Christian Idea of Man*. South Bend, Ind.: St. Augustine's Press, 2011.

————. *Happiness and Contemplation*. South Bend, Ind.: St. Augustine's Press, 1998.

————. *Leisure: The Basis of Culture*. New York: Random House, 1963.

Pollock, Frederick. "The History of the Law of Nature: A Preliminary Study". *Columbia Law Review* 1, no. 1 (January 1901): 11–32.

Poole, R. L. *Illustrations of Medieval Thought and Learning*. New York: Macmillan, 1920

Rager, Rev. John Clement. *The Political Philosophy of St. Robert Bellarmine*. Spokane, Wash.: Apostolate of Our Lady of Siluva, 1995.

Rahe, Paul A. *Republics Ancient and Modern*. Vol. 2, *New Modes and Orders in Early Modern Political Thought*. Chapel Hill: University of North Carolina Press, 1994.

————. *Republics Ancient and Modern*. Vol. 3, *Inventions of Prudence: Constituting the American Regime*. Chapel Hill: University of North Carolina Press, 1994.

Ratzinger, Joseph Cardinal. *Church, Ecumenism and Politics*. New York: Crossroad, 1988.

———. "Conscience and Truth". Presented at the Tenth Workshop for Bishops, Dallas, Texas, February 1991. EWTN. http://www.ewtn.com/library/conscience-and-the-truth-2468.

———. "Truth and Freedom". *Communio* 23 (Spring 1996): 16–35.

———. *Truth and Tolerance: Christian Belief and World Religions*. San Francisco: Ignatius Press, 2004.

Ratzinger, Joseph, and Marcello Pera. *Without Roots: The West, Relativism, Christianity, Islam*. New York: Basic Books, 2007.

Redpath, Peter A. *A Not-So-Elementary Christian Metaphysics*. Manitou Springs, Col.: Socratic Press, 2012.

Reid, Charles J., Jr. "The Medieval Origins of the Western Natural Rights Tradition: The Achievement of Brian Tierney". *Cornwall Law Review* 83, no. 2 (January 1998): 437–63. https://pdfs.semanticscholar.org/5602/bf20298571a0020f9e36820c975a65956819.pdf.

Reinsch, Paul Samuel. *English Common Law in the Early American Colonies*. New York: Da Capo Press, 1970. First published 1899.

Rommen, Heinrich A. "*De Legibus* of Francisco Suárez". *Notre Dame Law Review* 24, no. 1 (October 1948): 70–81, https://pdfs.semanticscholar.org/bd33/102b7b6081f5f58cfef14c138dfa4fb26e3d.pdf.

———. *The Natural Law: A Study in Legal and Social History and Philosophy*. Indianapolis: Liberty Fund, 1998.

———. *The State in Catholic Thought*. St. Louis: B. Herder, 1945.

Rosenthal, Alexander S. *Crown Under Law*. New York: Lexington Books, 2008.

Rossiter, Clinton. *Seedtime of the Republic: The Origin of the American Tradition of Political Liberty*. New York: Harcourt, Brace, 1953.

Ryan, John A., and Francis J. Boland. *Catholic Principles of Politics*. New York: Macmillan, 1952.

Sabine, George H. *A History of Political Theory*. New York: Holt, Rineheart, and Winston, 1961.

Sandoz, Ellis. "Classical and Christian Dimensions of American Political Thought". *Modern Age* (Winter 1981): 14–25.

———. *A Government of Laws: Political Theory, Religion, and the American Founding*. Columbia, Mo.: University of Missouri Press, 2001.

———. "Philosophical and Religious Dimensions of the American Founding". *Intercollegiate Review* (Spring 1995). https://home.isi.org/philosophical-and-religious-dimensions-american-founding.

———. *Republicanism, Religion, and the Soul of America*. Columbia: University of Missouri Press, 2006.

Sandoz, Ellis, ed. *Political Sermons of the American Founding Era: 1730–1805*. Indianapolis: Liberty Press, 1990.

Schall, James V. *At the Limits of Political Philosophy*. Washington D.C.: Catholic University of America Press, 1996.

———. "At a Moment of His Own Choosing". *Catholic Thing*, December 23, 2014. http://thecatholicthing.org/2014/12/23/moment-choosing.

———. *Christianity and Politics*. Boston: St. Paul Editions, 1981.

———. "Luther and Political Philosophy". *Faith and Reason* 8, no. 2 (Summer 1982): 7–31.

———. *The Mind That Is Catholic: Philosophical and Political Essays*. Washington, D.C.: Catholic University of America Press, 2008.

———. *On Islam: A Chronological Record*. San Francisco: Ignatius Press, 2018.

———. *The Politics of Heaven and Hell*. Lanham, Md.: University Press of America, 1987.

———. *Reason, Revelation, and the Foundations of Political Philosophy*. Baton Rouge: Louisiana State University Press, 1987.

———. *Roman Catholic Political Philosophy*. Lanham, Md.: Lexington Books, 2004.

Schmeeckle, John S. "Prelude to the Declaration of Independence: The Congressional Resolution of May 10 and 15, 1776". Academia. https://www.academia.edu/1479704/Safety_and_Happiness_The_American_Revolutionary_Standard_for_Governmental_Legitimacy.

Shah, Timothy Samuel, and Allen D. Hertzke, eds. *Christianity and Freedom*. Vol. 1, *Historical Perspectives*. New York: Cambridge University Press, 2016.

Sidney, Algernon. *Discourses concerning Government* (1698). Edited by Thomas G. West. Indianapolis: Liberty Fund, 1996.

Siedentop, Larry. *Inventing the Individual: The Origins of Western Liberalism*. Cambridge, Mass.: Harvard University Press, 2014.

Sigmund, Paul E. "Canon Law". *International Encyclopedia of the Social Sciences*. Encyclopedia.com. https://www.encyclopedia.com/social-sciences/applied-and-social-sciences-magazines/canon-law.

———. "Natural Law, Consent, and Equality: William of Ockham to Richard Hooker". Natural Law, Natural Rights, and American Constitutionalism. http://www.nlnrac.org/classical/late-medieval-transformations.

———. *Natural Law in Political Thought*. Cambridge, Mass.: Winthrop Publishers, 1971.

Skinner, Quentin. *The Foundations of Modern Political Thought*. Vol. 2, *The Age of Reformation*. Cambridge: Cambridge University Press, 1978.

Sokolowski, Robert. *Introduction to Phenomenology*. Cambridge: Cambridge University Press, 2000.

Somerville, J. P. "From Suárez to Filmer: A Reappraisal". *Historical Journal* 25, no. 23 (1982): 525–40.

Spragens, Thomas A., Jr. *The Politics of Motion: The World of Thomas Hobbes*. Lexington, Ky.: University Press of Kentucky, 1973.

Stark, Rodney. *How the West Won: The Neglected Story of the Triumph of Modernity*. Wilmington, Del.: ISI Books, 2014.

Strauss, Leo. *Natural Right and History*. Chicago: University of Chicago Press, 1950.

Strauss, Leo, and Joseph Cropsey, eds. *History of Political Philosophy*. 3rd ed. Chicago: University of Chicago Press, 1987.

Suárez, Francisco. *Selections from Three Works*. Edited by Thomas Pink and Knud Haakonssen. Indianapolis: Liberty Fund, 2015.

Tierney, Brian. *Foundations of the Conciliar Theory*. London: Cambridge University Press, 1968.

———. *The Idea of Natural Rights*. Grand Rapids: William B. Eedermans, 1997.

———. *Religion, Law, and the Growth of Constitutional Thought 1150–1650*. New York: Cambridge University Press, 1982.

Tocqueville, Alexis de. *Democracy in America*. Translated by Harvey C. Mansfield and Delba Winthrop. Chicago: University of Chicago Press, 2002.

———. *The Old Regime and the Revolution*. New York: Harper and Brothers, 1856.

Voegelin, Eric. *The Collected Works of Eric Voegelin*. Vol. 5, *Modernity without Constraint: The Political Religions, the New Science of Politics, and Science, Politics, and Gnosticism*. Edited by Ellis Sandoz. Columbia: University of Missouri Press, 2000.

———. *The Collected Works of Eric Voegelin*. Vol. 26, *History of Political Ideas*. Edited by David Walsh. Columbia: University of Missouri Press, 1999.

———. *From Enlightenment to Revolution*. Durham, N.C.: Duke University Press, 1975.

———. *History of Political Ideas: Renaissance and Reformation*. Columbia: University of Missouri Press, 1998.

———. *The New Science of Politics*. Chicago: University of Chicago Press, 1952.

———. *Order and History*. Vol. 1, *Israel and Revelation*. Baton Rouge: Louisiana State University Press, 1956.

———. *Science, Politics and Gnosticism*. Chicago: Regnery Gateway, 1968.

Waldron, Jeremy. *God, Locke and Equality: Christian Foundations of John Locke's Political Thought*. Cambridge: Cambridge University Press, 2002.

Walsh, David. *The Growth of the Liberal Soul*. Columbia: University of Missouri Press, 1997.

————. "Rights without Right". *First Things* (November 1996). https://www.firstthings.com/article/1996/11/002-rights-without-right.

Walsh, James J. *Education of the Founding Fathers of the Republic.* New York: Fordham University Press, 1935.

Washington, George. Inaugural Address (April 30, 1789), American Presidency Project, https://www.presidency.ucsb.edu/documents/inaugural-address-16.

Wells, William Vincent. *The Life and Public Services of Samuel Adams.* Boston: Little, Brown, 1865.

West, Thomas G. "Locke's Neglected Teaching on Morality and the Family". *Social Science and Modern Society* 50, no. 5 (September–October 2013): 472–76.

————. *The Political Theory of the American Founding: Natural Rights, Public Policy, and the Moral Conditions of Freedom.* New York: Cambridge University Press, 2017.

————. *Vindicating the Founders.* Lanham, Md.: Rowman and Littlefield, 1997.

White, Morton. *The Philosophy of the American Revolution.* New York: Oxford University Press, 1978.

Wiker, Benjamin. "Catholicism in the American Founding". *National Catholic Register,* July 3, 2013. http://www.ncregister.com/daily-news/catholicism-and-the-american-founding/#ixzz2Y688eLyM.

————. *The Reformation 500 Years Later: Twelve Things You Need to Know.* Washington, D.C.: Regnery, 2017.

Wilson, James. *The Collected Works of James Wilson.* Edited by Kermit L. Hall and Mark David Hall. Vol. 1. Indianapolis: Liberty Fund, 2007. Online Library of Liberty. https://oll.libertyfund.org/titles/wilson-collected-works-of-james-wilson-vol-1.

Wood, Gordon S. *The Idea of America: Reflections on the Birth of the United States.* New York: Penguin Press, 2011.

INDEX